THERESA REBECK
Collected Plays Volume I

1989–1998

THERESA REBECK

Collected Plays Volume I
1989–1998

CONTEMPORARY PLAYWRIGHTS
SERIES

SK
A Smith and Kraus Book

A Smith and Kraus Book
Published by Smith and Kraus, Inc.
PO Box 127, Lyme, NH 03768

First Edition: March 1999
10 9 8 7 6 5 4 3 2 1

The Library of Congress Cataloging-In-Publication Data
Rebeck, Theresa.
[Plays]
Theresa Rebeck: collected plays. —1st ed.
p. cm. — (Contemporary playwrights series)
ISBN 1-57525-172-8
I. Title. II. Series.
PS3568.E2697A19 1998
812'.54—dc21 98-53027

CONTENTS

FOR MY HUSBAND, JESS LYNN,
THE MOST WONDERFUL MAN I EVER MET,
WHO GOES THROUGH ALL OF IT WITH ME
AND SURVIVES.

THE FULL-LENGTH PLAYS

When I first started writing plays, I was a Woman Playwright. I was living in Boston at the time. One of my first plays, *Sunday on the Rocks*, had recently been produced to some acclaim in the Boston area and I was invited to a dinner party that included several local theatrical luminaries. One of the other guests, an accomplished director (male, mid-50s), turned to me and said, "Maybe you can tell me. Why can't women ever transcend their identities as women and just write as playwrights?" I said, "Do you mean, why can't we write like men?" and he said No, that wasn't what he meant at all. "Yes it is," said his wife, but he persisted in his position and went on to explain that male playwrights somehow, innately, are able to transcend their gender and write about the human condition, while women playwrights, also innately, are not. As a side note, let me add, this gentleman had never seen or read any of my plays. I was merely the woman playwright who happened to be at the dinner table.

Several months before this I had been in England doing some research on another project, and I had dinner with a fairly prominent British stage director (male, mid-40s). We had been introduced by a mutual friend, the brilliant South African playwright and director Barney Simon, and in reaction to Barney's recommendation of my work, this gentleman said, "Yes, but women don't make very good playwrights, do they?" I naturally disagreed and asked him in return how he could say such a thing without fear of being called a bigot. He replied that bigotry had nothing to do with it; it was a fact. Women made very fine novelists, he thought—better than men, even—but the essential nature of women is more interior, less active, and so they don't understand dramatic structure. In his opinion, history bore out the truth of these observations. Where are the women playwrights? He wanted to know. What were women doing all those centuries while men were writing great plays? The obvious conclusion, to him, was that women either hadn't been writing plays at all because it just wasn't anything they were interested in, or they'd been writing mediocre plays, which the unbiased judges of time and culture had rightfully dismissed.

Around the same time, another friend of mine, a theatre professional who hovered around and made half-stabs at being my mentor, suggested to me that I had to be careful not to let myself get "ghettoized" as a woman playwright.

My hackles went up. I pointed out that I was in fact a woman, and also a playwright, and I didn't see anything inherently wrong with being either, or both at once. My friend didn't have any sort of articulate response to that, but he was clearly a little embarrassed for me. He didn't want to get into a big gender discussion; he was just trying to be helpful. He wanted me to understand that it's rough out there and being considered a woman playwright was not, ultimately, going to stand in my favor.

He was right. A couple years later, in 1991, several theatres were considering my play *Spike Heels* for production. I came close many times, but no one had ever heard of me and producers were skittish about taking a chance on an unknown playwright, especially an unknown woman playwright. One producer passed on the play because, she told my agent, "Frank Rich will never give a good review to a feminist play." When this bit of information was passed on to me, I was surprised, because the fact is, I didn't know I had written a "feminist play." What I thought I was doing, what I was trying to do, was retell the *Pygmalion* story with contemporary, comic and sinister spin. There is an incident of sexual harassment at the center of the play, but I didn't consider writing about sexual harassment a particularly feminist gesture. Being a woman who in fact has been sexually harassed, I saw the experience as one among many on the human spectrum. To my mind, power and money and sex were things to be written about the way we might write about death, or love, or betrayal.

But my work, which at the time I considered to be fairly straightforward comic realism, was increasingly being branded as "feminist." People thought I was making a big political statement; mostly what I was really trying to do was write what I knew, which was what it means for this one person (me) to be a woman in the late twentieth century in America.

As a writer, I have always considered it my job to describe the world as I know it; to struggle toward whatever portion of the truth is available to me. I am a feminist in that I believe that women are as fully human as men and that their experiences are as worthy of representation, as universally significant, as men's. I believe that the hero's journey is both male and female. I believe that, as a rule, women are as deeply flawed as men are. I'm interested in writing about the way both genders make mistakes and the ways we grow, or don't grow.

Unfortunately, as we live in a sexist world, these beliefs are still perceived as radical and dangerous by some of those who have appointed themselves the protectors of the culture. Frank Rich's response to *Spike Heels*, an essentially dark comedy about sex and power which hinges on an episode of sexual harassment, was to compare it to pillow talk. He clearly didn't understand the play and dismissed it as half-baked fluff; four months later, when *Oleanna* opened off-Broadway he wrote "finally, someone has written a play about sexual harassment" and commended it as a searing commentary on our times. Apparently, when a woman writes about an actual incident of sexual harassment, it's pillow talk; and when a man writes about a woman lying about sexual harassment, it's a searing commentary.

At the time, I couldn't help but wonder why it's not okay for me to have a feminist agenda, but it is okay for Mr. Mamet to have a misogynist agenda. It is a question that plagues me still. Over the years the critical unease with women playwrights and what they might actually choose to write about has become apparent to me. One critic (male) actually chose his review of *Loose Knit* as an opportunity to lecture me, and in fact all women playwrights, on the subjects that would be appropriate for women to write about. Many of my friends, upon reading this, were enraged at such a patently patriarchal arrogance; I got lots of phone calls about how unfair it all was. Now, years later, I laugh about it. What are you gonna do? The ice occasionally starts to thaw; this year, women writers—two different ones, even—won the Tony and the Pulitzer for playwriting. At the same time, just last week, I had a producer gently castigate me for writing satires because, she sighed, "It makes you sound so angry." I pointed out that anger is not necessarily a bad thing for a writer to have. Dickens was angry. Sheridan was angry. Shaw was angry. Osborne was angry; Mamet is angry. *Angels in America,* the most celebrated play of my lifetime, is a very angry play. She shrugged; I was once again being obtuse. Apparently, if men are angry, that's cultural, but a woman's anger is something else altogether.

All of these things troubled me when I began writing for the theatre; they trouble me still. It troubles me most that we somehow are not permitted to engage in any sort of meaningful dialogue with our male colleagues on these matters. I have often thought that gender bias is the hidden sin of the American theatre. Then, in 1995, all my thinking and speaking about being a woman playwright abruptly came to a halt. I became a Playwright Who Wrote for Television.

In the spring of 1995, I was asked to write a piece for the Dramatist's Guild newsletter about anything I wanted. At the time, I had recently made the difficult decision to take a job writing for the television series *NYPD Blue*. I had worked briefly in television writing for sit coms in 1990–91, and I found the experience so harrowing I wrote a play about it, *The Family of Mann*. (The play was widely hailed as a "biting satire"; few people realized it

3

was actually a documentary. That's how crazy it is out there.) The idea of subjecting myself again to the madness that more or less rules T.V. Land was frightening to me, but I had a good offer to write for a show I admired a great deal, and I hoped that away from the madness of sitcoms I might find the work more satisfying. I also felt that there were some aspects of working in the theatre that finally weren't so different from writing for television. I felt, and still feel, that it is a mistake to merely romanticize the theatre and disdain all of what goes on in television and film; clearly, the situation is far more complicated than that, and it is possible to do good work or bad work in all three forms. I discussed all of this at length in the newsletter, and the column was subsequently reprinted in *American Theatre Magazine.*

I am still a little amazed at the extent of the response that was directed at that essay. Some people were angry with me for being openly unapologetic about writing for television. Others were grateful that I spoke clearly about some of the frustrations of working in the theatre. Others were angry that I spoke so clearly about some of the frustrations of working in the theatre. Four years later, people still talk to me about that piece.

Truth be told, I sometimes regret having written it. Having always considered myself a playwright, I was only ever marginally comfortable being called a woman playwright; that always seemed like a distinction that was more important to everyone else than me. I am not ashamed of being a woman, so I was willing to deal with it, and over time I found it interesting to think about. But in one fell swoop I became a playwright who wrote for television, and that's what people wanted to talk to me about. Newspapers would call and ask me for quotes about being a playwright who writes for television. I would get invited to theatre conferences to talk about writing for television.

And, depressingly, theatre critics began to use the fact that I sometimes write for television as a way of dismissing my plays.

I am interested in America's cultural unease with television; I think it's a subject worthy of much more thought than it has yet received. And I am proud of most of the work I have done in writing for television. But I am more particularly proud to call myself a playwright. If I were to be categorized at all, I would like to be called an American playwright.

I spend a lot of time thinking about America, who we are as a people and a culture and a nation, and I have always felt that the theatre is a truly appropriate place to examine these issues, the way David Hare examines what it means to be British, or Brian Friel examines what it means to be Irish. In writing *View of the Dome*, I was trying to consider the cultural idealism that graces our history—the spectacularly beautiful premise that underlies democracy, that all men, and women, are created equal—and how people of power dismiss that ideal without the briefest of considerations. What goes on in Washington, which is clearly power mongering of the highest order, has absolutely nothing to do with who we purport to be historically, which is why I think people are so tired of it all. We are taught that being an American means striving for justice and equality, and we're offended that so many of our leaders seem more interested in sniping at each other than trying to enact those principles into law.

After writing *The Family of Mann,* I came more and more to believe that the Hollywood condition—a defective group mind, a belief system so bizarre, social satire and documentary have become one and the same thing—had infected the country as a whole. This concern clearly informed the writing of *View of the Dome.* When the play was produced in New York, pre-Monica, it received controversial reviews, some of the critics vilifying it as too extreme. Post-Monica, when Chicago's Victory Gardens Theatre produced the play, it was hailed as a spot-on assessment of the national blood sport that politics had become. There was something both gratifying and disturbing to find out how right I actually turned out to be.

I am a woman, I am an American, I am a mother, I sometimes write for television, and I sometimes write movies; I play the piano, I knit, I rail at the universe; I am angry, I am sad; I am a comic realist, a misanthrope, and an idealist. There are many ways to categorize me, and my work. But for myself, I would most like to be considered a playwright.

SPIKE HEELS

ORIGINAL PRODUCTION

Spike Heels was produced in workshop by New York Stage and Film Company in association with the Powerhouse Theatre at Vassar, July, 1990.

Spike Heels was originally produced in New York by the Second Stage Theatre on June 4, 1992. It was directed by Michael Greif and had the following cast (in order of appearance):

ANDREW . . . . Tony Goldwyn
GEORGIE . . . . Saundra Santiago
EDWARD . . . . Kevin Bacon
LYDIA . . . . Julie White

Set Design . . . . James Youmans
Lighting Design . . . . Kenneth Posner
Costume Design . . . . Candice Donnelly
Sound Design . . . . Mark Bennett
Hair Design . . . . Antonio Soddu
Production Manager . . . . Carol Fishman
Production Stage Manager . . . . Jess Lynn
Stage Manager . . . . Allison Sommers

CHARACTERS
ANDREW
GEORGIE
EDWARD
LYDIA

TIME AND PLACE
The Present, Boston

ACT I
SCENE I

Loud classical music, Vivaldi or Mozart, on the radio. There is a long moment of pounding at the door. Lights come up on the main room of Andrew's apartment, the orderly environment of a scholar.

GEORGIE: *(Offstage.)* Andrew! Are you in there? Dammit, goddammit, are you home, goddam you—Andrew!

ANDREW: *(Overlapping, offstage.)* Wait a minute—I'm coming—

GEORGIE: *(Overlapping, offstage.)* Open up the goddam door—are you home or WHAT—Jesus CHRIST I am going to KILL myself I swear to God I will DAMMIT, ANDREW!
(Andrew crosses the stage quickly, wiping his hands on a towel, snaps off the radio and opens the door.)

ANDREW: What, what, what—
(He opens the door. Georgie barges in.)

GEORGIE: I have been on the stupid goddamn T for an hour and a half, squished between four of the smelliest fat men on earth, all of them with their armpits in my face, in high heels—Am I interrupting?

ANDREW: No, I was just making dinner. Lydia's coming over—

GEORGIE: Oh. I won't interrupt—

ANDREW: You're not interrupting—/

GEORGIE: *(Charging ahead.)* Goddammit, I hate heels. I have ruined my arches for the rest of my life just so a bunch of stupid men can have a good time looking at my fucking legs. *(She sits and takes off her heels.)*

ANDREW: Nice mouth. Very nice mouth.

GEORGIE: Oh, don't start. Don't even fucking start, okay? If I had a fucking car I wouldn't have to take the fucking T. Do you know how long I have been in transit? An hour and a half.

ANDREW: Edward let you off at 4:30? What, did he have a nervous breakdown or something?

GEORGIE: I hope so. I hope he totally loses his mind. I hope he has a vision of how useless his whole stupid life has been, and I hope he jumps out his spectacular little office window and into the fucking Charles River, that is what I hope.

ANDREW: Come on, he's not that bad.

GEORGIE: I wish I still smoked. Why the hell did I have to quit smoking? Do you have any cigarettes? How the hell are we supposed to survive in this stupid country without cigarettes? I mean, they invent this terrific little antidote to everything, *cigarettes,* and then after they get you hooked on it they tell you that it's going to kill you. And you know, the thing is, I think I'd rather be killed by cancer than by life in general. I really think that. *(She circles the room gingerly, trying to get some feeling back in her feet.)*

ANDREW: Are you going to tell me what happened?

GEORGIE: I threw a pencil at Edward, okay? He was getting on my nerves, so I said, fuck you, Edward, and I threw a pencil at him. *(She starts to laugh.)*

ANDREW: Oh, Jesus. Here. Give me your foot.

GEORGIE: Excuse me? I say I threw a pencil at Edward, and you say give me your foot? What is that supposed to mean? Are we having a conversation here, or is this like some sort of art film or what?

ANDREW: *(Crosses to the couch, throws her shoes aside and begins to massage her foot.)* No wonder you're in a bad mood. These shoes look like some sort of medieval torture device.

GEORGIE: Don't just throw those around, those cost a fortune. What are you—Andrew, excuse me, but what are you doing?

ANDREW: I'm massaging your foot. It's supposed to be soothing. Isn't it soothing?

GEORGIE: Yes, it's very—I don't know if soothing is what I would call this.

ANDREW: Supposedly the muscles in the foot are connected to almost every other part of your body. So it's important that your feet are always relaxed. That's why you're in a bad mood; you've been abusing your feet.

GEORGIE: That's not why I'm in a bad mood.

ANDREW: *(Pause.)* How's that?

GEORGIE: It's nice. It's very nice.

ANDREW: *(Pause. Andrew looks up at her for a moment, and becomes suddenly awkward. He quickly sets her foot down and moves to the kitchen.)* I better get to work on dinner.

GEORGIE: *(Watches him exit, then sits in silence for a moment.)* So how's Lydia?

ANDREW: *(Off.)* She's fine. Fine. She's good.

GEORGIE: Good. How's the wedding?

ANDREW: *(Off. Pause.)* Fine. It's still a ways off, so nobody's too hysterical yet.

GEORGIE: That's good.

ANDREW: *(Off.)* She wants to meet you.

GEORGIE: She does?

ANDREW: *(Off.)* Yeah. She's coming over for dinner later on. You should stick around. It really is ridiculous that you two haven't met.

GEORGIE: Yeah, that's ridiculous, all right.

ANDREW: *(Reenters, carrying a cutting board and vegetables.)* So can you stay?

GEORGIE: Right. She's gonna come over for some romantic little vegetable thing and find me. I'm sure. *(She starts to leave.)*

ANDREW: She said we should all go out sometime—

GEORGIE: Fine, we'll do that sometime.

ANDREW: Georgie—

GEORGIE: What? I'm all sweaty and gross. My shirt is sticking to everything and I stink. I can't meet Lydia smelling like a sewer. She'll faint or gag or something.

ANDREW: Don't start.

GEORGIE: I'm sorry. I'm just not up to it, okay?

ANDREW: So don't stay for dinner. She won't be here for another hour. Just stick around for a while.

GEORGIE: Look—these clothes are killing me. I need to go upstairs. I can come back tomorrow.

ANDREW: Go put on one of my t-shirts, they're in the top drawer of the dresser. Come on. You still haven't told me the details of your assault on Edward.

GEORGIE: Andrew—

ANDREW: There's some shorts in there, too.

GEORGIE: Oh, fuck.

(She heads off, peeling her jacket as she goes. Andrew cleans, puts away his books, etc.)

ANDREW: *(Calling.)* You'll be fine. It's just going to take a little while to get used to it all. You know, actually, you're doing great. I talked to Edward last week, and he said you're the best secretary he's ever had. So you should just chill out and be nice to him. He's not that bad, and he likes you a lot. As a matter of fact, I think he has a crush on you. *(He sees something on the coffee table, picks up a book and slams it down. He takes the book to a small garbage can by his desk and knocks the dead bug off.)* These goddam bugs are invading my living room now. Did you ever get a hold of Renzella? I thought he was sending somebody over. *(Pause.)* Georgie?

GEORGIE: *(Off.)* You got a regular boudoir in here. Lydia's been lending you some of her clothes, huh?

ANDREW: Hey, leave that stuff alone. *(Pause.)* Georgie?

GEORGIE: *(Off.)* I don't want to wear one of your t-shirts. I want to wear this. *(She appears in the doorway, wearing an elegant patterned silk dress. She slinks into the room.)*

ANDREW: I asked you not to start.

GEORGIE: Thank you. I picked it up at Saks. Usually I don't appreciate his line, but when I found this I was just devastated—

ANDREW: Take off the dress. Take it off now.

GEORGIE: I particularly like the bow.

ANDREW: I don't find this funny.

GEORGIE: I just thought I could pick up some fashion tips. So I look presentable when we all go out to dinner.

ANDREW: *This is not funny.*

    (Pause.)

GEORGIE: Okay. It's not funny. Fine. *(Pause.)* I didn't mean anything. I just meant—this is a nice dress. Silk, huh? Lydia's kind of loaded, huh? *(Pause.)* You think this looks good on me? I mean, I got some money coming in now, maybe I should try to dress better.

ANDREW: I think you should take it off.

GEORGIE: Yeah. I guess I look pretty stupid. *(She crosses back to the bedroom.)*

ANDREW: I'm sorry. That's her favorite dress. I just—you don't even know her. She's nothing like that.

    (Georgie exits.)

ANDREW: *(Calling.)* We'll set up a date this week and actually do it: we'll go out to dinner. The three of us. You two can spend the evening trashing Edward. It'll be fun. You'll be thick as thieves by dawn.

GEORGIE: *(Off.)* She doesn't like him either, huh?

ANDREW: Both of you, you're both heartbreakers.

    (Georgie reenters and stands in the doorway, without her shirt on, wearing a slip and a bra. She carries the t-shirt in her hands.)

GEORGIE: What is that supposed to mean?

ANDREW: Nothing. I told you, I think he has a crush on you. I talked to him last week, and—

GEORGIE: You talked to him? You talked to him. What did he say?

ANDREW: Georgie.

GEORGIE: What?

ANDREW: Put your shirt on.

    (Georgie puts the t-shirt on. It is long and loose, with sleeves and neck cut out. When she pulls it over her shoulders, her breasts are still largely exposed. Andrew points it out to her.)

GEORGIE: You talked to him?

ANDREW: I talk to him all the time. You know that.

GEORGIE: So what did he say?

ANDREW: He said he liked you.

GEORGIE: Great. That's just—and what did you say?

ANDREW: I said I liked you, too.

GEORGIE: That's what you said? You said, "I like her, too." That's all you said?

ANDREW: *(Perplexed.)* Yes. That's all I said.

(Pause.)

GEORGIE: Great. Well, you know, as far as I'm concerned, Edward can just go fuck himself. I mean, your little friend is just a prince, isn't he? He's just a delight. *(She goes back into the bedroom.)*

ANDREW: *(Calling.)* Look—he hired you. You didn't have any references, you didn't have any legal experience, you didn't have a college degree. And he didn't ask any questions. You might think about that.

GEORGIE: *(Reenters, carrying a pair of gym shorts. While she speaks, she takes off her slip and pantyhose.)* Oh, I might, might I? All right. I'm thinking about that. Nothing is coming to me, Andrew. What is your point here?

ANDREW: My point is, he gave you a job. I'm not saying the man is a saint. But he gave you a job.

GEORGIE: Yeah, right, he "gave" me the damn job. I fucking work my ass off for that jerk; he doesn't give me shit. I earn it, you know? He "gave" me the job. I just love that. What does that mean, that I should be working at McDonald's or something, that's what I really deserve or something?

ANDREW: You wouldn't last two hours at McDonald's. Some customer would complain about their French fries and you'd tell him to fuck off and die, and that would be the end of that.

GEORGIE: Bullshit. Fuck you, that is such fucking bullshit. You think I don't know how to behave in public or something?

ANDREW: *(Overlap.)* Georgie—could you put your clothes on—Georgie—

GEORGIE: *(Ignoring him, overlapping.)* Jesus, I was a goddam waitress for seven years, the customers fucking loved me. You think I talk like this in front of strangers; you think I don't have a brain in my head or something? That is so fucking condescending. Anytime I lose my temper, I'm crazy, is that it? You don't know why I threw that pencil, you just assume. You just make these assumptions. Well, fuck you, Andrew. I mean it. Fuck you. *(She takes her clothes in her hands and heads for the door.)*

ANDREW: You can't go out in the hall like that—

GEORGIE: I mean, I just love that. You don't even know. You've never seen me in that office. You think I'm like, incapable of acting like somebody I'm not? For four months I've been scared to death but I do it, you know, I take messages, I call the court, I write his damn letters. I watch my mouth, I dress like this—whatever this is; these are the ugliest clothes I have ever seen—I am gracious, I am bright, I am promising. I am being this other person for them because I do want this job but there is a point beyond which I will not be fucked with! So you finally push me beyond that point, and I throw the pencil and now you're going to tell me that that is *my* problem? What, do you guys think you hold all the cards or something? You think you have the last word on reality? You do, you think that anything you do to me is okay, and anything I do is fucked because I'm not using the right words. I'm, like, throwing pencils and saying fuck you, I'm speaking another language, that's my problem. And the thing is—I am America. You know? You guys are not America. You think you are; Jesus Christ, you guys think you own the world. I mean, who made up these rules, Andrew? And do you actually think we're buying it?

(*Pause.*)

ANDREW: Maybe you should sit down and tell me what's going on.

GEORGIE: Yeah, and maybe you should go fuck yourself. (*Pause.*) I'm sorry, okay?

ANDREW: Are you okay?

GEORGIE: Yes! No. Christ. I'm sorry. I'm sorry.

(*Pause. They stand for a moment in silence. Andrew crosses and puts his arm around her. She leans against him.*)

ANDREW: What happened at the office?

GEORGIE: I don't know. You got anything to drink around here? I mean, could I have a drink?

ANDREW: Do you want some tea?

GEORGIE: Tea? Are you kidding? I mean, is that supposed to soothe me or something? I hate to break the news to you, but I really think that that is like, just a myth, Andrew. I think that in reality vodka is far more soothing than tea.

ANDREW: I don't have any vodka.

GEORGIE: Bourbon works too.

ANDREW: I have half a bottle of white zinfandel.

GEORGIE: Oh, Jesus. Make me tea.

(*He exits to the kitchen. Georgie crosses, picks up the gym shorts and puts them on. Andrew reenters.*)

ANDREW: All right. Now tell me what happened.

GEORGIE: Nothing happened. I mean, it's stupid.

ANDREW: (*Pause.*) That's it? It's stupid? You can talk for hours about absolutely nothing, and now all you have to say about something that is clearly upsetting you is, it's stupid?

GEORGIE: I feel stupid.

ANDREW: What are you talking about, you feel stupid? You just walked in here and insulted me for ten minutes.

GEORGIE: That was different. I was mad./

ANDREW: You have to be mad to talk?

GEORGIE: No, come on—I don't know—/

ANDREW: I could make you mad.

GEORGIE: No, you couldn't. You're too nice.

ANDREW: Fuck you.

GEORGIE: —Andrew—

ANDREW: Fuck you. Come on. Fuck you.

GEORGIE: *(Calm.)* Yeah, fuck you too.

ANDREW: Fuck you.

GEORGIE: Fuck you.

ANDREW: Fuck you.

GEORGIE: You look really stupid saying fuck you—

ANDREW: Fuck you. Fuck you! Fuck you.

GEORGIE: *(Laughing. Overlap.)* Andrew, stop it. Cut it out. It sounds weird when you say it. You shouldn't talk like that.

ANDREW: You talk like that all the time!

GEORGIE: I'm different. I mean, I know how to swear. You don't. It's like, fuck you. Fuck you. Or, you know, fuck you. It's just—you know. You got to know how to say it.

ANDREW: Fuck you.

GEORGIE: Forget it. You look really stupid. You look the way I look when I try to talk like you.

ANDREW: You've tried it? Really? I must have missed that day.

GEORGIE: Oh, fuck you. You know I can do it; I can be as snotty and polite as anybody and it just makes me look stupid.

ANDREW: Georgie, it doesn't. You just—look. The English language is one of the most elegant and sophisticated languages on earth, and it will let you be whatever you want. If you use it carefully, and with respect, it can teach you things, it will allow you to uncover thoughts and ideas you never knew you were capable of; it will give you access to wisdom. Sophistication. Knowledge. Language is a gift that humanity has given itself to describe the world within, and without, with grace and wonder, and you can do that. Or you can use it badly and just be what you say you are. You can just be a, a fucking—cunt, if that's all you ever—

GEORGIE: UGGH. I can't believe you used that word. Oh, my God. You should see these words coming out of your mouth. It's so fucking weird. I'm not kidding, Andrew. I wouldn't swear if I was you.

ANDREW: Forget it.

(The tea kettle whistles.)

ANDREW: You want that fucking tea?

GEORGIE: No. I don't want the fucking tea.

ANDREW: *(Exits to the kitchen and turns off the kettle. He re-enters.)* You want to tell me what happened?

GEORGIE: Oh, God. It really is stupid. I mean, what do you think happened? He wants to screw me is what happened.

(Pause.)

ANDREW: Could you elaborate on that?

GEORGIE: What, you don't know what that means?

ANDREW: He propositioned you or he tried to rape you or what? You have to be more specific; "screw" covers a lot of ground.

GEORGIE: Well, in his own weird little way he tried both, okay?

ANDREW: *(Pause.)* Georgie, don't kid around with me now—

GEORGIE: Just sit down, Andrew. He didn't lay a hand on me, he just—Look. Last week he tells me we have to talk about my future with the firm so we go out to dinner and he tells me how amazing I am and I could be a paralegal if I keep this up. I spilled my soup, I got so excited. So then he took me home and asked if he could come up, and I said sorry, but I would like to keep our relationship professional. See, I do know how to talk like you assholes when I want to, so you can just stop acting like I'm a fucking idiot with words.

ANDREW: So he propositioned you.

GEORGIE: Last week, that was last week. Yesterday, he has me stay late, right? He says, "Georgie, could you stay late and type up some interrogatories." And I say, "sure." Then after everybody's gone he invites me into his office and asks me if I knew his couch folds out into a bed. So I say, "I have to get to work, Edward." But he wants to have a debate about the pros and cons of whether or not I should screw him. It was amazing, it went on for twenty minutes, I am not kidding. So I finally said, "Edward, I don't have to debate this with you. I don't have to be polite, you know? I'm not going to fuck you." So he says, he doesn't have to be polite either and he could just rape me if he wanted because everybody else is gone and the security guard isn't due until ten. And I stared at him—and, you know, I could see it in his little lawyer's face; he could've done it. *(Pause.)* I mean, on the one hand, it was no big deal; I just walked out of the office and took the stairs, 'cause I wasn't going to wait for any elevator. I mean, I was scared, but I didn't think he was going to do anything because it was pretty clear that in his own sick little mind, just saying it was as good as doing it.

ANDREW: You went to work today? You went to work after that?

GEORGIE: That job means a lot to me! *(Pause.)* What was I supposed to do, just quit and go back to—fuck, I don't know—I mean—I don't want to go back and be a waitress! What was I supposed to do? Quit because Edward is an asshole? I didn't care, I didn't think he'd try it again! I didn't; I thought that was it!

ANDREW: Wasn't it?

GEORGIE: Today, he comes out of his office at about 4:30 and asks me to stay late to type a pleading. And he kind of looks at me, you know? So I said, fuck you, Edward, and threw my pencil at him.

ANDREW: *(Pause.)* Why didn't you tell me? Dammit. Why didn't you tell me last night?

GEORGIE: He said something, it was something he said.

ANDREW: He said something *worse?*

GEORGIE: No. No. It was just talk. You know? It was just talk. I just—I didn't want to make a big deal about it./

ANDREW: It *is* a big deal. It's indecent. It's a big deal. *(He paces angrily.)*

GEORGIE: Andrew. You're mad. I've never seen you mad.

ANDREW: Yes, I'm mad! I'm mad! We'll sue him for harassment. We'll take him to court.

GEORGIE: What, are you kidding? He'll kill us. He's a really good lawyer.

ANDREW: I don't care. Dammit. Goddammit!

GEORGIE: You want some tea?

ANDREW: NO, I— *(Pause.)* I'm sorry. I shouldn't be yelling at you.

GEORGIE: It's okay. I mean, he didn't really do anything. It was just talk. Okay? Let me make you some tea.

(She goes into the kitchen. Andrew prowls the room angrily for a moment, then picks up the phone and dials. Georgie reenters with the tea.)

GEORGIE: Andrew, what are you doing? You're not calling him, are you? Don't call him, okay? Andrew. I mean it.

ANDREW: *(Into phone.)* Hi, Jennine, it's Andrew. Can you see if Edward is still there?

GEORGIE: *(Overlap.)* Andrew, I'm not kidding. Could you put the—would you put the fucking receiver down? Oh, FUCK.
(She crosses and pulls the cord out of the wall. They stare at each other for a moment, startled.)

GEORGIE: What, did you think I was kidding? Did you not understand that I was saying I do not want you calling that asshole? Do you not understand English?

ANDREW: *(Picks up the ends of the phone cord, angry.)* Have you lost your mind?

GEORGIE: No, I have not lost my mind! What the fuck kind of question is that? I asked you nicely to put the phone down. It was your little macho choice to keep on dialing, so don't go acting like I'm insane. I just don't want you talking to him right now! I don't need you doing some sort of protective male thing here! Just for a minute, okay?
(Pause.)

ANDREW: Okay.

GEORGIE: I'm sorry about your phone.

ANDREW: It's okay.

GEORGIE: I'll get you another one.

ANDREW: It's okay.

GEORGIE: God, I should just go home before I make everything worse—

ANDREW: No. It's okay. I'm sorry, okay?
(He takes her face in his hands for a moment; she pulls away nervously.)

GEORGIE: Okay. Let's talk about something else. Here's your tea. Chop those vegetables. Let's talk about—books. That'll cheer you up.

ANDREW: Georgie—

GEORGIE: No, come on, you're always beating me over the head to talk about books. I finished that one you gave me.
(She pulls a book out of her purse. They talk nervously.)

ANDREW: Already?

GEORGIE: It was good; it was a good read, you know? Reminded me of, like, Sydney Sheldon.

ANDREW: *The Iliad* reminds you of Sydney Sheldon. Great.

GEORGIE: Yeah, a lot happened, it would make a great mini series, you know? We should try the idea out on my sister; she's like the expert on junk TV. No shit, she lies around this apartment in the Bronx all day…What else you got?
(She picks up a book from the table. He takes it from her.)

ANDREW: No, you can't have that. I'm using that.

GEORGIE: Oh. Right. Right! How's your book coming?

ANDREW: It's fine.

GEORGIE: You should let me help you with that. I mean, I'm out of work now. I could come down and plug it into your computer for you. No kidding, I'm fast. I'll type it up for you; you'll be done in a week.

ANDREW: Right.

GEORGIE: I could, I could help! I mean, as long as you're going to do this Pygmalion thing, you might as well get something out of it.

ANDREW: Do what?

GEORGIE: Isn't that what it's called? I heard Edward—uh—you know, I heard That Guy we both can't stand right now tell one of the partners you were doing this pig thing. So I asked Donna about it. Some guy wrote a whole book; I bought it.

ANDREW: George Bernard Shaw.

GEORGIE: Yeah. I mean, it didn't exactly hit me as being the same thing here—

ANDREW: It's not the same thing. It's not the same thing at all. Edward doesn't know shit, okay? *(He takes the vegetables into the kitchen.)*

GEORGIE: *(Calling.)* Well—okay, he doesn't know shit, but I thought there were similarities.

ANDREW: *(Reenters with wash cloth and begins wiping off coffee table.)* It's not the same thing.

GEORGIE: Then what is it? *(Pause.)* I mean it. What is this?

ANDREW: What is what?

GEORGIE: This. This. All the dinners and the books and the lessons and the job. What is this, anyway? We been doing this for like, six months or something, you know? I mean—what's going on here, Andrew?

ANDREW: Georgie. We can take him to court.

GEORGIE: NO. I'm not talking about him. I'm talking about this. What is this?

ANDREW: It's—friendship.

GEORGIE: Friendship.

ANDREW: Yes.

GEORGIE: You're sure about that.

ANDREW: Yes.

GEORGIE: You get that mad whenever anybody fucks around with your friends, huh?

ANDREW: Yes.

(She looks at him. Suddenly, she crosses and sits very close.)

ANDREW: What are you doing?

GEORGIE: Nothing.

ANDREW: Georgie—

GEORGIE: I'm not doing anything. I'm just sitting next to my friend here with hardly any clothes on.

ANDREW: Come on. Don't do this. Please?

GEORGIE: Just once, Andrew. Don't you want to try it just once? Really. Don't you, kind of?

ANDREW: I don't think a one night stand is what you're looking for.

GEORGIE: Fine. We'll do it twice. She'll never know.

ANDREW: She's not the one I'm worried about. Georgie—oh, boy. Look, you're upset about what happened with Edward

GEORGIE: Do I look upset?

ANDREW: But this isn't going to fix that—

GEORGIE: I don't need to be fixed. Come on, Andrew, let's just do it today. I had a bad day. I'm not upset—but I had a bad day.

ANDREW: Georgie—no—If I—I would be just as bad as him if I—I'm not going to take advantage of you like that.

GEORGIE: Fuck, yes, take advantage of me. Please. Don't be noble, Andrew. For once, don't be noble.

ANDREW: Georgie, sweetheart—

GEORGIE: Andrew. She's going to be here in half an hour. We don't have a lot of time to talk about this.

(She slides her arms up around his neck. Protesting, he tries to pull her away. She resists and they wrestle for a moment; Andrew finally gets her turned around and holds her in front of him with her arms crossed under his.)

GEORGIE: Okay, okay, if you don't want to, just say so—

ANDREW: It's not that I don't want to! *(Pause.)* I want to, all right?

GEORGIE: You do?

ANDREW: Yes. Oh, yes.

(He buries his face in her hair for a moment. She waits, uncertain.)

GEORGIE: Okay. *(Pause.)* Are we waiting for something?

ANDREW: It's not that simple.

GEORGIE: Trust me on this one. It is that simple.

(She pulls away; he holds her.)

ANDREW: Not fifteen minutes ago, you were on a rampage; you were ready to murder me and every other man you've ever met. Now you want to make love?

GEORGIE: Sex is kind of spontaneous that way.

ANDREW: It's not what you want.

GEORGIE: I'm pretty sure it is.

ANDREW: Please. Listen to me. Will you please listen?

(She nods. He releases her. Pause.)

ANDREW: All right. Nietzche talks about the myth of eternal return.

GEORGIE: Oh, come on. Don't do this to me—

ANDREW: Thomas Hardy, historical repetition.

GEORGIE: Don't do this to me, Andrew—we don't have much time here!

ANDREW: *(Overlap.)* What history teaches is that people have never learned anything from history. Hegel. History is a nightmare from which I am trying to escape. James Joyce.

GEORGIE: *(Overlap.)* This is your fucking book. I don't want to hear about your stupid book now!

ANDREW: You better want to hear about it, because I'm not talking about my stupid book, I'm talking about your life. Historical repetition. One man treats you bad so you fall in bed with another. God. The system eats up people like you; you end up in dead end jobs, crummy apartments, bad neighborhoods, too many drugs, too much alcohol, meaningless relationships. They don't give you anything to live for, so you live for nothing! The complexities of what happens to the underclasses are so byzantine no one can make head or tail out of them anymore, we never could. We spin our theories, one after another, and it never amounts to anything; century after century we lose half the human race, more than half, to what? And why? I just didn't want to see you become a statistic.

GEORGIE: What does this have to do with whether or not we go to bed?

ANDREW: I will not become just another one of your lovers. We're both worth more than that.

GEORGIE: I didn't mean—

ANDREW: Relationships *mean* something. People *mean*. You don't sleep with every person you're attracted to; that's not the way it works. And aside from the crucial fact that I'm not about to betray Lydia, whom I love, I'm not going to betray you. You want to know what this is? I am not your friend, okay? I am your teacher. And you don't sleep with your teacher; it screws up everything. You don't do it.

GEORGIE: Fine. Okay, fine. I mean, I just wanted to sleep with you. I didn't mean to threaten world history.

ANDREW: Georgie. It's not that I don't want to.

GEORGIE: No, it's fine, I don't care, I shouldn't of— I'm no better than Edward, am I?

ANDREW: No. You are.

GEORGIE: What's Lydia like? Is she like you? I mean, is she gentle, like you?

ANDREW: I guess so.

GEORGIE: Edward is so full of shit. You know, he told me—He told me the reason he came on to me was because you told him to.

ANDREW: What?

GEORGIE: Yeah. I mean, I didn't believe him. Because it was so creepy, and you're not—I mean, you're so Not That, but it just made me sick to hear it, you know?

ANDREW: *(Pause.)* What did he say?

GEORGIE: I don't know. He said you told him I was on the make or something and he should—you know? Then today when I got here, you said you talked to him, so I thought—I mean, I didn't want to think it, but—I'm sorry. I just—I got freaked out. I'm sorry.

ANDREW: It's okay.

GEORGIE: What a creep.

ANDREW: Yeah. *(Long pause.)* It's getting late. We should—get going on this dinner.

(He picks up the dish rag and crosses to the kitchen. She watches him for an awful moment.)

GEORGIE: *(Quiet, filled with dread)* Andrew?

ANDREW: What?

GEORGIE: What did you say to him?

ANDREW: What?

GEORGIE: *(Pause.)* Oh, no. When I got here you said you talked to him. What did you say?

ANDREW: I said—I liked you. That was all I said.

GEORGIE: That was all?

ANDREW: Yes! I mean, no, I—of course, we talked about other things, but it wasn't anything—it wasn't—

GEORGIE: Why are you getting so nervous?

ANDREW: I'm not nervous! I'm trying to remember the conversation. He said—he wanted to ask you out, and I said I thought that would be okay. I told you might be—I told him I thought you might need someone in your life, you seemed—Look. I thought you were getting a kind of a crush on me, so it might be good for you—

GEORGIE: You gave me to him?

ANDREW: No. That's not what I did.

GEORGIE: What the fuck would you call it? Why was he asking your permission to go out with me in the first place? Am I like your property or something and he has to get your permission—

ANDREW: Georgie, no; it was a misunderstanding. He thought there was something going on between us and he just wanted to know—

GEORGIE: Something going on. Some *thing*, huh? Christ, Andrew. I am in love with you.

ANDREW: *(Pause.)* I'm sorry. I didn't know.

GEORGIE: You didn't know? How could you not know?

ANDREW: Please, believe me, if I had known, I never would have said—

GEORGIE: You never would have said what? You never would have said, go ahead, take her? You never would have said that, huh? I can't believe you. You—you're just the same as the rest of them, aren't you? *(She picks up her bag and goes to the door quickly, furious.)*

ANDREW: No! That's not—Georgie, you're upset, you're not being fair, you're not thinking—

GEORGIE: Don't talk to me about fair, just don't even start!

ANDREW: Don't walk out. We have to talk about this. Georgie—
(He grabs her elbow. She shoves him hard. They stare at each other.)

GEORGIE: Fuck that, Andrew. You don't like my language, and I don't like yours. I'm sick of talking, you know? You know what I mean? You guys—for all you know, you don't know shit. *(She exits.)*
(Blackout.)

SCENE II

Again, loud classical music on the radio; this time something more sinister— Stravinsky, Rachmaninoff. A bottle of scotch with a significant dent in it stands on the coffee table. Knocking on the door. After a moment, Andrew crosses into the room.

ANDREW: Yeah, yeah, I'm coming—
(He opens the door; Edward enters. Andrew stares at him, aghast.)

EDWARD: Hi. How's it going?

ANDREW: Edward.

EDWARD: Nice. Nice welcome. Listen, your security's great here; your front door is wide open.

ANDREW: Edward, what are you doing here?

EDWARD: I'm returning your calls. Sorry I didn't get back to you; I was in court all day. Anyway, I'm supposed to have dinner with Georgie, so I thought I'd kill two birds with one stone. I won't stay.

ANDREW: *(Quietly astonished.)* What? You what?

EDWARD: Christ, what a day I've had. Can I use your phone? *(He dials.)*

ANDREW: She's having dinner with you?

EDWARD: Yeah. Can you turn that down?

(Andrew crosses to the music and snaps it off. Edward speaks into the receiver.)

EDWARD: Georgie. It's Edward. *(Pause.)* No, no, I'm in the building. I'm at Andrew's. So, can you just meet me down here? *(Pause.)* Hello? *(Pause.)* No, I just—Andrew wanted to talk to me about something, so I—No, I just got here. *(Pause.)* It's okay—okay, take your time. *(Pause.)* Okay, great. Bye. *(He stares at the receiver, perplexed, and hangs up.)* Christ. You have anything to drink around here?

ANDREW: You're not staying.

EDWARD: *(Finds the bottle of scotch.)* Is this *scotch?* Andrew, congratulations. You learned how to drink scotch. *(He exits to the kitchen, delivers part of his speech there, reenters pouring scotch and sits.)*

ANDREW: Edward—

EDWARD: *(Calling.)* You would not believe the day I've had. I spent the entire afternoon in front of McGilla Gorilla trying to convince her that three Jamaican dope peddlers with a collective list of priors as long as the Old Testament had been denied their rights. Some of these judges—I mean, I didn't write the fucking constitution. It wasn't my idea to give everybody rights. That was our founding fathers, remember? If she doesn't like it, she can complain to the goddam supreme court. The stupid cop violated their rights. He pulls them over—get this, the cop pulls them over because they ran a red light—and they all get into an argument, so he pulls a search and seizure and finds six pounds of marijuana in the trunk. Marijuana, okay, we're not even talking cocaine. And can you show me probable cause in an argument about whether the light was yellow or red? Can you do that for me, please? Four hours I'm arguing this shit. I mean, I got assigned this crummy case; someone give me a fucking break! I hate this pro bono shit. If I'm going to defend criminals I really prefer that they have lots and lots of money.

ANDREW: *(Crosses and takes the glass from him politely. Quiet.)* Don't make yourself at home; you're not staying. I've been calling you all day to let you know that I want you to stay away from her. If you ever go near her again, I'll have you charged with assault. No. Forget that. If you go near her, I'll cut your throat out. Do you understand? Now get out.

(Pause.)

EDWARD: Well. That was aggressive. You want to tell me what this is about?

ANDREW: You know what this is about.

EDWARD: Well, no, really, I don't, but I can make some wild guesses. You talked to Georgie?

ANDREW: Yes. I talked to Georgie.

EDWARD: She told you about the fight we had, huh?

ANDREW: Actually, what she told me was that you threatened to rape her.

EDWARD: What? Oh, that is not—

ANDREW: Don't. Just don't even try to talk your way out of this one. You know, frankly, I never thought even you could sink this low. Christ, we've been friends for what, fifteen years, and I've seen you go through a lot of women and I'm not always crazy about the way you treat them, but this—if anyone had asked me, I would've said, no, he's bad but he's not that bad—

EDWARD: *(Overlap.)* Andrew. I didn't threaten her. I did not threaten her. Okay?

ANDREW: Spare me—

EDWARD: To the best of my recollection, in this country the accused is innocent until proven guilty, so can you give me a second here to tell you what happened?

ANDREW: Fine. Fine. Go right ahead.

EDWARD: Can I have my drink back, please?

(Andrew looks at him, hands him the drink.)

EDWARD: I'm glad to see you're bringing an open mind to this. Okay. You want to know what happened? I came onto her. I admit it. That's not a crime; she's an attractive woman. And as you'll recall, I told you about this ahead of time; I got clearance from you, pal.

ANDREW: Don't throw that at me—

EDWARD: *(Overlap.)* I asked you—

ANDREW: *(Overlap.)* You said you wanted to start seeing her!

EDWARD: Did you think that meant I was going to take her on a picnic?

ANDREW: I certainly didn't think it meant rape.

EDWARD: Oh, for—Nothing happened! I came onto her and she wasn't interested and I got mad. That's it. I got mad.

ANDREW: What did you say to her?

EDWARD: Please. Who remembers? It turned into a huge fight. The woman is screaming at me. I know very little.

ANDREW: What did you say?

EDWARD: Andrew—this woman makes Godzilla look like a Barbie doll.

ANDREW: What did you say?

EDWARD: I don't remember the specifics of the fight.

ANDREW: You did it, didn't you? You said it.

EDWARD: I did not threaten her, okay? I mean, we were having an argument, a discussion in my office, and I said some things that perhaps I should not have said, but I did not threaten her—

ANDREW: (Overlapping.) Oh, what, "some things that I should not have said," like I could just rape you—

EDWARD: All right, yes, perhaps I said that, that is not the same thing—

ANDREW: That's it. Get out.

(He grabs at the drink. Edward resists and the scotch goes flying, covering both of them.)

EDWARD: Do you think we can discuss this like rational adults?

ANDREW: No, as a matter of fact, I don't think we can.

EDWARD: When I walked in, you said you wanted to slit my throat. That doesn't mean you'd actually do it, does it?

ANDREW: Oh, it might.

EDWARD: I was having a fight with my secretary, Andrew. We both said things we shouldn't have said. *(Edward turns away and goes to the kitchen. He returns a moment later with a towel. He dries himself off and throws it at Andrew.)*

ANDREW: It wasn't a fight. It was sexual harassment.

EDWARD: Oh, don't even say those words. Everyone's so fucking sensitive these days—

ANDREW: (Overlap.) I don't give a damn what you—

EDWARD: (Overlap.) As a term, "sexual harassment" is so over defined it's almost meaningless. MacKinnon notwithstanding, at no point did I actually threaten her; and at no point did I suggest that her job security would be endangered by a failure to participate in a sexual act—

ANDREW: (Overlap.) Shut up. WOULD YOU PLEASE SHUT UP? *(Pause.)*

EDWARD: I'm sorry. I spend too much time in front of judges. *(Pause.)* Come on. Let's be reasonable about this. If I had threatened to rape her, would she be having dinner with me?

ANDREW: I don't know anything about any dinner.

EDWARD: You just heard me on the phone with her. I admit, we had a nasty fight, but she came back to the office today, we talked it out, and she went back to work. Now I'm taking her to dinner to smooth things over.

ANDREW: A dinner is supposed to smooth over rape?

EDWARD: I did not in fact rape her! Can we at least agree on that?

ANDREW: Fine.

EDWARD: Thank you. Now. May I take it that you object to this dinner?

ANDREW: Yes. I object to the dinner.

EDWARD: Why?

ANDREW: Edward—

EDWARD: Are you interested in her?

ANDREW: You know—she is not some thing we can pass around between us, Jesus—

EDWARD: You're objecting to a simple dinner. I'm trying to find out why. If there's something going on between you—

ANDREW: No, nothing is going on between us!

EDWARD: You don't want her, but you'd prefer that no one else had her?

ANDREW: I don't know what it is about you, but everything sounds so sleazy coming out of your mouth.

EDWARD: Yeah, they teach us how to do that in law school. I'm just trying to get a grip on this, man. I mean, it sounds to me like you want to fuck her.

ANDREW: Everything is not sex, you know?

EDWARD: I know. Do you want to fuck her or not?

ANDREW: Look, I'm engaged to another woman, I'm not about to—why am I even answering you? I'm not the one on trial here!

EDWARD: Oh, no. Not Lydia. I have told you, I absolutely refuse to believe that you are going to marry that woman—

ANDREW: We are not getting into this again—

EDWARD: Sleeping with Lydia is one thing, Andrew, but marrying her—

ANDREW: We are not discussing this—

EDWARD: Come on, the woman looks like a corpse! What happens when you dust her off and actually put her in sunlight?

ANDREW: You didn't object to her looks while you were going out with her! As I recall, before she dumped you, you thought she was "exquisite."

EDWARD: Ooooo. Nice shot. That's a three pointer. *(He exits to the kitchen and returns a moment later with fixings for hors d'oeuvres. He eats happily.)*

ANDREW: *(Pause.)* I don't know why I even talk to you anymore.

EDWARD: *(Calling.)* I keep you sharp.

ANDREW: *(Calling.)* You give me a headache.

EDWARD: *(Reentering.)* I love fighting with you. You're so earnest.

ANDREW: Oh, for—yes, I'm earnest. Jesus CHRIST, I'm earnest! This is not a game—

EDWARD: ANDREW. CALM DOWN. I know it's not a game. I'm just being a jerk, okay?

ANDREW: Well, cut it out. I mean, some things are not just food for another argument. We're talking about a woman's soul here—

EDWARD: A woman's soul? Andrew, come back. We're-not talking about anybody's *soul;* we're talking about whether or not I said something sleazy to my secretary. I'm not trying to be difficult; I'm just being realistic. I mean, I just, I don't want to have a little conversation about how we all should behave better so the world will be a better place. I'm not going to make the world a better place. The human race does not do that. We make it worse, we always have; if we're not killing each other, we're killing whales or buffalo or bald eagles, what have you, and if we're not doing that, we just pollute everything so nothing can survive here anyway. That is what the human race does; it's what we've always done. We have our moments. We have Shakespeare. The Declaration of Independence. The Taj Mahal. Smokey Robinson. We are capable of wisdom and compassion and genius, but most of the time we just throw it away. We yearn for meaning and then we squander our lives on drugs and television. We're corrupt. We are not good. I accept that. And this is why you're holed up in this nice little university teaching political philosophy, and I'm making $143,000 a year defending drug dealers. Because I like reality. And what is the moral of this story? The moral is: Georgie is real. She is *real.* And frankly, your impulse to keep her at a distance, physically, at least, strikes me as a little academic.

ANDREW: Don't give me that. What are you saying, I'm stupid or insipid because I want to preserve some integrity in my private life, because I believe it's possible to—to—to care about her without screwing her? I believe in human dignity so I'm an idiot, is that it? Well, fuck you, Edward. I mean it. That's a crock of shit. Next thing, you'll be telling me Ted Bundy is a national hero!

EDWARD: Don't twist my words. My position is offensive enough as it stands. Chill out. Have some scotch. *(He pours him a drink.)* Come on. We can talk about this. We've been through worse.

ANDREW: I don't know. I don't know. Sometimes, talking to you is like talking to a swamp.

EDWARD: It's a gift.

ANDREW: I have to admit, it is.

(They drink.)

EDWARD: This is good scotch. When did you start drinking scotch?

ANDREW: Last night.

EDWARD: Oh?

ANDREW: Yeah. We had a fight of our own. She blames me for the whole thing. As far as she's concerned, I gave you permission to threaten rape.

EDWARD: Well in a way—

ANDREW: Edward—

EDWARD: Sorry. I'm sorry. It's like a knee jerk reaction. I'm sorry.

ANDREW: Look. I admit this is largely my fault. I never should have sent her to you in the first place. I wasn't thinking. I thought you'd treat her differently because she came from me.

EDWARD: Andrew.

ANDREW: I know. That was pretty stupid, wasn't it? I am a stupid man.

EDWARD: Andrew—I'm sorry. I am sorry. I just don't know what I can do about it now. You want me to promise to behave myself? I can promise that.

ANDREW: Please don't take this wrong, but I would have to be crazy to trust your promises at this point. God only knows what the word "behave" actually means to you.

EDWARD: It has a series of definitions.

ANDREW: Exactly. I'll get her another job.

EDWARD: What?

ANDREW: Don't give me a hard time about this! If she goes back to work for you, it's like she's saying fine, treat me like dirt, I don't mind. Well, she's better than that, all right?

EDWARD: It's not like she's Joan of Arc, for God's sake.

ANDREW: I'm not going to argue about this anymore.

EDWARD: It just seems to me that complete relocation is a drastic solution to an essentially simple misunderstanding. I don't think it's necessary, okay?

ANDREW: Well, I think it is.

(Pause.)

EDWARD: Well, what you think isn't entirely relevant anymore, is it?

ANDREW: *(Pause.)* Excuse me?

EDWARD: *(Dangerous.)* Look. I spent the last four months training that girl and she is now a damn good secretary. I'm not going to let you just walk off with her.

ANDREW: Oh, now everything's business all of a sudden—

EDWARD: What else would it be?

ANDREW: Was it business when you threatened to rape her? And this dinner, that's business too, huh?

(Pause.)

EDWARD: You know, you're getting to be a real prick in your old age.

ANDREW: That's funny, coming from you.

(Pause.)

EDWARD: So what are you going to do? You going to tell her that she can't work for me anymore? You're going to tell her that, huh?

ANDREW: I'm just going to talk to her. She'll quit.

EDWARD: She isn't going to quit! She doesn't give a fuck about your moral codes, Andrew! She needs the damn job.

ANDREW: I'm just going to talk to her.

EDWARD: Tell you what. We'll both talk to her. When she gets down here, we'll just ask her. The two of us. We'll just ask her if she wants to quit.

ANDREW: I would prefer to talk to her alone.

EDWARD: Uh huh. I just bet you would.

ANDREW: Listen—

EDWARD: No, I understand. You two need a little privacy to work out the details of this decent little friendship you got.

ANDREW: It's not—

(Knocks on door.)

EDWARD: How much time do you need?

ANDREW: I don't—

EDWARD: It took me five minutes to get her to come back. How much time do you need to get her to quit again?

GEORGIE: *(Knocking.)* Hey, are you guys in there?

EDWARD: Ten minutes. Will that do?

ANDREW: You know—Lydia really is right about you.

EDWARD: I'll give you fifteen. That's ten more than I had. And I'll bet you, you still can't do it. How about it, Andrew?

ANDREW: I am not going to bet you—

GEORGIE: *(Pounding.)* You guys—

EDWARD: You're on. Come up with some sort of excuse, okay? Hello, my darling.

(Edward opens the door. Georgie enters; she is dressed to the nines in a provocative outfit. In her hands, she carries a pair of exotic spike heels.)

GEORGIE: Hi, Eddie. Have a little trouble with the door there? *(She crosses and puts on her shoes.)*

EDWARD: You're late.

GEORGIE: So fire me. The subway went insane yet again. It took me forever to get home. Hi, Andrew.

EDWARD: You should have said something. I could have given you a lift.

GEORGIE: No, it's okay, I love the subway.

(She puts on the second shoe and stands up a little too quickly. She staggers; Edward reaches out and steadies her.)

EDWARD: Steady—

GEORGIE: Sorry. I haven't worn these things for a while and you have to get used to them, you know? It's kind of like walking on stilts.

EDWARD: They're fabulous. You really look stunning, Georgie.

GEORGIE: I'm not overdressed, am I?

EDWARD: No, no. I mean, you don't have to be. *(Pause.)* That's not what I mean. I mean, we can go someplace elegant. If—we go out, I mean.

GEORGIE: What do you mean, if?

EDWARD: Nothing.

GEORGIE: Great. Let's go. *(She turns for the door.)*

EDWARD: Andrew?

GEORGIE: Andrew. Well, what a fun idea. Andrew. Why don't you come along?

ANDREW: I don't think—

GEORGIE: If you're not hungry, you can always watch us eat.

(Pause.)

ANDREW: No. Thank you.

GEORGIE: Suit yourself. *(To Edward.)* Andrew's in a snit, huh? He doesn't like it when I wear these shoes. He thinks they're bad for me. But you like them, don't you?

EDWARD: I have to admit, I do. Sorry, Andrew.

GEORGIE: I like them, too. I like the way they make my legs look kind of dangerous. And I like being tall. *(She laughs.)* I like being able to look you both in the eye. It's the only chance I get, when I'm wearing these things. *(She crosses to Edward and stands close, looking him in the eye.)* See what I mean?

EDWARD: It's perfectly delightful.

GEORGIE: Thank you. *(She looks back at Andrew.)* What do you think, Andrew?

ANDREW: I think they look sad and ridiculous.

GEORGIE: Then I guess it's a good thing you're not going out to dinner with us, huh? Come on, Edward. Let's hit the road.

ANDREW: What's your rush?

(Pause.)

GEORGIE: Excuse me?

ANDREW: You don't have to rush off, do you? Why don't you guys stay and have a drink first?

GEORGIE: I think we're in kind of a hurry.

ANDREW: One drink.

GEORGIE: Aren't we in a hurry?

ANDREW: Are you? Edward?

EDWARD: I don't think so.

ANDREW: Maybe you could run downstairs and get a bottle of wine.

EDWARD: Well, there's an idea. I'll be right back.

GEORGIE: No, Edward—I mean, I don't like wine. Look, Andrew has this scotch here. So Andrew, you've taken up scotch, huh? Forget the wine. I'll have scotch.

ANDREW: I'd really like some wine.

GEORGIE: What are you talking about? You're drinking scotch.

ANDREW: I'd rather have wine.

GEORGIE: Well, fine, then you go get it.

EDWARD: No, that's okay, I'll get it. What would you like?

ANDREW: I don't—Champagne.

GEORGIE: What?

ANDREW: We'll have champagne. It'll be fun.

GEORGIE: Fun?

EDWARD: I'll be right back.

GEORGIE: No, come on—I mean—okay. I'll go get it.

ANDREW AND EDWARD: *(Overlapping.)* NO. No, no—
    (Georgie stares at them.)

EDWARD: I mean—it'll just take a second. You two—can chat.

GEORGIE: I don't want to chat.

EDWARD: Chat.

    (He exits. Georgie turns and stares at Andrew for a second, then crosses and pours herself a glass of scotch.)

GEORGIE: Okay. What is going on?

ANDREW: I might ask you the same question.

GEORGIE: Hey, I'm not the one acting like the three stooges, okay?

ANDREW: What do you think you're doing?

GEORGIE: What do I think I'm doing? I think I'm giving Edward a hard-on. What do you think I'm doing?

ANDREW: I don't know. *(Pause.)* Are you trying to make me jealous?

GEORGIE: Is it working?

ANDREW: Yeah. Sure.

GEORGIE: Good. /

ANDREW: I can't believe you. You went back to work for him. After what he did, you went back to work—you're going out to *dinner*—

GEORGIE: You're suggesting we all have champagne together. So get off my fucking back, okay? It looks like we're two of a kind when it comes to Edward.

ANDREW: I was trying to get rid of him so I could talk to you for a few minutes!

GEORGIE: Really? Andrew, you're so sly.

ANDREW: Okay, fine. You're mad at me, you want to have a fight, fine—

GEORGIE: Gee, thanks for the permission, teach—

ANDREW: But don't go back to work for him! Don't have dinner with him!

GEORGIE: Why not?

ANDREW: He threatened to rape you!

GEORGIE: He apologized!

ANDREW: I would like to think that some things go beyond apology.

GEORGIE: Like what? Like betrayal, maybe? Listen—I know he's still slime, but you want to know what happened? I did go back to work, yeah. I went back in to get my stuff—I had all this shit in my desk, you know? So I go in at about ten to pick it all up, and it was amazing. Every secretary in the building has her own little story to tell me about how she almost did the same thing but never had the guts. I'm like this fucking hero, you know? So right in the middle of this big scene, there's like fifteen people crowding around my desk, right, Edward comes out and says he wants to talk to me. In his office. And he just stands there, and it's like this dare, you know, it's like this fucking dare, and everyone goes real quiet, just waiting to see what I'm gonna do. The whole fucking office is watching me. So we go in, and he apologizes. Swore he'd never do it again. Then he offers me a two thousand dollar raise. Well—the whole thing just started to seem kind of funny. Two thousand bucks? He never even touched me! I didn't even have to kiss him. I just thought— hey, you know, two thousand bucks. Jesus. So—I didn't quit. *(Pause.)* I didn't quit.

ANDREW: Do you believe him?

GEORGIE: Yeah. I believe he's going to give me a raise. He won't even feel it. Two thousand is like what he pays to have his car waxed.

ANDREW: That's not what I mean.

GEORGIE: I know.

(Pause.)

ANDREW: I can get you another job. Last night I called some people in the department and I found some leads—

GEORGIE: I don't need a job. I got a job.

ANDREW: You don't have to put up with it. He'll try it again, you know he will—

GEORGIE: I can take care of myself; I been doing it for years. I don't need you to like, worry about me.

ANDREW: I beg to differ.

GEORGIE: Yeah, well, tough shit for you.

ANDREW: (Pause.) This isn't about the job.

GEORGIE: I'm getting out of here; you make me crazy— (She goes for the door.)

ANDREW: Last night you said you were in love with me.

GEORGIE: Yeah. I remember

(Pause.)

ANDREW: Come here, Please? I can't talk to you if you keep trying to leave. Come on, sit down—

(He crosses to her at the door. Instinctively, her arms fly up, defensive.)

GEORGIE: Andrew, don't. (Pause.) I just—could you not get too close to me? (Wounded, Andrew backs off. She stands at the door and looks at him.)

ANDREW: I'm sorry about what happened. I didn't mean to betray you, and I certainly never meant to hurt you, and if that's why you're doing this—

GEORGIE: What exactly am I doing? (Pause.) You don't know, do you? You don't know if I'm just trying to make you jealous, or if this is just what is, you know, reality, why not sleep with him? Maybe this is me. Okay? I mean, I understand this. Hormones I get. Every man I've every had to deal with—I fucking know how to deal with that, okay? I know what to do, and when to do it, and how to get what I want. You know—I live in a whole different world from you. I'm in the receiver's position. I do what you guys tell me to; I always do it. Whether it's reading books or fucking, I do it. I make all this noise, you know; I scream and yell bloody fucking murder but I always manage to do what you say. That's the way we survive. I'm just being realistic, okay? And yeah, maybe I am trying to make you jealous, maybe I want to teach you something for a change, you could learn from me, but—fuck. Jesus. Forget it. (She crosses from him and sits.)

ANDREW: You're not that. You're not.

GEORGIE: Yeah, well then you tell me what I am because I don't know anymore.

Oh, fuck. Look—I'm sorry I'm being so awful, I don't—I'm just con-fused, okay? I don't want to talk about this. Fuck. I don't know what I'm doing, Andrew, I just don't know what else to—

ANDREW: It's okay. It's okay. *(Andrew crosses to her, tentative.)* Let me take those off. Please? Let me take your shoes off. /

(She looks at him, amazed, as he kneels and takes her shoes off, setting them aside. He holds her feet between his hands for a moment.)

GEORGIE: Andrew, don't. Come on. Don't. It's killing me, okay? I know it's nothing to you, but I can't take it.

ANDREW: *(Looks at her.)* It's not nothing. /

(He holds her by the elbow and slowly leans in to kiss her. The kiss begins to become passionate and physical when he suddenly pulls away. Confused, she clings to him for a moment; he gently releases himself.)

ANDREW: *(Pause.)* Oh, God. You scare me to death.

GEORGIE: What?

ANDREW: You—no. No.

GEORGIE: Wait a minute. Come on. Let's go back to this tender moment thing—

(She reaches for him; he pulls away.)

ANDREW: Look at that dress.

GEORGIE: What?

ANDREW: You look ridiculous.

GEORGIE: You just said—could you not fuck with my brain here? I get enough of that at the office—

ANDREW: Why are you wearing those shoes?

GEORGIE: Because they make my legs look good! Why are you yelling at me?

ANDREW: Because you're making a spectacle of yourself.

GEORGIE: Listen, the popular opinion is that I clean up pretty good, so don't get started on me here—

ANDREW: You don't care, do you? You're just going to go ahead and squander yourself. This is enough for you? The shoes, the dress, the fancy dinner. That's what you want, is that it?

GEORGIE: No. No, I don't want him, I don't want to do this, if you don't want me to, I won't do it—I—Why are you yelling at me? A minute ago you were kissing me, and you meant it. You meant it. Why are you yelling at me? What the FUCK is going on here?

ANDREW: *(Pause.)* It wouldn't work. We are too different. There is an abyss between us; not a crevice, not a difference of opinion. An abyss. The void. It would be a nightmare to negotiate, and you're not exactly the calmest person I've ever met, you know what I mean? Who do you think you'd take it out on?

GEORGIE: I wouldn't.

ANDREW: Who are you kidding? It's inevitable with you; there's no peace in you. The only reason we've lasted as long as we have is because we don't sleep together. I listen to you, and I feel battered. I wouldn't survive. I'm telling you, if it got to be any more than this, I would not survive. *(Pause.)* It doesn't have to be like this. Life doesn't have to be just this long scream of rage, Georgie. You're better than this. I made you better than this.

GEORGIE: What?

ANDREW: I'm sorry. I didn't mean that.

GEORGIE: What did you say? You made me better? Did you actually say that?

ANDREW: Please don't go off again, I cannot take any more of this—

GEORGIE: *(Picks up the shoes.)* Well, I won't be better. I won't be better anymore. I'll be as bad as I want. Why didn't you just leave me alone in the first place; why didn't you just let me be whatever I was? At least I was happy. *(She starts to put on the shoes again.)*

ANDREW: You weren't happy.

GEORGIE: Fuck you. I'm not happy now.

ANDREW: You were not happy. You were so bored with your life you were killing yourself. You came home drunk after every shift; you were sleeping with every guy who looked at you—

GEORGIE: That's what this is all about, isn't it? Fuck the abyss, this isn't about any abyss, this is about sex! All the guys. That's what bothers you, really. Isn't it?

ANDREW: Oh, for God's sake, I'm not judging you. Your apartment's right above mine. I couldn't help—the whole building knew about it. Christ.

GEORGIE: Why don't you just cut my heart out and get it over with? Compared to you, Edward really is a prince. Tell him I went upstairs to wait.

ANDREW: Georgie—

GEORGIE: TELL HIM I'M WAITING FOR HIM UPSTAIRS.

ANDREW: It won't prove anything.

GEORGIE: Oh, yeah. It will. Think about it, Andrew. Think about it tonight, while you're listening to your little ceiling here. Think about it.
(She exits. Andrew stands for a moment, then viciously shoves a pile of books off the bookcase. Blackout.)

END OF ACT I

ACT II
SCENE I

Loud music is heard on the boombox, Elvis Costello or Prince. The lights come up on Georgie's apartment, layout identical to that in Andrew's apartment, but all particulars—knickknacks, books, pillows, etc., different. This apartment is a comfortable mess. Georgie actually has more books than Andrew; they sprawl everywhere, as do her tapes. Edward and Georgie are discovered entwined in a serious clinch on the couch. Georgie's legs are wrapped around Edward's body, the spike heels clearly visible. After a moment, Edward suddenly pulls away. He looks down at Georgie for a moment, stands, crosses to the music and snaps it off. Georgie watches him, astonished. He remains standing by the silent boombox for a moment before she speaks.

GEORGIE: Is something wrong?

EDWARD: The music. It seemed a little loud to me.

GEORGIE: Oh. *(Pause.)* Well, then, why don't you turn it off?

EDWARD: Thanks, I think I will.

(Pause. He stands there, thinking. She looks at him.)

GEORGIE: Edward—

EDWARD: Could I have something to drink?

GEORGIE: Excuse me?

EDWARD: You invited me up for a drink. I'd like a drink.

GEORGIE: I'm sorry. I'm a little confused. I thought we got *past* the drink.

EDWARD: I'm kind of thirsty.

(Pause.)

GEORGIE: Okay. What would you like to drink?

EDWARD: I don't know, I—tea? Could I have a cup of tea?

GEORGIE: Excuse me?

EDWARD: I think I'd like some tea.

GEORGIE: Why?

EDWARD: Don't you have any tea?

GEORGIE: I don't know, you know, I kind of doubt it—

EDWARD: I'll look.

GEORGIE: Edward—

(He exits to the kitchen. Noise. Georgie looks after him, annoyed, then sits and stares at the coffee table for a moment. She suddenly picks up a pile of books and drops them on the floor, crosses to the table, pours herself a drink.)

GEORGIE: *(Calling loudly.)* I think you're going to have to settle for scotch, Edward. Personally, I have always thought scotch was much more to the point than almost anything else available in most situations.

EDWARD: *(Calling.)* I'd like to keep my wits about me, if you don't mind.

GEORGIE: *(Drinking.)* Oh, you plan on needing your wits? What for?

EDWARD: *(Reentering.)* One never knows. You know, your kitchen is a disaster area. And how old is this stuff? *(He carries a mashed box of tea.)*

GEORGIE: I have no idea.

EDWARD: That milk in there, you know, that stuff is really frightening. *(He goes back into the kitchen.)*

GEORGIE: *(Calling.)* Edward—

EDWARD: *(Calling, sound of dishes.)* Don't you ever wash your dishes? Andrew's always complaining about the bugs in this building; I don't see how you can just leave dirty plates lying around like this. It's like an invitation.

GEORGIE: Edward—EDWARD. You are not doing my dishes. YOU ARE NOT—

(She stands and crosses quickly. Edward meets her in the doorway.)

EDWARD: SHHHH. Could—would you be quiet, please? You are one of the noisiest people I've ever met. It's the middle of the night, people are trying to sleep.

GEORGIE: Not everyone. Some of them, I'm sure, are doing other things. People do all sorts of things in the middle of the night. Didn't you know that?

EDWARD: Yes. I know that.

GEORGIE: I thought maybe you did. So—what's the problem here, Edward? All of a sudden you're acting like—I mean, what, is this your first time?

EDWARD: No.

GEORGIE: You a little nervous? You want me to be gentle? I can be gentle. *(She starts to close in.)*

EDWARD: That's not necessary.

GEORGIE: I didn't think it was. So what's the problem?

EDWARD: I'm just trying to get a grip on this. I mean, not two days ago, you did tell me, and I quote, "Even if you were the last fucking asshole on the planet, Edward"

GEORGIE: Yeah, yeah, yeah. What can I say? I came to my senses.

EDWARD: Yes, well—

GEORGIE: You can be very persuasive.

EDWARD: I'm aware of that; still—

GEORGIE: You changing your mind about this?

EDWARD: No, that's not exactly—

GEORGIE: So what's the problem? *(She's getting close.)*

EDWARD: There's no problem. I just—I want that tea.

(He goes back to the kitchen. Georgie looks after him, seriously annoyed.)

GEORGIE: I swear, sex was never this complicated in high school. *(She looks at the floor. To floor.)* You getting all this?

(She glances back at the kitchen for a moment, then stomps on the floor several times. Edward enters with a mug of tea and watches her.)

EDWARD: Is something wrong?

GEORGIE: *(Starts.)* Oh. You know. Bugs. *(She takes off her shoe, crosses to the trash can and scrapes the bug off, puts the shoe back on.)* Got your tea there? Mmm, that looks delicious.

EDWARD: Could you turn down the sarcasm for just a few minutes, please? I mean, I would just like a minute, a tiny oasis of time that is not smothered in attitude. Just a moment of normal conversation. If you don't mind. I would like to talk.

GEORGIE: We talked at dinner.

EDWARD: No, we chatted at dinner. We had three hours of chat, and I'm feeling a little disoriented, and I would like to talk.

GEORGIE: Why?

EDWARD: What's the matter, don't you know *how* to talk?

GEORGIE: Of course I know how to talk. I talk constantly! I just don't want to talk now! Christ, you're as bad as Andrew!

EDWARD: Oh? How so?

GEORGIE: *(Pause.)* I don't want to talk about Andrew.

EDWARD: Why not?

GEORGIE: Edward—

EDWARD: What?

GEORGIE: You are driving me crazy.

EDWARD: Why are you getting so defensive?

GEORGIE: I'm not—I hate this.

EDWARD: I just asked a simple question—

GEORGIE: You did not, you—

EDWARD: Yes, I did—

GEORGIE: You're right, this talking is really fun. I'm so glad we're *talking.* Okay. So fine. So what was the question?

EDWARD: Actually, there was no question. The subject of Andrew came up and you got all tense.

GEORGIE: Why don't you pick a subject. You want to have a discussion here? Then pick a subject and let's get on with it all right?

EDWARD: All right. *(Pause.)* What do you and Andrew talk about?

GEORGIE: *(Pause.)* We talk about many things. Books and shit. America. You name it, we talk about it. Andrew and I have a very conversational relationship.

EDWARD: Does that bother you?

GEORGIE: *(Pause.)* What is that supposed to mean?

EDWARD: Nothing. He told me you had a crush on him, so I just thought—

GEORGIE: Well, he was wrong.

EDWARD: How did you two meet, anyway?

GEORGIE: Edward, what is it, I mean am I on trial here—

EDWARD: You have something to hide?

GEORGIE: NO, I—fuck. We met at the mailboxes. We live in the same building, I mean, it's not unusual—

EDWARD: What, did he try to pick you up?

GEORGIE: I hardly think so.

EDWARD: You tried to pick him up.

GEORGIE: Is there a point to this? 'Cause I got to tell you, you're kind of wrecking the mood here; you're like doing a demolition job on my hormones.

EDWARD: I just want to know how you two met! He never told me.

GEORGIE: He gave me a book. We were standing by the mailboxes, and he handed me this book and said, here, I think you'll like this. That was it. He gave me this book.

EDWARD: He gave you a book?

GEORGIE: Yes.

EDWARD: You didn't think that was a pickup?

GEORGIE: No, I thought he was a Jehovah's Witness.

EDWARD: What?

GEORGIE: I thought he was a Jehovah's Witness! I have this ongoing relationship with those guys; I'm like, a sucker for the Jehovah's Witnesses. So when this guy gave me a book I thought it was gonna be about the end of the world or what God really thinks or something. I mean, I got like the collected edition of those things—

EDWARD: You actually buy those?

GEORGIE: Yeah—well, yeah, I—I got a whole shelf of them.

(She indicates. He goes over to look at her books. He picks one up and pages through it, amazed.)

GEORGIE: What? They just get to me, okay? I mean, those fucking moonies, or the dianetics people, you can see it in their eyes, their brains are fried; they'd just as soon kill you as anything. But the Jehovah's Witnesses are always so nerdy I believe them. What? It's not like I go to their meetings or anything. I just talk to them. I like what they say. Resurrection. Life everlasting. It just sounds nice. I mean, I don't believe this shit at all, but I just—I end up listening because it's so—I don't know. They're always so kind. *(Pause.)* You can borrow that if you want. It's okay. You might like it. Some of it's very hopeful.

EDWARD: *(Looks at her and smiles.)* Thank you.

GEORGIE: So that's why I talked to Andrew. I thought he was a Jehovah's Witness. So. You want to do it or not?

EDWARD: *(Looks at her, startled and suddenly uncomfortable. The mood is seriously broken.)* Excuse me?

GEORGIE: Oh, come on, Edward. We both know why you're here.

EDWARD: *(Recovering.)* Yes, I guess we do, now. And I must say, I am stunned by your subtlety. I mean—never mind. Never mind. I think I will have that drink after all. The tea is not actually doing the trick. *(He picks the scotch bottle off the bookshelf, crosses to the kitchen and finds some ice and glasses.)*

GEORGIE: Oh, for God's sake. We're drinking now? Now we're drinking? Why are we drinking?

EDWARD: We're drinking because I want to drink!

GEORGIE: Are we going to have more conversation, too?

EDWARD: We will if I want to!

GEORGIE: Yeah, well, as long as we're taking a poll here, I gotta say, I'm not particularly interested in more conversation, Edward! I mean it. If you think this is going to go on all night or something, maybe you should just leave.

EDWARD: You're not throwing me out. *(He reenters, pours scotch into her glass and hands it to her.)*

GEORGIE: You say one more word, and I am.

EDWARD: No, you're not.

GEORGIE: Yes, I am.

EDWARD: Drink your scotch.

GEORGIE: Fuck you.

EDWARD: Yeah, fuck you too.

(They bump glasses in a forced toast. They both drink.)

GEORGIE: Now what? Should we have another? Maybe we should go out to dinner again. No, I know. How about a game of cards?

EDWARD: You know, I have to say, you really—your technique just leaves me breathless. Really.

GEORGIE: I gave you technique all night, Edward, and it didn't get either of us anywhere. But the gig is up. I don't know what's bugging you but it's time to get over it. You want to do it or not? This is your last shot.

EDWARD: *(Pause.)* My last shot?

GEORGIE: Yeah. This is it. This is the offer. So what's it going to be?

EDWARD: Well. Since you put it that way.

(He sets his drink down and looks at her. He does not move. After a moment, she crosses slowly, eases into him and almost kisses him. He speaks.)

EDWARD: Thank you very much, but since you put it that way, I'm afraid I'm going to have to decline your generous offer.

GEORGIE: *(Pause.)* Suit yourself. *(She crosses away from him, furious, and picks up her drink.)*

EDWARD: Please don't take this wrong. I just don't like being used.

GEORGIE: Oh, cut me a break. You want it; I'm saying here it is. Who cares about being used at a time like this?

EDWARD: I do.

GEORGIE: Yeah, I guess you can dish it out but you can't take it. Well, fine. That's fine. But trust me on this one: You just passed up the most interesting fuck of your life.

EDWARD: That may be. But it also may be that I prefer sleeping with one person at a time. Maybe I simply want to preserve as one of the ground rules of the increasingly neurotic relationship we seem to have established between us that if I ever do take you to bed, it will be on the condition that Andrew does not come along! *(He puts on his jacket and starts to leave.)*

GEORGIE: Andrew—fuck Andrew, I am tired of talking about Andrew!

EDWARD: What happened, he broke your heart so now you're bitter? You poor thing.

GEORGIE: Oh, shut up—

EDWARD: And now you're going to seduce his best friend to get back at him, is that it? That's the oldest trick in the book!

GEORGIE: Yeah, it's so old you almost fell for it.

EDWARD: What do you think you're doing? You think this is going to prove something? All it proves is what I suspected from the start. You are nothing but bad news.

GEORGIE: Look who's talking.

EDWARD: I am. And I know you. I know exactly who you are.

GEORGIE: You don't know the first thing about me.

EDWARD: I know everything about you. I see you every fucking day down at the courthouse, hanging all over your junkie boyfriend, screaming at your pimp!

GEORGIE: I don't know what you're talking about.

EDWARD: *(Overlap.)* I know where you grew up. I know your family. I know how your mother lays around the house all day because she can't hold down a job—

GEORGIE: This doesn't have anything to do with anything—

EDWARD: I know how she drinks! I know how she leeches money out of you! I know about all of it, the arrests—

GEORGIE: STOP IT. *(Pause.)* So what? So you listen in on my phone calls, so what is that supposed to prove?

EDWARD: I don't listen to your phone calls. I don't have to. You're a dime a dozen, Georgie; you are as common as dirt.

GEORGIE: Yeah, I'm so common you've been trying to screw me for four months.

EDWARD: You think that makes you something? That doesn't make you anything. This is all—this is a fucking game to guys like me; you're a piece of furniture, for God's sake! I could go through three of you in a week!

GEORGIE: *(Overlap.)* Shut up. SHUT UP.

EDWARD: Come to think of it, I will take you up on that offer. Why the hell not?

GEORGIE: SHUT UP. You SHUT UP

(She takes a swing at him. Edward grabs her arms; they struggle for a second.)

EDWARD: Christ—Georgie, for God's sake—

GEORGIE: Shut UP! Why don't you ever SHUT UP— *(She stops suddenly.)*

EDWARD: Georgie—

GEORGIE: Oh, shit, I can't see anything. Edward—

EDWARD: Oh, Christ—Here, put your head down—you're okay— *(He sets her on the couch and tries to put her head down.)*

GEORGIE: No, I need air— *(Scared.)* I can't see, Edward.

EDWARD: *(Starting to panic.)* You're okay. You're fine. Just shut your eyes for a second. Take a breath. Georgie?

GEORGIE: I can't see.

(She leans back on the couch. He puts his arm around her.)

EDWARD: You're okay. You're okay. Are you okay? Come on. Sweetheart. Are you okay?

GEORGIE: *(She suddenly shoves him away.)* Don't you touch me.

(He backs away, startled. Pause.)

GEORGIE: Just stay away from me, okay?

EDWARD: Yeah. Yeah. I'm sorry. I'm sorry, okay? I'm sorry. Christ. What am I doing?

(He sits. Pause. She watches him. He finally looks at her.)

EDWARD: Are you okay?

GEORGIE: Yeah.

EDWARD: I'm sorry. I don't know why I did that.

GEORGIE: Me neither.

EDWARD: Can you see me?

GEORGIE: Yeah. I can see you. It just went funny, you know? When you just see stars? It went funny. I couldn't see anything. It scared me.

EDWARD: Me too.

(She sits up. He starts for her, then stops.)

EDWARD: Come on. Just lie there for a second, would you?

GEORGIE: I'm okay.

EDWARD: You're not okay. You're drunk.

GEORGIE: No, I'm not. I didn't drink hardly anything. I just—I got—so mad at you. That never happened to me before. I mean, I'm, like, mad all the time, but that never happened before.

EDWARD: You just never had me around to provoke you. And that was nothing. Stick with me, baby. I'll *really* piss you off.

GEORGIE: It's not funny.

EDWARD: I know.

GEORGIE: You were being a big jerk.

EDWARD: I know. I'm sorry.

GEORGIE: Why did you do that?

EDWARD: *(Starts to cross again, and stops himself uncertainly.)* Don't think about it for a minute.

GEORGIE: Man. I have to stop getting so mad all the time.

EDWARD: You scared me half to death. Do you want a glass of water?

GEORGIE: What is this thing you have with liquids? Andrew's the same way; something goes wrong and he just dives for the liquids. I don't know, they teach you this in college? Is this a class thing?

EDWARD: I'll get you a glass of water.

(He goes into the kitchen. Georgie curls up on the couch. He returns a moment

later with a glass of water and a washcloth. He approaches her carefully, then feeds her the water as if she were a child. She resists for a moment.)

EDWARD: Come on, sweetheart. Just drink it. It's good for you.

GEORGIE: It's just water, Edward.

EDWARD: Water is very good for you—there you go. Here. Come on.

(She drinks. He takes the cloth and wipes her face.)

EDWARD: Is that better?

GEORGIE: Yeah.

EDWARD: Good.

GEORGIE: Why are you being so nice all of a sudden?

EDWARD: Look, I am a nice person.

(She laughs.)

EDWARD: I am! Ten percent of the time, I am a very nice person. *(He pats her face with the cloth again, then folds it neatly.)* You okay now?

GEORGIE: Yeah. Hey, Edward.

EDWARD: Yeah.

GEORGIE: What's she like? Lydia, I mean.

EDWARD: I'm not the person to ask. I don't like her.

GEORGIE: What, are you kidding? That makes you exactly the person to ask.

EDWARD: Lots of money, ancestors on the Mayflower, parents on Beacon Hill. That sort of thing.

GEORGIE: Yeah, yeah, yeah. Cut to the chase. What does she look like?

EDWARD: She's very pale. She's pretty, but pale and orderly. Quiet. I find her kind of sinister, to tell you the truth.

GEORGIE: You make her sound like Dracula.

EDWARD: Yes, she's very much like Dracula. Always meticulously dressed. You know, neat little dresses. Blouses with bows at the collar. Protruding bicuspids.

(He bares his teeth. She laughs, then starts to cry.)

EDWARD: Hey, hey, hey.

GEORGIE: Oh, perfect. He's gonna marry Dracula; that's just perfect. I'm sorry, I'm just—

EDWARD: Hey. It's okay.

GEORGIE: It's not okay. How can he do it?

EDWARD: It's what he thinks he wants.

GEORGIE: Well, why isn't it me?

EDWARD: I don't know. He's stupid.

GEORGIE: Don't talk down to me, Edward; I don't need you to act like I'm some sort of big baby here—

EDWARD: I'm not! I mean it. He's being really stupid.

GEORGIE: Yeah, right. *(Pause. She dries her eyes.)*

EDWARD: Look. I'm sorry I said those things, okay? I mean, those things I said before.

GEORGIE: No, it's okay. Some of it was true.

EDWARD: Still.

GEORGIE: Yeah. Hey, Edward.

EDWARD: Yeah?

GEORGIE: Can you put your arm around me for a second?

EDWARD: Georgie—

GEORGIE: Come on. I wouldn't ask except you've been nice for about two minutes or something and I'm afraid if I wait any longer, you'll, like, turn into yourself again.

EDWARD: You're not still doing this to get back at him?

GEORGIE: For heaven's sake. It's just a hug.

(He brushes her hair back from her face, and puts his arm around her. She hangs onto him for a moment, then pulls away a little. They sit, for a moment, with their arms around each other. She puts her head on his shoulder.)

GEORGIE: This is nice.

(Pounding on the door. Georgie jumps then clings to Edward for a second.)

EDWARD: Well. I wonder who that is.

GEORGIE: Oh, God. I can't handle this anymore.

EDWARD: Chin up. You can't give up now, sweetheart.

(The knocking becomes violent.)

GEORGIE: Edward—

EDWARD: You're fine. If he gets out of line, just throw a pencil at him.

(He opens the door. Lydia is there.)

EDWARD: Oh, no.

LYDIA: *(Biting.)* Hello, Edward. How lovely to see you again. *(She crosses into the apartment and glares at Georgie.)*

EDWARD: Lydia. What a charming coincidence. We were just talking about you.

LYDIA: That is charming.

EDWARD: Where's Andrew?

LYDIA: Who cares?

EDWARD: Oh, I think several of us, at least... *(He looks out in the hallway but Andrew is nowhere in sight.)*

LYDIA: How about you? Do you care?

GEORGIE: Well, I don't—

LYDIA: Oh, please. I have a little trouble believing that!

GEORGIE: Listen. I don't know who you are or what you think you're doing here, but—

LYDIA: Oh, I think you know who I am.

GEORGIE: Well, of course I know who you are! What are you doing here?

LYDIA: No. What are you doing here?

GEORGIE: I live here!

LYDIA: You know what I mean!

EDWARD: Excuse me, but where's Andrew?

LYDIA: Oh, where do you think he is? He's downstairs, shrouded in the shattered wreckage of his book, our marriage and my life.

EDWARD: Oh, Christ. *(He exits.)*

GEORGIE: Edward, hey! Hey, where are you going? Don't leave me here with her! Edward!

(But he is gone. Georgie turns and looks at Lydia, who is very steely indeed.)

GEORGIE: Look. It's been great meeting you, but you know, I am having one ripper of a day, you know, so—

LYDIA: Don't talk to me about bad days.

GEORGIE: Listen—

LYDIA: No. No. You listen. *(She puts down her purse decisively, crosses to the door and shuts it.)*

GEORGIE: HEY—

LYDIA: I don't know you. You and I have never met. And you are wreaking havoc on my life.

(Lydia crosses back to her purse, reaches in and pulls out Georgie's jacket, blouse, slip, skirt, pantyhose and shoes from the previous day. She folds these items and stacks them neatly as she speaks. Georgie watches, amazed.)

LYDIA: At first, I admired Andrew's interest in your welfare. He cares about people; he truly cares and I think that's wonderful. But these past few months, I must admit, I have become less interested in his interest. Not only do I listen to him talk about you incessantly, any time I come over to have dinner or spend the night here, I am bombarded by you. When you come home at night, we hear your little heels clicking on the ceiling. When you leave in the morning, we hear your little heels. When you go to bed we hear you brush your teeth, and talk on the phone, and listen to the radio and on certain evenings I could swear that we can even hear you undress. I am not enjoying this. For the past two months, I have been under the distinct impression that any time I spend the night here, I am actually sleeping with two people—Andrew, and yourself. In fact, when you came home with Edward tonight my first thought was, my God, the bed is already crowded enough; now we have to fit Edward in too? Now. I don't know what went on between you and Andrew.

GEORGIE: Nothing. Nothing at all.

LYDIA: Excuse me, but that clearly is not the case. And I want you out of my life! Is that understood?

GEORGIE: Where am I supposed to go?

LYDIA: I don't care! I'll find you a better apartment! It will be my pleasure!

(They glare at each other for a moment.)

GEORGIE: Listen, I am really sorry but I am just not up to this right now, okay? I mean, if I get mad one more time tonight I might just die from it. So, can we chill out for a minute? You want a cup of tea or something?

LYDIA: Do you have anything stronger? Scotch? Is that scotch?

GEORGIE: Yes. It is.

LYDIA: I'll have scotch.

GEORGIE: Fine. *(She exits to the kitchen and reenters a second later with a glass. She pours Lydia a shot of scotch.)* Here. You knock that back, you'll feel much better.

LYDIA: Thank you. *(She drinks and studies Georgie.)* That's an interesting outfit you have on.

GEORGIE: Excuse me?

LYDIA: I guess men really do like that sort of thing, don't they? You'd like to think some of them, at least one, or two, are above it, but that just doesn't seem to be the case. All of them, they're like Pavlov's dogs; you provide the right stimulus and the next thing you know, they're salivating all over you. Don't those shoes hurt?

GEORGIE: Yeah, as a matter of fact, they kind of do.

LYDIA: But I guess you don't wear them for comfort, do you? You wear them for other reasons. You wear them because they make your legs look amazing. *(She puts the second pair of heels on and walks around the room for a moment and picks up a large book under the table.)* And I see you're also studying law.

GEORGIE: *(Crosses and takes the book from her.)* No, I am not "studying law." I stole that from the library at work so I could figure out what the fuck was going on down there.

LYDIA: Really. How remarkable.

GEORGIE: Look—

LYDIA: Could I have another?

GEORGIE: Another?

LYDIA: Please.

(Georgie takes Lydia's glass from her and pours scotch into it, looks at her, and then continues to pour an enormous amount of scotch into the glass. She gives it back to her. Lydia looks at it, and knocks back a solid drink. Georgie stares.)

LYDIA: God, I wish I still smoked.

GEORGIE: You used to smoke?

LYDIA: Two packs a day. It was disgusting.

GEORGIE: You know—you're very different from what I thought. It's weird, meeting you. It's just—weird.

LYDIA: Oh, really? Well, what did you think I'd be like?

GEORGIE: I don't know. I mean, you're very—forceful. I guess I thought you would be kind of formal and polite. Maybe like Dracula, or something.

LYDIA: Oh. Edward told you that; that's where you got that. He is so awful. Ever since I dumped him he's been telling everybody I'm some kind of vampire. He thinks it's witty.

GEORGIE: Wait a minute. You went out with him, too?

LYDIA: Didn't you know that?

GEORGIE: Man, what do those two do, trade off girlfriends once a year or something?

LYDIA: It's certainly starting to look that way.

GEORGIE: Wait a minute, that's not what I—

LYDIA: *(Overlap.)* Really, there's no need to explain. In fact, I would prefer not to know the details.

GEORGIE: I'm just trying to tell you—

LYDIA: And I'm trying to tell you: What I've had with both of them is substantially more real than whatever this is, and I don't want to know about it. All right? I just want it to stop. All right?

GEORGIE: Right.

LYDIA: As long as we understand each other.

GEORGIE: Oh, I understand you all right. This part, I think I got down solid.

LYDIA: Good.

GEORGIE: *(Finally angry.)* But what I don't have, you know—what I want to know is—if you're so fucking real, Lydia, then what the hell are you doing here? I mean, if you're so much better than me, then why even bother? You could just wait it out and I'll drift away like a piece of paper, like nothing, right? 'Cause that's what I am. Nothing. Right? So why the fuck are you up here, taking me apart?

LYDIA: I don't think I have to justify myself to you.

GEORGIE: Oh, yeah? Well, I think you do. All of you. What an amazing fucking snow job you all are doing on the world. And I bought it! We all buy it. My family—they're like, all of a sudden I'm Mary Tyler Moore or something. I mean, they live in hell, right, and they spend their whole lives just wishing they were somewhere else, wishing they were rich, or sober, or clean; living on a street with trees, being on some fucking TV show. And I did it. I moved to Boston, I work in a law office, I'm the big success story. And they have no idea what that means. It means I get to hang out with a bunch of lunatics. It means I get to read books that make no sense. *(She pushes the law book off the table.)* It means that instead of getting harassed by jerks at the local bar, now I get harassed by guys in suits. Guys with glasses. Guys who talk nice. Guys in suits. Well, you know what I have to say to all of you? Shame on you. Shame on you for thinking you're better than the rest of us. And shame on you for being mean to me. Shame on you, Lydia.

LYDIA: *(Pause.)* I'm sorry.

GEORGIE: I think you'd better go.

LYDIA: Yes. Of course. *(Pause.)* I am sorry. I just—Andrew postponed our wedding tonight, and I'm a little—my life is in a bit of a shambles, tonight, and I know that's no excuse, but I'm just not myself. Please. Forgive me. *(She goes to the door.)*

GEORGIE: Oh, God. Wait a minute.

LYDIA: No. You're right. I've been behaving very badly. You're right. I'm sorry. *(She turns and opens the door.)*

GEORGIE: No, I'm the one. Come on, I'm being a jerk. He postponed the wedding? Fuck me. I'm sorry, you said that before and it went right by me. I'm sorry. I got a bad temper, and—whatever. Just sit down, okay? *(Georgie brings her back into the room. Lydia pulls away.)*

LYDIA: Really, I think I'd best go. Please. Please don't be nice to me. I don't want to be friends with you.

GEORGIE: Yeah, I don't want to be friends with you either. I'm just saying. I didn't mean to, like, yell at you. I think you better finish your drink. *(She hands her scotch to her. Lydia looks at it for a moment then sits and drinks.)*

GEORGIE: He's probably just nervous. Weddings make boys nervous.

LYDIA: I think it's worse than that. He—we haven't had sex in quite a while.

GEORGIE: You mean *none* of us are getting laid? No wonder we're all so uptight.

LYDIA: You mean you and Edward didn't—

GEORGIE: No.

LYDIA: No?

GEORGIE: No. I swear to God, I worked on him for four hours and I couldn't get him *near* the bedroom.

LYDIA: Edward? You couldn't—Edward?

GEORGIE: You didn't have that problem, huh?

LYDIA: As a matter of fact—never mind.

GEORGIE: He wanted it.

LYDIA: Yes, dear, he always wants it. Well. If he wouldn't sleep with you, I think you must've really made an impression on him.
(They laugh a little.)

LYDIA: And I know you've made an impression on Andrew.

GEORGIE: *(Awkward.)* Oh. I don't know.

LYDIA: Please. Could we not—? *(Pause.)* I'd prefer not to pretend. I'd also prefer not to talk to you about it, but I just don't know who else to talk to.

GEORGIE: Hey—

LYDIA: I'm not crying! It's just, I can't talk to my family about this; they'll simply gloat. They never liked Andrew. He wasn't "good" enough. Is that unbelievable? He's the best man I've ever met, and he's not *good* enough for them. He doesn't make enough money. And they certainly don't like his politics. Edward was the one they liked. Well. You can imagine. You know what my father told me, when Andrew and I decided to get married? Never trust a man who thinks he can change the world. That's what he said! I don't care, really, I don't—but how can I tell them this? I always told him, he didn't understand, just didn't understand. Andrew saved me. He is my best self; he makes me my best self. How can I tell them they were right?

GEORGIE: They're not.

LYDIA: No, I know. They're not. I know. It's just—I'm confused.

GEORGIE: Yeah. Me too. *(Pause.)* You want to dance? *(She crosses to the boombox and puts in a tape. Romantic music comes up.)*

LYDIA: Excuse me?

GEORGIE: Come on. Dance with me.

LYDIA: What?

GEORGIE: It'll make you feel better. I'll lead and you can just dance—

LYDIA: Oh, no—

GEORGIE: Come on. Let me do this. *(She unties Lydia's bow and takes her in her arms.)*

LYDIA: I don't—aw, no—I don't dance—

GEORGIE: No, it's not silly. It's just nice. Haven't you ever danced with a girl before? It's nice. Come on.

(Georgie takes her by the arms and they begin to slow dance.)

GEORGIE: I love to dance. It's so fucking romantic. You know? It always makes me want to have sex. Men are so dumb, they're so busy trying to get you in bed they can't even figure that out. I mean—I'm not making a pass at you.

LYDIA: I understand.

(Georgie nods, and they begin to dance more freely, Georgie leading and coaxing Lydia into the moves. As they turn through the room their movements become looser, more hilariously erotic. They laugh for a moment, and end up slow dancing. Suddenly, there are sounds of a loud struggle and pounding on the door.)

EDWARD: *(Off.)* Georgie! Open the door! Georgie!

GEORGIE: Oh, what now?

ANDREW: *(Off.)* LET GO OF ME!

LYDIA: Oh, no—

(Both women start for the door, then stop and stare at each other.)

GEORGIE: You know, we probably—probably we should just leave them out there.

(The struggle at the door sounds even more violent.)

EDWARD: *(Off.)* GEORGIE. OPEN THE GODDAMN DOOR!

(She goes to the door. Lydia turns off the music. Edward bursts in, dragging Andrew by the collar and sleeve. He throws him into the room. They all stare at each other.)

EDWARD: Hi, girls. How's it going?

GEORGIE: Edward, what are you doing?

EDWARD: I'm trying to keep us all out of court. Now, I think it's about time we talked this out. Andrew?

ANDREW: What?

EDWARD: Start talking.

GEORGIE: Actually, I think that now is not a good time, Edward.

EDWARD: Georgie, I am not going to let him do this to you anymore.

ANDREW: Let me, excuse me, let me? Who put you in charge here?

EDWARD: Just talk to her, Andrew.

GEORGIE: I mean it, you guys. Lydia and I were doing just fine here—

LYDIA: It's all right, Georgie—

ANDREW: No, it's not all right! I resent this! Who does he think he is, shoving everybody around?

EDWARD: I'm trying to help!

ANDREW: Help? You threatened to rape her, and now you think you can—

EDWARD: Wait a minute—

LYDIA: He what?

ANDREW: He threatened to rape her—

GEORGIE: You guys.

EDWARD: That is not exactly what—

LYDIA: Edward, for God's sake—

EDWARD: We were having a fight!

LYDIA: Oh, but really—

EDWARD: COULD WE NOT GO BACK TO THIS? I'M ALREADY PAST THIS POINT. *(Pause.)* Come on, Andrew. Deal with this woman.

ANDREW: Excuse me, but I don't need you to tell me what I have to do here—

EDWARD: Look, I'm on your side—

ANDREW: You are not on my—

EDWARD: Don't fight me, Andrew—

ANDREW: I will fight you if I want! *(He shoves him.)*

EDWARD: Don't you fucking shove me—

(He shoves him back. Georgie immediately leaps in between them.)

LYDIA: ANDREW.

GEORGIE: EDWARD.

(She stands in between them for a moment as they glare at each other.)

GEORGIE: I will not have this! *(She shoves them both away from each other.)* You are both driving me crazy.

(She storms into the kitchen. The other three stare at each other. Georgie reenters a moment later with a six pack of diet Pepsi which she passes around silently.)

EDWARD: What am I supposed to do with this?

GEORGIE: You're supposed to drink it, Edward. We are all going to just have a drink and calm down for a minute, okay? Drink it!

(Everyone pops their soda—and drinks. Pause.)

GEORGIE: Okay. So—could we not fight anymore? I mean, could we just like, finish our sodas and go to bed now?

EDWARD: Actually, going to bed may just be the most complicated action we could contemplate at this moment in time.

ANDREW: Georgie, can I talk to you alone? Would you two mind if I talked to her alone for a second?

LYDIA: I'd mind.

EDWARD: Yes, I think I'd mind too.

ANDREW: Oh, come on—

GEORGIE: Edward, I thought you wanted to help.

EDWARD: I do want to help, but I'm also a little mad right now, and besides which we all know what he's going to say anyway. Don't we?

LYDIA: I think we do.

EDWARD: So I think he should just say it. This involves all of us. So—just say it, Andrew.

ANDREW: Forget it.

EDWARD: No, come on. Say it.

GEORGIE: You guys—

EDWARD: You want to say it. Say it!

ANDREW: I don't want to say it.

EDWARD: Say it!

GEORGIE: Edward!

LYDIA: Please, Andrew. Just say it.

    (Pause. Andrew looks at her.)

LYDIA: Please. It's not like I don't already know.

ANDREW: Fine. Fine. *(To Georgie.)* You were right. I think I probably—my feelings for you are stronger—All right. I am in love with you. All right?

GEORGIE: All right.

    (Pause.)

LYDIA: Well, that is just great. *(She throws her drink at him.)*

ANDREW: Lydia—

LYDIA: I can't believe you said that! In front of me!

ANDREW: You told me to!

LYDIA: You're in love with her?

ANDREW: You said you knew!

LYDIA: You mean it, don't you? You're in love with her!

ANDREW: Well, of course I mean it. What else would I mean?

LYDIA: You could mean anything! I thought you meant—I don't know what I thought you meant! You jerk! You're in love with her! I mean, I can see sleeping with her, but falling in love with her?

GEORGIE: Watch it, Lydia.

LYDIA: I'm sorry—

ANDREW: I never slept with her—

LYDIA: Oh, please—

EDWARD: He didn't!

ANDREW: I didn't!

LYDIA: Well, you should've; it might've—you're in love with her?

ANDREW: Yes. *(Pause.)* I think we'd better call the wedding off altogether.

LYDIA: Yes, that would seem to be the next step, wouldn't it? You're in love with another woman; that could potentially interfere with our wedding plans.

ANDREW: Lydia, it's not you.

LYDIA: That much is clear, Andrew, I think I'm pretty straight on that point.

ANDREW: That's not what I—it's just me, okay? Things have not been—great with us for a long time, and I'm just saying, it's not enough, you're not— *(He stops himself.)*

LYDIA: Go on. I'm not enough what? I'm not wild enough? I'm not sexy enough? I'm not passionate, I'm not needy, I'm not—I am just what I've always been, Andrew. What is suddenly not enough?

ANDREW: We can't talk about this here—

LYDIA: What kind of a life do you think you can have with her? We have a life together, we have—Georgie, I'm sorry, I don't mean this to be as insulting as it sounds, but honestly. Do you think this is going to work out? Andrew. Do you honestly think that?

ANDREW: I don't think anything. I'm just not going to lie about it anymore. *(Pause.)* I'm sorry.

LYDIA: It doesn't matter. I can learn not to love you. You learned not to love me, I can—could you take your glasses off, please? Just take them off. *(He takes them off and looks at her.)*

LYDIA: There. You see? When you take them off, you look like a stranger, you look—I always think that when I see you in the morning. You look like a stranger without your glasses. Except you don't, really, I don't—

ANDREW: Lydia—

LYDIA: Could you please be quiet, please? *(Pause.)* It isn't working. Put your glasses on. *(He puts his glasses on. Pause. Lydia turns to Georgie.)*

LYDIA: Well, Georgie, he's all yours. If you want him, you can have him.

GEORGIE: Thanks. Yeah, thanks a lot, Lydia. And Edward, thank you. Thank you for helping us clear all this up. We all feel much better now. And Andrew, thank you for picking me up out of the gutter and teaching me how to talk and how to behave and how to read. It was really great of you. I'm just, so glad I've met you all. I'm really just—this is working out just *great*. *(She walks out the door, slamming it behind them. They all stare at the closed door.)*

LYDIA: She's right. *(She goes to the door, opens it, leaves. The men stare at the closed door.)*

EDWARD: Oh, great. They're teaming up. Now we're really in for it. *(Andrew looks at him. Blackout.)*

SCENE II

The next morning. The lights come up on Georgie's apartment, in much the same condition as the night before, except for the fact that Edward is sprawled on the couch, sleeping, and Andrew is sprawled on the floor, tangled in blankets and a pillow. He turns and gets himself even more tangled up. He has not had an easy night. He sits up, frustrated, untangles himself from the blankets, and looks at Edward, who is sleeping soundly. Andrew looks at his watch, looks at Edward, picks up his pillow, crosses to Edward, and hits him with it. Edward jolts awake.

EDWARD: What? What?

ANDREW: Get up.

EDWARD: Why? What time is it?

ANDREW: It's after ten.

EDWARD: Did she come back?

ANDREW: No.

EDWARD: Man. This couch is really comfortable.

ANDREW: Oh, shut up.

EDWARD: Hey, I didn't tell you to sleep on the floor. You could have gone downstairs and slept in your own bed.

ANDREW: Excuse me, but since you wouldn't leave—

EDWARD: You could've slept in her bed.

ANDREW: I didn't want to sleep in her bed. It would have been...

EDWARD: Disappointing, under the circumstances?

ANDREW: Shut up.

EDWARD: You think she's got anything to eat around here?
    (He stands and crosses to the kitchen. Andrew watches him, somewhat amazed.)

ANDREW: How can you think about food at a time like this?

EDWARD: *(Off.)* It's ten o'clock in the morning. It's a great time to think about food.

ANDREW: Don't you have someplace to go? Something to do? A judge to bribe? Some drug kingpin to get off on a technicality?

EDWARD: *(Reentering.)* Hey. Could you let me eat something before we get into this? Besides, it's Saturday. Courts are closed. *(He carries with him a box of cereal, which he pours into a bowl and starts to eat without milk.)*

ANDREW: That is just—what—how can you eat that without milk?

EDWARD: She doesn't have any milk. I mean, she has some, but it's alive. You don't want to pour it over your cereal.

(He hands Andrew a bowl and a spoon. Andrew watches Edward eat.)

ANDREW: Why are you still here?

EDWARD: I don't know. Why are you still here?

ANDREW: I'm still here because you wouldn't leave.

EDWARD: Well, I'm still here because you wouldn't leave.

ANDREW: That makes no sense.

EDWARD: You seemed to think it made sense when you said it.

ANDREW: Edward—

EDWARD: What?

ANDREW: Just leave. This has nothing to do with you anymore. You've done enough damage. Leave.

EDWARD: *I've* done enough damage?

ANDREW: LEAVE! WOULD YOU JUST GET OUT OF HERE?

EDWARD: I'm not even going to even respond to that. You know why? Because I'm getting a little tired of verbally beating the living daylights out of you.

ANDREW: Oh, is that what you've been doing?

EDWARD: As a matter of fact, it is. You and I fight, Andrew. This is the basis of our friendship. We fight, I win, and you lose. And it's getting old.

ANDREW: I lose?

EDWARD: That's right, buddy. So just eat your cereal and keep your mouth shut, because—

ANDREW: Lydia.

EDWARD: Excuse me?

ANDREW: I didn't lose then.

EDWARD: That had nothing to do with you. I mean, I admit that Lydia dumped me, but by then we were both sick of each other. That wasn't...

ANDREW: Wasn't it?

EDWARD: You didn't start seeing her until months after she and I...

(He stops himself. Looks at Andrew who looks back, deliberate. Pause.)

ANDREW: Lydia didn't want to hurt your feelings.

EDWARD: At the time, Lydia delighted in hurting my feelings. I don't believe you. If you were sleeping with Lydia while she and I were still together, I would have known.

ANDREW: Are you sure about that?

EDWARD: You were sleeping with her?

ANDREW: Yes.

EDWARD: You fucking creep. Don't you have any principles at all?

ANDREW: Did you actually say that? Mr. I Could Rape You If I Wanted—

EDWARD: Don't change the subject! You were sleeping with my girlfriend! Christ, you're no better than I am!

ANDREW: It was your own fault!

EDWARD: You were sleeping with my girlfriend at the time she dumped me! I think most people would agree I was the one getting screwed!

ANDREW: Don't play the victim. No one is going to believe you.

EDWARD: Yeah, well, don't you play the good guy. That's getting a little hard to swallow, too.

ANDREW: You didn't want her anyway!

EDWARD: That's not the point! You were supposed to be my friend! Well, fuck you. Just fuck you. I don't owe you shit. I'm getting out of here.

ANDREW: Thank God!

EDWARD: *(Looks for his jacket, starts to put it on.)* You know, just for the record, I did all of this for you.

ANDREW: What?

EDWARD: Yeah, that's right. As you'll recall, when you asked me to give Georgie a job, all I knew was she was some wild thing with no experience at all. Didn't even know how to *type*. But I gave her a job because you asked me to. And then, okay, after that, I wasn't exactly great for a while, but—

ANDREW: Wasn't exactly great. Excuse me, wasn't—

EDWARD: But at least I figured out what was going on and tried to stop it! I mean, I realized what an asshole I was being and I, I, I decided to change and try to make up for everything. So—

ANDREW: Oh, please!

EDWARD: I got you up here! I got you to admit how you felt about her! I mean, at least I got you to stop lying to everybody. And maybe it didn't feel so great, but at least now you have a chance at a real life instead of some—whatever—with Lydia. So don't go whining to me about what a big bad wolf I am. If it wasn't for me you wouldn't have anything right now.

ANDREW: I don't have anything right now!

EDWARD: Oh, that is complete horseshit. I mean, get a fucking grip, would you? Georgie adores you. You adore her. And all you can do is moan and gnash your teeth! I mean, I realize that relations between the sexes are confused nowadays, but they're not *that* confused. When she gets back here, you should just take her in your arms and take her to bed.

ANDREW: Well, thank you for your advice, Mr. Sensitivity. Take her in your arms and fuck her. That's very delicate and perceptive of you.

EDWARD: Oh, for—Do you want her or not, Andrew? Because if you don't, I'll take her, and this time, you won't get a second chance!

ANDREW: Forget it! I'm not giving her to you again!

(They stare at each other .)

EDWARD: I can't believe you said that.

ANDREW: You said it, too.

EDWARD: Jesus. We really are a couple of assholes.

(They sit for a moment, thinking about what assholes they have been.)

ANDREW: I don't know what's the matter with me. I don't know who I am anymore.

EDWARD: *(Pause.)* You were sleeping with Lydia?

ANDREW: Just once. We both felt so guilty about it she had to break up with you before we could do it again. She was going to end it anyway.

EDWARD: I know. That was my fault. I completely fucked up everything with her. *(Pause.)* Don't tell her I said that.

ANDREW: Edward, she's probably never going to speak to me again.

EDWARD: Oh, right.

ANDREW: What are we going to do?

EDWARD: I don't know. But I have this terrible feeling that we're not entirely in control of this situation.

ANDREW: We never were.

EDWARD: Oh, sure we were. I mean, remember when we could just blame everything on women? Not a specific woman. Just, women in general. The whole idea of women.

ANDREW: Women.

EDWARD: It was so nice. Just blaming everything on them. We didn't have to think about anything. We didn't have to fight amongst ourselves, unless we wanted to. Because it wasn't our fault. It was women. Fuck 'em.

ANDREW: Fuck 'em.

ANDREW AND EDWARD: FUCK WOMEN.

(They laugh at themselves.)

GEORGIE: *(At door.)* Well, that is lovely.

(The men stand quickly. Georgie enters, carrying clothes, a bag of groceries and a book. She wears blue jeans, a sweater and her heels.)

ANDREW: Georgie.

EDWARD: Georgie!

GEORGIE: I can't believe it. Are you guys going to torture me for the rest of my life?

ANDREW: We were just—

GEORGIE: I mean, what the fuck are you doing here? What the fuck is this? Well, fine. That's just fine. You think my whole life is your fucking property anyway. I guess it's no surprise to find you taking over my apartment. *(She crosses toward the kitchen, angry.)*

ANDREW: That's not what we were trying to do.

EDWARD: We were worried about you.

GEORGIE: Right. You guys probably spent the whole night deciding which one of you gets me.

ANDREW AND EDWARD: No! No, no, no, come on...

GEORGIE: You both are hopeless. *(She dumps things on the table.)*

ANDREW: Where have you been?

GEORGIE: I was at Lydia's.

EDWARD: I was afraid of that.

GEORGIE: Yeah, we had a great time. We listened to records. Smoked cigarettes. Had conversation. You know, she talked, I listened. I talked, she listened. Very different from what the three of us have been doing, I gotta say.

EDWARD: Aw, come on, Georgie, would you stop being such a pain in the ass? We're trying to be sensitive, we really are, and you're just—

GEORGIE: Oh, now you're sensitive and I'm the pain in the ass. I love that—

ANDREW: All right! Could we just not—do that, right away? I mean, could we just try to be civilized for—I don't know. Five minutes, maybe?

GEORGIE: Fine. The clock is ticking. Here, have a muffin. I'm going to make some tea.

(She hands a packet of muffins to Edward and goes to the kitchen. Edward concentrates on opening them. Andrew whacks him.)

EDWARD: What?

ANDREW: Go.

EDWARD: Now? I want to find out what happens!

(Andrew stares at him.)

EDWARD: Okay! I'll be in the bathroom.

(And he goes, taking the muffins. Georgie reenters and looks around.)

GEORGIE: Where's Edward?

ANDREW: He had to go to the, uh, the bathroom.

GEORGIE: Sly, Andrew. Very sly.

(She takes more groceries out of the bag. Andrew picks a book off the table.

As he speaks to her, she continues to move around the apartment, unpacking groceries, going to the kitchen, cleaning.)

ANDREW: What's this?

GEORGIE: *Pride and Prejudice.* Lydia lent it to me. She says it's about a bunch of girls and their boyfriends. I thought it sounded good.

ANDREW: So. You and Lydia got along.

GEORGIE: You always told me I'd like her. I mean, I doubt we're going to be best friends or anything, but you know. The three of us, we should all have dinner sometime.

ANDREW: I don't think that's going to be possible.

GEORGIE: Well, it's up to you.

ANDREW: That's not—Georgie, could you stop—could you stand still, for a minute? Please.

(He takes her by the arm and holds on to her for a moment. They look at each other. She looks away. Careful, he leans in to kiss her. She pulls away.)

GEORGIE: I don't think you should do that.

ANDREW: I'm sorry. Yesterday, you seemed to want me to do that.

GEORGIE: Yeah, well, things were different yesterday. I was kind of fucked up. I mean, yesterday, I was actually going to screw someone I didn't much like just to prove some sort of stupid point that I can't even remember what it was. It's the kind of shit I used to do all the time. You know? I'm just lucky Edward isn't quite as bad as I thought he was. Neither is Lydia. She's a very forgiving person. You should call her, right now. I bet she'd be really glad to talk to you.

ANDREW: What are you doing?

GEORGIE: I'm telling you. I think you better call Lydia.

(Andrew and Georgie stare at each other.)

ANDREW: You're changing your mind? *(Pause.)* You're going to do the decent thing and send me back to Lydia, the wronged woman who you've come to respect, even care for—

GEORGIE: I'm not doing this for anybody but myself. I just can't take it anymore, Andrew. Between you and Edward, it's like, you both want—it's always about what you guys want. And I'm just like some thing just spinning in the middle of it all. I can't even think, you know?

ANDREW: If you're saying you're confused, that's fine. I'm confused, too. We'll work it out.

GEORGIE: I don't want to work it out. I mean, I'm confused, but I do know I don't want to be this person you keep trying to make me. I mean, all these things about me that really bug you, they aren't going anywhere. Let's just walk away from it, huh?

ANDREW: I finally decided to confront it! I can't walk away now!

GEORGIE: Look, I'm never going to be good enough for you.

ANDREW: You are good enough!

GEORGIE: There's always going to be something you're trying to fix—

ANDREW: I wasn't trying to fix you! All I ever wanted was to help you see what is here! What your life can be. You needed to change; you said so yourself! And you did change. Because of me. What did I do that was so terrible?

GEORGIE: Well, you did a lot of things that were terrible. And a lot of things that weren't. And I did, too; I'm not saying I'm perfect. A lot of the time, I'm just a fucking mess. Mostly, I'm a fucking mess around you. I mean, when I'm with you, I'm always thinking about how to please you. How to make you happy. And then I hate myself when I don't. I need my life back.

ANDREW: I love you.

GEORGIE: *(Pause.)* You really should call Lydia.
(Pause.)

ANDREW: Can I say one more thing?

GEORGIE: What?

ANDREW: I like your shoes.

GEORGIE: What?

ANDREW: I like your shoes. Actually, I always kind of liked them. They look good on you. You have nice legs.

GEORGIE: Look. I'm sorry, okay?

ANDREW: Me too.

GEORGIE: You did help me.

ANDREW: I know. *(He exits.)*

GEORGIE: Oh, *fuck. (She takes her shoes off, throws them down, sits and holds her head in her hands.)*
(Pause.)

EDWARD: *(Off.)* Can I come out now?

GEORGIE: *(Pause.)* Yeah.

EDWARD: *(Appears, his mouth full of foam, toothbrush in hand. Tentative.)* How are you?

GEORGIE: Not so great. *(Pause.)* Is that my toothbrush?

EDWARD: *(Looking at it.)* Is yours the red one?

GEORGIE: Mine's the only one, Edward. This is my apartment, remember?
(She takes it from him and goes to the bathroom with it. Edward goes into

the kitchen, gets a glass of water and rinses out his mouth. Georgie reenters, trying not to cry. She starts to put groceries away again. He stands in the door of the kitchen and watches her.)

EDWARD: Here, let me help you.

(He starts to take them from her. She does not let him.)

GEORGIE: I'm fine. I'm fine! *(Pause.)* I'm not fine.

EDWARD: It's okay, honey. Come on. I'll make you some tea.

GEORGIE: *(She lets him take the groceries.)* Look, you probably should go check on Andrew, I think he's—

EDWARD: I'll get around to him. I'm more concerned about you right now. *(He takes the rest of the groceries into the kitchen.)*

GEORGIE: I hope he goes back to Lydia.

EDWARD: I'd say it's anybody's guess what he'll do.

GEORGIE: I really like her.

EDWARD: She's all right.

GEORGIE: No, she's kind of great and you have to stop running around telling everybody she's a vampire. It's not funny and you're a jerk, okay?

EDWARD: Okay.

GEORGIE: Okay.

EDWARD: *(Pause.)* That's a nice sweater.

GEORGIE: It's Lydia's.

EDWARD: I know. I gave it to her. *(He laughs. She stares at him.)*

EDWARD: Oh, come on. I'm just trying to lighten the mood here. It's funny in a way, isn't it? Well, okay, it isn't, but sort of it is. Never mind.

GEORGIE: No, you're right. It is kind of funny. You know, they were sleeping together before she dumped you.

EDWARD: Yes, I heard. Apparently, the whole world has heard. I don't know what the big deal is. It was only once.

GEORGIE: That's not what Lydia says.

EDWARD: What?

GEORGIE: Did he tell you that? It was only once?

EDWARD: How many times was it? Never mind. Don't tell me. I don't want to know. *(Cleaning, he picks up her shoes.)* These shoes really are beautiful.

GEORGIE: I'm throwing them out.

EDWARD: Oh, don't do that.

GEORGIE: They hurt my feet.

EDWARD: They're very beautiful.

GEORGIE: Look, Edward—

EDWARD: Sorry. Sorry. Go ahead. Throw them away. Do whatever you want.

GEORGIE: Sorry. I'm sorry.

EDWARD: Hey, come on, I'll make you breakfast. What did I do with those muffins?

GEORGIE: Listen, Edward, thanks, but could you just take off? I mean, I didn't sleep much last night, and I'm beat.

EDWARD: Sure. You're sure you're okay?

GEORGIE: Yeah. I'm fine. I am. I'm fine

EDWARD: Good *(He crosses to the door. Turns back and looks at her.)* So what are you going to do now? Move into a convent?

GEORGIE: *(Pause.)* I knew that's what you were after.

EDWARD: I'm just asking.

GEORGIE: I should have known. You got so nice, so nice and helpful and reasonable. That's a sure sign that you want something.

EDWARD: I never made any bones about that.

GEORGIE: This whole concerned mother act—

EDWARD: I am concerned.

GEORGIE: Yeah, I picked that up.

EDWARD: He is all wrong for you.

GEORGIE: Edward—

EDWARD: I just hope you're not having second thoughts.

GEORGIE: I am not getting into this with you, Edward.

EDWARD: We're already in it. Aren't we? *(He smiles at her.)*

GEORGIE: Oh, no. *(She picks up one of her shoes and wields it as a weapon.)*

EDWARD: Come on, Georgie. I'm not the enemy.

GEORGIE: You sure about that?

EDWARD: Ninety percent.

GEORGIE: Edward—we don't have the most romantic relationship here.

EDWARD: Neither of us is exactly indifferent. Come on. I'm not Andrew.

GEORGIE: That much I got.

EDWARD: And I'm not talking about a one-night stand.

GEORGIE: I don't care what you're talking about—

EDWARD: Don't you think people can change?

GEORGIE: *(Pause.)* Yeah. Yeah, as a matter of fact, I do.

EDWARD: Then what are you afraid of?

GEORGIE: *(Pause.)* Nothing. I'm not afraid of anything. *(She throws down the shoe.)*

(Pause.)

EDWARD: Good. *(Pause.)* Okay. You decide. And you let me know. *(He goes to the door.)*

GEORGIE: All right. All right. But if you want to try this, you gotta know, this isn't going to look anything like anything you've ever been in before.

EDWARD: I know that.

GEORGIE: I'm not kidding, Edward. I'm not playing any more of your games. I'm not taking anymore of your shit. This is on my terms.

EDWARD: Of course.

GEORGIE: One kiss. For now, that's all you're getting.

EDWARD: I accept your terms.

GEORGIE: Fuck you.

EDWARD: Yeah, fuck you, too.

(They kiss. The kiss goes on for rather a long time. She pushes him away. They look at each other.)

EDWARD: Now what?

GEORGIE: Now we—negotiate.

EDWARD: All right.

GEORGIE: All right. Make me an offer.

(Both start to smile. Blackout.)

END OF PLAY

SUNDAY ON THE ROCKS

ORIGINAL PRODUCTION

Sunday on the Rocks was originally produced at Long Wharf Theatre, May 3, 1994. It was directed by Susann Brinkley, unit set design by Hugh Landwehr, production stage manager was C.A. Clark, with the following cast (in order of appearance):

ELLY . . . . Kristin Flanders
GAYLE . . . . Jennifer Van Dyck
JEN . . . . Mia Korf
JESSICA . . . . Patricia Cornell

Set Coordination and Properties . . . . David Fletcher
Costume Coordination . . . . Patricia M. Risser
Lighting . . . . Kirk Matson
Sound . . . . Brenton Evans
Script Development . . . . Sari Bodi
Artistic Director . . . . Arvin Brown
Executive Director . . . . M. Edgar Rosenblum

CHARACTERS

ELLY: A talkative, excitable woman, thirty
GAYLE: A woman of few words, intelligent and wry, thirty-four
JEN: A loose, casual, very likable woman, twenty-nine
JESSICA: A slight, pretty, seemingly gentle woman with a will of iron, thirty. On the surface, she looks very much like any of the others—it is important not to distinguish her from them in terms of costume.

NOTE:

1. There is nothing self-pitying about these women. Although their conversation chronicles their past mistakes, they are good-humored about it all. The first act should be played lightly, almost like a comedy. There is nothing vicious about their laughter.
2. The description of Elly's mother within the text should be tailored to resemble the actress who plays Jessica.

SET

The back porch of a slightly weather-beaten house, not necessarily screened in. There is a small table set stage right, and the door to the house at the opposite end of the porch. Three wicker chairs are scattered about the porch. The door leads to a comfortable, quite tidy living room with a small couch, an easy chair, a floor lamp and stereo. Elly's purse and a couple of books have been set on the couch. A door to the left of the living room leads to the kitchen and the bedrooms upstairs. It is a beautiful Sunday morning in the early autumn. The day promises to be quite warm.

ACT I
SCENE I

Breakfast on the Back Porch

The lights come up on Elly, who sits on the porch, holding a large glass of scotch over ice. She takes a drink and shudders. Gayle enters from the house, carrying breakfast fixings and a half-empty glass of orange juice.

GAYLE: *(She notices the scotch.)* What are you doing?

ELLY: I'm drinking scotch.

GAYLE: You're drinking scotch.

ELLY: Yes, I'm drinking scotch.

GAYLE: El, it's nine thirty in the morning.

ELLY: I know, I'm having it for breakfast. Like F. Scott Fitzgerald. I read that about him, I think, he was such an incredible alcoholic he would have, like, scotch for breakfast.

GAYLE: Yeah, but you're not an alcoholic.

ELLY: Wait a minute. It might have been Hemingway. Was Hemingway an alcoholic?

GAYLE: I don't know, but—

ELLY: Maybe it was Dorothy Parker. It doesn't matter. A lot of writers were alcoholics, and I'm sure one of them drank scotch for breakfast.

GAYLE: But you're not a writer. You're in advertising.

ELLY: Other people do it, too. When I was in college, I knew all these guys who would go on binges and drink all weekend, non-stop. I'm not kidding. Also—ALSO, have you ever gone to one of those fancy Sunday brunches they have at these fabulous hotels? Waiters wander around the room with these bottles of champagne, you know, and everyone gets bombed at eleven in the morning. OR many people won't drink the champagne because it doesn't have enough kick, so to speak, and so they have Bloody Marys. And this doesn't only happen in fancy hotels, mind you; I've seen it in normal restaurants, people getting bombed on Sunday mornings. So this morning I am taking part in a long and honored tradition.

GAYLE: You've thought this through, haven't you?

ELLY: I've just never done it. You know, I have never had a drink before like four in the afternoon. I've never had a drink in the morning.

GAYLE: So why are you starting now?

ELLY: I'm pregnant.

(*Pause.*)

GAYLE: Oh. (*Pause.*) God, I'm sorry, El.

ELLY: Please don't be sorry. This is not something to be sorry about; it is not something to be happy about. It's just something that *is,* you know, something that happens to people. Some people get pregnant; some people drink in the morning. I really don't think there's any morality connected to the condition.

GAYLE: Oh, God. Are you going to start talking about morality?

ELLY: Why not?

GAYLE: Then I'm going to join you.

(*Gayle takes the bottle and pours herself a drink.*)

ELLY: Haven't you ever been curious about drinking in the morning?

GAYLE: I've done it.

ELLY: You have? When?

GAYLE: Give me one of your ice cubes. Many many years ago. I was very uptight at the time. God, Jessica is going to freak if she catches us.

ELLY: No, she's already gone. She went to church with Jeffrey.

GAYLE: Oh, great. She's going to come back all holy and find us getting hammered on the back porch.

ELLY: No, they were going to take a long drive in the country because it's such a lovely day. Perhaps late in the afternoon, they'll stop by a roadside inn and have tea—

GAYLE: Oh, that sounds very nice.

ELLY: Yes, they have—the perfect relationship.

(*Pause.*)

GAYLE: Does Roger know?

ELLY: About Jessica and Jeff and their perfect relationship?

GAYLE: Do you think you could not be coy about this?

ELLY: Yes, Roger knows. I told Roger last night, and now Roger knows.

GAYLE: What did he say?

ELLY: He said, I'm sorry. I don't know why, but whenever I tell someone I'm pregnant it brings out their need to apologize.

GAYLE: Who else have you told?

ELLY: No one. It's just that everyone at the gynecologist's office couldn't apologize enough. And try to imagine how stupid you feel, in a gynecologist's office, saying to everyone, "Hey—it's not your fault."

GAYLE: Did Roger say anything besides "I'm sorry?"

ELLY: Yes, he said, "What are you going to do about it?"

GAYLE: Oh.

ELLY: Look, could you stop saying "Oh" like it's the end of the world? It is not the end of the world.

GAYLE: I'm sorry. From now on, I'll say only the exactly right thing.

ELLY: I'm sorry.

GAYLE: Do you think you have enough scotch in you to talk about this yet?

ELLY: I don't know. Yes. I can talk about this. This isn't that big a deal.

GAYLE: Right. So what did Roger say?

ELLY: Roger. Roger, Roger. Roger said what are you going to do, I said I'm going to have an abortion—and—he offered to marry me.

GAYLE: He did?

ELLY: Yes, but I thought he was going to choke to death. You should have seen him strangling out the words; he was absolutely terrified that I would take him up on it. So I said, calm down, I'm not going to marry you, we don't have the money, we're not ready, etc., etc., and HE said, well, it's just that he could never bring himself to have an abortion.

GAYLE: He did.

ELLY: Yes. And I got mad.

GAYLE: You did.

ELLY: Yes. So I said, that's right, you fucking asshole, you couldn't bring yourself to have an abortion because you've never had to fucking think about it, because it's my fucking problem because it's my fucking body, and you can afford to just sit there and wash your hands of the whole damn thing because we're not talking about *your* being pregnant for nine months; we're talking about *me.*

GAYLE: What did he say to that?

ELLY: Oh, he went into this whole song and dance about how he would stick by me, la la la la la—he loves me—I told him to get lost—he told me I was flying off the handle—you know how these things go. So, at some point, I just got completely mad and left. Do you want some more scotch?

GAYLE: I have a lot.

ELLY: Have some more.

(*Elly pours more scotch into Gayle's glass. Jen enters from the kitchen, carrying the Sunday paper.*)

JEN: Oh, God, you're out here! I've been looking all over the house for you. I thought you guys deserted me and went out to get donuts or something. God, I would love a donut. Jesus, you're drinking scotch.

ELLY: Cocktails at brunch.

GAYLE: It's an old and honored tradition.

JEN: "Cocktails at brunch" is a Bloody Mary at 11. Scotch on the rocks at 9:30 is not the same thing.

ELLY: Do you want some?

JEN: I don't know. Where's Jessica?

(Jen looks around suspiciously, pushes Elly's feet off the chair and stares at it.)

ELLY: Gone for the day. Off for a jaunt in the country with Jeffrey. I'll get you a glass.

JEN: You punched a hole in Jessica's chair.

ELLY: They're not Jessica's chairs. They're *our* chairs. Remember? We all paid for them. They're OUR chairs.

JEN: Yeah, I know, but they're really her chairs, you know? I mean, *I* didn't want them.

GAYLE: Me neither.

ELLY: Well, I sure didn't want them. I hate wicker. Why do we do that?

JEN: I don't know. But she's going to throw a fit when she sees this hole.

ELLY: Well, fine. If she's going to inflict wicker on us, she can just take the consequences.

(Elly goes into the house. Jen sits down, looking at the newspaper, somewhat preoccupied.)

JEN: You know, it really is kind of ridiculous the way we let her push us around. I mean, it's not like she's our mother.

GAYLE: Jen.

JEN: I can't believe we're doing this. Can you believe this? The last time I got drunk in the morning I was in high school. Oh, God, I hope Richardson doesn't call. I mean, it's hard enough to talk to him when I'm sober. I guess he called about fourteen times yesterday while I was at the mall. Jessica left all these little notes on my bed—you know those little tiny white notes she leaves everywhere? It looked like it was snowing in there.

GAYLE: Jen—Elly's pregnant.

JEN: Oh, Jesus, no kidding. Really? God. That's really too bad. But you know, she better not tell Jessica. Do you want the comics?

GAYLE: Jen!

JEN: I heard you: Elly's pregnant. I just don't think it's that big a deal. Is she going to have an abortion?

GAYLE: Yes.

JEN: Well.

GAYLE: You know, this isn't a non-event.

(Elly reenters with a glassful of ice. She puts some in her glass, some in Gayle's

and pours scotch for Jen. She then reveals a pack of cigarettes and deals them out.)

ELLY: I don't think it's a non-event. I never said that. Here we have cigarettes. In honor of the scotch for breakfast, I bought a pack of cigarettes today.

JEN: Oh, God, I would *love* a cigarette.

(Jen and Gayle take cigarettes; Elly pulls out a lighter and lights them all around. Everyone enjoys their first puff with great relish. Elly crosses front and center and peers out toward the street.)

ELLY: With my luck, Jessica and Jeffrey will stop by after Mass to pick up sweaters or something. She'll take one look at this and kick me out. She's just looking for an excuse.

JEN: Isn't that the truth? God, she wanted to get rid of you over that stupid Campbell's soup thing.

(Gayle kicks her.)

JEN: OWWWW. What did you kick me f— Oh, Jesus, Gayle, it's not like Elly doesn't know. OOOOWWWW.

(Gayle has kicked her again, harder.)

ELLY: What did she say to you?

GAYLE: Nothing.

ELLY: What is the point of drinking scotch in the morning if you're not going to tell the truth?

JEN: She said just the sort of shit you'd expect her to. She said you weren't fitting into the spirit of the household—you know, stuff about integrity and Christian non violent resistance to the capitalist system—I don't know. What else did she say? She doesn't like the way you wash dishes. The same stuff.

ELLY: She wanted to kick me out over a fucking can of soup?

GAYLE: You knew it was going to make her mad when you bought it. I was with you. Jesus, that was *why* you bought it, to make her mad.

ELLY: I bought it because I like mushroom soup.

GAYLE: You could've bought Purity Supreme mushroom soup.

ELLY: Purity Supreme doesn't make—

GAYLE: Yes it does—

ELLY: No, it doesn't make the kind of mushroom soup that I like. I like golden mushroom soup. Purity Supreme makes cream of mushroom soup, and I don't like that kind.

GAYLE: You could have hid it in your room and had it some night when she was out. You put it in the pantry, you knew she was going to see it—

ELLY: I resent being told what I can eat and what I can't! And aside from the fact that she's the only person in America still boycotting soup, it was always a stupid boycott, I've tried to explain that to you—

JEN: Oh, no.

ELLY: There are two kinds of boycotts: Practical boycotts and ideological boycotts.

GAYLE: El—

ELLY: If it's a practical boycott, then you take part in it because you're trying to hurt the company's business. And those are *big* boycotts; you have to have a lot of people doing them or they don't work, like the Nestle boycott. The other kind, the ideological kind, you take part in because it's like your moral duty. You know you're really not making a dent, but you do it because it's the right thing to do.

JEN: I never understood this argument.

GAYLE: That's because it's a stupid argument.

ELLY: It's not! The point is, nobody ever believed in the Campbell's boycott, so if we're going to do it, it's only because of the ideological thing, because we, like, hate what they're doing to the farmworkers. But all the other canning companies are doing it to the farmworkers too, so we have to boycott everybody. If we boycott Campbell's, we have to boycott DelMonte, and Purity Supreme and Dole—if it's a moral issue it applies across the board, doesn't it? But nobody's going to give up canned everything, even Jessica likes her little can of beets.

GAYLE: El, this argument is stupid.

ELLY: No, it's not, if you think about it—

JEN: Who wants to think about it? It's not that big a deal to boycott Campbell's soup.

ELLY: *(Yelling.)* IT IS IF YOU LIKE GOLDEN MUSHROOM !

JEN: All right! I just don't understand what the big deal is—

ELLY: *(Ranting a little.)* It's the principal of the thing! God! If Jessica had a good reason for insisting that I boycott the fucking soup, I'd do it gladly, I'd picket the company, I'd quit my job and teach English to poor little migrant children for the rest of my life! But she doesn't have a good reason! It's the same damn thing with Roger! If he had a good reason that I shouldn't have an abortion, I wouldn't! I wouldn't! But he doesn't have any reason, he hasn't thought it through for a second. It's all just out there—boycott soup, don't have abortions, all these horrible things floating around the ozone, these *things* I'm not supposed to do because they make me a terrible person, and no one can really give me a good reason why. WHY?

GAYLE: Oh, come on, you know that's not true.

ELLY: I don't know that's not true.

GAYLE: You want reasons why? You want to know why you shouldn't have an abortion? Roger will give you reasons.

JEN: Jessica will give you reasons—

ELLY: No, they won't. They'll just go into some routine about murder or something. I mean, they just don't seem to be able to get it through their thick fucking skulls that this is not a moral issue, it's a *social* issue—

GAYLE: Jesus, El, would you listen to yourself? You don't really want reasons from people! You just want to argue! You just want to be right about everything—

ELLY: That's not true. I don't need to be right. I need to be *convinced.* If they're going to tell me I'm all fucked up and immoral, they better back up their arguments. I just think if you're going to judge somebody, you ought to be able to convince them too.

(Pause.)

GAYLE: *(To Jen.)* Did you follow that?

JEN: Kind of. But I just kind of think it's stupid, you know? I mean—people don't work like that. There's just always going to be somebody who thinks you're awful and there's nothing you can do about it. Can I have some more scotch?

(Elly pushes the bottle to Jen.)

ELLY: Well, coming from you, that philosophy is not entirely surprising.

(Pause. Jen puts down the bottle.)

GAYLE: *El.*

JEN: Oh. Is that supposed to be an insult? Are you trying to insult me?

ELLY: No, I just meant—

JEN: I know what you meant. You meant I sleep around a lot.

ELLY: No, I didn't—

GAYLE: Yes you did.

ELLY: I didn't mean anything, it just came out of my mouth.

JEN: I don't care if that is what you meant. I do sleep around, I don't sleep around alot. I sleep around. I have always believed that sex is just really, really fun, and I'm not going to change my attitude now. I like sex. That doesn't mean I'm a loon about it. I don't pick up guys on streetcorners. I don't parade total strangers through the house. I mean, I'm not Wilt Chamberlain, for God's sake.

GAYLE: No one said you were.

JEN: I sleep with my friends. I don't sleep with anybody I haven't known for at least two weeks. And I'm completely careful. I take every precaution in the book. Those people who say safe sex isn't fun? They've never met *me*. I've never had a venereal disease, I've never been pregnant—

ELLY: All right—

JEN: It's not like I'm a prostitute.

GAYLE: All right.

JEN: Jesus, I don't even have affairs with married men! Okay, okay, *once* I had an affair with a married man. But just once.

(Pause.)

ELLY: *(Curious.)* You did?

JEN: *(Admission.)* Yeah, so what? That hardly makes me a homewrecker.

GAYLE: When?

ELLY: I know who it was. It was that blond guy with the thinning hair—the one who wore suits, what was his name—

GAYLE: Bernard.

JEN: *(Overlapping.)* No, no, no—It was before I moved in here. It was two years ago, in Philadelphia. That was why I left Philadelphia.

ELLY: You left an entire city because of some guy?

JEN: I had to.

GAYLE: How long were you and he—

JEN: Three years.

ELLY: Three years? Three *years?* You? I'm sorry, I'm not trying to be as insulting as I'm sounding, but—you know, as long as I've known you—you don't exactly settle into relationships.

GAYLE: Going out with a married man is not exactly settling in.

JEN: No, it's not, is it? I was his mistress. Pretty weird, huh?

GAYLE: How did it happen?

JEN: You know how those things are. I don't know. I was his paralegal, right? And we're like—together all the time, we go to the law library together, we go to court together, we go to lunch together, we take a road trip to Pittsburgh together, and—you know? One thing leads to another. I'm not going to explain it. Shit happens.

ELLY: Three years?

JEN: Yeah, its was not good.

ELLY: So you had to move?

JEN: Yeah, it was like the only way to do it. So, here I am— sleeping around.

ELLY: Yes, here you are.

GAYLE: Here we are.

JEN: Here we are!

ELLY: Here we are.

(Pause.)

JEN: I haven't thought about that for a long time. It makes me feel weird—like I was some kind of villain. I used to feel that way all the time. It's funny—you can go through your life making mistake after mistake, but you always know, these are just mistakes, everybody makes mistakes. Then one day you realize that you're in the middle of a mistake that's something worse. It's not just another mistake anymore; suddenly you're a bad person. And it's so weird, it—happens without your even knowing it.

GAYLE: You're not a bad person.

ELLY: No, you're not a bad person. Still, I wouldn't tell that story to Jessica if I were you.

JEN: Yeah, she'd try to get rid of me.

ELLY: No, she wouldn't. She'd keep you around and pray over you. She'd make you stay up late and have long, meaningful talks about Jesus and His forgiveness.

JEN: She'd probably make me go to church.

GAYLE: For that? That is nothing.

JEN: Oh, you got a better story?

GAYLE: What? No.

JEN: Yes, you do. Don't you? You do.

GAYLE: I do not.

JEN: Look at the guilt on that face.

ELLY: Gayle—what did you do? Gayle!

GAYLE: I don't know what you're talking about.

JEN: Come on, spill it. Come on…

(Pause.)

ELLY: Oh, forget it. She never does anything wrong.

GAYLE: Oh, Honey.

ELLY: (Laughs.) Time for more scotch! And another round of cigarettes… (She pours scotch and passes the cigarettes, then the lighter, around.) This is fun. We should do this more often. This is really fun.

JEN: Except I'm not getting drunk. This is not good scotch.

ELLY: Yes, it is. It's great scotch. It cost me twenty bucks.

GAYLE: It's hard to get drunk in the morning. I don't know why that is, but it's true.

ELLY: Well, we'll just have to keep drinking. Okay, Gayle: What did you do?

GAYLE: (Deliberate.) I had sex with a man for money.

ELLY: You're kidding. *(Elly starts to laugh.)*

JEN: You what?

GAYLE: I had sex with a man for money.

JEN: You mean, you were like—a prostitute?

GAYLE: Yes. I was like a prostitute. I mean, I wasn't walking the streets and I didn't have a pimp or anything, it was just the one guy. But I did—he said he'd pay me for sex, so I did it.

ELLY: That is incredible.

GAYLE: No, it's not. It would be nice if it was incredible, but it's just a normal, sick story.

(Pause.)

ELLY: Well, are you going to tell the normal sick story?

GAYLE: Okay. I was doing temp work at this marketing research company, right? And the head of the project started coming on to me. So I told him to leave me alone and he said he thought it would be mutually beneficial for me to hear him out. So I did. And—he told me that he could put me down as a special consultant on the project, somebody he brought in, and get the company to pay me sixty dollars an hour instead of the $12.50 I'd get from the temp agency. Well, if you multiply that by 40 hours a week—

ELLY: My God. He wanted you bad.

JEN: Did he come through with it?

GAYLE: Yeah, I made him pay me half in advance, and then I got the rest at the end of the week.

JEN: You did it for a week?

GAYLE: Two weeks. It was a lot of money.

ELLY: You must be pretty good, Gayle.

(They laugh uproariously.)

GAYLE: Well, let's just say I was just willing to do alot for that much money. I made it worth his while to keep me on the payroll for an extra week.

JEN: *(Calming down a little.)* Oh, God. I'm sorry, I'm just—you know? That sounds kind of disgusting.

GAYLE: It was kind of disgusting. It was also illegal; it was embezzling.

ELLY: What did you have to do?

GAYLE: I think I'll leave the details to your sordid imagination, if you don't mind.

ELLY: Oh, come on, you're leaving out the best part—

GAYLE: I'm not going to give you details, El! I'm not that drunk!

(Pause. Jen hands her the scotch bottle.)

JEN: Why did you do it?

GAYLE: I needed the money. That was really just it. I was stuck, I was tired of living in New York, I was tired of working in these stupid boring offices—I was sick of it. I was just a mess. And he was offering me so much money. I mean, it was enough to go back to school and finish my degree, so, thanks to this sleezeball, I am now a social worker. You know? I don't know. It kind of makes me sick to think about it, but I might do it again if I had to.

ELLY: Better not tell that to Jessica.

GAYLE: Oh, she knows.

ELLY: You're kidding. You told her? Why on earth would you—

GAYLE: We were friends. Back before you guys moved in when we were living with Neil and Karen. So one day I told her. I needed to talk about it. But she couldn't really handle it.

ELLY: What did she do?

GAYLE: She didn't talk to me for two months.

ELLY: What do you mean, she didn't talk to you?

GAYLE: She—didn't talk to me.

ELLY: What a bitch.

GAYLE: It's kind of an extreme story for someone like her. I should have known better.

ELLY: Don't defend her.

GAYLE: I'm not defending her. I'm just trying to explain. She's different from us, you know?

ELLY: Yeah, she's a bitch and we're not.

JEN: Did she try to kick you out?

GAYLE: You know, she can't really kick any of us out. I don't know why we're always speculating on this. Everybody's name is on the lease. As long as we pay the rent and keep the kitchen clean, she can't do anything.

JEN: Then why does it *feel* like she can?

GAYLE: Probably what we should do, is move.

ELLY: No way. There's three of us and one of her. *She* should move.

GAYLE: She was here first. If we don't like her rules, we should go.

JEN: Yeah, but the rent here is so *cheap*. If I had to find another apartment, I'd have to pay real rent, and if I had to pay real rent, I'd have to get a real job.

ELLY: Me too.

GAYLE: Me too.

JEN: Let's face it, we're stuck with her.

ELLY: There's got to be a way around this. *(To Gayle.)* She stopped talking to you?

GAYLE: Yeah, I told her this terrible thing, and…she left me alone.

ELLY: That would be a way to go. Do you think if I told her I was having an abortion she'd stop talking to me?

GAYLE: No.

ELLY: Why not? That seems like a fair deal to me. You confess your sins to her, so she leaves you alone. It worked for you. I don't see why you should get the deal and not me. I mean, I'm as much of a sinner as you are—

GAYLE: That doesn't have anything to do with it. She wants to get rid of you because you're a ringleader.

ELLY: I am not!

GAYLE: You are too! Look at this! You're depressed, so we're all drinking scotch!

ELLY: I didn't force scotch on anybody.

GAYLE: I know, it's just sort of natural with you. Remember when we buried Irving in the backyard? Remember how that drove her crazy?

ELLY: Yeah?

JEN: I liked that. I mean, that was really cool.

GAYLE: Your hamster dies, and in no time flat you've got the whole household in the back yard, digging a little grave underneath the statue of Mary, reading a definition of "hamster" out of the dictionary as a eulogy—

JEN: A small rodent, with large cheek pouches. Amen.

GAYLE: See? Jen even remembers the definition.

ELLY: So what? Irving was a great hamster, he deserved a ceremony to mark his passing. I don't see why she had to get so nasty about it.

GAYLE: She's jealous. That's the kind of thing she's always trying to do, get us all together for little functions—like that seder she planned. I mean, maybe if we all, you know, went along with her more—

ELLY: We all went to her fucking seder. It was boring. A Catholic throwing a seder—I mean, it's stupid—

GAYLE: I'm just saying—

ELLY: I know what you're saying ! You're saying that I deliberately provoke her, that I act like some sort of rotten little rebellious kid around here—

GAYLE: No, I'm not—

ELLY: Yes, you are! And I do! I don't care! She fucking drives me crazy and I love getting on her nerves! And it's so fucking easy for me to do, I mean it's just a delight, frankly, to annoy that woman, because all I have to do is be myself, only a little more so. You know, all I have to do is leave a dirty pot on the stove, or suggest that we have lobsters for Thanksgiving, or get high in the living room, and she's seething—

JEN: Yeah, what Jessica needs is a good lay.

ELLY: Oh, you think there's a flaw in the perfect relationship? Jeffrey's maybe not so hot in bed?

JEN: She's not sleeping with Jeffrey.

ELLY: What? What are you talking about, she is too. He's here all weekend.

JEN: They sleep together but they don't have sex. Didn't you know that?

GAYLE: They sleep together but they don't have sex?

ELLY: They've been going out for four years. She's thirty years old!

JEN: Yeah, but it's some religious thing.

GAYLE: She told you that? When did she tell you that?

JEN: I don't know, about a year ago. She was complaining about all the guys I had over, and I said, well, you know, you have Jeffrey over every weekend. And she said, yeah, but they weren't having sex, and I was. So I said I didn't understand what that had to do with anything and she got mad so I just said okay, if I want to sleep with some guy I'll go to his place. I thought you guys knew.

ELLY: What a bitch.

GAYLE: El—

ELLY: I mean, that's sick, you know? Sleeping with Jeffrey for four years—and she's supposedly in love with him, right?—and not having sex? Don't you think that's taking the old Catholic notion of sin a bit too far?

GAYLE: I don't think it's any of our business.

ELLY: Why shouldn't it be our business? Everything we do is her business. She makes it her business if I drink Campbell's soup. And you can just bet this abortion is going to be her business; she'll probably try to have me arrested—

GAYLE: Come on, you can't tell her—

ELLY: You know what I hate the most about her? What I've always hated about her? She doesn't *hurt*. You know? She doesn't feel pain. She's so sure of everything in her life, it's like an armor with her, all that fucking Catholic righteousness. Can't you just see her in bed with him? I bet she sleeps naked except for a pair of panties. And anytime he goes for them, she gently holds out her little hand, chastises him nobly, saves herself for marriage and keeps the universe intact. It's that iron will, you know, keeping Jeffrey and the rest of us in place. Jesus, she's like some fucking medieval saint—

JEN: Elly, please, just forget it, okay? She's not here, and it's a nice day so let's just forget her and have scotch for breakfast—
(*Elly smashes the bottle away from her. It rolls off the table and onto the floor. Jen fetches it.*)
ELLY: I don't want anymore scotch! Why do you think I'm drinking this stuff? I'm drinking it because I half believe her! We all half believe that bitch just because she's so fucking sure of herself and none of us have a clue!
(*Pause. They all think about this.*)
JEN: Yeah. You know, we probably *should* move out.
(*They all look at each other.*)
ELLY: The rent here—
ALL: —is *so* cheap. (*They laugh.*)
JEN: Oh, well, You want some?
(*She holds up the bottle. Pause.*)
(*Blackout.*)

SCENE II

Men on the Telephone, Which is where They Belong

It is a couple of hours later. Gayle, Elly and Jen have moved into the living room. Music comes up, "I Will Survive," by Gloria Gaynor. All three are dressed up in sunglasses, hats and scarves. Gayle sings the lead while Jen and Elly perform a complicated back up routine. At some point, the whole thing dissolves into chaos.

GAYLE: "First I was afraid. I was petrified. Kept thinking I could never live without you by my side. But then I spent so many nights thinking how you did me wrong, and I grew Strong. I learned how to get along. And so you're back—"
JEN/ELLY: Do do do.
GAYLE: From outer space.
JEN/ELLY: Do do do.
GAYLE: You just walked in da da da da with that sad look upon your face
ALL: I should have changed that stupid lock, I should've made you leave the key, if I had known for just one second you'd be back to bother me, go on now, go—

(Et cetera. They are all camping it up royally and well into the second verse when the phone rings.)

JEN: Shit.

(Jen dances over to the phone. Gayle and Elly continue singing.)

GAYLE/ELLY: I will survive! I will survivvveee…

JEN: Hello. *(Loud.)* HELLO? OH, HI, RICHARDSON. *(Pause.)* WHAT? YOU'RE GONNA HAVE TO—COULD YOU—Just a minute. You guys—

(She rolls her eyes and points to the stereo. Elly dances over and turns it down, but she and Gayle continue to dance and sing with each other somewhat softly. Jen returns to the phone, but her mind is more on the music. She speaks loudly to be heard over the music.)

JEN: Sorry…No, we're just sort of hanging out…Elly and Gayle…What? I don't know, I'm kind of into hanging out here…Huh?

(She covers the phone and rolls her eyes at Gayle and Elly. Elly dances over and gives her a drink.)

JEN: God. He wants to come over. Bigtime.

ELLY: No way. I cannot fucking deal with Richardson today.

JEN: *(Into phone.)* What?…no, I don't—Elly's not feeling very well…

ELLY: Don't lie to him. I feel fine. I just don't want to see any men.

JEN: No, we're just hanging out. Listening to records and shit…

GAYLE: We're bonding. Tell him we're female bonding.

JEN: *(Getting irritated.)* What…Well, we can talk tomorrow at work. We'll have lunch…Okay, fine, I know, but today's not good…I know what I just said, Richardson, you don't have to repeat it back to me. I just want to—What could be so fucking important— *(Snapping at Elly.)* COULD YOU TURN THAT OFF FOR A SECOND?

(Elly turns the music off. She and Gayle watch Jen. Jen continues into receiver.)

JEN: Now, what is it?…Well, I'm sorry but you're getting on my last nerve here…Well, if you're not going to even tell me what it is you want to talk about I don't see why I should—…Yeah? What about it?…Well, I did, I thought you were completely off base, I'm not going to apolo—

ELLY: Hang up on him.

JEN: *(Unbelieving, into the phone.)* What? You have got to be kidding…I don't care what you think, that is the craziest thing I've ever heard…No way. No…WHAT?…First of all, I didn't say that, but—

ELLY: HANG UP ON HIM!

JEN: RICHARDSON, YOU ARE A TOTAL LOON AND I AM NEVER GOING TO SLEEP WITH YOU…Oh yeah, then what are you saying?

…You know what your problem is? You are fucking neurotic. *(She slams the phone down and stares at it.)* What an asshole.

ELLY: I never could stand him.

JEN: WHAT A FUCKING ASSHOLE. *(Jen paces furiously for a moment.)*

GAYLE: What did he say?

JEN: I can't believe he just did that to me!

ELLY: He's crazy. How many times have I told you he's crazy?

JEN: Do you know what he just said to me? He just told me—you're not going to believe this. We had lunch Thursday, right?

GAYLE: Yeah?

(Elly grabs the bottle of scotch and pours drinks, then passes ice around while Jen tells her story.)

JEN: So we're sitting there in the cafeteria and this Chinese guy, Billy, we know him from the mail room, he comes up and asks if he can eat with us. So I say of course, not realizing that stupid Richardson is *mad* at Billy for reasons which are completely beyond my imagination. So Billy sits down and Richardson starts sniping at him, this poor Chinese guy who can't even speak the language. And he's getting pretty loud, you know, everyone's sort of looking at us? So I say, you're getting kind of aggressive here, Richardson, and Billy's just smiling away because he doesn't even know what's going on, and Richardson tells me he's not being aggressive, he's being *assertive*—isn't that just perfect, it's like straight out of fucking therapy, you know? Christ. So I said, I think you're confusing assertiveness with machismo here, Richardson. And you know what he just told me on the phone? He wants to get together to talk about this because I was making like this personal statement about his fucking sexuality, and that means something like I've been lying to him all along and subconsciously I want to sleep with him.

(Elly starts to laugh.)

JEN: It's not funny! You know, I think going into therapy was the biggest mistake of his life. His stupid therapist keeps telling him to let it all out. I'm sorry, but I don't think Richardson should let it all out. Doesn't it worry you that there are all these therapists out there telling weirdoes to just let it all out?

GAYLE: Oh, God, Something else to worry about.

JEN: You know what he said to me last week? He told me I was afraid of my sexuality. I use casual sex as a shield against real sex. That's what he told me.

GAYLE: What's real sex?

(Elly and Gayle are laughing hysterically.)

JEN: I'm not kidding. He gets all this shit from his therapist.

GAYLE: Has he told you you're a lesbian yet?

JEN: I think he's building up to that.

ELLY: Why do you hang out with this lunatic?

JEN: I don't know. He tells good stories. He's nice—

ELLY: Excuse me, but this is not nice!

JEN: Okay, he used to be nice. Before he went into therapy he was all fucked up, but he was really nice.

ELLY: Well, he's not nice anymore. You should just tell him to fuck off and die.

JEN: I can't do that. He's in love with me.

(Elly starts to laugh.)

JEN: I knew you would do that. *(Protesting.)* He says he's in love with me. I feel awful about it.

GAYLE: That's not love.

JEN: What would you call it?

ELLY: Who cares what you call it; it's totally bizarre. Stay away from him.

JEN: I can't just dump him. I feel bad.

ELLY: It's not your fault he fell in love with you.

JEN: Yes, it is. Isn't it? I mean—isn't it, kind of?

GAYLE: Did you lead him on?

JEN: Who knows? I probably flirt with him sometimes, but—

ELLY: You flirt with everybody.

JEN: That's what I mean! So maybe I led him on. But I don't think so. I mean, I am *so* not interested in him. Anytime he brings it up, I just tell him face to face: I don't want to be insulting, but I am not interested in sleeping with you.

GAYLE: What does he say to that?

JEN: I don't know, some bullshit. You know what he did last week? He went around and asked all these people if they thought I was in love with him. It was like he was collecting opinions for a case. And everybody said yes. Can you believe that? They said *yes.*

ELLY: Who did he ask?

JEN: He wouldn't tell me. So I said: Look, Richardson, if all these people think I'm in love with you its because I really do *love* you. But you don't always fall in love with people you love. Shit happens, or it doesn't.

ELLY: I don't know why you're so nice about it. He's a serious loon. He's dangerous.

JEN: He is not.

ELLY: The only thing he'll understand is total rejection. Stay away from him.

JEN: Oh, that's nice. That's real compassionate.

ELLY: In the twentieth century, compassion is a luxury you cannot afford. Unless you're getting off on this—

JEN: Mind your own business, Elly! *(Pause.)* I was really awful to him on the phone. Shit

GAYLE: He left you no choice!

JEN: I didn't have to yell at him. I mean, I just—I don't think it's his fault he's crazy. I think his parents fucked him up when he was little.

GAYLE: You think they abused him?

ELLY: Hold it right there. I don't want to have this conversation. I don't care what happened to him when he was four years old. Whatever it was, it doesn't give him the right to do these totally bizarre things to Jen. I mean, everyone has their reasons, even Jessica has her reasons, but that does not mean we have to go along with every weird, sick thing that they do.

GAYLE: Oh, come on. I thought you were into reasons. I thought that was all you wanted out of life—a couple of good, solid *reasons*.

ELLY: What?

JEN: That's right, before, when you were screaming about having an abortion, you said—

ELLY: That was different. And I was not *screaming*.

GAYLE: You said that if Jessica and Roger could give you decent *reasons* you wouldn't have an abortion—

ELLY: I know what I said! I was talking about a different kind of reason.

GAYLE: Oh, please—

ELLY: Those kind are *rational* reasons, the kind you use like in arguments and talking about issues and stuff. This kind of reasons, Richardson's reasons, are just psychological excuses for totally off the wall behavior.

JEN: You always do this. You, like, make up these rules about what everything means—

ELLY: I'm not saying Richardson's reasons aren't valid; I'm just saying they're twisted and I don't want to hear it!

JEN: Oh, that makes a lot of sense. Valid but twisted. I get it.

ELLY: LOOK. Here we have little Adolph Hitler, right? And his mother hits him a billion times and his father hits his mother, and his uncle teaches him that—I don't know, that Jews murder babies and drink their blood, and God knows what else the Hitlers do, but what with one thing and another, little Adolph decides he's got to murder six million Jews. OKAY? DO YOU GET IT? EVEN ADOLPH HITLER HAD HIS

REASONS, BUT I DON'T CARE, THAT DOESN'T EXCUSE WHAT
HE DID!

(Pause.)

GAYLE: God. Hitler is always such a conversation stopper.

(They all start to laugh again.)

GAYLE: It's true. Anytime things start to get a little messy, someone says, well, what about Hitler? And everybody shuts right up.

ELLY: Well, what can you say? The man was a monster.

JEN: Yeah, it's a good thing he never went into therapy. Think of what would have happened if some therapist told him to "let it all out."

(They all laugh. The phone rings.)

JEN: Oh, God, It's Richardson. Oh, shit.

ELLY: Just don't talk to him. I'll get it.

JEN: No wait, not wait—what are you going to say?

ELLY: I'm going to tell him to fuck off and die.

JEN: NO, you can't—

ELLY: I'm kidding. I'll tell him you're in the shower.

GAYLE: Oh, that's a great idea. He'll believe that one.

ELLY: I'll tell him you're drunk. I'll tell him four of your old boyfriends come over and you all got drunk and now you're upstairs fucking your brains out so you can't come to the phone.

JEN: Oh, God, he'll just tell me I'm doing it because I'm afraid of my sexuality—

GAYLE: Are you going to answer it? I'll answer it.

ELLY: I want to answer it!

JEN: No wait—tell him—tell him—I went out.

ELLY: Oh, that's a great excuse. Very specific.

JEN: Tell him I went out for donuts.

ELLY: I'm just going to tell him you don't want to talk to him! *(Elly picks up the phone.)*

JEN: Elly, no—

ELLY: Hello? *(Pause.)* He hung up.

(Elly sets down the phone. They all look at it for a moment.)

JEN: He hung up? He couldn't hang up.

ELLY: What do you mean, he couldn't hang up? He hung up.

JEN: Then it wasn't Richardson. He lets the phone ring for about twenty times before he hangs up.

ELLY: Is that who that is? He's the one who does that?

GAYLE: Didn't you know that? Don't you answer it?

ELLY: Not when I don't feel like it.

JEN: Why don't we have a phone machine?

ELLY: Jessica thinks they're immoral.

GAYLE: Come on, it's not that she thinks they're immoral. She just doesn't want to spend the money until she finds the exact right one.

ELLY: Oh, the exact right phone machine. What is the exact right phone machine?

GAYLE: One that's made of wicker.

(They laugh.)

GAYLE: Who do you think it was?

JEN: He'll call back.

GAYLE: It might be a she.

JEN: No, it's never a she around here. Only boys call us. None of us have any girlfriends.

GAYLE: That's ridiculous.

JEN: It's true!

GAYLE: My mother calls.

JEN: Oh, come on, you can't count mothers.

ELLY: Why not?

GAYLE: We don't have girlfriends? That can't be true.

ELLY: Wait a minute, Sarah calls me all the time.

JEN: She's your boss.

ELLY: Yeah, but she's my friend, too.

JEN: You can't count her.

GAYLE: It's not true that only men call here. It's just true that those are the only calls you count.

JEN: You're right. Oh, well, What can I say? I like men better than women.

ELLY: Jen! What are you doing saying things like that? Haven't you ever heard of feminism?

JEN: Of course I've heard of feminism. It really put me in touch with my feelings, and what I feel is, I like men better than women.

GAYLE: Isn't that interesting? I think they're mostly shitheads.

ELLY: I know.

GAYLE: I can't stand them.

ELLY: I know. They're such idiots.

GAYLE: Everything is their fault.

(They break up laughing.)

ELLY: Why are we laughing? It's true.

(They laugh even harder. Elly reaches for the bottle of scotch.)

ELLY: Oh, you guys. We're running out of scotch.

JEN: What do you mean. We have a lot—

ELLY: No, no, no. We're running low. I'll go get more— *(Elly crosses to the stairs.)*

GAYLE: Elly—no, Elly, you can't go out; you're drunk.

ELLY: I AM NOT DRUNK!

JEN: How can you not be drunk? I am completely smashed—

ELLY: I AM NOT DRUNK! *(Elly disappears into her room.)*

GAYLE: You can't go out! We can't let her go out in this condition. She'll get arrested.

JEN: Can you get arrested for being drunk?

ELLY: *(Off.)* I AM NOT DRUNK! *(Elly staggers back on, carrying a full bottle of scotch.)*

GAYLE: You are so drunk. You are totally looped.

ELLY: I am not looped. I am tight. That's what they call it in Hemingway novels. Tight. I am tight.

JEN: You are schnockered.

ELLY: No, you are schnockered. I am—

GAYLE: Blitzed.

ELLY: I am TIGHT! I am tight and Gayle is—trashed.

GAYLE: No, I'm not. I'm—wasted.

ELLY: Okay. I am tight, and Jen is schnockered, and Gayle is wasted. That's pretty good.

JEN: I don't want to be schnockered. I want to be—Wait a minute. You have another bottle?

GAYLE: You have another bottle? You bought two bottles?

ELLY: I felt it was an emergency.

JEN: Wait a minute! You shouldn't be drinking at all! You're pregnant—

GAYLE: Jen—

ELLY: No, no, hey, it's okay. That's *why* I'm drinking. Because I'm pregnant. I'm trying to anesthetize the little fella. *(Talking to her stomach.)* How's it going in there? Have you passed out yet? You won't feel a thing.

JEN: You think it's a boy?

ELLY: Honestly, Jen, I've heard of cradle robbing, but really—

JEN: Yes, ha ha, very funny. Seriously, you think it's a boy?

ELLY: I don't know, I guess—yeah. I think it's a boy.

JEN: You should have him. There's a shortage of men, you know. Some girl could need him someday.

ELLY: I can't have a baby. What would I do with a baby?

JEN: I don't know, I just—

GAYLE: You would raise him, you moron. People do it all the time.

ELLY: I don't know. Sometimes I think I do want to have a baby. I want to have, like, a baby and a dog. We could go places together. Elly and her baby and her dog. The Elly Team. I think that would be nice. *(Pause.)* Shit. I want a baby.

JEN: Then have it!

ELLY: I can't have it. I'm too fucked up.

JEN: You'll sober up.

ELLY: That's not what I *mean*.

JEN: Well, if you're going to do the abortion thing, you better take a couple of bodyguards along. You can get killed going into an abortion clinic these days. Those Right to Lifers are dangerous. Huh. That's kind of ironic, isn't it?

ELLY: It's occurred to people, Jen.

JEN: Well, at least it's still legal. If the Republicans were in charge, the three of us would probably be sitting here, trying to figure out how to operate a coat hanger.

ELLY/GAYLE: Oh, God, that's—Jen—

JEN: What, it's true!

GAYLE: I don't want to talk about politics.

ELLY: Especially in such graphic detail. *(She starts to open the bottle then stops herself.)* You know, I really don't want any more scotch.

GAYLE: Me neither. Time to make COFFEE. *(Gayle tries to stand and can't.)*

JEN: You know what we should do? We should make cookies.

GAYLE: *Cookies.*

JEN: We could make oatmeal cookies.

GAYLE: Oatmeal cookies…

JEN: This is great. I've decided: Getting drunk and making cookies is the perfect thing to do on a Sunday afternoon.

GAYLE: Sunday afternoon… *(Pause. She sits bolt upright.)* SHIT. It's Sunday afternoon. *(She leans over quickly and reaches for the phone. She picks up the receiver, stares at the phone for a second, then sets down the receiver. Then she picks up the receiver again.)* Shit.
(Pause. Gayle sets the receiver down again. Jen and Elly stare at her.)

ELLY: Is something wrong?

GAYLE: NO. No. What time is it?

ELLY: *(Looking at her watch.)* Quarter after twelve.

GAYLE: SHIT. What time was that phone call? The one we didn't answer?

JEN: It was, like, ten minutes ago. What, you think it was for you?

GAYLE: What? No, no, I just—nothing. I don't know. You know?

ELLY: You were expecting a call?

GAYLE: No. I mean, maybe. I don't know. Shit.

JEN: Yes you were. You were expecting a call from a man.

GAYLE: No. I just—I forgot about something.

ELLY: Call him back.

GAYLE: Who was it?

GAYLE: It wasn't anybody.

ELLY: Gayle!

GAYLE: What?

ELLY: You always do this.

GAYLE: I'm not *doing* anything.

ELLY: Oh, come on. Why can't you just tell us—

GAYLE: There's nothing to tell. It was just—nothing. Forget it.

ELLY: I thought alcohol was supposed to make people talk.

JEN: Leave her alone, Elly.

ELLY: Don't you trust us? *(Pause.)* Oh, great. That makes me feel just *great.*
     (The phone rings. Gayle jumps.)

ELLY: Gee, I wonder who that is? Probably nobody. It's probably not even
     worth answering. It's probably nothing.
     (The phone rings again. Gayle stares at it.)

JEN: Gayle! Answer it!
     (Gayle quickly picks up the receiver.)

GAYLE: Hello?…Oh, hello. Oh—I'm not sure. Just a minute, I'll check.
     *(Gayle covers the receiver with her hand and looks at Elly. Pause. Elly reaches
     for the phone.)*

ELLY: Hello?…Hi. *(Pause.)* Yeah, I'm sorry too. It's just—this is really weird
     for me—What? I can't hear you, you have to— *(Pause.)* I can't right now.
     I just need to—I need to think for a little while, okay? *(Pause. The phone
     call becomes progressively more difficult for her. She covers her face with her
     free hand.)* Yeah, yeah, I'm still here. It's just— *(Pause.)* Roger, we can't
     talk about this over the phone— *(Pause.)* I know, but I just think you're
     getting— *(Pause.)* I don't know. It doesn't sound like a real good idea to
     me—Well, because marriage is serious, my God, that's not something
     you just dive into. You were always the one with commitment paranoia.
     (Gayle and Jen stand to leave. Elly gestures them to sit down.)

ELLY: You guys— *(Into phone.)* What? Roger, this is too serious to decide over
     the phone. I am not going to decide to marry you over the phone. *Yes, I
     know that abortion is serious too, I never said it wasn't*—Fuck. Fuck. Look.

I don't want to marry you. Okay? I don't want to marry you, Roger. I don't want to spend the rest of my life with you. I don't want to have your child. Okay? Okay? I don't want to marry you. I am not in love with you OKAY?

(Gayle and Jen look at each other, and begin to leave again. Elly reaches out and grabs Gayle's hand to stop her. She leans against her suddenly, cradling the phone against her chest.)

(Blackout.)

SCENE III

Gods and Mothers

The lights are lowered and the blinds are drawn. A half filled plate of oatmeal cookies sits on the floor in front of the couch next to a disgustingly full tray of cigarettes. The easy chair has been dragged over to the couch, and Jen and Gayle sit holding a Ouija board on their knees. Elly lounges full length on the couch and watches them. The cursor moves rapidly across the surface of the board.

JEN: You're pushing it.

GAYLE: I'm not, I swear!

JEN: N—E—Y—Barney. We're talking to Barney, is that right?

GAYLE: *(Watching board.)* Yes.

JEN: I have never had a Ouija board work this good.

GAYLE: What do you want to ask him? Hi, Barney.

ELLY: Barney? We're talking to a male spirit? Wouldn't you know. Tell Barney we don't want to talk to men today.

JEN: Elly, no—shit, she doesn't mean it, Barney. Are you still here? *(She watches.)* Yes. Thank God.

(Elly giggles.)

JEN: Stop it, Elly. This is very serious and if he thinks you're a nonbeliever he'll go away. You can't just fool around with this.

ELLY: Okay, okay. I have a question. Ask him—if Gayle's new boyfriend is going to call back.

GAYLE: Elly—

JEN: Yes. It says yes.

GAYLE: You're pushing this—

JEN: I would never push a Ouija—

ELLY: I knew it! I knew it was a guy.

GAYLE: It was just a date.

JEN: Come on, come on, we have to ask him another question. Think of a question. Gayle. I want to know—let me think, I want to know—

ELLY: Is there sex in the afterlife?

(The cursor moves wildly from one end of the board to the other.)

JEN: Great. Oh, great. That's what it does when it knows there's an unbeliever present. Barney, no, we believe in you.

ELLY: No, we don't, Barney.

GAYLE: It's saying something. Look, it's spelling something.

JEN: God, we didn't even ask a question. This is amazing—

(Pause. They all watch.)

GAYLE: Go.

JEN: Go. Go where?

ELLY: Go fish.

JEN: Elly—

GAYLE: No, come on, pay attention, it's saying go outside and do something—it's a beautiful day out—

JEN: Wait a minute. You are pushing this, aren't you?

GAYLE: Of course I'm pushing it! For heaven's sake, let's get out of here! We've been lying around all day—

JEN: That's great. That's just great. You guys are both jerks. *(Jen starts to throw the Ouija board back into the box.)*

ELLY: No, come on, come on, I want to ask it a question.

JEN: Just forget it, Elly. You made your stupid point.

GAYLE: Look, I'm sorry. I just thought—

JEN: You shouldn't fuck around with this, I'm telling you—

ELLY: I'm not fucking around. I have a question. I want to know—I want to know if I can use this thing to talk to my mother.

JEN: Oh, ha ha, that's real funny.

ELLY: I'm not kidding!

JEN: You can only talk to dead people with a Ouija board, moron.

ELLY: No kidding, moron.

(Pause. Gayle takes her hand off the cursor and looks at Jen. They all look at each other.)

GAYLE: Oh, Jesus, Jen. You're kidding, right?

JEN: Your mother's dead? When did she die?

ELLY: What? Four years ago. Are you kidding? She died four years ago.

JEN: Your mother's dead? You didn't tell me your mother was dead.

ELLY: I've been living with you for a year. How could you not know?

JEN: Why didn't you tell me?

(Pause.)

ELLY: That is so depressing.

JEN: Well, we don't exactly see each other a lot. Just weekends and shit.

ELLY: Yeah. It just makes you wonder. I mean, who knows what kind of shit we don't know about each other?

JEN: God, I know. I mean, like, think about it. How did we meet?

ELLY: God help us all. Jessica picked us.

JEN: That's my point. The three of us, we could be anybody, you know. I saw this movie, where this girl got a roommate through the personals, who tried to *kill* her—

GAYLE: Jen!

JEN: What?

GAYLE: Come back.

JEN: Oh. Sorry. *(Pause.)* So—how'd your mom die?

ELLY: Oh—she was killed in a car accident. Some moron ran a red light at fifty miles an hour and smashed into her. He was driving this Oldsmobile station wagon, and she was in a Chevette. She didn't stand a chance.

JEN: Do you miss her?

ELLY: Oh, yeah.

JEN: That's nice. I mean, it's not nice that she's dead; it's nice that you miss her. If my mother died I think I'd have a party.

GAYLE: Jen!

JEN: What? My mother's a bitch!

GAYLE: Well, my mother's a bitch too, but I wouldn't throw a party.

ELLY: My mother was cool.

GAYLE: Yeah?

ELLY: Yeah. She was very loving and compassionate and she loved being a mother. And—she was very spiritual, you know—

JEN: Jesus. She sounds like Jessica.

ELLY: What?

GAYLE: I don't want to talk about Jessica again…

ELLY: SHE WAS NOTHING LIKE JESSICA.

(Pause. Both Jen and Gayle are a little startled at the force of this outburst.)

JEN: Jesus.

ELLY: I just don't see how you can say that.

GAYLE: El, would you calm down? You've been flying off the handle all day.

ELLY: My mother listened to people! She *listened.* And she understood that we are all fucked up. The entire planet. She used to say, we're all sinners—

JEN: Yeah, I've heard that. Jessica says that all the time.

ELLY: But when Jessica says it, she means that we're sinners and she's perfect, and when my mother said it, she meant that we're all a little fucked up and it's no big deal.

GAYLE: *(Irritated.)* Look, I wasn't kidding. Do you think we could stop trashing Jessica for maybe, I don't know, five or ten minutes?

ELLY: Oh, I'm sorry. That's right, you and Jessica are such close friends. Ever since way back when—

GAYLE: I just don't think she's all that bad.

ELLY: She is too.

GAYLE: She is not! If she were, she wouldn't bug you so much.

ELLY: She bugs you too.

GAYLE: She does not.

ELLY: She does too!

JEN: You guys—

GAYLE: She does not! I admire the woman—

ELLY: She is a self righteous prima donna!

GAYLE: Yeah, well, so are you.

(Pause. They look at each other for a moment, then Elly looks away, stung.)

JEN: Do you guys want a cookie? *(Pause.)* How about some more coffee? I want more coffee… *(Jen exits to the kitchen for coffee.)*

GAYLE: I'm sorry. I just think, you know, that you're pissed off because you're pregnant and you're taking it out on Jessica.

(Elly picks up a knife and begins to play with it.)

ELLY: Oh, no, my dislike for her is very sincere. Every night as I go to bed, I fantasize about skewering her in any number of ways, like one of those medieval saints she's so fond of imitating. You know, after living with her, I'm starting to understand why they all ended up the way they did.

GAYLE: All right. It's a given, you hate her. Why don't you move out? Just move out.

ELLY: Real job, real rent.

GAYLE: You could get a real job and pay real rent, El. You're thirty years old! It's not unheard of!

ELLY: Hey. I'm an American. We're a nation of professional adolescents. Why buck a trend?

GAYLE: Because life is passing you by.

ELLY: No, I'm passing it by, remember?

(Jen reenters with coffee.)

GAYLE: All right, let's talk about that, then. You're pissed off about this baby.

ELLY: On the contrary. I delight in the knowledge that my reproductive system actually works. After all these years of fooling it, I've wondered.

JEN: How did you get pregnant, anyway? I mean, nobody gets pregnant anymore.

(They look at her.)

JEN: Nobody who doesn't want to, I mean. A little bit of birth control goes a long way.

ELLY: The diaphragm, if used properly, is ninety-eight percent successful. Well, meet Miss Two Percent.

GAYLE: And that doesn't make you mad.

ELLY: No. Because it doesn't matter. I'm going to have an abortion, and that's that.

GAYLE: What would your mother think about that?

ELLY: My mother is dead.

GAYLE: What would she think, El?

JEN: She would hate it. She was Mother Earth Goddess, remember?

GAYLE: Jen—

JEN: I just think you should stop playing shrink. I'm just sitting here waiting for you to say, "El—let it all out…".

GAYLE: All right.

JEN: I mean, personally, I think abortion is a bad idea, but if she doesn't want to talk about it—

ELLY: You do?

JEN: God, yes.

ELLY: You?

JEN: Are you kidding? After what I've learned about babies this year, I would never have an abortion.

ELLY: Great.

JEN: Babies are big business.

ELLY: Oh, no.

JEN: Oh, yeah. Everybody wants one. They were kind of cheap for a while, but the ceiling has really come off in the past couple years. We did five surrogate mother contracts, just this month.

ELLY: This does not help me.

JEN: Listen, all sorts of shit goes on nowadays. I know a guy who set up this deal where he got a pregnant teenager to give her baby up for adoption to this very nice yuppie couple in exchange for medical and living expenses during the pregnancy. Bill came to $50,000.

GAYLE: That isn't legal.

JEN: Oh, grow up. There are plenty of ways around the law, and the market is so hot right now no one really knows what's going on. So the way I look at it, if you don't want this kid, you could make somebody else real happy and end up with a few bucks in the bargain.

ELLY: Sure. Everybody wins.

JEN: You could quit your job. You hate that job. Take a few months off, get some desperate sterile couple to foot all the bills…

ELLY: You could set up one of these deals for me?

GAYLE: El!

ELLY: I'm kidding! I could never sell my baby. I'd rather kill it. *(Pause.)* That's what I love about contemporary society. Options.

JEN: Oh, come on, that's not what I said.

GAYLE: You said, babies are big business.

JEN: Yeah, but you're making it sound sleazy. It's a good thing.

GAYLE/ELLY: Jen!

JEN: What? I'm just being realistic! We live in a market economy. Money is power. Now babies are money, so babies are power. You guys are the ones who are always screaming about women's rights and rah rah feminism, well, that's fine but I'm telling you, I've been working in law offices for four years now and those guys are not going to just hand over their money and their power and their little offices. No way; they live for that shit. Now all of a sudden, these guys have decided they want babies, too—they want something we've got, right? So all I'm saying is: Let them pay for it. And you can both stop looking at me like I crawled out of the woodwork somewhere. I make a lot of sense and you know it.

ELLY: Oh, you do. I'm just wondering how come you're so practical about some things and such a moron about Richardson.

JEN: Would you leave Richardson out of this? He's none of your business. I swear to God, you're obsessed—

ELLY: I just think he's—

JEN: I already told you, I don't care what you think!

GAYLE: You guys, come on, Richardson's got nothing to do with whether or not Elly should sell her baby.

JEN: I didn't say sell! I said put it up for adoption for a profit.

GAYLE: Fine. I'm disgusted either way.

ELLY: I'm not. I think it's kind of funny. Babies for cash. I can't wait till they start advertising. I could do a lot with this. Buy a baby and build a family—shoot for an upper, middle upper consumer…fifty thou isn't that big an investment—it's much cheaper than a house—

GAYLE: Okay, we get the point.

ELLY: You realize, of course, that this could put abortion clinics out of business. The Right to Lifers will win, not because they're right, but because having babies became economically feasible! But they won't care! Because in the embrace of capitalism and morality, ALL ARE WINNERS! WE HAVE ACHIEVED UTOPIA! YES! YES! YES!

(Elly laughs maniacally, then falls into natural laughter again. Both stare at her.)

GAYLE: Are you all right?

ELLY: Don't you think it's funny?

GAYLE: No.

ELLY: How could you not think this is funny? We were laughing at Hitler before. If Hitler is funny, this is funny.

GAYLE: I never said Hitler was funny.

ELLY: You were laughing.

GAYLE: I was not—

ELLY: Laugh, Damn you! It's funny! LAUGH.

(Elly jumps her and tickles her viciously. Jen joins in. Gayle screams laughs for a moment, then they collapse in a heap on the couch.)

JEN: God. Do we have any aspirin?

ELLY: Or alka seltzer?

GAYLE: I'll get it.

(Gayle goes to the kitchen. Elly stands and wanders to the window.)

ELLY: We should go outside, it's so nice— *(Pause.)* Shit. Hey, hey, what kind of car does Richardson drive?

JEN: Oh, please, please could we not talk about him? Please?

ELLY: No, no kidding, Jen, I think—

JEN: Gayle, she's doing it again!

(Gayle reenters with ginger ale and aspirin.)

GAYLE: Cut it out, El.

ELLY: No, listen—

JEN/GAYLE: *(Overlapping.)* SHUT UP! CUT IT OUT!

ELLY: All right, but don't blame me—

JEN/GAYLE: *(Overlapping.)* SHUT UP!

ELLY: *(Overlapping.)* ALL RIGHT!

(For one instant, everyone is screaming simultaneously. They start to laugh, then pass around the aspirin.)

ELLY: I still want to talk to my mother.

JEN: Your mother probably went to heaven, or whatever you want to call it, so we're not going to be able to get her on the Ouija board. The Ouija board is for low-rent spirits.

GAYLE: What did you want to tell her?

ELLY: I don't know. I wanted to tell her how much I loved her. And I wanted to tell her that I'm all fucked up.

JEN: You could pray to her.

ELLY: What? Come on, that's stupid.

JEN: Why is that stupid? I don't think that's stupid at all. It might be stupid for me to pray to my mother because she's alive and she's a drunk and I hate her, but you really loved your mother.

ELLY: I hate God. *(Pause.)* I hate God for killing my mother.

GAYLE: Some moron in an Oldsmobile station wagon killed your mother.

ELLY: You think I haven't told myself that a billion times?
(Pause.)

JEN: So why pray to some stupid God? Pray to her.

ELLY: What if she doesn't answer?

JEN: She will.

ELLY: Jen—

JEN: No, you can't feel stupid. Come on, we'll all pray to her. Okay. Let's see. We should all hold hands.

ELLY: Jen, come on.

GAYLE: No, I want to do this, too. *(Gayle sits and grabs Elly's hands.)*

JEN: Okay, okay, we have to close our eyes.

ELLY: You guys—

GAYLE: CLOSE YOUR EYES!
(They do.)

JEN: Okay—now, Elly, you have to tell us what she looks like so we know who we're praying to.

ELLY: Well—um, okay. She had blonde hair and brown eyes—her hair was long, kind of, and straight—and people used to say I looked like her, but I don't think I really did. And she used to wear this funny little hat, it was kind of like this little fisherman's cap, you know— *(Pause.)* I can't, Jen.

JEN: That's okay, that's good enough. Okay. Here we go. *(Calling.)* Mrs. Stewart—

GAYLE: No, you can't call her Mrs. Stewart. You have to call her Mom.

JEN: Oh, right. Okay. *(Calling.)* Mom—Mom, we're down here and we're fucked up and we need to talk to you!

GAYLE: We're confused, Mom!

ELLY: And we're a little drunk! I'm pregnant, Mom!

GAYLE: Things are a mess!

ELLY: We need you to tell us that we're okay, Mom!

GAYLE: We need some advice!

JEN: We need courage! We need support!

ELLY: Mom, are you there?

GAYLE: Mom?

ALL: *(Calling, in unison.)* Mooooommmmm!

JESSICA: *(At doorway.)* Just what is going on here?

(Pause. All of them open their eyes and look at her. Jessica stares at them. Jen and Gayle are somewhat abashed; Elly is suddenly defensive. Freeze.)

(Blackout.)

END OF ACT I

ACT II
SCENE I

What's He Doing Out There?

It is a few seconds later. Jessica stares at the mess.

JESSICA: What are you doing? Look at this place!
   (Jen and Gayle scramble to clean.)
JEN: *(Overlap.)* Shit. Sorry, Jessica—
GAYLE: *(Overlap.)* Jessica—I'm sorry about the mess. It's not as bad as it looks. We didn't expect you back this early—
JESSICA: *(Overlap.)* Look at this place! What did you guys do, sit around and drink all day? Oh, God, you've been smoking in the house—you guys—
JEN: Not very much. We were mostly smoking outside. We just, it's just that we brought the ashtray in, and it was full of cigarettes—shit, I'll just go get the air stuff—
GAYLE: *(Overlap.)* Things just got away from us a little; we'll clean it right up—
JESSICA: Oh, forget it. It's okay, Gayle—GAYLE, IT'S OKAY. I don't care. Jen—forget it.
JEN: Forget it?
JESSICA: It's fine, we can clean it up later. Listen, Richardson's out front. He's across the street in his car. He wants to talk to you.
JEN: What? *(Jen crosses rapidly, angrily to the porch.)*
JESSICA: He came by to talk to you because he said you had a fight or something. I told him I'd tell you he was out there.
JEN: *(Overlap.)* He WHAT? That jerk—Oh, that is just fucking great. This is unbelievable.
JESSICA: No, now come on, you're just getting all… *(Calling.)* He just wants to talk to you—why are you overreacting like this? He just said that you had some sort of disagreement and he wants to…
ELLY: *(Overlap.)* Aren't you mad about this?
JEN: *(Screaming from porch.)* WHAT IS HE DOING OUT THERE? What a dweeb. I mean, what a fucking weenie. It's not enough that he has to follow me around the office like some kind of retarded shithead, now he's got to, what, park on my street? This is an invasion of privacy, an invasion of my private fucking spaces, you know? Shit. I mean it, I say we arrest him. This has to be illegal. WOULD SOMEONE PLEASE

PAY ATTENTION TO ME? GAYLE! ELLY! SOMEBODY CALL THE FUCKING COPS!

GAYLE: *(Overlap.)* We'll clean this right up— *(Gayle picks up several dishes.)*

JESSICA: *(Overlap.)* Gayle, it's okay, leave it. Apparently we have a disaster on our hands. Richardson looks like death warmed over—What did she do to him? Is she sober?

ELLY: She's fine.

JESSICA: She certainly doesn't sound fine.

(Gayle crosses to the door, Jessica following. They all pile out on the porch and stare off at Richardson.)

JEN: Can you believe this?

GAYLE: He's just sitting there.

JEN: He's such a jerk

ELLY: What is the big deal? I say we ignore him.

GAYLE: Isn't he even going to get out of his car?

JEN: Okay, Jessica, what did he say?

JESSICA: He said he wanted to talk to you.

JEN: If he wanted to talk to me, why didn't he come to the door? I mean, *normal* people come to the door.

JESSICA: I didn't ask.

ELLY: Ignore him. Believe me, this works with men.

GAYLE: Wait a minute. He's getting out of the car. He's—no, he's just tying his shoe or something.

JEN: What else did he say?

JESSICA: He didn't say anything else. I told him I'd send you out. He's very upset.

JEN: Well, so am I. This is totally off the wall.

ELLY: Yo! RICHARDSON! *(Elly waves wildly.)*

JEN: Elly! Stop it!

ELLY: I'm just trying to get him to wave. He won't even look at us.

JEN: I thought you wanted to ignore him!

ELLY: I changed my mind.

GAYLE: He looks bad. He kind of looks like a zombie, doesn't he?

JESSICA: *(Overlap, to Jen.)* Do you want to change? Maybe you should change.

ELLY: Jessica, would you cut it out? She looks fine.

GAYLE: How long do you think he's been out there?

JESSICA: Well, he was there when I got home. I talked to him for a few minutes and then I pulled around the corner, so—

GAYLE: That's not what I mean. I mean, he was just sitting there, right? So he could have been there all afternoon for all we know.

ELLY: He's been there at least fifteen minutes; I saw him.

JEN: Why didn't you tell me?

ELLY: I tried! You told me to shut up!

GAYLE: So he's been out there for a while. God. If you hadn't come home, he might have stayed there all night.

ELLY: He looks like he's about to start sprouting things. Moss. Mushrooms.

(Gayle starts to snicker.)

JESSICA: I don't think—

ELLY: I know, I know. It's not nice to make fun of crazy people. I'm sorry.

JESSICA: Richardson isn't crazy. He's upset. Jen—

JEN: DON'T PRESSURE ME. I'm thinking! *(Pause.)* He is such a shithead.

JESSICA: I thought you cared about him.

JEN: Of course I care about him!

ELLY: That's not the issue.

JESSICA: If you love a person you don't put him through this kind of pain, no matter what he said or did in the middle of a fight. Besides, you were drinking—

ELLY: Oh, come on—

JEN: Shut up, Elly.

(Jessica crosses and sits with Jen.)

JESSICA: I'm not trying to pressure you. I've had my share of fights with Jeffrey, and I know how awful they can be, but I think it's a mistake to let this go any further. You and Richardson have been close for a long time, and I don't think either of you wants to sacrifice that.

JEN: I know, it's just—he kind of scares me.

GAYLE: Jessica. If she's scared of him—

JESSICA: What is there to be afraid of?

JEN: I don't know. Nothing.

ELLY: Why don't you leave her alone?

JESSICA: I happen to think she could use a little help.

ELLY: It just seems to me that Jen is perfectly capable of deciding for herself what she wants. I mean, she's not one of your little high school students, you know?

(Pause. Jessica stands up and begins to cross to the door.)

JESSICA: Fine. I'm sorry I said anything.

(Jen stands, alarmed.)

JEN: Where are you going? Jessica!

JESSICA: I'm going to tell Richardson you don't want to talk to him. That's what you want, isn't it?

JEN: I don't know what I want!

JESSICA: Look, I told him you would come out and talk to him. I didn't realize it was going to be such a catastrophe.

JEN: I'm sorry but—

JESSICA: If you don't want to talk to him, I think he needs to know that, so he doesn't wait around anymore. Is that all right with you?

JEN: No, come on, that'll just make him mad—Oh, Geez. *(Jen stands immobile, confused.)*

GAYLE: Jen, don't do anything you don't feel comfortable doing.

JEN: Oh, come off it, Gayle! You're sounding like a therapist again and it doesn't help, you know?

JESSICA: *(Overlapping.)* What are you afraid of? He loves you very much—

JEN: Would you just stop saying that word? Jesus!

ELLY: He doesn't love her—

JESSICA: I don't think you know anything about it.

ELLY: I don't know anything about love?

JESSICA: Elly—I only meant you don't really know Richardson well enough to say that.

ELLY: And you do.

JESSICA: I think I know him better than you do, yes. We've talked.

ELLY: Wait a minute. Wait a *minute*. You talked to him?

JESSICA: Yes, I like Richardson and sometimes I talk to him. Is that all right with you?

ELLY: That depends on what you said. Did you tell him she was in love with him?

JESSICA: What?

ELLY: Richardson went around taking a poll, asking everyone if Jen was secretly in love with him. And he tells Jen that everyone said yes. Were you in on that?

JESSICA: I don't know anything about a poll. All I know is he's been very upset about the fights they've been having, so we had lunch last week, and—

ELLY: You did. You told him she was in love with him.

JESSICA: I told him the truth. Jen obviously loves him much more than— *(Jessica stops herself. Pause.)*

ELLY: Than all the men she fucks? You realize, of course, that that's what he wants. All he wants is to fuck her. And that's what the whole problem is: She won't fuck him.

GAYLE: El, for God's sake.

JESSICA: I don't think you know anything about it.

ELLY: I think I do.

JEN: You had lunch with him? You mean—you've been talking to him behind my back?

JESSICA: I wasn't trying to interfere. He's your boyfriend; I respect that. I was only trying to help.

JEN: (Overlap.) HE IS NOT MY BOYFRIEND! HE HAS NEVER BEEN MY BOYFRIEND, HE WILL NEVER BE MY BOYFRIEND. Did he tell you that? Did he tell you he was my boyfriend?

JESSICA: I don't care what you call it—

JEN: I care what you call it! (Jen stands suddenly and stomps off the porch.)

ELLY: Jen, come on, don't—Jen!

JEN: MIND YOUR OWN BUSINESS, ELLY! GOD. Both of you—I wish you would both mind your own business once in a while.
(Jen exits. They watch her.)

JESSICA: I hope she doesn't hurt him.

ELLY: What? You hope *she* doesn't hurt *him*?

JESSICA: Elly, come on, would you calm down? This isn't the end of the world. I mean, I'm not asking her to marry him. I just think they should talk to each other.

ELLY: You can't talk to him.

JESSICA: Of course you can. I talk to him all the time. He's weird, but he's not crazy.

ELLY: He *is* crazy.

JESSICA: He is not!

ELLY: He's off the deep end. He calls her sixty billion times a day to scream at her; that is not, to my knowledge, the way sane people behave—

JESSICA: He calls her up and screams at her because he's worried about all these men she sees. He's afraid she's going to get AIDS. If she hasn't gotten it already.

ELLY: She's not going to get AIDS.

JESSICA: Elly, come on! You know as well as I do that she's at risk!

ELLY: She says she's careful.

JESSICA: Careful isn't good enough anymore.

GAYLE: (Looking off.) Oh, God. She's getting in the car with him.

JESSICA: Why shouldn't she get in the car with him?

ELLY: Gayle, tell her what he's been doing!

GAYLE: Jessica—it's just that he seems so angry with her—

JESSICA: You've never gotten angry at someone you love?

ELLY: You know, you do—you keep saying that word like it's some sort of magic formula. It's like you think all this LOVE is going to solve something.

JESSICA: I'm not going to apologize for that.

ELLY: But the problem is, this thing between Jen and Richardson isn't about love, it's about sex, a subject you— *(Pause.)* haven't fully considered.

JESSICA: Maybe I haven't. And maybe I am too idealistic about those two. I just—I think they really love each other. I'd like to see them end up together.

ELLY: Do you even listen to her? She's not interested in him. She's said it a million times—

JESSICA: Yes, but that's not how she acts. You've seen them together. They're adorable.

ELLY: All they do is yell at each other!

JESSICA: That is not all they do. When they get along, they're like a couple of kids. Remember when he was always bringing her lunch? He was sure she wasn't eating right—

ELLY: Yeah, she was on a diet and he kept bringing her macaroni and cheese. She was ready to kill him; she gained five pounds.

JESSICA: Well, she didn't have to eat it if—

ELLY: Oh, come on, who's going to say no to macaroni and cheese?

JESSICA: Now you're just being ridiculous—

ELLY: He's trying to control her!

JESSICA: Well, maybe she could use a little control in her life. And she's not the only one.

ELLY: I beg your pardon?

GAYLE: You guys—just don't go there, okay?

JESSICA: You're right. I'm sorry.

(Jessica smiles at Elly, who looks away and goes into the house.)

JESSICA: *(To Gayle.)* I'm sorry. I'm not going to let her get to me today. I feel too good. What a day. It's almost like summer, isn't it?

GAYLE: It's better than summer. I love this kind of weather.

JESSICA: This is the end of it, though. It's supposed to freeze tonight.

GAYLE: Really?

JESSICA: That's what the paper said. And the trees are all pretty much past their peak. *(Jessica turns her face to the sun.)*

GAYLE: Did you have a nice drive?

JESSICA: It was great. Jeffrey and I went all the way up to Manchester and walked on the beach. When we started out this morning, we were only going to go as far as Andover, but the day was so warm we just kept driving. I had no idea it was so close. So we took our shoes off and went walking in the surf.

GAYLE: Sounds great.

JESSICA: It was. *(Pause.)* We had a good talk. *(Pause.)* We talked about getting married.

GAYLE: What? Jesus. Are you kidding? What is going on today? It's got to be the weather.

JESSICA: Thanks a lot.

GAYLE: I'm sorry. I didn't mean that the way it sounded. It's just—somebody else I know got proposed to today. I think it's kind of weird is all.

JESSICA: Well, he didn't—Jeffrey didn't propose—

GAYLE: Well, what did he say?

JESSICA: He just wanted to talk about it, you know—generally.

GAYLE: Generally?

JESSICA: Yes, generally.

GAYLE: Oh, Jessica—come on, is he doing this to you again?

JESSICA: What do you mean? I think we're ready to talk about marriage now; before it just wasn't the right time.

GAYLE: How long are you going to let him do this to you?

JESSICA: I don't know what you're talking about. We're just trying to work things out. We both think it's important not to rush—

GAYLE: I know, I know. I'm sorry.

(Pause.)

JESSICA: I guess I sound pretty defensive, don't I?

GAYLE: No, I shouldn't have said anything. It's just—I'm having such a weird day. *(Pause.)* Look, Jessica, I don't want to rain on your parade; I don't, but at some point don't you just have to give it up? I mean, I like Jeffrey; he's a sweet guy, and I know you love him, but he's been waffling for so long. Don't you just want to—I mean, some days, don't you just want to take *charge* of your life, give him his walking papers or an ultimatum or something, just take *control*— *(Pause.)* Don't you want that?

JESSICA: So—what are you saying? You think that breaking up with Jeffrey will give me control over my life? Is that what you're saying?

GAYLE: I don't know—yes. Yes. I think it would be a good thing—

JESSICA: So I break up with Jeffrey, and what happens then? Then I start looking around again? My friends fix me up, or I join one of those agencies?

GAYLE: No, that's not what—you don't have to do that shit.

JESSICA: Okay. Let's say I break up with Jeffrey and join a health club. Or take classes at UMass. Or start going to bars. I'm not going to do that, Gayle. I'm just—it's so humiliating. I won't do it.

GAYLE: You're a beautiful woman. You won't have any trouble finding someone.

JESSICA: It's not easy for me. It's never been easy. It takes me a long time to feel comfortable with people. And I don't have a lot of time anymore. All right?

GAYLE: You're only thirty years old!

JESSICA: I'll be thirty-one next month.

GAYLE: That's young.

JESSICA: Not if you want children. *(Pause.)* I want to have children. I've always wanted children. It's late for me; I can't— I don't have a lot of years to keep looking anymore.

GAYLE: But—I mean—what if Jeffrey decides—Jesus, Jessica. He's been waffling for so long.

JESSICA: I don't know why we're even talking about this. I love Jeffrey. We just need time to work a few things out. That's what we talked about today; we're working things out and in a year or so we're going to get married. Gayle—don't look at me like that. This is one of the happiest days of my life. Why don't you believe me?

GAYLE: I do. I'm sorry, I just—I'm so confused today. On the one hand, thirty seems young, on the other hand, thirty seems old. I think we should all be getting on with our lives, and I have no idea what that means anymore. So what did Jeffrey say?

JESSICA: Well—it wasn't so much what he said. We were walking in the ocean, and the water was freezing; we were kind of laughing about that…and there was this little girl running up ahead of us, chasing the waves in and out—you know, how kids do—and she had this giant piece of seaweed that she was swinging around, waving over the ocean. She looked like she was blessing the waters. So we started talking about kids, and how there were probably kids all over the world chasing waves, playing with seaweed—the human connection felt so powerful. Thinking about all those people, all those children, on all those other shores. So we started talking about that, and—I don't know. He brought it up—we started talking about getting married. I guess that sounds a little crazy.

GAYLE: *(Dry.)* No. It sounds very romantic. Jeffrey's a very romantic guy.

JESSICA: Then when we were driving home, we took all these back roads to avoid the traffic, and we ended up driving through what must be the wealthiest suburbs in the country. It was appalling. I kept thinking about how the earth is being destroyed, about how many beaches aren't safe anymore because everything's getting so polluted because American capitalists cannot see past their wallets or their lovely little lawns—. I mean, how do you think these grand fortunes are made? They're built out of the ruined lives of South African blacks, or Brazilian peasants, or Korean factory workers. And I just wanted to stop and say to these people: We are sharing this planet. All of us, we're all in this together. You have no right to be doing what you're doing. I wanted to tell them to go look at that ocean. Do you know what I mean?

GAYLE: I'm—not sure.

ELLY: I have no idea what you are talking about.

(Jessica starts. Elly has stood at the screen door through much of Jessica's last speech. She crosses casually out onto the porch. Both watch her uneasily.)

JESSICA: The only reason they can live in these palaces is because halfway around the world someone is working eighteen hours a day on a coffee plantation, or in some Godforsaken copper mine, or who knows what. Americans don't realize that in order to live this wonderful, opulent life, they have to destroy the rest of the world.

ELLY: I don't know. Maybe those people in the mansions aren't exploiting Brazilian peasants. Maybe they inherited their money and now—now they're running vast philanthropic empires from these modest New England estates. I mean, you never know.

JESSICA: Never mind. What did you do today, Gayle?

GAYLE: Well—

ELLY: Oh, this and that.

JESSICA: How could I forget. You had a seance. Honestly, Elly, I don't know where you get these ideas.

ELLY: It wasn't a seance; we were praying. And it wasn't my idea—it was Jen's.

JESSICA: What were you yelling? Mom?

(Pause.)

ELLY: Yes. We were praying to my mother.

JESSICA: Oh.

ELLY: We got an answer, too.

JESSICA: Really? Oh, no, look at this—when did this happen? *(Jessica examines the hole in the wicker chair.)*

ELLY: Who knows? Wicker's so fragile. We probably should have bought something more sturdy. Like plastic.

JESSICA: I'll get Jeffrey to look at it. He's learning how to do caning, did I tell you? He's making me a rocking chair. I'll take this downstairs, then we should probably get started on that living room. You guys made quite a mess.

GAYLE: We'll clean it up, Jessica.

JESSICA: I don't mind helping. *(Jessica exits with the chair.)*

ELLY: Can you believe that? She drives by somebody's house, a total stranger, and decides that they made all their money out of the blood and tears of South American peasants. She doesn't even know these people!

GAYLE: El, don't pick on her politics. She's right and you know it.

ELLY: And what is it with Jeffrey? Is the man trying to work out his sexual frustration in wood? This place is turning into American Arts and Crafts: We have the dulcimer Jeffrey made, the bookshelves Jeffrey made, the rocking chair—

GAYLE: Elly, would you just stop it? You are really driving me crazy.

ELLY: Me? What about her?

GAYLE: What about her? She walked in on us trashing the living room, holding a black Mass as far as she can tell, and all she did was offer to help us clean it up! Jessica is not the problem today.

ELLY: Oh, yes, she's just a saint. It was just saintly the way she sent Jen off with the Local Psychopath. That was very compassionate.

GAYLE: It's not going to hurt Jen to talk to him. Jessica's right, they should work this out.

ELLY: What is it with this About Face?

GAYLE: It's just—this is not a good day to pick a fight with Jessica. Apparently Jeffrey said something to her, I don't know what—

ELLY: I can give you an educated guess. "Please fuck me, Jessica, please—"

GAYLE: Lay off it, Elly. I mean it. Leave her alone today.

ELLY: You know, those two really are perfect for each other. She won't have sex with him and he won't marry her.

GAYLE: I SAID LAY OFF.

ELLY: Right. Lay off. Saint Jessica comes home, and everybody falls right back in line. Just this morning, you were telling me what a bitch she was when you wanted to talk about this prostitution thing, but now—

GAYLE: God, I wish I'd never told you that.

ELLY: Why? I'm on your side!

GAYLE: Because I'm ashamed! I'm *ashamed* of what I did! And Jesus, if there is a right side, it's hers. She had a right to condemn it.

ELLY: She was a total bitch—

GAYLE: She was right! What I did was not okay. I mean, we can sit here and say, oh, everybody makes mistakes, but that's no excuse. A mistake is not something you just ignore, as if it never happened. A mistake is a mistake, you know? Jessica had a right not to like it.

ELLY: No one has a right to condemn another person like that.

GAYLE: You've been doing it all day!

ELLY: That's different.

GAYLE: Forget it. I just don't want to fight anymore, okay?

ELLY: She fucking thinks she's better than us—

GAYLE: Well, maybe she is!

ELLY: God, you are such a wuss; she walks in the door and you turn into jello! "Oh, she's so much better than us—"

GAYLE: Fuck you.

ELLY: Yeah, fuck you too.

GAYLE: Forget it. I am not getting caught in the middle of this anymore.

ELLY: You live here. You are in the middle of it.

GAYLE: I AM NOT GOING TO LET YOU DO THIS TO ME!

ELLY: You let her do it. You listen when she trashes me. You had a whole household meeting about throwing me out over a can of soup!

GAYLE: Yeah, and maybe we should have done it.

ELLY: Yeah, maybe you should have. *(Pause.)* You know what gets me? You both—you and Jen—you'd rather live with me. But even so, if it came to a choice—she would win.

GAYLE: This is not a war—

ELLY: Yes it is. *(Elly crosses and looks through the screen door.)*

GAYLE: Elly, please. *(Pause.)* I'm warning you—

ELLY: FUCK OFF.

JESSICA: *(Calling as she enters living room.)* Who's going to do the dishes?

ELLY: *(Cheery.)* I will!

(Elly returns to the living room. When she speaks her manner is quite friendly. Gayle follows her, somewhat confused and wary.)

JESSICA: Oh—that's okay. I'll do them.

ELLY: It's our mess. I'll do them.

JESSICA: It's no trouble.

ELLY: Do you want to do them?

JESSICA: Sure. I don't mind.

ELLY: I know you don't mind, but do you want to do them?

JESSICA: Yes. I want to do them. *(Jessica picks up glasses.)*

ELLY: Then why did you ask who was going to do them?

JESSICA: It was just a rhetorical question.

ELLY: "Who's going to do the dishes" is a rhetorical question. I see.

JESSICA: I'll do them; I don't mind—

ELLY: But I'll feel guilty if you do them. I'll do them.

(Elly reaches out and takes the glasses from Jessica, who does not give them up immediately. For a moment, the two women stand with their hands on the glasses, then Jessica lets them go. Elly stands before her, holding the glasses for a moment, but Jessica turns and begins to put together the Ouija board. Gayle crosses quickly and takes it from her.)

GAYLE: I'll get that, Jessica.

(Jessica nods and starts to move furniture back in place. Elly sets down the glasses deliberately, crosses to stereo and drops in a tape. The Temps, "Just my Imagination" comes on. She dances for a moment, Jessica watching and becoming more and more impatient. Jessica finally picks up the glasses and goes to kitchen.)

ELLY: *(Sweet.)* Jessica, I said I'd do the dishes. This is our mess. You really should let us clean it up.

JESSICA: I don't mind.

ELLY: But I told you I'd get them. *(Elly takes glasses from her and crosses to the kitchen.)*

JESSICA: Just—be sure to do the glasses first. If you do them last, they spot because the water gets dirty.

(Pause. Elly exits.)

JESSICA: I'm always afraid to say something; she's so defensive. But honestly, it's like she doesn't even see the dirt. I hope we can get some air in here before it gets too cool. This place smells awful.

(Jessica props open the screen door; she and Gayle clean for a moment. Elly reenters, crosses to the cassette and snaps it off.)

ELLY: Jesus. The Temps can be so fucking sentimental.

JESSICA: Oh, don't turn that off. I love that song.

ELLY: *(Muttering.)* Tough shit.

JESSICA: I beg your pardon? *(Pause.)* Did you hear me? I like that song.

ELLY: So?

JESSICA: Eleanor.

ELLY: What did you call me?

GAYLE: Listen Elly, I like the Temps. Jessica likes the Temps. When Jen comes home we'll see how she feels about them. But the best you could hope for is a split decision, so for now could you put them back on?

ELLY: Jessica, I have to tell you something.

GAYLE: El—

ELLY: Gayle, you said you didn't want to be in the middle of this. So stay out of it. Jessica, yesterday morning I found out that I'm pregnant, and I've decided I'm going to have an abortion. I know you don't approve, I know you probably think that it's murder or something, but—I'm going to do it, and I'm not apologizing for it. I've decided that it's not a good idea to get too apologetic about who you are. So—that's why I'm telling you this. Everybody says your baby is a part of you; well, this abortion is a part of me, and I want you to know about it. *(Pause.)* Okay, that's all. That's it. I'm done. *(Pause.)* Aren't you going to say anything?

JESSICA: I'm sorry.

ELLY: Jesus Christ.

JESSICA: *(Pause.)* What did Roger say?

ELLY: He doesn't like it.

JESSICA: I'm not surprised.

ELLY: What do you mean, you're not surprised? Have you been having lunch with him, too?

JESSICA: No, I just—I was remembering the day he brought his little niece over here. He was very sweet with her. I thought he would be a good father.

ELLY: Well, if you want to know the truth, the thought never crossed his mind until last night, when I smacked him across the face with the imminent possibility.

JESSICA: But he wants to have this baby—

ELLY: Yes, Roger wants to marry me and set up house, although I'm sure you and everyone else cannot imagine why. I'm the one. I don't want to marry him. I am not in love with him.

GAYLE: Elly, I don't think—

ELLY: I don't want to talk about Roger.

JESSICA: I don't believe that. I don't believe you don't love him. I've seen you together; you seem so happy. I mean—it's natural that you're frightened by this, but I'm sure it would all work itself out once you were married. Children are wonderful; when the baby is here, I'm sure—

ELLY: It's not that simple.

JESSICA: Do you not want children? You could put it up for adoption. So many people want children, Elly, so many really good people—

ELLY: That's not the issue.

JESSICA: Issue? What are you talking about, issues? This isn't about issues! We're talking about a child—

ELLY: No, we're not. It's not a child.

JESSICA: Then what is it?

ELLY: I don't know. It's not—look, I don't—

JESSICA: You don't want to do it. Why else would you be so unhappy about this? You just need some time to think.

ELLY: I don't have time.

JESSICA: You do. You won't have to go through this alone. We'll all be here for you. You could even—if you wanted to raise it yourself, if you needed to quit your job for a while—

ELLY: *(Overlapping.)* No!

JESSICA: *(Overlapping.)* You wouldn't be alone! I know—I know we haven't been getting along, but we could try. I know you're a good person—

ELLY: NO, I'm not a good person—please, God, please don't be nice to me!

JESSICA: You're just confused. You don't really want to do this—

ELLY: I do! I want to do this! I don't want this baby to exist in the world. I don't care how awful that sounds; it's the truth. I'm tired of the way my life is just happening to me, all this stuff just keeps happening. My job, wicker furniture, Campbell's soup, my boyfriend, who, I'm finally able to admit after much too much time, I don't love—it's all blurred together, and you think that some of this has got to be more important than the rest, but it gets to a point where you just can't make anything out. And I'm not saying that the world is a bad place to be; I'm not saying I wouldn't want a kid in the world. But my life is too blurred right now; it's like one of those bad dreams that just keeps going on and on and on and you just wish like hell that you'd wake up but it just keeps going; it's one cryptic, meaningless, confusing thing after another. But at some point, you have to say, hold it. Hold it. And I'm saying it now. A baby is not something that should just happen. This baby is not going to happen.

JESSICA: Elly—I understand.

ELLY: You do not; even I do not understand that and I said it. Look, I don't want to talk about this!

JESSICA: *(Suddenly steely.)* Well, I do. You brought it up, now you can just deal with what I have to say. This is not about me, or the fact that I see the world differently from you. You're not a child. You're confused, I understand that, but that's tough. Things do happen. Big decisions come up. And you don't just muddle through them and hope it all ends well! Your life *isn't* a blur. It's a life. You own it. And you're talking about denying that right to another human being. I know you're in pain, but if you just run away from this because you're hurt, or angry, or scared, you're never going to grow up. So stop whining and *deal.*

(Jessica exits. Pause.)

GAYLE: Are you okay?

ELLY: Oh, Jesus. What if she's right?

GAYLE: Maybe you're both right.

ELLY: We can't be. We can't both be right, can we? God. How does anyone anywhere decide anything?

GAYLE: I don't know.

ELLY: She was so nice.

GAYLE: Yeah, she was. Why wasn't she nice to me? It would have made such a difference.

(Pause.)

ELLY: Aw, she's full of shit.

GAYLE: *(Pause.)* Come on. We have to finish cleaning this up.

(They stand and look at the mess for a minute, then at each other.)

ELLY/GAYLE: Nah.

ELLY: Lord. Look at this sunset. It's almost enough to make you believe in God.

(They go out onto the porch.)

ELLY/GAYLE: Nah.

ELLY: Gayle—who was this guy on the phone?

GAYLE: What?

ELLY: The guy who called today.

GAYLE: It probably wasn't him.

ELLY: You like him, huh?

GAYLE: He's just this guy from work.

ELLY: What's his name?

GAYLE: Phil.

ELLY: What's he do?

GAYLE: He's a shrink.

ELLY: You're kidding.

GAYLE: See, I knew you'd do this.

ELLY: You're going out with a shrink. Of course.

GAYLE: We're not going out. He just said he might call today.

ELLY: So why didn't you call him?

GAYLE: It was very tentative. It was no big deal.

ELLY: But he called—

GAYLE: It probably wasn't him. It was probably Richardson calling back.

ELLY: Call him back. Ask him out to dinner.

GAYLE: El, I'm not going to do that.

ELLY: You like him? What's he like?

GAYLE: He's nice. He's a nice guy.

ELLY: Yeah, but what's he like?

GAYLE: He's not a nerd, and he's not an asshole.

ELLY: CALL HIM UP.

GAYLE: See, I knew you were going to do this. That's why I didn't want to tell you.

ELLY: What? What am I doing? I'm telling you to call this nice guy on the phone, what's wrong with—

GAYLE: You're making a big deal out of nothing. He's just a guy, and you're working up this big romance here so if I ever do go out with him it's going to be totally anticlimactic.

ELLY: I'm just saying you should call him. How's he supposed to know you're interested—

GAYLE: I'd just like to wait and see what happens, okay?

ELLY: That's a mistake. I'm telling you. If you have a chance at something that might mean something to you, I'd take it.
(Pause.)

GAYLE: What are you going to do, El?

ELLY: I don't know *(Pause.)* Mom? I'm going to have an abortion. Mom?
(They look at the sunset, waiting for an answer.)
(Blackout.)

SCENE II

I'm Sorry, Violence Is Just Not Cool

Elly lies on the couch in semidarkness. The nearly full scotch bottle and a half glass of scotch sits on the coffee table. We hear Lou Reed singing "Busload of Faith."

ELLY: "You need a busload of faith to get by...busload of..."
(Jessica stands in the doorway, watches Elly for a moment. She crosses into the room cautiously.)

JESSICA: Excuse me—do you mind if I turn the music down? I was about to go to bed.

ELLY: Oh, sure. I'm sorry. *(Elly jumps up and turns off the stereo.)*

JESSICA: Oh, that's—I didn't mean that you had to turn it off, I just—

ELLY: That's okay, I wasn't really listening to it.

(They both stand awkwardly for a moment, then Elly crosses back to the couch.)

JESSICA: Well. Good night.

ELLY: Jessica—I'm sorry I was so awful this afternoon. I was really out of line.

JESSICA: That's okay. You were upset.

ELLY: Still.

JESSICA: Would you like to talk about it?

ELLY: No. I really wouldn't.

JESSICA: It might help, it might really help you get some perspective—

ELLY: *No.* Thank you. I just—thank you. No. *(Elly puts her feet up and picks up a magazine.)*

JESSICA: I just meant—I'm sorry, could you take your feet off the couch, please?

(Pause. Elly takes her feet off the couch.)

JESSICA: It's just—that fabric marks up very easily. And it's hard to clean.

(Elly looks at her.)

ELLY: Sorry.

JESSICA: *(Chilly.)* Well. Goodnight.

(Jessica exits. Elly shakes her head, takes a hit off the scotch, leans back and puts her feet back on the couch. She hears someone on the back porch, sits up, and looks. Jen enters, staggering against the doorframe in the darkness. Elly reaches for the light.)

ELLY: Oh, Jen. Hi.

JEN: No, Elly, it's okay, don't turn on the light. I'm fine—

(Elly has snapped the light on. In the light, severe bruises can be clearly seen on Jen's face. She supports herself against the door for a moment.)

ELLY: Oh, my God. Oh, Jesus, Jen.

JEN: I'm okay.

ELLY: *(Very upset.)* Oh, fuck. Oh, shit— *(Elly stands and brings Jen to the chair.)*

ELLY: Sit down, Jesus—oh my God, he hit you—

JEN: I'm okay. I'm gonna be fine.

ELLY: Shit. GAYLE! Oh, God, Jen, what do you need? Do you need anything? Yes. Ice. You need ice. Oh, shit. GAYLE! COME ON! GAYLE!

JEN: Elly, don't, there's nothing you can do about it now—

ELLY: Yes, we can, we can put ice on it and call the police and have the fuck-ing asshole castrated, sweetheart—Oh, God, look at you. GAYLE!

JEN: Elly, I'm okay. He didn't rape me or anything, he just hit me.

ELLY: *(Bitterly sarcastic.)* Oh, well, yes, that is something to be grateful for. GAYLE!

(Jen leans back and touches her face gently as Elly dashes to the kitchen. Gayle appears in the doorway in a robe. She looks at Jen for a moment, stunned. Elly returns, fumbles with ice and a dishcloth.)

ELLY: Here. Put this on—I don't know, put it on your eye, I guess—

JEN: It's okay. I'm okay, Elly.

GAYLE: What happened?

ELLY: Gayle, what do we do? You work in a hospital, do this—

GAYLE: I'm not a nurse, I'm just a social worker— *(Gayle crosses and helps with the ice.)*

JEN: Ouch. Be careful.

ELLY: Sorry. Jesus. I told you, I *told* you he was dangerous—

JEN: He just hit me.

ELLY: He hit you A LOT.

JEN: Well, yeah, he hit me a lot. What a jerk.

GAYLE: Have you called the police yet?

ELLY: We were just getting to that.

(Elly crosses to the phone. Jessica enters.)

JEN: Elly—

JESSICA: What's going on—oh, my God. *(Jessica stands immobile in the doorway.)* What happened?

JEN: Richardson and I got into a fight.

JESSICA: Oh, look at you—come on, you have to lie down.

JEN: Could I just have some aspirin? I have a splitting headache.

(Gayle crosses to the kitchen and returns with aspirin and water a few moments later.)

JESSICA: Is anything broken? Did you pass out or anything?

JEN: No, and it's a miracle. I'm telling you, the last thing you need after drinking all day is a bash in the head.

JESSICA: Richardson did this?

ELLY: All that love that he feels for her burst forth in a rapturous outpouring of abuse. You know how love is.

JESSICA: What happened? He's so gentle—

ELLY: Yes, he's a very gentle psychopath.

JESSICA: Who are you calling?

ELLY: The police.

JESSICA: The police—Don't you think we should find out what happened first?

ELLY: No, I think we should call the police first.

JEN: Elly, come on, I don't want to call the police.

GAYLE: Jen, we have to take you to the hospital and get you checked out. They're going to want to know what happened.

JEN: I'm not kidding, no cops!

JESSICA: Okay, okay, it's okay—Elly for heaven's sake, put the phone down—

ELLY: We can't take care of this ourselves, Jessica. She's been assaulted.

JESSICA: We don't know that.

ELLY: What do you mean, we don't—what do you mean?

JESSICA: I just want to find out what happened before anyone goes flying off the handle!

ELLY: You want to know what happened? TAKE A LOOK AT HER. THAT ASSHOLE ASSAULTED HER. What do you think, she assaulted him?

JESSICA: *Please don't yell—*

GAYLE: Would you two shut up so we can find out what happened?

JEN: I don't know what happened! I mean it was weird, you know. You know how Richardson is. He hardly ever makes total sense. You can say to him, like, A B C, Richardson, and he'll say something like—One hundred ten. Forty-three. I don't know.

GAYLE: Where did you go after you left here?

JEN: Yeah. You know, I didn't want to go anywhere with him. I went out there and told him to totally leave me alone; I told him I was really tired of how weird he was getting and I never wanted to talk to him again. I did. And he said I wasn't being fair because you don't just cut off friendships like that. So I said the problem is, you don't want to be my friend, Richardson, and he said we couldn't talk about it here because you guys were watching us. So—Jesus.

GAYLE: So you went with him.

JEN: I thought I owed it to him. We've been friends for two years.

JESSICA: Then what happened.

JEN: Then we went out to dinner. We went to Christopher's. And that was okay for a while, because he was talking about other things—I mean, he kept talking about this guy Billy from work and what Billy did, and the kind of people he hung out with—and finally, I said, I don't really think Billy is the issue. And he said he just wanted to warn me about Billy because he thought he had AIDS. And that made me kind of mad, because first of all I don't think it's true, and second, I'm not going to sleep with Billy. I mean, it's not like I sleep with every man I know. So I said that and we started arguing again, and Richardson got so loud the manager came over and asked us to leave.

GAYLE: My God.

JEN: No kidding. It was really embarrassing and kind of scary, you know? So we were standing in the parking lot and I said look, I'm going home, and he said—He said we still had to talk. So—we went back to his apartment.

ELLY: Jesus, what were you thinking?

JEN: How was I supposed to know he'd do this?

JESSICA: What happened then?

JEN: Well—we got inside, and he got really uptight.

ELLY: He got *more* uptight.

JEN: Yeah. His roommate wasn't there, he told me that about twelve times. And then he kept sort of hovering around me and asking me what I wanted. It was really weird, he kept saying, What do you want? What do you want? And I said, you know, a cup of tea, maybe? I mean, I didn't know what was going on. Oh, boy. So he got mad at me and he said I was being cruel to him, so I said, Richardson, just get the tea, I just want some tea here. And he said, what about what he wanted. He said nobody cared what he wanted. And I said that wasn't true, that I did care, I said that was why I was even there, because I cared about him. So then he kissed me. And I let him. I let him, just for a second, because—I don't know why, I just—then when I tried to get out of it he freaked out, he—do I have to tell you this part?

GAYLE: No, it's okay, we get the picture.

JEN: He's such a fucking shithead.

GAYLE: I know. It's okay.

JEN: I've been stuck in his apartment for three hours. I locked myself in his stupid fucking bathroom for three hours while he sat out there and told me he was sorry. Three solid hours.

ELLY: How did you get out?

JEN: He left finally. I told him I wasn't going to come out until he left.
(The phone rings.)

JEN: It's him. Don't answer it.
(Jessica crosses to the phone.)

JEN: Jessica, please don't answer it!

JESSICA: Hello? *(Pause.)* Yes, she's here. She's—she's going to be fine. *(Pause.)* I don't think that's a good idea. She's upset. *(Pause.)* Yes, I know. I'll tell her. *(Pause.)* Please, don't—I know. I know. I'll tell her. We'll call you back. *(She hangs up.)* He's very sorry.

ELLY: We are calling the cops.

JESSICA: I don't think that's necessary.

ELLY: The hell it's not. He tried to rape her and now he's calling to say he's sorry? Well, I'm sorry too, but we're calling the cops and making sure he never comes near her again.

JESSICA: He didn't try to rape her.

ELLY: What would you call it?

JESSICA: It certainly was not rape and getting hysterical about this is not going to help anyone. *(Pause.)* I mean, I'm as sorry as anyone that this happened, I really am, and I'm not excusing Richardson; there is no excuse for what he did, but—

(Pause.)

ELLY: But?

JESSICA: Nothing. I think we should all go to bed now. We're all upset, and tired, and I think we should talk about this in the morning.

ELLY: Talk about what in the morning? What's to talk about?

JESSICA: I just think we should go to bed.

ELLY: Well, I just think we're a little too wound up to go to sleep right now. So I want to hear what you have to say. You obviously have something to say. I want to hear it.

GAYLE: Jessica—what is it?

JEN: I want to hear it, too. I mean, I told you what happened. What, do you think I'm lying or something? Is that what you think?

JESSICA: No, of course not. Of course not, Jen—it's just, a few things aren't clear to me. That's all. We'll talk about it in the morning.

JEN: What? What's not clear? What did that asshole say to you? I told you what happened! What did he say?

JESSICA: He didn't say anything. He was crying, he was apologizing. He said it was a misunderstanding. He just kept saying that.

ELLY: A misunderstanding. That's great. "Oh, look, my fist is in your eye, I just can't understand how it got there—"

JESSICA: *(Snapping.)* Please don't make jokes about this; there is nothing funny about this!

(Pause.)

ELLY: I'm so sorry. You were going to tell us about Richardson's misunderstanding.

JESSICA: I guess I just—I think they misunderstood each other.

JEN: What do you mean? I didn't misunderstand anything. I was trying to be nice to him, so he hit me! You explain it; it's Richardson's dazzling logic—

JESSICA: Jen, you said it yourself, you let him kiss you. My God. What do you think that said to him?

JEN: It was just a kiss! I felt sorry for him!

JESSICA: Don't you think that misled him?

JEN: I don't know! Maybe, but I didn't mean—look, I told him a million times—

JESSICA: You told him you cared for him, you kissed him—

JEN: I told him—

JESSICA: *(Overlap.)* —and he took that to mean you would sleep with him. Can't you understand why he thought that?

ELLY: I knew that's what you were thinking.

JEN: Elly, shut up, I can defend myself. I don't have to defend myself. *He* hit *me.*

JESSICA: I'm not accusing anyone.

JEN: Then what are you doing?

JESSICA: I'm just saying—I think you both made mistakes.

ELLY: And what was her mistake? I missed that part. What did she do to him?

JESSICA: I think she knows.

JEN: No, I don't. I don't.

ELLY: We don't know, Jessica. You're going to have to tell us.

GAYLE: That's enough. We have to stop this before somebody says something we all—

ELLY: *(Overlapping.)* Let her say it, Gayle. *I want to hear her say it.*

JESSICA: How do you think he feels? How do you think he's felt all these years while she's been just stringing him along? You don't know, you never bothered to think. I know. I know! He loves her; he wants a life with her and she—she just tramples on that like it's nothing, like it's—Well, I'm not surprised he finally—if you want to know the truth, I'm surprised this didn't happen sooner. She brought this on herself with all these games she plays. Sex is not a game.

ELLY: *(Pause.)* What do you know about sex?

(Pause.)

JESSICA: I don't think my private life has anything to do with this.

ELLY: I think it's got a lot to do with it.

JESSICA: Well, I don't choose to discuss it with you.

ELLY: I wasn't giving you a choice. You don't give us choices. I mean, we boycott soup because you say so, not because we choose to. We bought all that fucking wicker because you said so. I'm just saying. Living in this house isn't always about choices, is it?

JESSICA: I can't believe this. If you're unhappy here, this is hardly the time or the place to discuss it.

ELLY: This is exactly the time and place, but that's not what we were discussing. We were talking about you, and sex and control. We were talking about your remarkable observation that Jen was asking for this because she sleeps around.

JESSICA: I never said that.

ELLY: Oh, you said something pretty damn close, Jessica; it flew right out of your mouth and we all heard it. And I was just wondering what it is in your life that plants these ideas in your head when you see your roommate sitting in front of you with a black eye.

JESSICA: I don't have to answer you.

ELLY: We told you he was dangerous. We told you and told you, all three of us, and you wouldn't listen.

JESSICA: Yes, I know you would love for this to be my problem; well, it's not my problem.

ELLY: *(Overlap.)* You can't stand the idea that you were actually wrong about that lunatic, so this has to be her fault! Reality has to conform to you! Where the hell do you get off?

JESSICA: You're ridiculous. You're hysterical and ridiculous—

ELLY: You're so pure, you're so *right,* you're the fucking virgin mother, aren't you? And we're just a mess ! But you love that; we're just you own little chorus of sinners that you keep around because we make you feel so fucking pure.

JESSICA: That's enough—

ELLY: No, it's not enough. It's not near what I have to say to you—

GAYLE: *(Overlapping Elly.)* Really, really, you guys. She's hurt, could you just…

JESSICA: You can't stay here.

ELLY: What?

JESSICA: I know you're going through a hard time right now, but this is just— too much. I don't have to listen to any more of this. I want you out tonight. Do you hear me? Tonight.

(Jessica starts to push by Elly to leave the room. Elly suddenly picks up a small, sharp knife from a cheeseboard on the coffee table and raises it calmly, at a distance from Jessica. There is an uncertain, shocked pause.)

ELLY: Yes, you do have to listen to this.

GAYLE: Elly, stop it. EL.

JEN: Jesus Christ, Elly, have you lost your mind?

(Elly closes in on her as Jessica tries to back away.)

ELLY: On the contrary. I'm just in the middle of a misunderstanding, Jessica and I have misunderstood each other, and then she provoked me, and now I'm going to hurt her, but then we're all going to forget about it because it was really her fault to begin with. That's the way it works, isn't it?

JESSICA: STOP IT—

(Jessica tries to bolt away from Elly; but Elly grabs her arm and brings the knife up before her face. Jen and Gayle bolt forward, then hang back.)

JEN/GAYLE: Elly—Elly, Jesus Christ—ELLY.

ELLY: What do you think? Should I hurt you, Jessica? Will it help? If I hurt you, will you understand that you are one of us? You're just as bad as we are, Jessica. YOU. ARE ONE. OF US.

GAYLE: Elly, put the knife down. PUT IT DOWN.

(Suddenly bewildered, Elly backs away from her, then drops the knife on the coffee table.)

ELLY: What am I doing? What am I doing?

(Pause.)

GAYLE: Jessica, are you all right?

JESSICA: No. I'm not. I'm not.

ELLY: Jessica—

(Jessica suddenly bolts from the room. Elly starts after her then stops. Pause.)

ELLY: Oh, shit.

JEN: I cannot believe you did that.

GAYLE: That was weird.

JEN: Did you see that?

GAYLE: I saw it.

ELLY: I just pulled a knife on my roommate. That is really no way to behave.

JEN: You were excellent, Elly.

ELLY: Jen! My mother did not raise me to act like this!

JEN: Oh, come on, it wasn't a sharp knife. Besides, she was really being a bitch.

ELLY: I can't believe I did that!

JEN: *(To Gayle.)* Wasn't that excellent?

GAYLE: Well, "excellent" isn't the word that popped to *my* mind—

ELLY: What was I doing? What did I say to her? I pulled a knife on her! How could I do something like that?

GAYLE: Elly. It's okay. You didn't hurt anybody.

ELLY: I have to go talk to her.

GAYLE: I don't think that's a good idea.

JEN: No, hey, I think she heard you. Pick up a knife, and everybody listens.

ELLY: Well, we have to do something!

GAYLE: We will do something, just give me a minute to figure out what!

ELLY: I'm going up.

GAYLE: Elly, no, if anyone's going up there, it's not you—

> (Gayle turns to go upstairs just as Jessica enters the room. She wears a light coat over her pajamas and carries her bag. The two women back away slightly, watching each other cautiously.)

JESSICA: I need my keys. My car keys. I left them on the bookcase. (Pause.) Please get out of my way.

ELLY: I'm sorry, Jessica. I don't know why I did that. I just lost it. You were hurting Jen, you were blaming her, and I just—

JESSICA: That's not why! That's not what you said.

ELLY: No. I guess it wasn't.

JESSICA: All those things you said. They're not true. You don't know me. Both of you, you just trample on everything I value. You throw it away as if it were nothing, as if it were dirt, and then you expect me to just applaud you, to say, yes, that's fine, that's wonderful, throw it away, I don't care! This man loves her, he—I know, I know I was wrong about him he's troubled, he's—I was wrong. But he loves her so much, and I—Jeffrey and I—I'll never have that. You think I don't know? You could have a child. And you want to kill it. I may never have that, and you—let me by! (Elly does. Jessica gets her keys.)

ELLY: Where are you going? Are you going to Jeffrey's? You can't go over there.

JESSICA: You attacked me!

ELLY: Oh, come on, it wasn't a sharp knife! (Beat.) Well, it wasn't. I should-n't've done it, but we're all making mistakes tonight. Let's just calm down and work this out. I can't believe these words are coming out of my mouth…

GAYLE: She's right, Jessica.

ELLY: I am, Jessica. Come on. We're all in this together, so could we just—

JESSICA: No. We're not. I'm not one of you, and I don't intend to be. You're lost. All of you. I'm not lost. I'm not one of you.

> (Jessica goes. The three stand there for a long moment of silence.)

JEN: We're lost?

ELLY: She's right. We are lost.

GAYLE: Yeah. I guess we are. *(Beat.)* But at least—we know it.

ELLY: And at least we have a sense of humor about it, geez—

JEN: No shit. *We're* lost? She's going to fucking Jeffrey's—

ELLY: She rejected *us* for Jeffrey? What kind of fucked up is that?

GAYLE: Well, you did pull a knife on her.

ELLY: I apologized!

JEN: Hey, you think this means we'll get the house?

GAYLE: Jen!

JEN: What? She thinks we're lost, she's not one of us; it sounds to me like we're gonna get the house.

ELLY: Sounds that way to me.

JEN: Yes! I think that's excellent.

(Elly and Jen give each other the high five.)

GAYLE: We're not getting the house! Or, maybe you are. But I'm moving out.

JEN: You are?

GAYLE: Yes. I am.

ELLY: Gayle—

GAYLE: We'll talk about it on the way to the police station.

JEN: The police station? Why are we going to the police station.

ELLY: You got beat up!

JEN: Oh, yeah. But you know, I'm not kidding, you guys. We can't go to the cops because they'll arrest the wrong person. Richardson looks worse than I do.

GAYLE: He does?

JEN: I pounded him. Well, he won the fight. But he looks *bad.*

ELLY: Good. I'm glad you punished that jerk. We're still going to the police.

JEN: Elly—

ELLY: Jen, it's just that if he got violent once, he can get violent again, and— *(Beat.)* Shit.

JEN: It's okay, Elly.

ELLY: No, it's not. I mean violence is not good. It's not just a mistake, you know? *(Beat.)* I am a bad person, aren't I?

GAYLE: No, you're not a bad person. But if you ever pull a knife on me, I'll murder you.

ELLY: Fair enough.

GAYLE: *(Beat.)* But for now we are going to take this girl to the hospital, and I don't want any more arguments about it. I have no intention of ever going through a day like this again, so starting tonight, we are going to fucking deal. We're going to the hospital, I'll check you in myself and we can fill out the police report from there.

(They all stand, gathering jackets, shoes and keys.)

ELLY: If you move, can we come with you?

GAYLE: We'll talk about it on the way to the hospital.

JEN: Real rent, huh? You think we're capable of real rent?

GAYLE: I think we're capable of anything.

JEN: Hey, can we stop for doughnuts? What? If you guys are going to take care of me, then do it right.

ELLY: Hey, is your new boyfriend going to be there?

JEN: What boyfriend? Where?

GAYLE: Elly—

ELLY: *(To Jen.)* Gayle's new boyfriend works at the hospital.

GAYLE: He's not—

ELLY: He's a shrink. His name is Phil. Keep your eyes open.

GAYLE: You have the biggest mouth!

ELLY: Big mouth? Me?

GAYLE: You're not moving in with me.

ELLY: Come on…

(The door slams as they leave.)

(Blackout.)

END OF PLAY

LOOSE KNIT

ORIGINAL PRODUCTION

Loose Knit was originally presented in workshop by New York Stage and Film Company in association with the Powerhouse Theater at Vassar. *Loose Knit* premiered in New York City during the 1992–93 season of Second Stage Theatre, Carole Rothman, Artistic Director; Suzanne Schwartz Davidson, Producing Director. It was directed by Beth Schachter and had the following cast (in order of appearance):

LIZ	Mary B. Ward
LILY	Patricia Kalember
PAULA	Tamara Tunie
GINA	Kristine Nielsen
MARGIE	Constance Shulman
BOB	Reed Birney
MILES	Daniel Gerroll

Set Design	Santo Loquasto
Lighting Design	Frances Aronson
Costume Design	Elsa Ward
Sound Design	Mark Bennett
Production Stage Manager	Jess Lynn
Hair Design	Antonio Soddu

CHARACTERS

LIZ: White, early-thirties, loose, easy going, intelligent, emotional, Lily's sister

GINA: White, mid-thirties, holds herself in, matter of fact, a lawyer

PAULA: Black, late-thirties, well-adjusted, sharp intelligence

LILY: White, mid-thirties, very feminine, very controlled, married

MARGIE: White, early-thirties, quite lovely but a bit scattered and erratic, always at the end of her rope

BOB: White, late-thirties, Lily's husband, not ambitious

MILES: White, mid-thirties, carries himself with all the assumptions of power and money, although it is never clear where he got it

TIME AND PLACE
The Present, New York City

SETS
A variety of locations: the apartments of Lily, Liz and Gina, and a small Japanese sushi restaurant. A large wooden table is the centerpiece of all three apartments. A small table representing the sushi restaurant stands to one side.

ACT I
SCENE I

Lily's apartment. Three women sit draped on furniture, knitting. A fourth, Lily, stands among them holding a plate of banana bread. They stand in tableau for a moment, an almost archetypal image of womanhood. As the lights change, the tableau breaks and they move with dreamlike gestures as they examine their knitting pieces over the table. Lily bends and sets down the banana bread. Liz suddenly tears at her knitting and throws it on the floor.

LIZ: Fuck.

LILY: Oh, dear.

PAULA: I told you that was going to be too hard.

LIZ: You said it was easy.

PAULA: I said it was a lovely stitch.

LIZ: You said it was easy!

LILY: No, I think I said that. I thought it looked easy. *(She takes the knitting from her.)*

LIZ: I'm sorry, but I just think this knitting racket is a total fucking drag. You spend weeks just shoving needles and strings at each other until you've got a whole bunch of knots. What a great way to pass time.

GINA: You should have started with a scarf.

LIZ: Scarves are boring.

GINA: You hate knitting anyway! What do you care if you're bored?

LILY: What a mess.

LIZ: Oh, leave it alone. I don't like that pattern anymore. I'm not going to finish it.

LILY: *(Takes the knitting and tries to unravel it.)* Calm down. Everything's such a catastrophe...

LIZ: I didn't say it was a catastrophe. I just don't want to finish it. It's too short. Those little sweaters that hit you at the waist are never flattering. You think they're going to be and then they're not. And I don't like this girl in the picture. She looks smug.
(She studies the instruction magazine in her hand and then shows the picture to Paula, who nods.)

LILY: Now, Liz, you always do this when you're about to quit and I'm not going to let you quit this time.

LIZ: Ahhhh! Lily, please! I spend so much time avoiding Mom and Dad and then you just take over for them. I don't know why I bother.

LILY: Since you mention it, I did see Dad the other day.

LIZ: So how is the old shithead?

PAULA: I love it when you two talk parents.

LILY: He'd like to see you.

LIZ: What he'd like to do is kill me. He'll settle for locking me in his apartment and screaming at me for a couple of hours.

(She and Paula laugh.)

LILY: I still don't understand why you're so mad at him.

LIZ: Oh, for heaven's sake, you do too. I'm mad at him because he dumped Mom and married his secretary. I mean, it's all so tawdry and predictable, I'm downright embarrassed. His *secretary?* He has no imagination. And maybe Mom is no saint but the woman is over sixty and alone now—

LILY: *(Overlap.)* Really, Liz, that was over a year ago, and it's not like it came out of the blue; he and Mom were making each other miserable for years. No one can live with her, you say it more than anyone, when was the last time you even went to see her?

LIZ: Who wants to see her? She's always depressed because Dad dumped her! *(Pause.)* I'm sorry. You're right. I'll go see her.

LILY: What about Dad?

LIZ: I will go see Mom, okay?

LILY: Would anybody like tea?

(Behind her back, Liz sticks her tongue out at Lily.)

PAULA: That would be great.

LIZ: Yeah, sure. Tea, mmmm.

LILY: Hang onto that for a second, Liz; I think I've figured it out. It's just like that top I made for Adelaide last year. It's a leaf pattern.

GINA: Where is Adelaide tonight?

LILY: She's at her play group. And guess what? They're learning how to knit.

GINA: *(Appreciative.)* Awwwww.

LILY: You should have seen her going off with her little needles in her little Laura Ashley dress. You know, their children's clothes are the only things you can buy any more. It's a shame, but last week I was looking at their women's dresses, and they just have too much up at the neckline now. You know, collars and bows, it's too much. I like something that's more open, you know, with all those flowers, you need a little bit more of a neckline. I think it's because she died. Did you know that? Laura Ashley died two years ago. Fell down a flight of stairs.

(She exits. Liz watches her go.)

LIZ: Whenever she does that, I'm never sure if she's kidding.

GINA: So where's Margie?

LIZ: I don't know. *(Calling.)* Hey, Lily, where's Margie?

LILY: *(Calling.)* She should be on her way.

LIZ: Good. I have to admit, I just, you know, I don't feel comfortable until she's here. She's the only one who's a worse knitter than I am.

PAULA: Why do you see this as a competition?

LIZ: Oh, Paula, don't start.

PAULA: Don't start what?

LIZ: Don't start asking questions. I know you. One thing leads to another and all of a sudden my neuroses are spread all over the room.

PAULA: Your neuroses are spread all over the room anyway.

LIZ: That's not true. Is that true? Oh, well. I can't help it. I get lied to all day so on my off hours I end up with this pathological urge to be honest. No shit, every day I am, like, bombarded with lies. Last Tuesday, I interviewed a certain extremely well-known and promiscuous rock star who lied to me twelve times in twenty minutes. I counted.

PAULA: Really?

GINA: Who?

LIZ: Oh, who cares, they all do it.

GINA: Stop complaining. You have the most glamorous job of any of us, and all you do is complain.

LIZ: I spend half my life hustling stories and I'm always broke. It's not glamorous!

GINA: You meet movie stars.

LIZ: They're a bunch of liars.

GINA: So? I hang out with lawyers. They lie too. And, they're mean and boring and they're not on television. Your job sounds good to me.

PAULA: If you really want to meet liars, you should become a therapist. People will pay you hundreds of dollars an hour so they can come in and lie. It's astonishing. I'm going to write a book about it.

LIZ: Really? They come in and lie?

(Lily reenters and silently serves tea while Paula speaks.)

PAULA: Well, they don't know they're lying—or no, some of them do. You know. It's like anything. I just sort of listen and hope it's not my fault.

(Margie enters, breathless, dumps her stuff all over the floor and kisses Lily. She shakes off rain and peels off rain coat.)

MARGIE: I'm sorry, I'm sorry I'm so late—I hate this city—

GINA: Join the club.

LILY: Yes, we're all being very morose tonight.

MARGIE: Really? You guys are morose? You don't look morose.

PAULA: We got started talking about reality. That'll depress anybody.

LILY: *(To Margie.)* Something came up at work?

MARGIE: No, I had an appointment at a dating service. Took forever.

LILY: You went to a dating service?

MARGIE: Yes, I went to a dating service.

LIZ: You did not.

MARGIE: What? Why shouldn't I go to a dating service? You go to a bar and you don't know who you're talking to; you could be talking to some serial killer or something. This way, if I end up getting murdered by my date I can at least sue somebody. Besides, what's wrong with just admitting you want to find a man? Is there something wrong with that? It's just, you know, the primal urge, and there's no reason we have to be ashamed of it. You go to a bar, all you do there is pretend that you want a drink when what you really want is a date, and the next thing you know, you're an alcoholic, and you're fat. I mean, no thanks, okay? It's time to be an adult.

LIZ: I didn't mean anything.

MARGIE: I'm just saying. You reach a point, reality sinks in.

LILY: I think it's a good idea.

MARGIE: You do?

LILY: Yes.

PAULA: Me too. It's a control issue. Now you've got control.

LIZ: So, what was it like?

MARGIE: Well, given the fact that it was the most humiliating moment of my life, they were very nice. I mean, it was kind of like joining a cult, you know? Everybody smiled all the time and asked extremely personal questions. I don't know. It's probably just as big a waste of time as anything, but as long as you're wasting time you may as well live with hope, you know? I mean, I can't imagine, from what they asked me, that they're going to hook me up with an actual human being, but, you know, they might. Someone with biceps, he's out there somewhere, and they'll find him, with their little computer, and then I'll have a date with him. Biceps. That could be nice, huh?

PAULA: I went out with a guy in college who had biceps. He was a pig.

MARGIE: Oh, for heaven's sake. I mean, come on. Geez.

PAULA: What? I'm just saying…

MARGIE: No, you're not just saying. I'm trying to have some hope here, you know, I'm trying to not be completely depressed about, you know, and you're just, I mean, you've got a problem, Paula. You do. For a therapist, you are not very sensitive.

PAULA: I'm sorry.

MARGIE: Forget it.

GINA: So, how's the sweater coming?

MARGIE: Oh, all right. I don't know. It's starting to look kind of funny. I think I'm decreasing wrong.

(Bob enters, carrying a box of Tide.)

BOB: Okay, quilters, brace yourself, there's a penis coming through—

LILY: Bob, please.

MARGIE: Hey, Bob—

BOB: Can someone explain to me, again, how much detergent I'm supposed to throw into these machines—hey, Liz—

LIZ: Hey, Bob.

LILY: Bob, I've asked you—

BOB: I know, but you said you wanted the laundry finished and I couldn't remember—

LILY: I told you before anyone got here—

BOB: Yeah, but I mean it, I can't keep it all straight. It's the fabric softener that screws me up; I get so worried about throwing it in at the right point in the cycle everything else just goes out of my head. Can someone help me? Gina? Liz?

LIZ: Oh—

LILY: I'll do it.

BOB: I can do it; I just need someone to help. Liz can help.

LILY: It will be easier if I do it.

(She exits with box of Tide, Margie stands and follows.)

MARGIE: You actually do fabric softener? Can I watch?

PAULA: You want to watch?

MARGIE: I want to know how to use that stuff. I can never figure it out.

PAULA: You should just use those little sheets in the dryer.

MARGIE: Those don't work.

PAULA: Yes, they do. *(She follows.)*

LIZ: Where are you going?

PAULA: I want to watch, too. I've never seen anybody actually use that shit either.

(They exit. Bob settles in to talk with Gina and Liz.)

LIZ: It's all too complicated. We should just go back to whacking wet clothing against rocks.

GINA: Everything would lose it's shape.

BOB: Besides, how would you bleach anything? I mean, I mixed the bleach in with the fabric softener because—

GINA: You put bleach in with the fabric softener? Oh, no. Lily. Lily!
(She runs after them. Liz looks at Bob.)

LIZ: Very clever.

BOB: Thank you.
(He smiles and comes very close to her. She pushes him away.)

LIZ: I am going to kill you, Bob. How obvious do you want to be?

BOB: How obvious do you want me to be?

LIZ: She's in the next room!
(Laughing a little, he kisses her briefly once, then again. She gives in, then pushes him away just as Paula and Margie reenter, oblivious. Liz pulls away; she and Bob cover quickly.)

MARGIE: Well, that was not the thrilling event it is cracked up to be.

LIZ: No?

PAULA: I'm sticking with those little sheets.
(Gina and Lily reenter. Lily carries a bottle of fabric softener.)

LILY: Bob, Gina tells me some wild story about bleach, and you're doing a load of colors. What on earth are you using bleach for?

BOB: No, I wasn't…I was going to use it for the whites.

GINA: You said you mixed it—

BOB: I can't remember what I was doing. Let me look.
(He exits quickly. Lily follows him.)

MARGIE: I have such a crush on him.

GINA: Me too.

PAULA: Yeah, there's something about a man doing laundry that just pushes my buttons.

LIZ: *(Guilty.)* He's not doing the laundry. Lily's doing the laundry.

MARGIE: Yeah, but he tried. That's so sexy. Oh, man. That's what I should have told that stupid dating service. I'm looking for a man who'll do laundry.

GINA: I'm looking for a man who knits.

MARGIE: That would be good, too. Long romantic evenings, knitting by the fire. I can see it. Then again, I haven't had a date in so long I can see just about anything. God, this is beautiful, Liz. *(She looks at Liz's knitting.)*

LIZ: Oh, shut up. I'm such a failure.

MARGIE: No, I mean it; it's gorgeous—

LIZ: I know it's gorgeous! Lily fixed it. I just made a mess of it.

LILY: *(Reentering.)* You did not make a mess of it. You were just twisting the yarn around the wrong way. Here, look *(She demonstrates to Liz.)*

LIZ: I don't know, Lily.

LILY: You'll get it.

LIZ: No, look, I should just go. I don't belong here…

PAULA: You're leaving?

LIZ: I'm a lousy knitter.

LILY: Your knitting is fine. You were just twisting it around—

LIZ: It's hopeless, Lily.

MARGIE: No, it's not. Come on, Liz, you have to stay. This knitting thing is all the rage now. Plus, it's so politically correct.

LIZ: It is?

MARGIE: Yeah, I saw Gloria Steinem on Oprah the other day. She says women should have knitting groups for, like, support and all.

LILY: Well! An endorsement from Gloria Steinem.

LIZ: I guarantee you, Gloria Steinem does not knit.

MARGIE: I know, it's weird, but that's what she said. I mean, I thought this whole thing was a really stupid idea when Gina told me about it—

GINA: You did?

MARGIE: Well, Gina, you gotta admit it was kind of odd. A total stranger in a grocery store says, do you like to knit—

PAULA: You guys met in a grocery store?

LIZ: Gina, you picked her up in a grocery store?

GINA: Lily said we needed another person for the group, and I thought she looked nice.

PAULA: You met in a grocery store? I thought you were old friends or something.

LIZ: *(Amused.)* We've been knitting for a whole month with a total stranger! Margie, you could be anybody.

MARGIE: Yeah, but I'm not. I mean, you guys aren't going to kick me out now that you know, are you? I mean, you could be anybody, too.

LIZ: Yeah, but at least we went to college together. And Lily and I are related.

MARGIE: Oh, now there are rules? Great, you can't even join a knitting group without it getting all complicated. This is worse than that dating service.

LILY: No one's getting kicked out. I think it's nice that people can still make friends in the grocery store.

MARGIE: Yeah, me too. I mean, it was weird, but nice.

PAULA: So nobody's going anywhere, right?

LILY: No.

PAULA: Good.

MARGIE: Look at this, is this right?

(She holds up a piece of knitting which goes straight up one side and slopes in dramatically on the other. It looks like absolutely nothing. All stare at it.)

GINA: I don't think that's right, Margie.

LILY: Oh, dear. What did you do? *(She studies it.)*

MARGIE: I just followed the instructions.

PAULA: That can't be right.

MARGIE: I did, I followed the instructions. It said decrease every other row, so that's what I did.

LILY: No, you're supposed to decrease on alternate rows of each side. It's a raglan sleeve; it's supposed to slope in so you can set the sleeve—

MARGIE: That's what I did.

LILY: Clearly, that is not what you did.

MARGIE: I followed the instructions! You told me it was like a recipe. I mean, I work for a caterer, you know, I know how to follow a stupid recipe—

LILY: Well, then, you read the recipe wrong. *(She pokes through Margie's bag and comes up with instructions.)*

LIZ: Oh, God, isn't that the way it always goes? I swear, on my deathbed, someone is going to just look at me and say, but sweetheart, you read the recipe wrong, and it's all going to be just clear, in a flash, I'm going to get it, and then I'm going to die. I just know that's going to happen.

MARGIE: What?

LIZ: It's a metaphor, Margie.

MARGIE: I know, but I don't get it.

LIZ: Never mind.

MARGIE: No, I'm trying to—

LIZ: All right, look. This weekend I went on a press junket. Which means I spent the entire weekend in a hotel, with about seventy-five other hacks, and they stuffed us all full of food, and then we filed in for our inter-views, one after the other, you get five minutes alone with Schwartzenegger. Or whoever, I also interviewed his co-star, and I'm in this room with this woman, and she starts to tell me about America. This is a woman whose brains are all in her *hair,* and she's telling me things like, "Americans have forgotten how to dream. That's what my life is about. Showing people that dreams can come true." I want to kill this woman, Margie. But I write this shit down, and hand it in, and you know what my creepy editor says about it? He says, nice job, Liz. She's pretty smart. And what a set of knockers. See? Somewhere along the line I read the fucking recipe wrong.

MARGIE: No, I don't see. What does that have to do with anything?

LILY: I really don't understand why you don't try to do something more productive, Liz. Dad always says, it's a crime, with your brains—

LIZ: Oh, fuck Dad.

LILY: Liz!

LIZ: What? I'm not going to quit. I mean, I am not about to give him the satisfaction of doing what he wants me to do.

GINA: Listen. I come here to knit.

LIZ: What?

GINA: I just don't want to get into this, all right? I come here to *knit*.

LIZ: Well, the rest of us come here to talk.

GINA: No, you come here to complain.

LIZ: Gloria Steinem says that's good.

GINA: Gloria Steinem doesn't have to listen to you.

LIZ: Well, excuse me—

GINA: I don't think I will—

LILY: *(Overlap.)* You guys—you guys—could we all relax a little?

GINA: *(Snapping.)* I'm a little TENSE, all right?
   (Pause. They all look at her.)

MARGIE: *(Pause.)* And you know, the stupid part is, if I had a man, none of this would matter.
   (They all look at her. Blackout.)

SCENE II

The outline of an elegant Japanese sushi bar. In tableau, a man gestures a woman into a seat at a tiny, single table. As the lights come up, we see that the woman is Margie and the man is Miles. She sits and smiles nervously. Miles does not respond to Margie's remarks, but jots down a few notes in a large leather binder.

MARGIE: Oh, this is a great place. I love this. It's so...you know, it's really nice. The atmosphere. I mean, the party was great, too, but we didn't get much of a chance to talk, so it's nice that...yeah, this is great. *(Pause.)* I love your car. It's so…big. I mean, it's…never mind. *(Pause.)* Excuse me, but are you taking notes on me?

MILES: Excuse me?

MARGIE: I'm sorry. It just…it looks like you're taking notes on me.

MILES: Oh. I'm sorry. Please, forgive me. It's an insufferable habit. I don't know where I picked it up.

MARGIE: That's okay.

MILES: Sometimes I don't even know I'm doing it. *(He writes.)*

MARGIE: Oh. *(She laughs, uncomfortable.)* You're doing it!

MILES: *(Laughing.)* I'm sorry. Here. You take a turn.

(He holds the pencil out to her. She laughs.)

MARGIE: No, it's okay, really. It's fine.

MILES: You're sure?

MARGIE: Sure.

MILES: You're very sweet. *(He writes.)* And I must thank you for letting me drag you to that awful cocktail party. All that business talk could not have been much fun for you.

MARGIE: Are you kidding? It was great. I mean, I had drinks with the mayor! I thought he was very nice. Short, though. I mean, he looks taller on television. But I have to say, the Donald looked just like I thought he would. And did you get a load of that blonde he was with? I swear, he just keeps going out with different women in the same body, doesn't he?

MILES: *(Laughing.)* Well, I never actually thought of it that way.

MARGIE: Oh. I'm sorry. He's probably a friend of yours, isn't he? I'm sorry. Gee, I didn't mean anything…

MILES: Are you nervous, Margie?

MARGIE: What?

MILES: You seem a little tense.

MARGIE: No! I mean, well, maybe. Blind dates are always a little nerve wracking, I guess.

MILES: They don't have to be. Actually, over the past year or so, I've begun to rather enjoy blind dates.

MARGIE: Really?

MILES: Yes. There's always something—surprising, or challenging that comes up. It's very much like business negotiations, the first flush of battle, where you don't know who your opponent is, what he—or she—wants, what the bottom line is. It's fascinating. The mystery. Don't you find that to be true?

MARGIE: Well…I don't know. I don't do this a lot. I mean, I did just sign with a dating service, but nothing's really come of that yet, so—

MILES: A dating service? *(He writes this down.)*

MARGIE: Is that a problem?

MILES: It's just not the way I do things. I prefer personal references. A dating service carries with it an air of desperation, doesn't it?

MARGIE: I don't know. I—gee—

MILES: Am I being too personal?

MARGIE: No, I don't know. You're right. I mean, I signed with this dating service, and I've been apologizing for it ever since, so you must be right, right?

MILES: I'm sorry if I touched a nerve. I didn't mean to. *(He smiles at her.)*

MARGIE: So. You like blind dates, huh?

MILES: Well, of course, not always. During my twenties I really didn't have a lot of time for dating. I did crave companionship but it wasn't exactly romance I was looking for.

MARGIE: Oh.

MILES: I hope you don't mind my frankness.

MARGIE: No, no. It's very…refreshing.

MILES: In any event, it was time.

MARGIE: Time?

MILES: To take your gender more seriously.

MARGIE: Oh.

MILES: How much do you weigh?

MARGIE: What?

MILES: I hope you don't mind my asking.

MARGIE: Well, a little.

MILES: Do you have a weight problem?

MARGIE: No. I just…I don't know. It makes me self conscious.

MILES: Why?

MARGIE: Geez, I don't know. Do you tell everybody how much you weigh?

MILES: It depends on why they're asking.

MARGIE: Well, why are you asking?

MILES: I find you attractive, and I'm curious, that's all.

MARGIE: Oh. Well. I don't really know how much I weigh. I like, avoid the scale, you know?

MILES: I see. *(He writes.)*

MARGIE: I mean, it's probably around, one-fifteen, or something.

MILES: Would you like a drink?

MARGIE: You know, I really would. That's a great idea

MILES: *(He waves at the waiter. To Margie.)* I hope you like sushi?

MARGIE: Love it.

MILES: Good. They have a wonderful chef here. Stole him from the emperor's nephew.

MARGIE: The emperor?

MILES: Of Japan.

MARGIE: Oh, sure. Right. The emperor of Japan! I didn't know he had a nephew.

MILES: Well, he does. And his chef is a genius.

MARGIE: Really? Wow. This is amazing, you know, this is—you must make a shitload of money. Oh. I'm sorry.

MILES: No, it's fine. I do make a shitload of money. When I was twelve years old, I decided I was going to make my first million before I was thirty. And I've done that.

MARGIE: And now you're on to your second.

MILES: *(Laughing.)* That's very sweet. Anyway, I don't think a lot about it anymore. After a certain point, money ceases to have meaning.

MARGIE: I've heard that. Well, Miles—I didn't quite get what you do, exactly.

MILES: Mergers, acquisitions, that sort of thing. It's complicated.

MARGIE: But legal, I hope! *(She laughs.)*

MILES: What is that supposed to mean?

MARGIE: I don't know. It means I hope…the stuff…you do is…legal.

MILES: Of course it's legal. I'm an American.

MARGIE: Oh, I didn't mean—

MILES: I respect the law, Margie. And I take my responsibilities as a citizen quite seriously. In fact, if more Americans felt as I did, I believe this country would be far more stable.

MARGIE: I was just kidding.

MILES: Why? Why, kidding? I mean, I really don't care about the money, but I'm not quite sure why you need to joke about this. A person works hard, and is successful, that's funny? Most Americans don't think that's so funny.

MARGIE: I didn't mean anything. Really. I'm sorry.

MILES: It's fine. *(He writes.)* And you…cook.

MARGIE: Actually, I'm an actress. I mean, cooking is what I do to keep myself together, you know. Do you have to write? I'm, uh, a little…

(He stops and deliberately puts the pen down.)

MARGIE: I'm sorry. Go ahead.

MILES: No. Please. You're an actress. Might I have seen you in anything?

MARGIE: I doubt it. I mean, uh, *Carrie?* Did you see *Carrie,* the musical?

MILES: No.

MARGIE: I was in that.

MILES: Really.

MARGIE: Yes. *(Pause.)* You have a very nice car!

MILES: Thank you.

MARGIE: I've never actually seen a Silver Shadow before. I mean, it's so, you know, decadent, it's great.

MILES: Decadent.

MARGIE: I don't mean decadent, I mean, decadent in a good way. I mean, you know, decadent, excessive, wasteful—no, that's not what I mean. I don't know what I mean. Forget I said it.

MILES: *(Cold.)* I do think it's important to have beautiful things in your life. Is that what you mean?

MARGIE: Yes! That's what I mean! I mean, it's great to have beautiful things in your life and while that might seem kind of decadent to a lot of people, it's not, really, because unless you have too much money, which is not really possible, because then you can have, like, beautiful things. You know what I mean. *(Pause.)* Don't you?

MILES: No.

MARGIE: *(Abashed.)* Oh. I was hoping you did.

MILES: No.

MARGIE: Well. I do think it's nice to have beautiful things. In your life. I wish I had beautiful things in my life. I wish I had your car in my life. I mean, I'm glad it's in my life. It's in my life tonight, anyway, and I find that really just—wonderful. And I find you fascinating, but I also want to tell you to fuck off. Do you know what I mean? I mean, I don't really want to tell you to fuck off, really what I want to do is have sex in the back seat of that amazing car, but frankly, I don't know, I'm really just so stunned by all this, stunned and repulsed you know? The thought of kissing you makes my blood run cold but on the other hand, I'm really hoping that you'll pick me. Pick me, Miles. Pick me. Let's not waste time. That's why I signed up for that stupid dating service, because I didn't want to waste any more time, I don't have any more time to waste, but women aren't supposed to do that sort of thing, we don't choose, do we, you guys are the ones who do the choosing. Well, sometimes we FORGET THAT, ALL RIGHT? I wish I would shut up; I really do but I just don't think that's going to happen. What is the matter with me?

Why can't I do this? I'm really sorry. It's just, you know—you can't just be like this, but you are, and I—I want you. I want to fuck you in the back seat of that car. You make me sick.
(Pause. They stare at each other. Blackout.)

SCENE III

Liz's apartment. In tableau, a man and a woman lean in and kiss each other. As the lights come up, we see that it is Liz and Bob. She breaks the kiss.

LIZ: Bob, come on, this is crazy, she's going to be here any second.
(He pulls her back and kisses her again. They end up on the table. This kiss begins to get passionate. Bob is clearly trying to take off Liz's clothes.)

LIZ: *(Laughing.)* Oh, God, what are you doing? Bob—
(He dives. She holds him at bay.)

LIZ: Bob, this is clinical. I mean, do you want to get caught, much? What are you doing here?

BOB: I'm picking up the car. She's driving here and I'm supposed to drive away.

LIZ: See, this is my point.

BOB: *(Nuzzling her.)* I want to marry you.

LIZ: Yeah, well, I want world peace.

BOB: Lizzie…
(She holds out her hand and looks at him. After a moment, she pushes him away.)

BOB: Well, so, what's going on here? I mean, what, are you having second thoughts about this?

LIZ: Second thoughts? No, I'm not having second thoughts. What I'm having is more like heart failure. What I'm having is like, guilt, of Biblical proportions.

BOB: *(Reaching for her.)* Lizzie…

LIZ: No, Bob—what are we doing? What are we—we can't do this! You're married. To my sister. God help me; you're married to my sister. I'm going to hell.

BOB: So, we'll go together.

LIZ: Bob, we have to stop. Now. Before it's too late.

BOB: Before it's too late? What was last week?

LIZ: Last week was a big mistake, and it can't happen again.

BOB: Look, my marriage with Lily has been a mess for a long time. We're just going through the motions. Sex is completely mechanical—

LIZ: Don't tell me this. Would you please? I don't want to know about my sister's sex life.

BOB: You are so cute when you're terrified.

LIZ: Bob, cut it out. I mean, God knows Lily and I have never had much use for each other, but this—I mean, this is just one step too far, okay?

BOB: *(Pause.)* So, is that why you did it? To get at Lily?

LIZ: What?

BOB: I mean—ha. I'm sorry, I just thought—we've only been flirting with each other for *years.*

LIZ: *(Overlap.)* NO. That's—ri*dic*ulous. How could you even *suggest* such a thing?

BOB: *(Overlap.)* I mean, call me crazy, but I kind of assumed you had some *feelings* for me—

LIZ: Of *course* I have feelings, for God's sake, don't do this to me!

BOB: Well, I'm *sorry* to inconvenience you.
    (Pause.)

LIZ: I'm sorry. I'm sorry *(Pause.)* Of course I have feelings for you, Bob, you're my best friend, but this—frankly, it scares me that we did this. This isn't just some little indiscretion, or, I don't know, you know, some family *quirk.* This is the sort of thing that people get very upset about. Sleeping with your wife's sister? This is like, how Greek tragedies start.

BOB: I think it's much more common than people admit.

LIZ: Nevertheless!

BOB: You have to admit, there's a certain *thrill*—

LIZ: Bob! It's a bad thing. It happened, okay, it just— happened, and it was great, but we can still walk away from it. It's not like we *chose* it. It's not like we deliberately were trying to hurt anybody. It just happened. But now, I have to get myself back on track. *(Pause. Liz moves away.)*

BOB: You know, she knows.

LIZ: What?

BOB: I said, she knows. And you know she knows.

LIZ: How could she know? We only did it once!

BOB: Twice!

LIZ: Okay, twice, that's still—I mean, what, did you tell her?

BOB: Of course not.

LIZ: Did she say something?

BOB: No.

LIZ: Then—

BOB: I'm just saying, she knows. And as long as she already knows, what's the point of quitting before she finds out?

LIZ: *(Pause. She looks at him.)* The really scary thing is, that kind of makes sense to me.

BOB: I was hoping it would. *(He reaches for her.)*

LIZ: Bob. Go downstairs. I mean it. I don't want her to find you here.

BOB: Oh, lighten up. You didn't expect me to just give up without a fight, did you?

LIZ: I expect you to be reasonable about this.

BOB: Oh, for—be reasonable? What for? Life isn't reasonable. You work and you work, you put everything in place, you have a beautiful home, money in the bank, a lovely wife, a sweet little girl, and the next thing you know, you're bored and miserable, you didn't get tenure, your wife hates you, and your daughter thinks you're a geek. And you were reasonable, you were! Then—something else happens, and there's one thing in your life, one place you can go for comfort, and passion…Why the hell should I be reasonable?

(His head is in her neck. She looks down at him, sad and affectionate.)

LIZ: Oh, Bob…

(She rocks him for a moment. There is a brief knock on the door. Paula enters as they leap apart.)

PAULA: Boy, I love your security, Liz. The front door is wide open—Bob. Hi.

BOB: Hi, Paula.

(The tension is so thick you could cut it with a knife. Paula watches them, surprised.)

PAULA: Well. Well, well, well.

LIZ: Well, what?

PAULA: Well, everybody else is right behind me. And you missed a button.

(Liz checks her clothing, desperate, as in a flurry, Lily, Margie and Gina enter through the open door behind them.)

LILY: Really, Liz, this is New York. Security is generally considered to be a good idea in this city.

LIZ: There's something wrong with the super; he gets hot and props everything open—hi, hi—

(Lily crosses to Bob and gives him keys. They kiss.)

MARGIE: I can't believe you still live here. This is hell, you know; you live in hell. Drug addicts are shooting up in front of your mailboxes.

LIZ: It looks worse than it is—

LILY: *(To Bob.)* I thought you were going to wait for me outside. So that I didn't have to park the car.

BOB: Oh, I just…I thought I'd come in and say hi to Liz.

LILY: Oh. And did she say hi back?

BOB: I'll try and be home in time for the news.

LILY: Pick up some milk, would you?

BOB: Sure. Have a good time quilting.

GINA: It's knitting. We knit.

LILY: He's trying to be funny.

GINA: Oh. *(She laughs politely at Bob.)*

MARGIE: Where are you going, Bob?

BOB: Basketball game. *(He is gone.)*

MARGIE: Of course. Even Bob. Even the perfect man.

LILY: He's hardly perfect.

(Liz looks at her.)

PAULA: *(Covering a little.)* Men and sports! I have clients who come in and talk to me about sports for hours, and I always want to say, I'm sorry, even though I am your therapist I am also a woman. Could we talk about dreams or something? I do much better with dreams.

MARGIE: Women don't talk about sports?

PAULA: Never. Not ever. And men don't stop talking about it. They talk about sports more than they talk about women. They talk about sports more than they talk about sex.

MARGIE: That does not surprise me at all. They're all gay. Every single man on this planet is gay; that's what the problem is.

LIZ: What?

MARGIE: Oh, come on, haven't you ever suspected that? I mean, are you telling me that it has never crossed your mind that they all were gay? Secretly?

LILY: No, I can't actually say that it has.

MARGIE: That's why they're so hostile. They don't want us here, really, at all. They wish we didn't exist. They just want to fuck each other. They just want to fuck themselves.

PAULA: Margie, I must say, even for you this is unusually grim.

MARGIE: It's true. What? It's true. Even when they're controlling us they can't be sure, you know, they just can't be sure, and they hate us for that. Any little gesture you make, any little slip, you know, and they know you're not what they want, as hard as you try, you're not what they want, you're something else altogether, and that's it. They can't take it. It's a lost cause.

(They all stare at her except for Gina, who keeps knitting, oblivious.)

LIZ: Margie, are you okay? You want a beer or something?

MARGIE: You have beer? I'd love a beer.

PAULA: I'll have one too.

(Liz exits to kitchen. Margie pulls at her knitting, clearly upset. Paula and Lily watch Margie, confused. Gina knits.)

LILY: Did you get a chance to work on that stitch I showed you?

MARGIE: Don't condescend to me, Lily.

LILY: I wasn't—

MARGIE: Just because I can't figure out some stupid knitting thing doesn't mean I'm some sort of major failure as a woman, all right?

LILY: I didn't mean—

MARGIE: I'm doing the best I can, ALL RIGHT?

LILY: Oh, dear. Margie?

(She sits next to her and touches her. Liz reenters and passes around beers.)

MARGIE: What?

PAULA: What's the matter?

MARGIE: Nothing. *(Pause.)* I had kind of a weird date last night.

PAULA: What happened?

LIZ: Who was it? Did he hurt you?

MARGIE: No. Nothing happened. I don't know what happened. I just kind of lost it. He was fine. I just—lost it.

(She drinks. Paula, Lily and Liz stare at her. Gina knits.)

GINA: I swear, I hate binding off worse than anything. Everything changes, you know, once you bind off, the whole shape of the thing changes and you're just not sure of what you have. No matter how carefully you count the stitches or check the gauge, you always seem to end up with pieces that don't look the way they're supposed to, or don't quite fit together and then there's that sort of awful moment where you're just not sure you can ever get the whole thing together. I really hate that.

(Pause. They all stare at her.)

MARGIE: I never seem to get that far. I mean, I always quit first.

GINA: You finished that scarf.

MARGIE: Big deal. A scarf. That's all I'm capable of, a stupid scarf.

(She starts to cry. Lily puts her arm around her.)

LILY: Hey, hey, hey.

MARGIE: I'm sorry. I'm sorry, Lily. I blew it.

LILY: It's all right, honey.

MARGIE: It's not all right! Why aren't I a lesbian? Lesbians have it easy. Everybody listens to them. They're relevant and politically correct and even tempered because they don't sleep with those jerks! But am I a lesbian? No! I have to like men, and just be a total loser at getting one! Paula?

PAULA: Yeah?

MARGIE: Is it okay if I come by your office tomorrow? I mean, can I come talk to you about some stuff?

PAULA: *(With some humor.)* That might be a good idea

MARGIE: Okay. Okay, Lily, can you show me how to do this again? I think I did it right a couple of times, but then I started screwing it up again—

LILY: Of course. It's just following directions. Like following a recipe.

MARGIE: Okay.

(Lily picks up Margie's knitting and demonstrates for her.)

LIZ: So...so what happened?

MARGIE: Oh, nothing, you know, the same old stupid stuff. I keep taking stitches off one side and not the other. I don't know why it's so confusing.

LIZ: No, I don't mean about the knitting, I mean about the guy.

MARGIE: What guy?

LIZ: The guy! The guy!

LILY: Liz...

LIZ: What? One second she's losing it and the next second we're all knitting! I mean, could we have a reality check here?

MARGIE: This is real. This sweater is real, or at least it will be if I ever figure it out.

LIZ: What happened with this guy?

MARGIE: How come men are real and knitting isn't?

PAULA: If Margie doesn't want to talk about it, I don't think we should push her.

LIZ: But she's still upset about it.

PAULA: If she doesn't want to talk about it—

LIZ: Paula, Christ, it sounds like she was almost raped—

MARGIE: I wasn't raped!

LIZ: Well, what happened?

MARGIE: I don't want to talk about it, all right?

LIZ: Fine. *(Pause.)* I'm just saying—

PAULA: Liz, if you have such a powerful need for conversation, then you talk.

LIZ: What?

PAULA: Are you seeing anybody?

LIZ: No, I—

PAULA: Do you want to talk about that?

LIZ: Paula—

PAULA: Does it bother you?

LIZ: I am not the one with the problem here!

LILY: Are you sure about that?

LIZ: *(Pause.)* Never mind. *(Pause.)* Never mind.

   (She looks away. They all knit silently. Blackout.)

SCENE IV

The Japanese restaurant. In tableau, a man and a woman stand before the table, bowing. As the lights come up, we see that it is Paula and Miles. Paula stares off.

PAULA: I've never seen them do that before.

MILES: Excuse me?

PAULA: I've never seen a waiter serve sushi like that. Like an offering. It's quite—remarkable.

MILES: I know. It's a little embarrassing. They call it the Imperial Feast, and the show comes with it. Sort of like those waiters who sing to you in pizza joints.

PAULA: I didn't think you went to pizza joints.

MILES: I don't. I come here. *(He starts to serve her.)*

PAULA: I hope you don't mind my asking, but don't you find this all a bit...overstated?

MILES: Don't you like sushi? I love sushi.

PAULA: That's not what I meant. It's just, most people I know would be uncomfortable with the politics of all this. I mean, I've had a wonderful time tonight; meeting the governor was really exciting, and the opening at the Whitney was nothing short of dazzling. But to tell the truth, I'm beginning to find this all a little unnerving.

MILES: Really? How so?

PAULA: Well, you know, all of it together is so—all right. Your air of patronage, the subservience of everyone in the restaurant, your car—I mean, don't you guys read the newspaper? This sort of thing is going out of style.

MILES: Do you really think so?

PAULA: Yes. I do.

MILES: I think you'd be surprised. The imperialistic structures which seem to disturb you so much have stood at the heart of the American culture for centuries. In fact, these structures, and the assumptions they are built upon, are the very things which have made culture possible. In America and throughout the world.

PAULA: Well, that may be, but—

MILES: Here, I think you'll appreciate this; it's a combination of abalone, salmon roe and mahi mahi. Only two people in the world know how to make it. It's exquisite, really.

PAULA: Thank you.

(*He places it on her plate and hands it to her, then makes a note in his notebook. As he interviews her, he continues to make notes.*)

PAULA: What are you doing?

MILES: Just making a few notes to myself, that's all. It's a business habit. Annoying but harmless. I picked it up from my father.

PAULA: (*Friendly.*) Really? What was he like?

MILES: No, no, no. I was warned about this. You're famous for this. No prying about my parents until the second date.

PAULA: You can't blame a girl for trying.

MILES: (*Laughing.*) I hope you don't mind my saying so, Paula, but this is the first time I've dated a woman of color. I find it quite stimulating.

PAULA: Really?

MILES: Don't you think so?

PAULA: Well, I've dated white men before.

MILES: So the novelty's worn off.

PAULA: I guess.

MILES: (*He writes this down.*) Do you have many white friends?

PAULA: Yes. Do you?

MILES: Well, it's less of an issue for me, isn't it?

PAULA: You tell me.

MILES: (*Laughing.*) Therapists. All I meant was, clearly, it's important for blacks to assimilate themselves into the high culture. Which you seem to have accomplished admirably.

PAULA: What?

MILES: An attractive black woman achieves a position of authority in a predominantly white profession? That looks like assimilation to me.

PAULA: Yes, well, just for the record, I'm not particularly interested in being assimilated into the "high" culture.

MILES: You're not?

PAULA: No. Most of my "friends" are black. And, as you may or may not realize, my family is black. You might want to write that down, too.

MILES: Do you see them often?

PAULA: Yes. I do.

MILES: How often?

PAULA: Often enough.

MILES: And your "black friends"? How often do you see them?

PAULA: I don't keep track of how often I—

MILES: And your white friends? How often do you see them?

PAULA: Often.

MILES: More often than you see your black friends?

PAULA: *(Pause, cold.)* Maybe.

MILES: That's the beauty of America, isn't it? Social mobility. *(He writes this down.)*

PAULA: Okay. What's going on here?

MILES: We're trying to get to know each other.

PAULA: Is that what we're doing?

MILES: Don't you want to know me, Paula? Because I find you fascinating.

PAULA: You're pretty fascinating yourself, Miles.

MILES: Thank you. So. You're a psychologist. How many patients do you have? *(Beat. Cautious, Paula decides to answer.)*

PAULA: They're not patients, they're clients.

MILES: White?

PAULA: Would it make a difference if they were?

MILES: You tell me. You're the one who doesn't want to be assimilated.

PAULA: *(Pause.)* Yes. Most of them are white.

MILES: Do you like them?

PAULA: Oh, man. You know, we probably shouldn't talk about my work.

MILES: Why, are you feeling defensive about it?

PAULA: Why, do you want me to?

MILES: *(Laughing.)* Therapists…

PAULA: *(Also laughing.)* Guys…like you…

MILES: So. You were saying—

PAULA: I was saying, mmm, this sushi looks good. Is this blowfish? That's the stuff that'll kill you if it isn't cooked right, isn't it? Here, have some, Miles.

MILES: Thank you. It's tuna You were saying you had some trouble dealing with your white patients.

PAULA: Actually, no, I did not say that.

MILES: Well, but it must feel odd to have white people come in and complain to you all the time.

PAULA: No, it feels just fine.

MILES: I think you're being coy.

PAULA: Yeah, well, I think you're attacking me.

MILES: I'm just trying to get to know you, Paula. And I really am interested in the whole therapeutic enterprise.

PAULA: Then maybe you should try it. I know a couple of people who might be able to help you with this notebook thing.

MILES: *(Smiling a little.)* I'll think about it. So, how long, on the average, do you work with any given client? One year? Two? Five? Ten?

PAULA: Yes.

MILES: Have they gotten better?

PAULA: Oh, my God...

MILES: Is that a delicate question? I'm sorry. I just don't understand why someone would need your services for ten years. I mean, it's a treatment, right? What good is a treatment if it doesn't make you better?

PAULA: *(Steely.)* Well, Miles, some people have been terribly damaged by life. Their souls have been—wounded, whether by their family, or events, or just the world—

MILES: Well, Paula, I'm sure you're good at what you do, but I'm not convinced that talking to you is going to heal my soul or even make me a successful member of society. I've just never understood why anyone thinks that discussing their problems will make them go away.

PAULA: No one thinks that.

MILES: Don't they?

PAULA: No.

MILES: I thought they did.

PAULA: Well, and so what if they do? The world's a hard place. Once in a while, even the best of us needs an ear, and a little shot of compassion. Is that so awful?

MILES: If you require a person to pay for it, is it still compassion?

PAULA: Why are you attacking me?

MILES: Why do you see this as an attack? On the contrary, I have nothing but admiration for the shrewdness of your whole enterprise. You convince people they're dependent on you for their happiness and then you charge them for that dependency. It's brilliant.

PAULA: That is not what I do!

MILES: Oh, I've touched a nerve. I'm sorry. Have you tried the eel?

PAULA: No.

MILES: You should. *(Pause.)* Go ahead, try it. *(Pause.)* Try it.

(She reaches for it. He smiles. She sets down the sushi.)

PAULA: All right, Miles. All right. I think we've talked about me quite enough for one evening. I'd like to hear about you. Why don't you tell me what kind of dreams you have?

MILES: You're interested in my dreams?

PAULA: Very.

MILES: *(Pause.)* All right. *(Pause.)* There's one I have where I'm in my office above the city, and there's a document in the computer that I can't get out. So I look in my desk for the key to the computer and it looks like a knife, or a letter opener; it's quite sharp, but just as I'm about to put it into the computer, a white rat comes along and steals it out of my hand. So I chase it up and down the halls, and then I hear it behind me, so I turn, and hold out my hand, and the knife is in it—the key, I mean— but it's a different rat, a black rat, only now she's covered in blood because I've stabbed her. Because I had the key all along. *(Pause.)* Actually, I've had that dream several times.

PAULA: Really.

MILES: Do you know what it means?

PAULA: No. No. I have no idea. *(She stares at him.)*

(Blackout.)

SCENE V

Gina's apartment. While once again the table is the centerpiece of the room, this space is cluttered, swamped, with knitted items, piled on the floor, hanging from the ceilings. It is a maze, a jungle of knitting. All the women stand in the midst of the knitting, looking about. Tableau. As the lights change, the women start to turn, taking in the spectacle with wonder.

LIZ: Wow, Gina, this is—you been knitting a lot lately, huh?

GINA: I've had some extra time on my hands.

LIZ: I guess so.

GINA: Lily, this is that stitch I wanted to show you—

(She picks up a sweater from a pile and shows it to Lily, who takes it gingerly.)

LILY: Why, yes, oh, it's lovely—

PAULA: Gina, when did you do all this?

GINA: Last week. This week. The past couple weeks.

PAULA: Yes, but—

MARGIE: I could knit twenty-four hours a day, and I'd still...

LIZ: I don't know, Gina, this is—

GINA: Are we knitting or not? I thought you guys came here to knit.

(Pause. She knits. They watch her.)

LIZ: To tell you the truth, I'm not sure why I'm here, Gina.

MARGIE: Gina—how are things?

GINA: Fine.

MARGIE: Really?

GINA: Oh, sure.

PAULA: How's your family? How's work?

GINA: Work? Oh, come on, Paula. I'm through with all that.

LIZ: All what?

GINA: Everything.

(They all look at each other uneasily.)

GINA: What? What is the matter with you guys? This is America. No one starves in America. Look at the news, would you? Do you ever see starving people on the news? Well, okay, you do, but they're somewhere else. Ethiopia. Calcutta. Americans, Americans take care of each other.

LIZ: They do?

LILY: Liz.

GINA: You see it on television all the time. Someone will take care of you. Peter Jennings. The lady from Citibank. Your mother. You don't have to worry. You live in America. Maybe you live in a cave, but you also live in America. And that makes it all right. I mean, is there anywhere else in the world where you could be more free? If you were more free, you would die. Right?

LIZ: Well, when you put it that way.

LILY: Gina—do you have any juice, any apple juice or something? My throat's a little dry.

GINA: Oh—I'm sorry. Of course. Does anyone else—

LIZ: No.

MARGIE: I'm fine.

PAULA: I'd like some juice, too.

GINA: Okay. Great.

(She exits to the kitchen. The others speak quickly, furtively.)

LIZ: What the fuck is going on?

LILY: Look at this place—

LIZ: Paula, I think you should handle this—

PAULA: Handle what? I don't know what's—

MARGIE: Well, something's wrong—

PAULA: That is not my—

LIZ: Paula—

PAULA: WHAT? She is not one of my clients! And even if she were, I don't know if I—just because I have a fucking degree does not mean I have all the answers to everybody's problems, all right? All right? I don't have answers to anything. I don't have answers to shit.

GINA: (Calling from kitchen.) I can hear you.

LILY: What?

PAULA: (Quiet.) I'm sorry. I'm not myself today.

GINA: (Off, overlapping.) I can hear you talking about me!

LILY: Oh, no, we were just admiring all the work you've—

PAULA: (Overlapping.) I had a bad night last night, and right now I don't think I'm the person to handle this. I mean, look at this place! I can't solve this!

GINA: (Reentering.) I don't need to be solved. I'm a lot happier. And I've been getting a lot of knitting done.

MARGIE: Well, it's just—okay, look. I'm a little slow, all right. So what's going on? Did you get fired or something?

GINA: Oh, no. I didn't get fired. I was let go. They let me go. Like a balloon. (She hands drinks out. They all watch her.)

LIZ: When did…

GINA: IT DOESN'T MATTER. (Pause.) I don't care. We're streamlining the department, see, and that's just that. I put my time in, eighty hour weeks, I work hard, my research is better than anybody's, and I'm the only person in the entire building who knows how to run the computers. And it doesn't matter. They don't care. You want to know why the city is falling apart? Because they fire everybody who knows what they're doing. It's policy. If you know what you're doing, you get fired.

LIZ: But don't they have to…

GINA: They don't have to do anything. They only have to do what they want.

And Morrison doesn't like me because I'm a woman. It's also because I know what I'm doing, but she'd be able to handle that if I weren't a girl. She's one of *those* women, you know, one of the ones who only likes men? What am I talking about; we're all the same. You're all, the first thing you think is that I screwed up somehow, that's the way the logic works. Women are the worst, and that's the truth. We're always watching each other like sharks; they don't have to do it to us anymore because we're only too willing to do it to ourselves. And who comes into the picture but little Mr. Harvard Law. The kid's killing time! Everybody knows it. In six months he's going to land a spot with Debuvoise and Plimpton, whatever, he's out of here, he's doing his public service time so he can have a nice little mark on his CV. We're a SLOT on his RESUME and she thinks he's God's gift. I don't care. If I were black, you can bet it would be different. I'm sorry for being a racist, Paula, no one wants to be a racist but these morons making the decisions don't leave you any choice! Davenport stays because he's black, and Mr. Harvard Law stays because he's Mr. Harvard Law, and I go because I'm a single white woman in my thirties and it doesn't mean shit what I do. Let's face it. We're the most useless group of people history has ever heard of; we're a bunch of fucking spinsters, that's what we are. I wish I was married. I wish I was black. Or no, you know what I wish? I wish everybody who got in—you know, everybody who got *in*—would turn into white men. All of them. Those Asian women newscasters, and those sleazy black male weather guys, all those snappy little white girls who look great in power suits—I wish they would just turn into white men over fifty. I wish all of them would turn into Bill Buckley. Because then we would *know.* We would know who the good guys were, and who the bad guys were. We would just know who was who and what was what. *(She starts to unravel her knitting.)* But it's fine, okay? Everything is fine. If this were, you know, India or something, *Iran,* maybe then I'd be in trouble. Not only would I be out of a job, I'd have to wear one of those stupid black things over my face. Right? But this is America. It's better here than anywhere in the world. Everything is fine.

LIZ: Gina, when did this happen? How long have you been out of work?

GINA: I don't know. A few weeks. Three weeks. Something.

MARGIE: Why didn't you tell us?

GINA: I thought I did. I don't know. I forgot.

MARGIE: We could've helped, Gina.

GINA: But I don't come here for help. I come here to knit. *(She continues to unravel her sweater.)* This yarn is beautiful. Isn't it? It's so beautiful I can't stand to finish this sweater, so I keep pulling it out and knitting it over again. Someone else did that, didn't they? Some woman. Kept knitting the same thing, for years and years?

PAULA: Penelope.

GINA: I understand her now. I think I really understand her.

LIZ: We'll get you a lawyer.

GINA: I am a lawyer.

LIZ: Well, then you should know what your fucking rights are.

GINA: I do.

LIZ: Gina, you have to fight.

GINA: Why?

LILY: Liz—

LIZ: No! Christ! This is our problem, anytime someone steps on us, we go, I don't want to make waves, it's too much work, it's not worth it. Well, the perfect man is not going to come along and make this all right! We have to do it ourselves!

GINA: God, you are so full of shit, Liz.

LIZ: I am not—would you, goddammit, would you put the fucking knitting down for a half a second and deal with reality; this is your life I'm talking about, you stupid woman—
(She grabs the knitting in Gina's hands and tries to pull it away from her. Gina hangs onto it.)

GINA: Leave me alone. LEAVE ME ALONE.

LILY: For God's sake, Liz, leave her alone!
(Lily pulls Liz away. Gina shrouds herself in her yarn.)

LIZ: I'm sorry. I'm sorry. *(Pause.)* I'm sorry, Gina. *(Liz sits, confused.)*
(Pause.)

MARGIE: Well, I think I finally figured out this sleeve! Lily, look. I mean, I had to take it apart about fifty times but I finally got it! Sort of like Penelope, huh, Gina?
(Gina does not respond.)

LILY: It's beautiful, Margie.

PAULA: It's looking great.

MARGIE: Yeah. I love this color. Good thing, too, huh? Otherwise I might be pretty sick of it by now. I mean, it's taking me long enough, right? Everything takes so long. Doesn't it? I mean, some days it feels like, you know, life is just going to go on forever. Well, you know. You're fast,

Gina, geez, I couldn't knit this much in eight hundred years or something.

(Gina does not respond. The others knit. Pause. Liz watches her, becoming alarmed.)

LIZ: Oh, shit. You guys. She's lost it.

PAULA: Liz, *please.*

LIZ: No, I mean it. She's lost it. She's not here. Gina.

LILY: Gina?

(Gina looks at them but does not respond.)

LIZ: Oh, shit.

MARGIE: What? What?

PAULA: Gina. Can you hear me? Gina. Lily—

MARGIE: Should we call a doctor?

LILY: No, she's fine. She's fine. Gina. Come on, Gina. Are you all right? You're all right. Do you want to go lie down?

(Gina looks at her.)

LILY: Come on, Gina. Let's go lie down.

GINA: *(Very soft.)* I'm fine.

LILY: I know you are. You're just a little upset. Did Liz upset you?

(Gina nods.)

LILY: You just wanted to knit, and Liz upset you.

GINA: I thought we were going to knit.

LILY: That's what we came here for.

GINA: Liz—

LILY: Liz just made a mistake.

GINA: If she doesn't want to knit, she shouldn't come.

LILY: I'll talk to her about it.

GINA: I'm embarrassed now.

LILY: You don't have to be.

GINA: I'm sorry, I'm just—I'm embarrassed.

LILY: Come on. Let's just go into your bedroom for a minute and talk. Do you want to do that?

GINA: Yes, please.

LILY: Come on.

(She helps her stand. Gina looks around at the others for a moment.)

GINA: I'm sorry.

(She and Lily exit into her bedroom.)

LIZ: Christ.

MARGIE: I've never seen anything like that. I mean, she lost it. Major. We're talking planet ten.

PAULA: She'll be fine.

LIZ: Paula, she *lost* it.

PAULA: I KNOW SHE LOST IT. BUT SHE'LL BE FINE.

LIZ: For God's sake, could you not blow up—I mean, you're the therapist here; why don't you do something?

PAULA: *(Overlap.)* Don't you fucking tell me how to handle this; if you hadn't pushed her so hard none of this would have happened!

LIZ: *(Overlap.)* You're not going to blame this on me!

PAULA: And you are not going to make this my problem!

LILY: *(Reentering.)* That is ENOUGH. What is the matter with you?

LIZ: Sorry.

PAULA: How is she?

LILY: *(Crosses and picks up Gina's knitting, which was left on the floor.)* Somebody look in the bathroom and see if she's got any tranquilizers around here.

LIZ: Tranquilizers? That's the last thing she needs; she's already a fucking zombie—

LILY: Paula?

PAULA: Right. *(She exits to the bathroom.)*

LIZ: Lily—

LILY: Margie, see if there's anything in the kitchen. Warm up some milk or tea or something.
(Margie goes.)

LIZ: Oh, fuck, Lily, she's having some kind of breakdown. You can't fix this with a cup of warm milk and a hug—

LILY: Liz, just sit down and shut up. Or leave. Please.
(She exits into the bedroom. Left alone in the living room for a moment, Liz is lost. She sits, confused, and picks up a piece of knitting. She looks at it, shakes her head, sets it aside. Paula reenters.)

PAULA: She doesn't have anything here. I'm going to run up to my place and get her some Seconal.

MARGIE: *(Reentering.)* She doesn't have *anything* here. Should we call somebody? Her parents or somebody? Maybe we should call the police.

LIZ: Great. They can arrest her. That'll be a big help.

MARGIE: Look, Liz, you don't have to be such a shit, you know, I'm just trying to help.

LIZ: I'm sorry, okay?

MARGIE: I mean, you shouldn't have pushed her.

LIZ: I didn't know!

PAULA: *(Has her purse and keys.)* Margie, you come with me. I'm going to go get her some drugs. We can pick up some groceries on the way.

MARGIE: Okay, yeah, sure.

PAULA: Are you going to be okay here, Liz? I mean, do you want us to drop you somewhere?

LIZ: No, I'm—I'll just stay here. Just in case.

PAULA: Okay. *(Pause.)* Good luck.

(She and Margie exit. For a moment, Liz picks up Gina's knitting, stares at it, and sets it back down, distracted. Lily enters and watches her.)

LILY: Are you all right?

LIZ: What?

LILY: You seem upset.

LIZ: No. I, uh, yes, I'm upset. I feel like this is all my fault.

LILY: Oh.

LIZ: Yeah.

LILY: Well, it's not.

LIZ: It's not?

LILY: Of course not. She lost her job, and she didn't have anything else to fall back on.

LIZ: She had us.

LILY: Well. Apparently, that wasn't enough. Gloria Steinem notwithstanding.

LIZ: Paula and Margie went to get some food, and some drugs.

LILY: That's not what she needs.

LIZ: Isn't it?

LILY: No. She feels like she's floating. At least, that's what she told me. She's floating in the universe. She doesn't know her family anymore. She has no husband, or children. She doesn't feel grounded. Her work grounded her a little. But now she doesn't have that. So, now, she feels like she doesn't exist.

LIZ: Oh. Really? Well. I understand that.

LILY: Do you?

LIZ: Of course. I mean, let's face it. I don't have much going for me these days, and every time I try to make things better…I just make bigger messes. All this yelling I do, I don't know what it's about half the time. I just, I can't seem to put my life together. My work is stupid, I don't give a shit about it, and…I don't have anyone.

LILY: No one?

LIZ: No. *(Pause.)* Not all of us are as lucky as you are.

LILY: I'm not so lucky.

LIZ: *(Pause.)* Look. I know you know about—

LILY: *(Stopping her.)* Well, you should have someone.

LIZ: I should?

LILY: Men aren't the solution to everything, but they help.

LIZ: Do they?

LILY: I think so. They can. They're supposed to. They do run the planet. It doesn't hurt to have one or two of them on your side.

LIZ: I guess not.

LILY: I have a friend.

LIZ: What?

LILY: I have a friend who I thought you might like to meet. A male friend.

LIZ: Lily…

LILY: He lives in Daddy's building. I met him in the elevator there. I think he's extraordinary.

LIZ: Lily, I don't know…

LILY: I like him very much. He's come over to the apartment for tea a couple of times, and I like him very much. And, he's looking to settle down. Would you like to meet him?

LIZ: Christ. Lily. I can't think about this now, tonight, I mean, Gina…

LILY: This isn't about Gina. This is about you. I want you to be happy. I want to be happy, and I want you to be happy. I don't want you to float. I want you to be in the world. Isn't that what you want?

LIZ: *(Pause.)* I don't know what I want.

LILY: *(Pause.)* His name is Miles. *(Pause.)* He has a great deal of money.
(She leaves as Miles turns in his chair to stare at Liz. He smiles at her. Tableau. Blackout.)

END OF ACT I

ACT II
SCENE VI

The sushi bar. In tableau, we see Liz standing behind Miles. She is dressed elegantly, and she is holding his head in one hand and a dinner knife in the other, as if she is about to slit his throat. Tableau. The lights come up as she lowers the knife, sliding it up his chin slowly.

LIZ: Apparently, it was considered very erotic. It was just as important as sex, so you had to learn how to do it right. Geisha 101. Shaving your master.

MILES: *(Tense.)* Really.

LIZ: You don't think this is erotic?

MILES: Well, actually—

LIZ: Miles. You need to learn how to relax.
(She twists his head violently. He allows his neck to relax.)

LIZ: That's better. Good. *(She runs the back of the dinner knife slowly across his throat.)* See? What'd I tell you? The Japanese really know how to live. *(She sets the dinner knife on the table and sits.)* Of course, I myself know nothing about it. If this really was a razor, instead of a dinner knife, I'm sure I would have cut your throat.

MILES: I see. *(He writes this down.)*

LIZ: So. You're interested in Japanese culture.

MILES: Certain aspects of it, yes. I am less familiar with Geisha techniques than perhaps I might be.

LIZ: Well, you should look into it. I bet you'd enjoy it. They were really into subservience.

MILES: Yes. I will do that. *(He writes.)*

LIZ: So how many pages of notes have you taken?

MILES: Excuse me?

LIZ: Well, you've been writing for something like two hours now. I was just wondering how many pages you filled. As you know, I'm a journalist—more or less—so I'm just kind of curious about how many pages of notes you've taken on me.

MILES: Five.

LIZ: Five.

MILES: Yes.

LIZ: I guess you've got other women in there, too, huh? I mean, that notebook looks pretty full.

MILES: Yes. I have notes on other women as well.

LIZ: Do you have notes on Lily?

MILES: No.

LIZ: Why not?

MILES: It wouldn't be appropriate.

LIZ: Oh, and this is? *(Pause.)* Come on, I'm just trying to figure this out. I mean, if you don't mind my saying so, this is all…it's fucking weird, if you want to know the truth. I mean, God knows it was pretty funny meeting the vice president, but overall this is hardly a dream date, you know what I mean?

MILES: You're very different from your sister, aren't you?

LIZ: Yes. I am.

(He writes.)

LIZ: So, are you going to take notes on me all night? I mean, if this, like, suddenly turned into a really glorious evening of sexual adventure, and we made it back to your fabulous penthouse and I started ripping off your clothes, would you need to take notes on that, too?

MILES: Does this bother you?

LIZ: Well, yeah, it kind of does.

MILES: Why?

LIZ: Because, Miles, frankly, it's been my experience that when you write things down, sooner or later, people start to lie.

MILES: Really?

LIZ: That doesn't bother you, huh?

MILES: Not particularly. I don't expect people to tell the truth. Whether I write it down or not.

LIZ: *(Cool.)* That's…really sad.

MILES: I beg your pardon?

LIZ: That was a sad thing to say, Miles. You strike me as a very sad person.

(Pause. He looks at her.)

LIZ: Listen, I'm going to take off, okay? Clearly, this isn't working out, so I'm going to go find myself a cab.

MILES: No. Please. Continue.

LIZ: Why should I? If you don't care if I'm telling the truth, why should I keep talking? I mean, I could say anything, right, and it might be the truth, or it might be a lie, and you'll write it down, and that will make it real. And then I won't matter anymore; I won't even exist; the only thing that will exist is this story, on your page. *(Pause.)* I mean, just between you and me, I'm a little bit of an expert on this kind of thing, and I don't particularly like being on this side of the pencil.

MILES: Why not?

LIZ: The temptation to lie just might get the better of me. It was interesting meeting you. *(She stands.)*

MILES: Then you're easily tempted? To lie, I mean. I'm sorry, have I touched a nerve?

LIZ: Weren't you intending to? *(Pause.)* Everyone lies at one time or another.

MILES: I don't.

LIZ: No?

MILES: No.

LIZ: That's quite a feat.

MILES: Why don't you stay? I'll tell you all about it.

LIZ: What do you want, Miles?

MILES: Conversation. You seem to have a philosophical mind, and I love a good debate. Please. Sit down.

(Pause. She stares at him. He holds up his pencil, shows it to her, and sets it down. She reaches over, picks it up and breaks the pencil in two. She sits.)

MILES: You know, you should never walk away from a fight you may be winning.

LIZ: Excuse me?

MILES: Never walk away from a fight you may be winning. And if you're going to walk, don't come back. And if you're going to come back, get more of a concession than the pencil. I didn't really give you anything, did I? *(He opens the notebook and pulls a pen out, then writes.)*

LIZ: Boy, you really know how to romance a girl, don't you? I mean, that, you know, that really makes me hot.

MILES: You sat down, didn't you?

LIZ: Yes, I did, and if you keep this up, I may just fuck you right here in the restaurant. *(Pause. She laughs.)*

MILES: I fail to see what is so amusing.

LIZ: You are. You are really ridiculous, don't you know that? I mean, can I be frank? What am I saying, of course I can. You're Mr. Honesty, aren't you? Wouldn't it be more of a challenge just to be a real person, Miles? I mean all this power shit. Don't you think it's a little too easy? I'm just saying. You might want to think about developing a personality one of these days. The rest of us find them useful, particularly if you want to get laid, which is usually one of the points of a fucking date. I mean, I got a little power tip for you, Miles. Never lose sight of your goal.

MILES: *(Pause.)* I see. You're a radical. I should have known. Lily told me you were the second child. I should have suspected.

LIZ: Suspected what?

MILES: Suspected this. The arrogance, the foul language, everything. No, I was wrong. *(He shuts his notebook.)* You may go.

LIZ: Excuse me? What happened to the fun of a good debate?

MILES: I said, you may go.

LIZ: Oh. Well gee, thanks. I'll just get right on that. Now that you've dismissed me, I'll just scamper right out of here. Yes, sir. I'm scared. I'm running.

MILES: Do you know who you're talking to?

LIZ: No, Miles, I have no idea. Do you know who you're talking to?

MILES: Yes, I do.

LIZ: No, I don't think you do.

MILES: Yes, I think I do.

LIZ: No, I don't think you do!

MILES: *(Pause.)* I can have you removed.

LIZ: Well, great. Why don't you do that? I mean, that will really break my heart, since I was about to walk out on my own two minutes ago. You fucking creep.

(There is a terrible tense moment. Miles looks at her, quietly furious.)

MILES: You are nothing like your sister.

LIZ: No shit, Miles. I've spent most of my adult life being not my sister. I'm glad I've managed to achieve something.

MILES: Your sister is the finest woman I have ever met.

LIZ: Yeah, you and my father. Christ. I mean, this is, Jesus, this is so fucking classic I can hardly...are you an only child, Miles?

MILES: I would like you to leave.

LIZ: Miles, if you don't want to talk to me, why don't you leave? I mean, it's a free country, right? This is America! Walk out the door! What's the problem?

MILES: I would like...*you* to leave.

LIZ: Yeah, well, that's the problem with America, isn't it? We all want different things. You want me to leave, and I want you to be not such a huge fucking shithead.

(Miles stands. Liz stares at him.)

LIZ: *(A taunt.)* Going somewhere, Miles?

MILES: *(He stares at her. After a moment, he sits.)* Well. Well, well, well. This is interesting. We have a situation here, don't we?

LIZ: Is that what you call this? I was pretty sure it wasn't a date.

MILES: No, it's a date all right.

LIZ: Some date. This is like going out with my father.

MILES: It's my understanding that many girls dream about going on dates with their fathers.

LIZ: Yeah, well, it's my understanding that that is a big old male fantasy.

MILES: Oh, now we get to talk about male fantasies. I'm glad I stayed.

LIZ: Miles, you're starting to cross some lines here. And I thought you were such a good boy.

MILES: Well, I know you're not a good girl. I mean, it's been a long time since a real lady offered to fuck me in a restaurant.

LIZ: You pissed me off.

MILES: Yes, I did, and apparently you found it quite stimulating. I'll keep that in mind.

LIZ: You want to make a note about it? *(She offers him the broken pencil.)*

MILES: No, thank you, that detail I think I can hold onto. Unless it would really piss you off, in which case I'm prepared to write a whole novel.

LIZ: What are you doing?

MILES: I'm flirting with you. And what's more, you're enjoying it.

LIZ: Don't tell me what I'm feeling.

MILES: I beg your pardon. What are you feeling? Tell the truth.

LIZ: The truth is, you're starting to give me a headache, Miles. You make my father look like Mahatma Ghandi.

MILES: I understand that in his private life, Ghandi was a nightmare. Would you like to take a drive?

LIZ: What?

MILES: The only way to see New York is from the back seat of a Rolls.

LIZ: Excuse me, but it's not the only way. It's one way among many, and the majority of us enjoy New York just fine from the curb.

MILES: I'm sorry. That was an arrogant and presumptive thing to say. I'm sorry. *(Pause.)* I also have a Mercedes.

LIZ: Are you flirting again?

MILES: I'm just trying to point out that there are pleasures that come with having money. It's rare, very rare, that I feel like sharing them. You're clearly an intelligent and provocative woman. It's not—insane—that I should want to share them with you.

LIZ: Listen, this is not what I want. I only came on this stupid date as a favor to my sister, so—

MILES: Oh, you owed her a favor? What for?

LIZ: Never mind.

MILES: In any event, you're here now. And you've decided several times not to leave. If this isn't what you want, then why are you still here?

LIZ: I'm still here because you told me to go.

MILES: If I told you not to take a drive with me, would you come?

LIZ: Why don't you try it?

MILES: Are you flirting?

LIZ: No, I'm—I don't know what I'm doing...

MILES: All right. Let's stop this. We could joust with each other all night, but that's not what you want. What do you want?

LIZ: You wouldn't understand.

MILES: Do I strike you as a stupid man? Try me.

LIZ: I want...something authentic.

MILES: Liz, there's little in this world that is more authentic than a Rolls. I'm kidding! I'm sorry. I was just trying to make you laugh. I'm sorry. Clearly, you're a woman who cares about integrity. You're also an iconoclast. I admire that. I want to respect that. Tell me. What are you so angry about?

LIZ: *(Stares at him.)* The world isn't what I want it to be. *(Pause.)* I'm not the person I want to be.

MILES: That's right. You're a liar, aren't you? And you hate liars.

LIZ: Yes. I do.

MILES: Why don't you let me help you with that? I think I understand truth in a way that you might find useful.

LIZ: It's okay, Miles, really, I should...

MILES: It's simple, really. It's all about defining your terms instead of letting them define you. For example, let's say you're having an affair with your sister's husband. Hypothetically. Some people might say that makes you a liar and an adulterer, a bad person, but you know you're not a bad person. Whatever your reasons were, you did it. Hypothetically. You took an action. You broke a rule. From a certain point of view, that's actually honest. You knew what you wanted and you took it. You made the most authentic choice of all. You're not a liar. That is a truth as real as any. So that is the truth you choose. It's the truth I would choose. *(Pause.)* I told you it was simple.

LIZ: Oh, man. *(Pause.)* I should go. Really. I should get out of here.

MILES: Why?

LIZ: Because...because you're a bad guy, Miles. You're really, you know, I think you're a bad guy.

MILES: And you're a bad girl. *(Pause.)* Isn't that true?

LIZ: You just said I wasn't.

MILES: No, I didn't. Are you ready for that drive?

LIZ: I don't...

MILES: Elizabeth. While it is true that there are many different versions of America, mine is clearly the most desirable. Think of it as stock. I own preferred, you own common. And tonight, I'm offering to share my stock with you. Come along. Take a ride around the city with me. What else are your options? Going back to your apartment and doing things you shouldn't? Railing at the human race because it's not what you want it to be? All your anger hasn't gotten you anywhere. All you've done is endangered everything and everyone who matters to you. Take a ride with me. Clearly, we're more alike than we first thought. We both love power. I want to win you, and you want to win me.

LIZ: No. I just want to win.

MILES: Close enough. *(He kisses her.)*

(Blackout.)

SCENE VII

Gina's apartment, still draped with knitting. Four women surround the fig-ure of a man, hovering a bit like harpies. As the lights come up, we see that the man is Bob; he is holding half a sweater up to his chest. All are studying it. Tableau. As the lights change, their movements become quickly busi-nesslike as they pull and shape the sweater against Bob's chest.

GINA: No, the color is...I made a mistake about the color.

MARGIE: I like it!

GINA: It's much too long...no... *(She tries to take it from him.)*

LILY: You can't use Bob as a model for length. He has a funny body. He's very short waisted.

BOB: Thanks a lot.

LILY: Well, you are, Bob, you're very short waisted.

PAULA: I don't know, Gina. I think it's quite striking.

GINA: You do?

BOB: Looks good to me.

GINA: It does?

BOB: *(Hands it to her gently.)* You have a real gift, Gina.

GINA: I don't know.

MARGIE: Oh, you do too. You're like the queen of knitting. Look at this place. The only thing wrong with you is you just let all these sweaters pile up here. It's a crime, you know? People would pay good money for this. The homeless or something.

LILY: The homeless can hardly afford hand-knit sweaters, Margie.

MARGIE: You know what I mean. We could give some away, and we could sell the rest to rich ladies on the upper east side. They live for this shit.

GINA: They do?

MARGIE: Oh, yeah. Last week I worked at this place, this lady had a whole bedroom that she was using for a closet. I walked into it by mistake when I was looking for the bathroom. These people, they're completely out of touch. You could charge them like a thousand dollars or something for one of these, and they'd tell all their friends what a bargain they got.

LILY: I hardly think so.

MARGIE: No, really.

LILY: I hardly think the rich are "out of touch." Otherwise, I doubt that they would be rich.

MARGIE: Yeah, that's what I thought, too, but I'm telling you, Lily, I've talked to a lot of these people, and they're like, most of them are on a totally different planet. You know, like that friend of yours? I been thinking about him, and—

LILY: That's *enough*, Margie. *(Pause.)* I'm sorry. Gina, do you mind if I make us all some tea?

GINA: Oh, I'm sorry, I always forget. What kind do you want?

LILY: It's all right. I'll do it. *(She exits.)*

MARGIE: What's eating her?

BOB: I don't know.

GINA: Bob, do you think I should give my sweaters to the homeless?

BOB: No, Gina, actually, I agree with Margie. I think you should sell them for thousands of dollars to rich dingdongs on the upper east side. Take them for every penny you can get.

MARGIE: I'm telling you, Gina, it's a great idea. I could be your sales representative and all you'd have to do is sit around and knit all day. Which is what you do anyway.

GINA: That's true.

MARGIE: Then you could use the profits to buy more yarn.

GINA: You don't think it would be bad for me to just, you know, run away like that?

PAULA: Actually—

MARGIE: Oh, so what if it is? Look, let's face it, Gina. You played by all the rules and got fucked. Running away seems like a pretty good option to me.

PAULA: Margie, I don't think you should be—

MARGIE: What? It's true. My therapist tells me this shit. That guy you sent me to, Paula, I mean it, he's great. He says avoidance is like a great tactic for a while because it gives you time to get your shit together before you go back to war. He says life really is a war, and women don't quite get that because they're different from men, but that's the way men see it, so we better get used to it. I love this guy. He tells me the most useful shit.

PAULA: Be that as it may; what's useful for you is not necessarily as useful for Gina.

GINA: It sounds useful.

MARGIE: Oh, yeah, it's great. I feel much better.

GINA: So I could just stay home and knit all day.

MARGIE: Yeah.

GINA: That sounds useful, Paula. Margie, what's this guy's name?

MARGIE: I got his card here somewhere. *(She hunts in her purse.)*

BOB: *(Desperately casual.)* Where's Liz?

PAULA: I think she had a date tonight.

BOB: A date, huh? So who'd she go out with?

PAULA: I don't know.

BOB: *(Quiet, to Paula.)* Come on, Paula, give me a break. I've been trying to get a hold of her for two weeks. She won't even talk to me.

PAULA: Well, maybe she's come to her senses. Granted, that's unlikely with you guys.

GINA: Are you talking about me?

PAULA: No! Gina, of course not.

GINA: I wouldn't blame you if you were. I lost it last week. Did they tell you?

BOB: Well, Lily did mention it.

GINA: Complete crackup. It was quite a scene.

BOB: I'm sorry I missed it.

PAULA: Bob was just wondering where Liz was. Because it's our knitting night.

MARGIE: Oh, Liz isn't very serious about knitting. I mean, she's even worse at it than I am. If that's possible.

GINA: She doesn't take it seriously. She doesn't understand.

BOB: I know, I just thought… *(Intimate, to Margie.)* A date, huh? So who'd she go out with?

PAULA: *(Loud.)* Why don't we ask your wife?

LILY: *(Reenters.)* Ask me what?

PAULA: Who Liz went out with tonight.

LILY: *(Abrupt.)* I don't know.

MARGIE: Dates. Man, I am so over that. I told that dating service to go jump in the lake, did I tell you?

LILY: Good for you, Margie.

MARGIE: Yeah, therapy is much more rewarding. I'm just going to do this father-mentor transference thing for a while. It's so much easier than dealing with men. Present company excepted, of course.

BOB: Thanks, Margie.

MARGIE: So, you ready to learn how to cast on?

BOB: Oh. I guess so.

MARGIE: Gina, you show him. I'll just confuse him.

GINA: *(Shy.)* He doesn't really want to know how to knit.

BOB: Sure I do. That's why I'm here.

GINA: Really?

LILY: Oh, really, Bob, don't you think you're carrying this just a bit—

BOB: I want to learn how to knit, Lily. If it's not too much trouble.

LILY: *(Pause.)* I just think your time might be better spent working on your book, or applying for other positions. Daddy says that it's not going to be easy for you to come up with something in this market, especially if we want to stay in the city.

(Pause.)

BOB: Well, tell him thanks for the advice, would you, hon? I never thought of that.

(Bob and Lily stare at each other for a brief, tense moment. Margie tiptoes away. The others notice but do not comment.)

BOB: Gina. How about that lesson?

GINA: Oh. Okay. We'll start you off on big needles because they're a little easier to handle, and also the knitting goes faster, so it's more fun, you know; you start seeing progress right away. You'll be knitting a scarf. *(She hunts through her basket and comes up with a big pair of needles and some yarn.)*

BOB: Okay.

GINA: Now, first what you should do, even before I show you how to cast on, is hold the needles, just hold them, one in each hand, for just however long it takes to get used to them. Feel the metal. It's nice, isn't it? Feel how smooth they are. They're your friends. *(She puts the needles in his hands and holds them there.)*

BOB: They are?

GINA: Yes. Actually, that's the problem Liz always had with knitting. She never made friends with her needles. She thought they were her enemies.

BOB: She did?

GINA: Well, she's not a very peaceful person.

BOB: No, she's not.

GINA: She's very combative.

BOB: Yes, she is.

GINA: Have you made friends with your needles yet?

BOB: Well, just a second…okay. Okay. I think I'm ready.

(She looks at him to make sure. He smiles at her calmly. Pause. She smiles back.)

GINA: You're a very nice person, Bob.

BOB: *(Gentle.)* Thank you, Gina.

LILY: Yes, my husband is a real prince.

GINA: *(Startled, unsure.)* Well, he is.

LILY: *(Suddenly pulls sharply at her own knitting, which seems to have a knot in it. The yarn snaps.)* Oh, damn it.

(They all stare at her.)

MARGIE: Is something wrong, Lily? You seem like, kind of uptight or something.

LILY: No. I'm sorry. I'm sorry. I'm just a little preoccupied. I was thinking about something else.

LIZ: And what would that be, Lily?

(All jump a little, startled. Liz steps out from behind a pile of sweaters that obscures the door. Her clothing and hair are quite tousled. She smokes a cigarette and stalks into the room. In one hand she carries the notebook.)

MARGIE: Liz! What are you doing here?

LIZ: Well, I was just kind of cruising the city with this guy I had dinner with, and I realized I was in the neighborhood. So I had him drop me off. Hi, Bob.

BOB: Hey, Lizzie. How was your date?

LIZ: Oh, it was interesting. You're taking up knitting, huh? I hope you're better at it than I am.

BOB: By all reports I could hardly be worse.

LIZ: Boy, that's the fucking truth, isn't it?

GINA: Liz, could you not smoke in here? It gets into the yarn, you know, and it's very hard to get out.

LIZ: Oh, sure. *(She drops the butt on the floor and steps on it.)*

GINA: *(Irritated.)* Liz! Not on the—my God, you have no, you just— *(Gina picks it up.)*

LIZ: *(Cool.)* Sorry.

LILY: I'll go get that tea.

LIZ: Oh, fuck the tea, Lily. Don't you want to hear about my exciting date?

LILY: Not particularly. *(Pause.)* You're a mess.

LIZ: Yeah, no kidding. I just had a little bit of a tussle with this guy in the back seat of his car. A big, pretty Rolls. He had something I wanted. And when I got it, guess what I found out? I found out that where I was, my friends had been before me. *(She looks through the pages for a moment and hands several to Margie.)*

MARGIE: What? Where'd you get this?

LIZ: From your pal Miles. Actually, I guess he's Lily's pal. Here, Paula, I thought you might like a souvenir. *(She hands her her pages.)*

PAULA: Thank you.

LIZ: You did very well, actually; he thought you were quite intelligent and striking, for a black woman. He was going to give you a call back but decided that his Japanese associates would never understand. Don't take it too hard; he really hated Margie. He thought she was pathetic.

GINA: What are you guys talking about?

MARGIE: *(Reading.)* He doesn't say pathetic. He says I'm lovely, in a pathetic way. I mean, geez, Liz—

LIZ: For crying out loud, Margie—

MARGIE: Oh, so what? The guy was a creep.

BOB: I'm sorry; I'm having a little trouble catching up with this. What are all these pages?

LIZ: They're notes. Miles takes notes.

(She throws the notebook onto the table. Bob looks at it, confused.)

PAULA: Lily, what is this? You set us all up with this guy?

BOB: What guy? Miles? That creep from your father's building?

LIZ: Yeah. All three of us have been on dates with the creep from Daddy's building. All right, Lily. I'm willing to give you the benefit of the doubt. You meant well, didn't you? You didn't know you were setting me up on the date from hell. Right?

LILY: I guess that means you two didn't get along.

LIZ: Lily! I told you I was a complete mess, and you sent me on a date with the Terminator!

LILY: Well, I'm sorry it didn't work out. I'll give this back to him when I see him. *(She takes the notebook from Bob and puts it with her knitting things.)*

LIZ: You did. You knew about all of it. You've even read that notebook, haven't you?

LILY: Miles is a good friend. We share everything with each other.

MARGIE: Lily—

PAULA: *(Overlap.)* What were you thinking?

GINA: So you set everybody up with this guy except me?

(They all stare at her. The tea kettle whistles in the kitchen.)

LIZ: Gina. Go make us all some tea.

LILY: It's all right, I'll do it.

LIZ: No, you stay here. I have some questions for you.

(Pause. Liz and Lily stare at each other. Gina does not know what to do.)

LIZ: Gina! Get the fucking tea!

GINA: All right! *(She exits to the kitchen.)*

LILY: Really, Liz, I don't know what you're so worked up about.

LIZ: I'll tell you what I'm worked up about. You've been pretending to take care of all of us while setting us up on dates with a guy who hates women!

LILY: Really? He seems rather fond of me.

LIZ: Lily, he's one step away from a sociopath—

LILY: He took each of you to an exquisite restaurant. I hardly think that makes him a sociopath.

LIZ: He treated us like bugs. He would've taken blood if there was a socially acceptable way to do it. He's probably back at that restaurant right now, trying to figure one out…

LILY: *(Overlap.)* This is classic. All my single friends constantly complain about how there are no good men out there, and I actually find one, rich, powerful, handsome and all you can do is complain about his table manners! Well…

LIZ: *(Overlap.)* …Do I ask her for it politely, or just suck it out of her veins while she's not looking?

LILY: *(Overlap.)* …Perhaps if he had been married you would have gotten along better!

(Pause.)

LIZ: Oh, that's what this is about, isn't it?

MARGIE: That's what what is about?

PAULA: Margie, maybe you and I should—

LILY: I don't know what you mean.

MARGIE: Neither do I.

LIZ: I was fucking Bob, and she's mad about it.

> *(Pause.)*

MARGIE: Oh.

GINA: *(Enters with a tray with several teacups, a teapot, and a box of cookies.)* Okay, here's the tea. It's just Lipton, I hope that's okay. And there's some cookies that Lily brought. You're much better at this than I am, Lily, I just get so wrapped up in the knitting I forget the other part of it. But this should do us, huh? Okay. Dig in! So. What did I miss?

MARGIE: Uh...actually, Gina...

PAULA: Apparently, Liz has been sleeping with Bob.

MARGIE: And she thinks Lily is mad about it. So...that's what we were talking about.

> *(Pause.)*

GINA: Really? Oh. *(Pause.)* Bob? You were sleeping with Liz? But—

BOB: Yeah, Gina, I know.

GINA: Lily? Did you know about this?

LILY: As a matter of fact I did, Gina, and it's really not my concern. *(She sits and starts pouring tea.)*

GINA: It's not?

LILY: No. It's none of my business.

MARGIE: Aren't you mad about it?

LILY: Not particularly.

MARGIE: Oh, come on, Lily—

LILY: Margie, really, I don't care! *(Lily picks up her knitting and knits.)* Really. It doesn't matter. If you want details, you'll have to ask Liz and Bob. I had nothing to say about it while it was happening, and I have nothing to say about it now that it's over.

BOB: Who said it was over?

LILY: Oh, I'm sorry. Liz lead me to understand that you two had decided not to see each other anymore. That's not true?

BOB: No. That's not true.

LILY: That's not what Liz told me.

LIZ: Bob.

BOB: What?

LILY: Oh, did you two get your signals crossed? What a shame. And it didn't work out with Miles, either! Really, Liz. You just have a terrible time with men, don't you?

LIZ: Not all that terrible. Miles liked me a lot. I mean, how do you think I got that notebook?

(Pause.)

LILY: I have no idea.

LIZ: I'll give you this; he's a good kisser. He was interested in taking things further, but you know, it actually occurred to me, against all odds, it occurred to me that I was about to become everything I hate. So I stopped it. He was fine about it. He may have even been relieved; I have a feeling he was getting worried that I was going to scratch the interior of the Rolls.

MARGIE: So what happened then?

(Paula whacks her.)

MARGIE: What? This is better than the movies!

LIZ: He's sending the car back for me. We're going to rendezvous in that restaurant. Apparently, those little booths can be used for all sorts of activities.

LILY: No. Not you. You are not the one he wants.

LIZ: You are amazing. You are just—I mean, what, was I supposed to fail, is that the turn on for you, watching this guy go through us, one after the other? Well, I didn't fail, all right?

LILY: Good for you. I'm sure I'll read all about it.

BOB: Okay, okay, this is...I'm sorry, Lily. It should never have come to this. Come on, Liz. We'd better go.

LIZ: What?

BOB: I think the decent thing to do is go back to your place and let things cool down.

LIZ: That's not going to cool things down! Besides...Bob, I don't want you at my place. It's not going to solve anything, Bob.

BOB: Lizzie.

LIZ: Bob. Go.

(Pause.)

BOB: *(To all.)* I'm sorry. This is...a little disorienting and, uh...I, I'm going to take a walk. *(He turns to go.)*

LILY: Bob?

BOB: *(Pause.)* What?

LILY: Don't go home. All right?

BOB: Lily…

LILY: No. When I go home, I don't expect to see you there.

(After a moment, Bob is gone.)

GINA: Bob, wait— *(He is gone.)* He forgot his needles.

LILY: It's all right; I'll give them to him, Gina.

LIZ: Look, Lily, I'm sorry about what happened with Bob. I really am.

LILY: I have NOTHING to say to you. *(She takes the needles from Gina.)*

GINA: Are you going to see him, though?

LIZ: I was trying to end it—

LILY: Not as hard as you tried to begin it.

LIZ: That's not true!

PAULA: We should go.

(She stands, nudging Margie. Gina grabs the needles back.)

GINA: I mean, you told him not to go home.

LILY: Oh for God's sake, Gina!

PAULA: Gina, I don't think this is any of our business. In fact, the three of us should go.

MARGIE: Oh, for crying out loud, what kind of therapist are you? Things really start to heat up and all you want to do is leave.

GINA: Besides, why should I leave? I live here.

MARGIE: I think you should go back to the sushi restaurant, Liz. Take Miles for the biggest ride of his life.

PAULA: Margie!

MARGIE: What? I know, I said rich people were crazy. They are crazy. But, they have a lot of money. Why shouldn't she take advantage of it? If she goes after Bob, she's just going to have to live with the fact that she stole her sister's husband. I mean, they even have a kid. She can't do that! But, if she goes with Miles, she ends up with a guy who, like, owns half the city.

LIZ: Oh, and you don't think the fact that I find him completely repulsive is going to get in the way?

MARGIE: It hasn't so far. Come on, Liz. You can do it. It's your only chance.

PAULA: Chance for what?

MARGIE: I don't know! Chance for anything! What else is she going to do, fucking knit for the rest of her life?

PAULA: I think she has a few more options than—

MARGIE: I don't think she does!

GINA: She has Bob!

PAULA:

You're telling her to
sell herself to the highest
bidder!

MARGIE:

You bet I am! She could
be one of those trophy
wives, only with brains.
Think about it! She'll be
like a spy in the White
House or something. Like
Nancy Reagan, only on our
side.

MARGIE:

For whatever reason,
she's the one he wants, and
that's the only way to
control these guys. Like,
they hate women, but they
love sex. So you get in
there and distract them,
then whammo.

PAULA:

Christ, what has that
guy been telling you? Two
weeks in therapy, and
you're a complete monster!

MARGIE:

Paula, confrontation is a
good thing.

LIZ:

I don't have Bob, and I
think this is all a little
more complicated than
which boy I end up with!

GINA:

Well if you don't want
Bob, can I have him?

LIZ:

We are not passing
around men here!

GINA: Why not, they do it to us.

LIZ:

Margie! Gina, that
doesn't make it right!

GINA:

Right, wrong, who
cares, can I have Bob?

LIZ:

Look. This is not about
men! My God, I am sick to
death of discussing my life
in terms of those assholes
when my sister and I would
gladly kill each other if
given half a chance! It
seems to me that that is at
least worth a passing
mention!

LIZ: Besides, there are more than two men out there!

MARGIE: Yeah, but the rest of them are gay.

PAULA: So what if they are! We don't need them! We live most of our lives
without them anyway! If you get ten minutes of their attention a day,

you got a successful marriage on your hands! The rest of the time, they're reading the sports page or doing their little deals or slapping each other's behinds! Don't tell me about men, I know men! They do without us just fine. And we do without them. I say we leave it that way.

MARGIE: My point exactly. Any way you look at it, they're going to make you miserable, so you might as well take the one with the money.

PAULA: Honestly, Margie—

MARGIE: What? If you hate men so much why did you go on that damn date in the first place? Why did you sit there, letting him take notes on you?

LIZ: Why did any of us?

GINA: Because we're polite. And nobody wants to be alone.

(They look at her.)

GINA: What? I'd rather have Bob, but I'd at least go on a date with Miles. I mean, there's always a chance, isn't there? That you'll be the one he's nice to. There's always hope.

(They all sit and think about this.)

LIZ: What do you think, Lily?

LILY: I think you slept with my husband, Liz.

(Pause.)

LIZ: I'm sorry.

LILY: *(Reaches for her knitting.)* Yes, you should be. And if you don't mind, I would really prefer not to talk about this anymore. I mean, I just, it's my life, you know, and you're all just tossing it around as if it were nothing, as if—never mind. What a mess. *(She starts to clean.)*

GINA: That's okay, Lily, I kind of like it like this.

LILY: Don't be ridiculous, Gina. There is a mess here, and I will clean it up. That's the kind of person I am. You can't live in messes. Of course, I am living in the middle of a big mess, but I will take care of it! *(She continues to clean violently.)* That's your whole problem, Liz, you don't have anyone to take care of. You're just floating and drifting, with nothing to hold you down. You're just like a man, aren't you? That's what's wrong with you. That's the only thing the matter with any of you. If you had someone. A daughter. A husband. Someone to take care of. That's all we need. To be happy.

(Liz reaches over to touch her. Lily shrugs her off.)

LILY: I could have been happy. I am happy. It wasn't *my* failure. Liz! The perfect man. I hardly think so. The perfect man doesn't let everything, work, family, everything, he let it slip away like it was nothing, like…My father is paying our mortgage. Did you know that? It's humiliating! Liz won't take money from him, and we have to! And then there's Liz. Well, I don't care, all right? I don't care!

LIZ: Lily?

LILY: I'm fine! But it's not easy listening to you all complain about Miles. If it had been me, none of this would have happened. If it had been me, it would have been fine! He's the one I understand! If I were with Miles, I could have another child. Did you ever think of that? We'd have the money for everything, pre-school, piano lessons, college. Everything. Miles is the person who takes care of those things. You all act as if he were…but if he weren't there, what do you think would happen? To any of us? None of it worked! Nothing. I don't know what's going on. I don't even like my daughter anymore, she's like a stranger, she's just another woman, she's…

LIZ: Lily. Lily. Shhh. Shh. *(She holds her.)*

LILY: You're the one they want. No matter what I do. Why?

LIZ: No, I'm not, Lily. It was always you. I'm just a big old mess. And you were always so good.

LILY: Oh, people hate you when you're good. I would've tried being bad, once in a while, but I could never be as bad as you, so what was the point? *(She suddenly pushes her away and turns away. Liz does not know what to do. Lily looks at all the others. They look back.)*

LILY: Oh, dear. Now you're all staring at me. Yes, it's true. I'm as big a mess as the rest of you.

(They all laugh a little.)

GINA: Not me.

(They stare at each other. Blackout.)

SCENE VIII

The sushi restaurant. Two men stand in profile with their arms akimbo, as if they were about to draw their weapons. The lights come up, revealing that it is Miles and Bob. Tableau. They break tableau and shake hands.

BOB: Miles.

MILES: Bob, is it?

BOB: Imagine. Bumping into you like this. Mind if I join you? *(He sits.)* So, you've been having a little raw fish, huh, Miles?

MILES: Yes. I have.

BOB: It's kind of the new machismo, isn't it? Nobody eats steak anymore. It's all raw fish. Why is that, I wonder?

MILES: It's good for you.

BOB: There you go! How about a drink? *(He pulls out a small bottle of scotch and pours two drinks into glasses on the table.)*

MILES: Well, I don't, usually, but perhaps I'd better.

BOB: So. Miles. I'm glad I ran into you. It's nice to finally have an opportunity to get to know you a little. I mean, Lily raves about you. As far as she's concerned, you walk on water.

MILES: I'm very fond of your wife. She's been a good friend to me.

BOB: Oh, Lily's terrific.

MILES: She's the finest woman I know.

BOB: Don't I know it. She's the perfect wife. Of course, Liz is something else altogether. Have you met Liz? Lily's sister?

MILES: As a matter of fact, that's who I'm waiting for.

BOB: Really? You know Liz.

MILES: Yes.

BOB: She's great.

MILES: Yes, she is.

BOB: I've slept with them both, you know.

MILES: *(Pause.)* Yes, I did know that.

BOB: Oh. You did.

MILES: Lily and I are friends. She tells me everything.

BOB: Well, isn't that cozy?

MILES: Are you all right, Bob?

BOB: No, as a matter of fact, I'm not all right. This morning I was all right. This morning, I had a wonderful wife, and a wonderful daughter, and a wonderful girlfriend. And tonight, I don't have anything. So, I'm not all right.

MILES: Perhaps you wanted too much.

BOB: Hey. Don't you talk to me about wanting too much, Mr. I Own Everything. I just got a real good look at your car out there. And might I add, that's quite a parking space. So, don't talk to me about wanting too much.

MILES: Shouldn't you go home, Bob?

BOB: Yes, Miles, I probably should, but that's the problem. I don't have a home anymore! So, I thought I'd come talk to you instead. Everyone seems to be quite concerned with you, so I thought I'd try to figure out why. You don't seem so great.

MILES: Neither do you.

BOB: Well, touché to that. Have some more scotch. These glasses are much too small. I'm drunk. *(He pours them both a drink.)*

MILES: Yes, I can see that.

BOB: Well, aren't you perceptive. What a gift. Don't we all wish we were you, Mr. Miles Perfect Wonderful.

MILES: What are you doing, Bob?

BOB: I'm picking a fight! I'm trying to get you to punch me in the nose!

MILES: That's not likely, Bob.

BOB: No?

MILES: No.

BOB: Well, then maybe I'll punch you in the nose!

MILES: That's not likely, either.

BOB: You don't think so, huh?

(Bob swings or shoves Miles, who moves quickly out of the way, causing Bob to trip into a big pratfall. Miles picks him up.)

MILES: All right. I've had just about enough of this. Just understand: The only reason I'm not taking you apart is because I'm expecting someone, and I don't want to mess up my suit. But you're leaving. Now. *(He shoves him out of the restaurant, sits, and pours himself a drink.)*

BOB: *(Off.)* She's not coming!

MILES: I think I was very explicit about what's supposed to happen now, Bob.

BOB: *(Reentering.)* She's standing you up. How do you think I got here? The Rolls came back for her, and brought me instead. By the way, you're going to need to restock your wet bar.

(Bob sits, waving his bottle. Miles looks at him coldly.)

MILES: What did you do?

BOB: I didn't do anything. You underestimated her, Miles.

MILES: I'm really very irritated with you, Bob.

BOB: You kiss well, but other than that, she wasn't impressed. Compared you to a mosquito. Or maybe it was just a kind of generic blood sucker. I can't remember the specifics. But she's not coming back. She's standing you up.

MILES: That's not possible.

BOB: Possible or not, your chauffeur and I got along famously. Yeah, women are a mystery, and that's the truth. I mean, I thought when I married Lizzie, I...no, she's not the one I married. I married the other one, didn't I? Huh. Even then I wasn't sure why. Even then, I sort of wanted the other one. There was something so sad about her. I mean, you should have seen her in that dress. It was all pink, and it had this puffy stuff around the shoulders. She was supposed to be the maid of honor, you know, and she kept sneaking off to smoke a cigarette. Her father caught her. I saw it. She was out in the hallway, smoking a cigarette, and he came out and sort of took her by the arm, you know, and he said something, and then she said something, and then he smacked her, right on the face, he hit her, and she didn't flinch, she stood her ground, but she looked so—I shouldn't have seen it. I was supposed to be making the rounds with Lily. And Lily looked great; she was perfect. All in white. Lace, something. It could have worked out. If I'd finished my book in time. If Lizzie hadn't worn that pink dress. It all just, it left room for doubt, you know? And now here I am, trying to explain it to you, and and you have no soul. Why am I here? Why don't you have a soul, Miles?

MILES: Frankly, Bob, I find your questions fatuous and irrelevant. If your marriage and your career have not gone as smoothly as you might have hoped, that's not my concern. I do what I have to to get what I want; I am what I say I am, and I never pretend to be anything else. So if you're having a problem here, I suggest you deal with it and stop whining. You people. When it doesn't work out with me, all of you, you comfort yourselves with the idea that I have no soul. But I have a soul. It's you who are lost. I have what you want. Power. Money. Status. All of these things that you yearn for, I worked for and I claimed. Look at history. What do we remember? War. What do we care about? Power. What do we live for? Money. Am I getting through to you, Bob? I have more soul than any of you, because I know who we are. I know what we are. I alone am real.

BOB: *(Sincere.)* That's the saddest thing I've ever heard. You're a very lonely person, aren't you?

MILES: Bob. I think you should tell me what Liz is up to, then go home and save your marriage.

BOB: I can't. It's over. I'm lonely, and you're lonely, Miles. Women. They're the ones who brought us to this. The world would be a better place without them. And I like them. I mean, I'm one of those guys who actually likes them. But even I can't help thinking: What would it be like, without them? If there were no women? You and I could just get together, have a few drinks, slug it out, and then have babies. That's probably how it would work.

MILES: Look, are you going to tell me what Liz is doing, or not?

BOB: Forget about Liz! What do I know about Liz? I want to talk about Lily! You've been sleeping with my wife, haven't you?

MILES: *(Pause. Steely.)* That would be adultery, Bob. Some people don't believe in adultery.

BOB: Oh. I forgot.

MILES: Yes. You did. *(Pause.)* God, she is wasted on you.

BOB: What?

MILES: Lily! I've said to her, your husband is a loser. He is an invertebrate! It's inexplicable why anyone would even talk to that bozo. She claims that occasionally, you have a certain charm. I don't see it. Anyway, the fact is, she's used goods. But, she has a sister, and the sister turns out to be an interesting woman. A pain in the ass, but in a very interesting way. We almost do it. In the car. But she has reservations, and I'm a little worried about the upholstery. So we postpone it. But she's late, Bob. She was supposed to be here, and she's standing me up, so all of a sudden, I'm stuck on a date with you, and not only that, I'm thinking, she'll sleep with him, but not with me? You want to know something, Bob? I resent you. Times are changing, and I don't like it. Women are going for pathetic losers like you. WHY?

BOB: I think it's because we talk to them.

MILES: Yeah, right. *(He pours himself some more scotch.)*

BOB: Lily said, I have a certain charm?

MILES: Shut up. *(Impatient, he drinks from the bottle.)*

BOB: Maybe she does still love me. Who else would put up with me?

MILES: You're not coming home with me, Bob.

BOB: You think she'd take me back? Lily, I mean.

MILES: Oh, for heaven's sake, which one of them do you want?

BOB: I don't know! If I did, do you think I'd be here on this stupid date with you? I mean, Lizzie's great, but Lily's been my life! Lily and Adelaide. Adelaide's a good kid. Sweet. Thoughtful. Always watching, you know those kids who don't say much but you know they see everything. She's going to be in therapy forever. Oh, God. What am I going to do?

MILES: Well, if you want Lily back, you could try making a little more money. Get a job with her father and buy her a nice dress once in a while, would you?

BOB: God knows I'm sick of academia. And it might be nice to actually make a little money for once.

MILES: Duh, Bob.

BOB: Lily and I used to get along great. We could again! All I have to do is…make more money. I don't know. It seems to me it's got to be more complicated than that.

(Miles shakes his head.)

BOB: Women. They're a mystery, all right. If only I could figure out what I want from them…What do you want from them, Miles?

MILES: (Thinking about this.) Comfort. Beauty.

BOB: (Excited.) Comfort! Beauty!

MILES: A nice meal once in a while.

BOB: A nice meal…

MILES: Sex.

BOB: Well, yes, there's always that. Sex.

MILES: Besides. A man shouldn't be alone.

BOB: No. We shouldn't. I think they'll take us back. They will.

MILES: You're making this up as you go along, aren't you?

BOB: Miles, I know women. And believe it or not, they're just as confused as we are.

MILES: They are?

BOB: Completely lost. Like us. In fact, in a lot of ways, they're like us. Except that they're also…very forgiving. They'll take us back. And until then, at least we have each other.

(Miles stares at him. Blackout.)

SCENE IX

Lily holds out a plate of banana bread to Gina and Paula, as in scene one. Margie stands to one side, holding her knitting. All three take banana bread and start to eat it.

LILY: I tried a new recipe this week. I hope you like it.

GINA: Really? A new recipe!

PAULA: It's delicious, Lily.

LILY: Do you like it?

GINA: Oh, it's wonderful.

LILY: It has chocolate chips in it. At first, I was a little worried that it might be too rich. I mean, too much sugar can drive you a little crazy, can't it? And there really is an awful lot of caffeine in chocolate. Also, I read an article about food allergies in the *Times* this week, and some people are terribly allergic to chocolate, did you know that? There was a teenager in Florida who *died* from eating a bowl of chili because there was the tiniest bit of chocolate in it. Chocolate in a bowl of chili, who would've thought? Deadly.

(Beat. They all set their banana bread down.)

PAULA: So, where's Liz? I tried calling her this week, but her machine was on—

MARGIE: Yeah, when I called it just rang—

LILY: Really? Gina, look, I've started a new sweater.

GINA: You have?

LILY: Yes, I finished that one for Adelaide. She looks adorable in it.

GINA: How is Adelaide?

LILY: Oh, she's fine. Just great.

PAULA: How's Bob?

LILY: He's fine too. He's home now. And guess what, Gina? Adelaide's teaching him how to knit!

GINA: *(Appreciative.)* Awwww!

MARGIE: Yeah, that sounds healthy.

PAULA: So how's Liz? Did you two get a chance to—

LILY: Gina, could you look at this for me? I'm not sure which way I'm supposed to loop it.

GINA: Oh, sure…

MARGIE: Lily, why are we—

LILY: How's your sweater coming, Margie?

MARGIE: It's coming along just fine, Lily. Thanks for asking. I was just kind of looking at the different pieces the other day and thinking, you know, this really is lovely, in a pathetic way.

PAULA: You know, it is!

MARGIE: Yeah, yours looks good, too.

PAULA: I think it's quite intelligent and striking.

PAULA AND MARGIE: For a black woman. *(They laugh.)*

LILY: I don't know what's the matter with the two of you tonight.

MARGIE: Well, what's going on here? I mean, are we supposed to just keep knitting like nothing happened?

LILY: I don't know what you mean.

PAULA: Oh, come on, Lily. Last week—

LILY: Last week is over.

MARGIE: No it's not. I talked to my therapist about you, Lily.

LILY: Oh, good.

MARGIE: He thinks what you did is really fucked up.

LILY: I'm so glad you sent Margie into therapy, Paula. Really. It's always so wonderful to hear what a total stranger thinks about my life—

PAULA: *(Overlap.)* Maybe you should try it yourself, Lily. I agree with Margie. What you did *is* fucked up!

GINA: *(Overlap.)* You guys. You guys!

MARGIE: *(Overlap.)* And where's Liz, anyway? Is she, like, just out of the group now? I mean, do we get to say anything about anything anymore?

LILY: *(Overlap.)* I don't know where Liz is and I really don't care!
(Liz enters.)

LIZ: Hey, you guys! Sorry I'm late. I got stuck on the subway. Wow. What's this, chocolate chips?
(They all stare as she drops her knitting, picks up a piece of banana bread and eats.)

LILY: What are you doing here?

LIZ: It's our knitting night.

LILY: You're not welcome here.

PAULA: Lily!

LIZ: Gina, is that true? I'm not welcome?

GINA: Oh! I don't—oh—

LIZ: Lily, you can refuse to talk to me on the phone—

LILY: Gina?

LIZ: —and you can not let me into your house, but you can't kick me out of Gina's apartment.

LILY: Gina? If Liz stays, I'm going to have to leave.

GINA: Oh. Can't we just knit?

LILY: No, Gina. We can't. It's Liz or me.

MARGIE: Come on, don't pick on Gina—

LILY: I'm not picking on anyone. *(Pause.)* Fine. *(She starts to pack.)*

LIZ: Aw, Lily, please don't do this. I just want to talk.

LILY: What you want, Liz, is not a high priority with me right now.

LIZ: Come on! What happened was bad, but we could work through it. Last week, when you were falling apart we were almost communicating—

LILY: Oh, now you want me to fall apart again! That's lovely—

LIZ: Please! Do we have to go back to this?

LILY: One hug and I'm supposed to forgive you everything, is that it?

LIZ: You're just supposed to talk to me! We never talk! We just—resent each other, and, and pick at each other, all our lives, that's all it's ever been! You're my big sister! I want you to like me!

LILY: And that's why you slept with my husband, I suppose. Very effective reasoning, Liz. Once again, your logic is right on track.

MARGIE: You guys?

LIZ: Look, I'm not the only one at fault here. I mean, all this shit with Miles was hardly innocent.

LILY: I set you up on a bad date! You slept with my husband! It's not exactly the same thing!

LIZ: I'm *sorry*, okay? That just *happened*, I didn't—

LILY: It didn't just happen! You did it deliberately! You're so obsessed with honesty, why don't you just try it yourself once in awhile.

PAULA: You guys.

LIZ: *(Overlap.)* Could you stop accusing me and just—TRY? To communicate! God—I mean—we're sisters! Can't we just try?

LILY: *(Overlap.)* No. I don't want to try. I don't want to understand you. Frankly, I don't even want to know you.
(Pause.)

LIZ: Fine. That's fine with me. I never liked you anyway. Now, at least I don't have to pretend.

LILY: You're self-centered and thoughtless.

LIZ: Yeah, well, you're controlling and frigid.

LILY: You're a hypocrite and a liar!

LIZ: Not anymore! I admit it, ALL RIGHT? I fucked him to get at you! I fucked your husband, and the whole time, I was thinking about *you*.

MARGIE/GINA/PAULA: Liz! Geez, Liz…For heaven's sake! Liz!

LIZ: *(Abashed.)* Sorry.

MARGIE: You know, you guys, I could be wrong, but when Gloria Steinem said we should get together and communicate, I don't think this is what she meant.

PAULA: Me neither. I'm out of here.

GINA: You're going? Already? Are we meeting here next week?

PAULA: You may be, Gina. But I think I'm gonna pass.

MARGIE: Me too.

LILY: What?

PAULA: You heard me. I mean, what the hell are we coming here for? So we can sit around and listen to you two take each other apart? I mean, Jesus. It's hard enough just living in the world without getting jerked around by your knitting group.

MARGIE: Especially if you can't even knit.

PAULA: *(To Liz and Lily.)* Whatever this is—I hope you two work it out. *(She starts to pack.)*

GINA: Margie?

MARGIE: Sorry, Gina.

GINA: No, come on, you can't go! It's just Liz, again, unraveling everything—

LIZ: Would you give me a break? That's not what it is this time! I came here to try to put things back together for once! I know I've been a shit! I know! But I was hoping...I don't know what I was hoping. Just don't go.

PAULA: It's not just you, Liz. Lily's been lying to everybody. And enough is enough.

GINA: Lily.

LILY: What?

GINA: Say something. Say something to keep them here.

LILY: I don't care if they go.

LIZ: Yes, you do.

LILY: No, I don't!

GINA: Well, I do. What would have happened to me if you weren't here? Paula? Margie? Lily, ask them to stay. Please. Go. Tell them you're sorry. *(Pause.)*

LILY: I'm sorry.
(Pause.)

PAULA: That's it? Man. Don't you know anything about human behavior? I want to stay! I don't want to go! But you got to give me something here. Come on, Lily. Would you give us a little something?

LILY: All right. I admit that maybe Miles is...a little...hostile.

MARGIE/LIZ/PAULA: *(Overlaps.)* A little? A LITTLE? A little.

LILY: Okay! He is hostile. And maybe...I was feeling competitive. And maybe... it made me feel...superior...to see him...reject you.

MARGIE: *That's* supposed to keep us here?

LILY: I thought you wanted the truth!

MARGIE: Maybe we should go back to lying.

LIZ: Lying is what got us here.

PAULA: I prefer the truth. *(To Lily.)* Thank you.

LILY: I'm sorry. I shouldn't have done it. It's just—I was feeling so terrible. Things were going wrong even before Bob...you know. And then I met Miles, who was always so—

MARGIE: Rich.

LILY: Wonderful. He made me feel...perfect. Then he asked if I had any friends. Since I wasn't available. I didn't want him to want any of you. I wanted him to want me, and see that no one else would do. My husband was having an affair with my sister. Being with Miles was the only thing that made me feel worth anything at all.

LIZ: Lily…

LILY: I know, that doesn't make it all right for him to be mean to everyone else. I'm sorry. In spite of everything, I've always found men like that to be such a temptation.

LIZ: Hey. Don't talk to me about it. He embodies everything I hate, and I still spent half an hour making out with him in the back seat of his car. *(Pause.)*

LILY: What was it like?

LIZ: Lily…

MARGIE: Oh, come on, Liz, we're all dying to know.

PAULA: *(Overlap.)* I have to admit to more than a passing curiosity…

GINA: *(Overlap.)* I wanted to ask, but I thought it might be rude…

MARGIE: *(Overlap.)* Spill it!

(They all clamor and sit around her.)

LIZ: *(Sad.)* It was wild. You feel the city all around you, just spinning by, and all of it, it's all yours. It really made me think about all those rocks stars and movie moguls I always complain about, and I realized: Groupies are not as stupid as they look. It scared me, how great it was. Just letting some guy give you things, take care of you, make you someone just by being with him. *(Pause.)* And now he keeps calling me.

PAULA: He does?

LIZ: Well, he doesn't actually call. He sends the Rolls by. Every night, I watch it from my window, cutting slowly through the drug addicts like a big silver shark. He thinks he's going to win me. *(Pensive.)* And who knows? Maybe he will.

MARGIE: Either that, or he's going to lose his hubcaps.

PAULA: Liz, I have one word of advice for you: Don't be such a fucking moron! Stay away from that guy! He's bad news! Act like an adult for once in your life, would you?

LIZ: I'm trying! I'm here, aren't I?

MARGIE: Yeah, what do you need him for? We have Gina.

LIZ: What?

MARGIE: The woman's a gold mine. Look at this place. We're going into business. You could get in on the ground floor.

LIZ: I could?

(Margie helps her into a sweater.)

MARGIE: Look at the quality of the work here. You won't find that in any department store. For a mere five hundred dollars, that sweater can be yours.

GINA: Margie, you said a thousand.

MARGIE: *(Handing out sweaters.)* I priced them out at Missoni. We gotta be realistic. I mean it, we're gonna do this, Gina. I talked to my therapist about it, and he thinks it's a great idea. He says self-empowerment is the way to go here.

PAULA: Margie, if you're just doing what this guy tells you to do, it's not self-empowerment.

MARGIE: What?

LILY: I don't know, Margie. When we started this group, it was supposed to be a haven, not a business.

MARGIE: Yeah. Some haven. Besides, Lily, you have to be practical. That guy Miles may have a big old Rolls, but we've got sweaters. Which would you rather have on a cold winter night?

LILY: Yeah, that's a tough one.

(Gina stares at them, transfixed by the sight of the women in sweaters. As she speaks, the others get their knitting out.)

GINA: I can't believe it. It's so wonderful to see people wearing them. I never expected it somehow. And every piece of yarn went through my fingers. It's like having my arms wrapped around all of you. You see? We're fine. We don't need men. Well, we do, actually, but you know what I mean. We have each other, and that's enough! Well, it's not, actually, but you know what I mean! We have our knitting! Here, Liz. These are your needles. They're your friends.

(She holds needles out to Liz who reaches for them. The lights start to fade.)

LIZ: Okay. So who's going to teach me to cast on again?

MARGIE: I'll give it a whirl.

LIZ: Oh, great. The blind leading the blind.

LILY: Oh, Paula. I found an old book of Irish knits you might want to look at…

PAULA: Yeah?

LILY: Beautiful, beautiful sweaters…

(As they bend over their knitting, the lights fade to a lovely golden glow. Tableau and blackout.)

END OF PLAY

THE FAMILY OF MANN

ORIGINAL PRODUCTION

The Family of Mann premiered on June 28, 1994 at the Second Stage Theatre. It was directed by Pamela Berlin and had the following cast (in order of appearance):

ED/DAVE . . . . David Garrison
BILL . . . . Richard Cox
BELINDA/SISSY. . . . . Julie White
CLARA . . . . Lisa Gay Hamilton
REN/BUDDY. Robert Duncan McNeill
SALLY/GINNY . . . . Anne Lange
STEVE/UNCLE WILLY . . . . Reed Birney

Scenic Designer . . . . Derek McLane
Lighting Designer . . . . Natasha Katz
Costume Designer . . . . Lindsay W. Davis
Original Music & Sound Design . . . . Jeremy Dyman Grody
Production Stage Manager . . . . James Fitzsimmons

CHARACTERS

ED: the Executive Producer, mid-forties, large, friendly, a king
REN: Thirty-one, boyish, good looking, likable
BELINDA: Thirty-one, smart, opinionated, extremely emotional
BILL: mid-fourties, the director; a hatchet man
SALLY: early fourties, feminine but determined
STEVE: mid-fourties, a fierce has-been
CLARA: mid-twenties, black, deferential but observant

THE SITCOM

DAVE	Played by Ed
GINNY	Played by Sally
BUDDY	Played by Ren
SISSY	Played by Belinda
UNCLE WILLY	Played by Steve

The actress playing Clara grows wings in the second act. Although no one comments on them, she should wear them in every scene.

TIME AND PLACE

The Present, Los Angeles

ACT I
SCENE I

First Read Through

The lights come up, bright on an ambiguous space. Ed sits at a large table, everyone else slightly behind him. Everyone holds script binders in their hands.

ED: Before we read through today's script, I just wanted to take a moment to welcome our actors, our production personnel, our talented staff of writers—all of you—to *The Family of Mann*. I think we're all excited to be here today, embarking on a project which will hopefully say something we can all be proud of, and maybe give us all a couple of laughs in the bargain, since that's what we're being paid for.
(He laughs easily. Everyone else does too.)

ED: If you've seen any of the other shows we've worked on here, hopefully you realize that what we're trying to do is quality television that people can watch without being completely, egregiously offended morally and intellectually. It's a crazy idea, but we like to kid ourselves that stories about people living relatively decent, normal lives, the kind of lives I think most of us had in our childhood, might be of interest to America. Anyway, it's of interest to me, and I've had some success with this approach, so we're going to try it again and see if we can prove to the networks that Americans are not merely interested in amoral, sex-crazed psychopaths, or whatever it is they're putting on the air this week. Now, before we get started, I want to explain a few things about our organization. We really do consider ourselves a family here; mostly what we're interested in is creating a world where people can just enjoy coming in to work. If it's not fun, then I'm not interested in it, and I don't think you should be either. So I hope we can all just relax and enjoy each other and make some comedy here!
(There is scattered applause.)

ED: I give you our director, Bill.
(Everyone holds pencils and opens identical scripts. Bill, the director, starts to read.)

BILL: Okay, here we are in the Mann family kitchen. It's a Saturday morning, the day is bright and lovely and Ginny, the lovely wife of Dave Mann, is talking to her husband. Scene one.
(Lights change.)

SCENE II

BELINDA: The Writers' Room

Scene changes to the writers' room. All the writers sit around the table, scripts open before them. Everyone speaks very quickly.

ED: He's as big as a fucking cow. I mean, the last time I saw him was at the pilot, he looks great, and today, what, he's put on thirty pounds in two months.

SALLY: I put a call into his agent.

ED: Fuck his fucking agent. The man's old enough to know when he looks like a pig. Fucking actors. I can't believe this. He gets paid sixty thousand dollars a week to stay in shape and he shows up looking like Orson Welles.

REN: We have the same lawyer, I had lunch with him last week? First thing he says, so, how much weight has Jim put on? His last show, every hiatus he put on thirty pounds. Apparently he does this all the time.

ED: Oh, Jesus. *(To Sally.)* Did you know about this?

SALLY: Of course not—

BELINDA: I don't think he looks bad—

ED: You put a camera on him, he's a mess. Six months ago, the guy is America's perfect father. This is making me sick. Get his agent on the phone.

(Sally picks up the phone.)

SALLY: *(Into phone.)* Clara, can you get Andrew Stein for me, please? *(She hangs up.)*

STEVE: *(Overlap.)* The script's in good shape.

ED: The script's phenomenal. As long as Jim doesn't sit on it.

(Bill enters as the phone rings. Sally picks it up and speaks while Bill and Ed speak.)

ED: How's it going?

BILL: Fine, except for the fact that Jim is as big as a fucking house.

SALLY: *(Overlap.)* Andy? Oh, wonderful. Yes, it went very well; everyone's very excited. The network is very happy. Listen, Andy, we're a little concerned about Jim's weight.

ED: Could you believe it when he walked in? The guy's supposed to be our leading man, his gut is hanging over his—

BILL: And he's eating donuts, he doesn't pass the fucking table without picking up something, I think he's already had four or five.

ED: Jesus.

SALLY: *(Overlap.)* So he is aware of it?

BILL: He's stuffing himself.

SALLY: Well, Ed's not sure—here, let me have you talk to Ed—

ED: Fuck him, I don't want to talk to some fucking agent. I want to talk to his trainer. If he's so fucking aware of it, how come he's still fat? The guy's being paid sixty thousand dollars a week to stay thin—

SALLY: *(Into phone, overlap.)* Andy, we just wanted to make sure something was being done. Is he seeing a trainer, or—oh, good, good. So you'll tell him that we are concerned? Good. Okay. *(She hangs up.)*

BILL: I've seen this before. This is bad, this is fear of success. You can't start like this; if you don't come out of the gate like a fucking maniac it's all over.

BELINDA: I don't think he looks bad. He's incredibly appealing. My mother has the hugest crush on—

ED: Oh, Jesus, I feel sick. Can we get some lunch menus in here?
(Sally picks up the phone again.)

BILL: *(Overlap, to Belinda.)* You don't understand; you can't start like this. If you start like this, it's all over. He's sabotaging the whole show.

ED: I didn't want to cast him in the first place. The guy looks like a weasel. Now he looks like a fat weasel.
(He and Bill laugh.)

SALLY: Clara, can you bring the lunch menus in? Thanks. *(She hangs up.)*

ED: Fuck him. The script's phenomenal; it's going to be a great show. We'll just keep the camera on Monica all week, is she a beautiful girl or what?

REN: She has the most beautiful skin of any girl I have ever seen. She glows. She actually glows.

ED: What a punim. She good?

BILL: Unbelievable.

ED: Terrific.

CLARA: *(Enters with a book of menus.)* You guys ready to order lunch?

ED: Skip the menus, do we need to see menus? Just pick up a bunch of pizzas. Six or seven, I don't care. Jesus, this is making me—and stop off at Victor's for chocolate cake. We'll sit here and stuff our faces and make fun of how fat Jim is.
(He and Bill laugh. Blackout.)

SCENE III

ED: The Family of Mann I

A suburban kitchen. Dad sits at a table, reading the newspaper while Mom chatters. They perform in a bright, skittish, sitcom style.

GINNY: Maybe I'll write a novel today.

(Dad gives her a look. The laugh track chuckles.)

DAVE: You're going to write a novel, today? What are you going to write tomorrow, an encyclopedia?

(More laughter.)

GINNY: I mean it, Dave. I want to do something *big* today.

DAVE: How about we paint the living room?

(More laughter. She glares at him.)

DAVE: What? we have a very large living room!

(More laughter.)

GINNY: Dave, we're finally free! We could do anything! We could travel or go back to school, or learn how to ski!

DAVE: Go bungee jumping.

GINNY: Anything! Now that the kids have finally moved out, I feel so energized! Dave. We finally got rid of them.

(More laughter.)

DAVE: You sound like you hate your own children.

GINNY: No, hate would be too strong a word. Or maybe it wouldn't…

(More laughter.)

DAVE: Ginny!

GINNY: Dave, now that they're adults, it's time we faced facts. We have the most annoying children in America.

DAVE: I like them!

GINNY: I like them too, when they're not driving me crazy. Twenty-two years of "Mom, it's your day for car pool." "Mom, will you press my new blouse?" "Mom—"

BUDDY: *(Off.)* Mom, what's for breakfast?

GINNY: *(To Dad.)* Yes, I especially hated that one. Mom, what's for breakfast? In that annoying nasal twang Buddy has. You sounded just like him for a second there.

BUDDY: *(Entering.)* Mooooom! What's for breaaaaakfast?

GINNY: *(Laughing.)* Oh, stop! How do you do that?

(Dad stares at her. She gets it, leaping to her feet.)

GINNY: Buddy! What are you doing here?

BUDDY: I thought I'd come by for breakfast.

(He sits, expectant. Mom is confused.)

GINNY: You live in Chicago, sweetheart. Why would you come all the way to Minneapolis to have breakfast?

BUDDY: Well, see, there's this little thing called a recession, Mom. Could I have some orange juice?

(More laughter. She stares at him.)

SISSY: *(Off.)* Moooooom!

(Mom turns, desperate.)

GINNY: Sissy!

(Sissy enters, weeping, and throws herself on Mom's shoulder.)

SISSY: It's so awful—oh, Mom—

GINNY: What is it, sweetheart, what's the matter?

SISSY: My husband is the most hateful man that ever lived.

GINNY: *(Sympathetic.)* We've all known that for years, sweetheart. Why are you crying?

(More laughter.)

SISSY: Can I stay here, Mom?

BUDDY: Mom, I lost my job and my apartment, and I'm broke. It's okay if I stay here, isn't it?

GINNY: Oh, my poor sweet babies. I'd rather stick my fingers in a waffle iron than let you move back home.

(More laughter. Beat.)

SISSY AND BUDDY: Daddy?

DAVE: Oh, she's kidding. Of course you can stay! Isn't this great. We're a family again!

(He puts his arms around Buddy and Sissy. After a moment, Ginny makes a running jump and leaps on Sissy, trying to strangle her. All try to pry them apart. Laughter and applause. Blackout.)

SCENE IV

BILL: It's Not Real Enough

The writers' room. Everyone is sitting around the table. There is food and Coke cans everywhere.

ED: This doesn't, it just doesn't start right.

STEVE: Well, we talked about her, you know, her feeling of liberation when—

ED: Yeah, but a novel, it's too literary, everyone in America's going to be going who are these fucking people, writing novels, it's not real—

BELINDA: My mother tried to write a novel once.

ED: *(Not listening.)* That's the mistake everybody makes, like all this sniping at each other, that's not real. Once you give into that sort of shit, you're dead.

STEVE: Well, we don't have to start with the novel, I just thought it would give a sense of her, you know—

ED: Yeah, but it's got to be real. This show is—we're bringing the family together in adulthood, now, we're showing Americans moving out of their adolescence into a deeper maturity.

BILL: I think we should start with Sissy and Buddy, that's where the heat is going to be. Either one of them could be a breakout. I say we just start with the heat.

REN: What, do you mean open with them already there?

BILL: Yeah, some sort of funny scene with the two of them plotting to get their old rooms back or something.

REN: Except he's after her room. Just getting back in the house isn't enough, he's—

ED: You mean, she's got the room with the view of Minneapolis?

REN: Something like that. A spectacular view of downtown Minneapolis, and he's after that room.

SALLY: Ren, that is a great idea.

BELINDA: So they get into some totally moronic juvenile fight about it? That could work. I mean, they start out as children and then—

ED: Yeah, but it's still—there's something not right about the tone. These people should not be mean to each other. They tease each other, but without meanness.

BELINDA: Well, if we started with the brother sister thing we would lose the section where Dave picks on Ginny, that's where I thought it was sounding kind of—

ED: No, that part's okay. It was the stuff about her not liking her kids that I thought really went too far.

BILL: The attitudes are reversed. Dave should be the one who doesn't want the kids back; that's where the comedy is. She's gotta be thrilled to see them.

ED: Yeah, this stuff about not liking her kids doesn't work.

BELINDA: *(Cheerful.)* Well, I don't know. My mother hated me all the time. Didn't your mother hate you?

ED: No, I don't think—you're very nosy. Is this why your mother hated you?

BELINDA: It was just a periodic thing. You know, when you date drug addicts and come home trashed, parents tend to get upset. And isn't that like what we're going for with these two, that they're both—

ED: No, they're good kids, they aren't—

BELINDA: Well, I was a good kid too. I was just a good kid who got arrested a couple times. *(She laughs.)*

REN: You got arrested?

BELINDA: Oh, for buying cocaine. Big deal. I was a minor. It's not like I have a record or anything.

ED: Well, that's a big relief. You were buying drugs, but you were underage. I feel much better.

BELINDA: So, let's give Sissy a drug phase.

STEVE: Drugs aren't funny.

BELINDA: They're not?

ED: These are good kids. They're not drug addicts.

SALLY: Maybe if the opening is just more about Ginny's realizing the kids are gone—

ED: I need more coffee. CLARA! Is there coffee? CLARA!

CLARA: *(Enters.)* I'm in the next room, Ed. You don't have to roar.

ED: We need coffee.

SALLY: *(Overlap.)* She doesn't know what to do with herself...

CLARA: I just made a pot fifteen minutes ago. *(She picks it up and looks at it, pours it into his cup.)*

ED: Oh, this is fresh? I didn't know this was fresh.

SALLY: *(Overlap.)* There's a sense of confusion and loss—

ED: Oh yeah, those confusion and loss jokes are always such a scream. *(The guys laugh.)*

SALLY: No, I mean, if we tried to play it comedically—

ED: Comedically. Ohhhh. Now, everything is clear. *(Of coffee.)* This stuff is phenomenal. How do you make this?

CLARA: Well, you put the little white filter in the machine. Then you open the little silver bag and pour the coffee in.

ED: Phenomenal.

CLARA: I can't believe they pay you so much and me so little.

ED: I adore this girl.

BILL: Could I have some of that?

(Bill holds out his cup. As Clara pours, he puts his arm around her.)
ED: She's phenomenal, isn't she?
BILL: Fantastic.
ED: So what do we have? Comedic confusion and loss.
BILL: I just think we gotta be careful not to lose Dave in all this. What I want to know is where Dave is.
ED: As played by Jim, Dave is standing in the corner with his fist up his ass.
  (The guys all laugh.)
REN: Sitcom for the nineties. *(Doing Jackie Gleason.)* "Norton! How would you like my fist up your ass?"
  (The guys howl.)
BILL: "Alice! Why, I oughta just shove my fist up Norton's ass!"
REN: *(As Alice.)* "You do whatever you want, Ralph. Trixie and I are going to go lick each other dry."
STEVE: *(As Norton.)* "Hey, Ralph, Ralperoonie, the girls are going to…lick each other dry! Don't you think we should, uh…watch?"
REN: *(As Alice.)* "Why that's a great idea, Norton. You coming, Ralph?"
BILL: "Alice…you're the greatest."
  (They are laughing uproariously. Belinda watches, puzzled, and Sally smiles politely. Clara does not respond.)
BILL: Oh, God. Oh, God…
REN: *(As Ralph.)* "Norton!"
  (They all laugh even harder.)
ED: So what do we have, Dave is standing around with Norton's fist up his ass? Well, at least it's funny.
  (They continue to laugh. Lights change.)

SCENE V

BELINDA: Reality
  Ed and Belinda are in his office.

ED: You like it here? I mean, everything's going okay? Need anything?
BELINDA: No, it's great. Everything's great.
ED: It's an amazing job, isn't it? I mean, the first show I got, I thought, they have to be kidding. I couldn't imagine how anybody would be willing to pay me for this. They put me in a room with three other guys and said,

all right, entertain yourselves all day, eat as much as you like, and while you're at it, if you write a few things down, we'll put them on television for you. Oh, and by the way, we'll pay you a zillion dollars for this. It's like stealing money.

BELINDA: It's pretty amazing. I mean, it seems—I'm still getting used to it, but, you know—I'm writing for a TV show! I'm sorry, I'm sounding like a moron—

ED: No, no—

BELINDA: Anyway, thank you for the opportunity. And, I hope I wasn't crossing lines in there, with the drug stuff—

ED: Not at all.

BELINDA: I just thought that might be an area for comedy, so I was—

ED: You'll figure it out.

BELINDA: I just, you know, I'm real excited about being here, so I want to do a good job, and I get—anyway. And on top of it all, to be making so much money, I—

ED: No, you can't do it for the money. That's the first mistake everybody makes. If you do it for the money, you're lost. If it's there, if it's not there, you have to be the same person.

BELINDA: *(Laughing a little.)* Well, some day I hope to be the same person with a lot more money.

ED: You need money?

BELINDA: Oh. No, that's not—I'm fine. I'm doing fine. Thank you.

ED: I mean, the money's good. It's a good thing. To be able to support your family, and take care of the people you love. You don't have that worry right now, but you will. But for now, it's good that you can just learn the craft, and enjoy the opportunity. Television is so powerful; there's no other form of entertainment that reaches so many people. That's what's so great about what we do. We make a difference. We literally affect people's lives.

BELINDA: It's quite a responsibility.

ED: You're a talented girl. You're going to do fine out here. Los Angeles takes a little getting used to, but really, it's a wonderful place. It's possibly the last great cauldron of the American character, do you know what I mean? We're creating a landscape, creating an art form, creating ourselves. It's the essence of America. That's what I like most about Los Angeles. It allows you to create your own reality.

BELINDA: Oh. But—wow. I don't know. If you create it, is it real? I mean, I thought we were creating fantasies.

(She laughs, friendly. He stares at her. Lights change.)

SCENE VI

ED: Did You See My Name?

Belinda is at home. She is lit by the blue light of a television set. She is talk-ing on the phone and drinking a beer.

BELINDA: *(On phone, excited.)* Did you see it? Did you see my name? *(She laughs.)* I know, it was wild, wasn't it? Did Grandma like it? *(Pause.)* She thought it was too racy? Well, what do you want, she's near death, every-thing's racy to her. Mom. I'm kidding, Mom. Hi, Daddy! Yeah, it was great wasn't it? Well, not great, but for my first episode on television—yeah, it was exciting. It looked so *real.* And it's so weird, because that's *not* real, you know, but there it is on the television screen, and it's like, man, it's like you exist. It's so…Dad? Oh. Hi, Gigi! Yeah, it was great, wasn't it? Uh huh. Uh huh. No, I didn't write that, I didn't write that part. Well, you know, as a group, we rewrite things, and—*(Pause.)* No, I—I didn't write that, either. Yeah, Ed wrote that. *(Pause.)* Yeah, I wrote some of it— *(Lying.)* yeah, I wrote that. That was my line. Good, yeah, I—Uh…who is this? Mrs. Markgraf! Yeah, it is fun being in Hollywood. No, uh, no I—I haven't met Tom Cruise. Could you put my dad back on? Thanks. *(Pause, laughing.)* Dad, how many people are there? Well, yeah, but—of course I did. I had a, a bunch of friends came over and we watched it together. They're in the other room. Okay, you go back to your party and I'll go back to mine. Yeah. I love you too. 'Bye. *(She hangs up. Beat. Calling to no one.)* Be right there. *(Beat.)* I'm sooo pathetic. *(Lights change.)*

SCENE VII

BELINDA: Phenomenal
Ed and Bill are in Ed's office.

ED: You see the reviews?

BILL: Phenomenal. We're gold.

ED: I can't believe it. You see *The New York Times?* The network guys, they're telling me they've never seen reviews like this. Not since *All in the Family.*

BILL: It just goes to show, people are hungry.

ED: Yeah, but now we gotta hit a home run every week. We gotta keep the heat on until we see what the numbers look like.

BILL: I'm not kidding, this is it, Ed. This is the way I felt the first week of *Family Business*. When it works, it works. We're going seven years.

ED: You think so?

BILL: If Jim goes on a diet.

ED: Fuck him. He can lose the weight or he's out of here. This isn't fucking *Designing Women,* or *Rosanne,* for that matter. Anybody can be replaced. Just make sure he knows that.

BILL: No, he's fine, he's going to the gym, he's going to be—

ED: Is he pulling anything? Come late to rehearsals or anything?

BILL: No, he's scared to death. He's desperate for this show to survive; he's got something like four mortgages to pay off. He's not going to fuck up.

ED: Is that why he's doing all those fried chicken commercials?

BILL: I guess.

ED: Jesus.

BILL: How's the table?

ED: Great. I mean, I'm still not sure this is Steve's kind of show, and Sally's not—you know, we're stuck with her, what are you going to do? They're friends; no one else will give them jobs. But Ren and Belinda are phenomenal. You read their scripts?

BILL: Phenomenal.

ED: First time out for both of them. Unbelievable.

BILL: Where'd you find her?

ED: In a stack. I mean, her spec came in over the fucking transom, I don't even know why I read it. I just pulled it out of a stack one day on a whim, and I thought, fuck, this is good, let's just hire her. She's got a fucking Ph.D., did you know that?

BILL: You're shitting me.

ED: Taught English at some university and got sick of it. I'm going to call fucking Cosby and say, fuck you and your Ph.D. I got a *story* editor with a Ph.D., take that and shove it up your ass.

BILL: *(Laughing.)* That's perfect. You should, you should do it.

ED: Fucking Cosby and his fucking Ph.D. Anyway, I read her script, and I think, you know, she's good, and then that afternoon, I go to this psychic, who tells me, out of the blue, that a woman named Linda is going to come into my life and make a huge impact.

BILL: Linda?

ED: Is that amazing? I mean, it's not exactly the same, but—

BILL: No, but—you didn't—

ED: Nothing. I was there to ask about whether or not I should buy another house, Deb and I are thinking about buying a place in Santa Monica because the beach house is so far, and there are so many people at the house in Brentwood all the time we can't be alone, with the gardener, and the housekeeper and Becky and the kids—

BILL: Yeah, yeah—

ED: So I hadn't said anything about hiring writers. I mean, we weren't even sure the show was going at that point.

BILL: That's wild.

ED: Yeah. A woman named "Linda." And what about Ren, he remind you of anybody?

(Bill looks at him, actively thinking.)

ED: Me! Doesn't he remind you of me? About twenty years ago?

BILL: Oh—

ED: Yeah, I went back to that psychic today, to talk about the show, and you know what she told me? That I was going to have a son. Out of the blue, she says, I see a son coming into your life. A prince among men. And, you know, Deb's forty-six, she's not—

BILL: Well, you never—

ED: I know, but be realistic. I mean, with these psychics, you can't always be literal. She says a son, but that might mean a lot of things. So when I got back to the lot today, I bumped into Ren, and I thought: This is what she was talking about. A prince. Of course, I didn't know that when I hired him. This just happened today.

BILL: Ren's great. His script is phenomenal.

ED: And what a jump shot. Did you see him yesterday, making that shot from the corner?

BILL: See him? I was trying to stop him. I'm going, all of a sudden he's Michael Jordan—

ED: He played college ball.

BILL: You're shitting me.

ED: You didn't know? He made it to the Final Four. Twice.

BILL: Jesus.

ED: That's why I hired him.

(They laugh. Lights change.)

SCENE VIII

REN: The Numbers
> *Ren and Steve and Belinda are in the writers' room. Clara enters, carrying yellow sheets of paper.*

CLARA: The numbers came in.
> *(Steve and Ren jump, take the sheets eagerly.)*

STEVE: All of them?

CLARA: Just the overnights. We won our slot.

REN: All right! *(He gives Clara a high-five.)*

STEVE: *(Studying sheet.)* Not by much. Jesus. Not by much at all. A tenth of a point.

BELINDA: Now how do you read these?

REN: *(Pointing.)* This number is the percentage of available sets that were tuned into our show, and this one is—percentage of viewers. Of the sets that were turned on, this is how many watched us.

BELINDA: What?

STEVE: This is not good at all.

CLARA: Bill says we'll bounce in the nationals.

STEVE: You didn't take these down to the set, did you?

CLARA: No, he came by before he went over—

STEVE: Never let an actor see a number. It makes them completely insane.
> *(Ed and Sally enter. She is trying to show him Polaroids.)*

SALLY: You can't tell from the Polaroids, Ed. We have to go over there. It'll take ten minutes—

ED: I told you; I don't care what they wear.

SALLY: You say that, and then on show night all of a sudden nobody looks right—

CLARA: The numbers came in. *(She hands sheets to Sally and Ed.)*

SALLY: Oh, no. We fell four points off our lead.

STEVE: That fucking black show is a piece of shit, and then they blame us because everybody turns it off in the middle.

ED: It doesn't matter. Those assholes at the network will do whatever they want anyway. You have to ignore this shit. Is there coffee?

CLARA: What's the magic word?

ED: Clara, my love, is there coffee?

CLARA: Ed, sweetie, for you, there's always coffee. *(She goes to get it.)*

SALLY: I love your shirt, Ren. That's a terrific color on you.

REN: Thanks.

SALLY: All right, I'm going to wardrobe. I'll be back in ten minutes; don't start without me. *(She goes.)*

BELINDA: *(Still trying to figure it out.)* This number is the percentage of what?...

ED: You can't pay any attention to them. Jesus, these numbers are for shit. Steve, look at what *Empty Nest* did, and that's a fucking hit.

STEVE: Back in the eighties, no one could stay on with these numbers.

ED: The networks are going down. Fuck 'em, they deserve to; they're as bad as the car companies. They put shit on year after year, it serves them right that people finally won't watch it. Shit, I don't want to talk about the numbers. Belinda, how's your script coming?

BELINDA: I'm proofing it over lunch. You'll have it this afternoon.

ED: Great. Did you put in that stuff we talked about? About Dave interfering with Sissy's boyfriends?

BELINDA: Yeah. It's a little creepy, but I think I figured out how to make it work.

ED: Creepy?

BELINDA: Ed, she's twenty-nine years old and her father won't let her date.

ED: So, what's your point? *(He laughs.)*

BELINDA: Right. So, I put that in and moved the dog food run to the top of the D scene; it's much hotter there—

ED: Great—

BELINDA: And I cut four pages out of the second act and reconceived Jimmy.

ED: Jimmy? I liked Jimmy.

BELINDA: He wasn't funny enough.

ED: Is he funny now?

BELINDA: This guy is so funny, he makes Robin Williams look like a big bore.

ED: You think Williams is funny?

BELINDA: Not as funny as you, Ed.

ED: I love this girl.

BELINDA: Yeah, yeah, yeah... *(She goes.)*

ED: *(To Ren.)* She's great, isn't she? She's a machine. How's your new script coming?

REN: Great. You'll have it by the end of the week.

ED: She's gaining on you.

(Ed laughs. Ren laughs with him, sort of.)

STEVE: Ed, I probably should get going on a second script, too. I mean, I haven't really done much since that first script and I have a couple ideas.

ED: Oh, well, yeah, sure Steve. Put them together and we'll talk.

STEVE: Well, is now a good time? I could pitch 'em now. It shouldn't take too long.

ED: *(Looking at the sheets again.)* No, why don't you hold onto them for a few days. Now is not really a great time.

STEVE: Oh. Okay.

ED: Fucking numbers. Ren, you want to go do some editing?

REN: Sure.

ED: Your episode is looking phenomenal. We just have to get another thirty seconds out of it.

REN: Great.

(They go. Steve sits alone for a long moment. Sally enters. She looks around.)

SALLY: Where is everybody? I thought we were working.

(Steve looks at her. Lights change.)

SCENE IX

SALLY: The Best Place To Work In Hollywood

Sally arranges flowers on her desk. There is also a teapot and cups. Belinda looks around.

BELINDA: What a lovely office.

SALLY: Thank you. I like to keep it pretty, so there's at least one place on the lot I can come to for a little—comfort, I suppose. Would you like some tea?

BELINDA: Oh, sure, that'd be great.

(Sally pours and hands her a cup.)

SALLY: So, how are you liking it here?

BELINDA: Well, you know, it's great, I just, a lot, it's real different.

SALLY: From the university?

BELINDA: Well, from anything, as far as I can tell. *(Pause.)* I didn't know you knew about the whole...university thing.

SALLY: Oh, I'm sorry. Was it a secret?

BELINDA: No, of course not. I just—actually, I did ask Ed not to mention it. He found out about it through my agent, I didn't—

SALLY: Oh, Ed's telling everyone. You should be proud. It's quite an accomplishment.

BELINDA: Thank you. I just didn't want people to think I was an intellectual snob, or anything.

SALLY: Not at all. Well. A drug phase and a Ph.D. You're a very interesting person, aren't you?

BELINDA: It was a very small drug phase, I don't know why I even—

SALLY: You must miss teaching. *(She hands her a cup of tea.)*

BELINDA: Well, yeah, I guess I do. There actually was something really comforting about discussing Victorian novels for twelve hours a day.

SALLY: I'm sure it was a much more intellectual environment.

BELINDA: Oh, no—I mean, yes, of course, but—

SALLY: We read too.

BELINDA: Oh, I know. I didn't—I really don't miss it that much. I was constantly broke and the politics—I didn't actually fit in.

SALLY: Oh, no. You're lovely! I'm sure you fit in everywhere you go.

BELINDA: Well, thank you. But I never actually felt comfortable as an academic. I mean, I loved teaching, but the faculty…I felt like this populist in elitist heaven. I prefer Dickens to Henry James.

SALLY: Really.

BELINDA: Yeah. And I just thought, writing for television, if Dickens were alive today, that's where he'd be, so—

SALLY: Well, you're very lucky to be with us on your first show. This is one of the best places to work in Hollywood. Ed is one of the few truly decent and supportive people in the industry, and he really does want you to consider this a home. You're lucky.

BELINDA: *(Cautious.)* Everyone's been great. And I really am thrilled to be here.

SALLY: Well, good.

BELINDA: Of course, it's pretty different than I thought it would be. I guess I thought it was going to be sort of like the *Dick Van Dyke Show,* and, you know, it's really not.

SALLY: It does get a little rough sometimes. You must find that hard, coming from your ivory tower.

BELINDA: Oh, no. I love three hours of fist up the ass jokes. We used to kid about that all the time back at the old ivory tower. In between all the drugs we did.

(Sally looks at her. Belinda laughs. After a moment, Sally laughs back.)

SALLY: My first job, on *Happy Days,* the first day I was there, one of the other writers unzipped his pants, put his cock on the table and told me to suck it. *(Pause.)*

BELINDA: You're kidding.

SALLY: I was the only woman in a room of ten. They all thought it was hilarious, of course. I was twenty-four years old.

BELINDA: What did you do?

SALLY: Well, I certainly didn't oblige him. I laughed in a slightly uncomfortable way. *(She demonstrates.)* After a month or so the joke wore thin and he went on to something else. The whole trick is going along with it, but not really. You know.

BELINDA: I don't think I do.

SALLY: You can't protest, because that would get in the way of the room's energy, but you also can't just pretend that you're one of them. Because, we're not. Are we?

BELINDA: Apparently not.

SALLY: Anyway, you don't have to worry about the really overt stuff here. Ed wouldn't tolerate it.

BELINDA: He wouldn't.

SALLY: Absolutely not. He's actually rather traditional.

BELINDA: Traditional?

SALLY: On the last season of *Family Business,* we had a staff writer, a woman, who told the filthiest jokes in the room. She also tried to play basketball with them in one of their pickup games. She didn't last the season.

BELINDA: *(Pause.)* Are you warning me about something?

SALLY: I'm just trying to help. Ed is a complicated person. I hope you understand that.

BELINDA: You're kind of complicated yourself, aren't you?

SALLY: Not really. All I want out of life is to make a lot of money. More money than I can count. So much money that everyone will have to kiss up to me, and I can treat anyone I want like dirt. *(She laughs.)* More tea? *(She pours.)*
(Lights change.)

SCENE X

BELINDA: The Family of Mann II
Sissy and Buddy are reading a newspaper. Sissy is circling items. Ginny bustles about the kitchen.

SISSY: *(Wistful.)* I miss Benny.

BUDDY: Benny? The guy who chained you to the kitchen counter until you learned how to make a pie crust?

SISSY: That wasn't what it looked like.

BUDDY: It looked like about sixty pounds of wrought iron.

(Laugh track.)

SISSY: You never liked him.

BUDDY: Well, no I didn't. And now that I find out he's been married to another woman the whole time he was married to you, I like him even less.

SISSY: Nobody's perfect!

(More laughter.)

BUDDY: I know nobody's perfect, but Benny isn't even in the ballpark! Why are you defending him?

SISSY: I just think that everyone has a good side, that's all.

BUDDY: Yeah, well, Benny's good side belongs in a federal penitentiary.

(More laughter.)

SISSY: What do you know about it?

(They start to argue. Ginny laughs.)

GINNY: Okay, you two! I don't want to have to separate you! *(Smiling.)* Kids…

(More laughter. Uncle Willy and Dave enter.)

DAVE: Hey! Look who I found!

SISSY: Uncle Willy!

UNCLE WILLY: I was in the neighborhood, thought I'd stop by, visit my favorite brother and his gorgeous wife. You look fabulous, Ginny.

GINNY: Thanks, Willy. Have you had lunch?

UNCLE WILLY: Lunch! That would be terrific. Lunch, dinner, whatever. Breakfast. A chance to visit with my favorite niece and nephew for a few hours. A couple of days, weeks, months. Whatever! I'll just settle in a corner somewhere; you can throw me a bone once in a while. Sissy! You look fabulous.

(Laughter.)

DAVE: *(Threatening.)* Willy…

UNCLE WILLY: *(Begging.)* Just for a little while, Dave, till my trail cools off. I mean, till I get back on my feet.

DAVE: All right. Everybody out! Not you, Willy!

(The others go. Willy turns, desperate, to Dave.)

UNCLE WILLY: Dave. Dave, don't hit me, Dave. I'm not in a lot of trouble. A little, tiny misunderstanding with a loan shark.

DAVE: I'm sick, Willy. I just found out. I may be dying.

UNCLE WILLY: *(Pause.)* What?

DAVE: I don't know how to tell Ginny, or the kids. I know we haven't always gotten along, but—you are my brother. Can you help me?
(They hug. Blackout.)

SCENE XI

REN: Real Money
The writers' room. Exhausted, Ren and Belinda are going through a mass of orange pages, copy editing with a pencil. Periodically, they pass pages back and forth. They keep reading as they talk.

BELINDA: What time is it?

REN: It's a little after two.

BELINDA: Oh, fuck. Jesus, fuck me. Where's the rest of this scene? *(She paws dully through the pages.)*

REN: What is it?

BELINDA: G. G. G, G, G. I only have half of it.

REN: That's the whole scene.

BELINDA: It's not the whole scene. What happened to the part where he tells them he's not dying?

REN: That's there.

BELINDA: No, it's not.
(She hands the pages to him. Ren reads.)

REN: Oh, shit. Did we cut that? *(He starts pawing through the pages.)*

BELINDA: How could we cut it? The whole episode is about whether he's dying or not.

REN: Where is the old draft?
(They both are pawing through white pages by now.)

BELINDA: Fuck. Fuck me. We're going to be here all night. It's a good thing they pay us a fortune.

REN: My deal is fucked. I have a terrible deal. Ed is—I mean, he's a great guy, he's been great to me, but he's—you know, he's made a lot of promises that he doesn't keep. I was supposed to be a producer on this show.

BELINDA: Oh, yeah? And instead you're just a shitty little story editor like me.

REN: No, I mean, it's great being here, I'm just saying. I'm never going to make any real money here.

BELINDA: We're making four thousand dollars a week. That's not real money? What's real money?

REN: Four thousand dollars a week is not real money.

BELINDA: How did you end up here, anyway?

REN: My sister-in-law was a regular on *Family Business* the last season. She played the nun who tried to teach the twins to tap dance.

BELINDA: Oh, right. I missed that.

REN: So Ed and I got to know each other. We started playing basketball together.

BELINDA: Then you never did this before.

REN: Well, you know, I had a couple guest spots on *Who's the Boss?* and *Full House.* Here it is. Is this it? *(He reads off of some pages.)* Dave says, "I just sat there and heard the doctor say, you don't have cancer. It's nothing. And then I thought, if it's nothing, how come you're charging me an arm and a leg?"

BELINDA: Oh, God, did we leave that terrible joke in there?

REN: Hey. I wrote that terrible joke.

BELINDA: Oh. I'm sorry—

REN: It's okay. It is a terrible joke. But it's two-fifteen, and it's all we got. Where's the first half of the scene?

BELINDA: No, come on, we gotta fix it. I mean, there's got to be a way to fix this. *(She takes the page and stares at it.)*

REN: Belinda—

BELINDA: How about if we just take it out?

REN: Belinda.

BELINDA: *(Preoccupied, looking at the page.)* That'll work. Actually, this is a moment that should not have a joke at all, rhythmically it doesn't—He's facing his mortality, I don't want to hear one-liners… *(She starts to block out a cut on the page.)*

REN: We can't just change the script on our own! Ed is going to throw a fit—

BELINDA: Ed is gonna love this. Look, it clears out a moment for the two of them, and, you know, if we don't build an emotional context—

REN: An emotional *what?*

BELINDA: Look, just because it's a sitcom doesn't mean it has to be shit. This will make it better, so what's your problem?

REN: Well, excuse me. I mean, it's just my script. What would *I* know about it?

BELINDA: Ren, you said yourself it's a bad joke! Why are you fighting for it?

REN: Why are you fighting against it? It's two in the fucking morning!

CLARA: *(Staggers in.)* Are you guys okay?

BELINDA: Yeah.

CLARA: Are you almost done?

REN: Yes.

BELINDA: No.

CLARA: You know, we're not writing *The Brothers Karamazov* in here.

BELINDA: We're just working on a few...

CLARA: Great. I'm gonna be here till three.

(She goes. Ren stares at the pages, grim and exhausted.)

BELINDA: I'm sorry. I just, I taught writing for so long, you know, freshman comp, I spent so many years telling undergrads how important good writing is, and so many people watch television, I just keep having this vision in my head of all these people gathered around it like a campfire and we're the storytellers, and... *(Pause.)* Never mind. We'll just leave it.

REN: No, take it out. You're right. It's better without it. It is.

BELINDA: I'm sorry, I didn't—

REN: It's fine.

(He takes the pages from her and crosses the section out. She watches him.)

REN: Okay, Clara, we're done—

CLARA: *(Enters, yawning.)* Who won?

REN: Belinda.

BELINDA: It wasn't—

REN: Yes it was.

CLARA: Just don't start up again. Man, I'm tired...

(She takes the pages as Ren and Belinda collect their things. Completely energetic, Ed enters.)

ED: Hey! It's my two favorite writers! Clara, my love, is there coffee?

CLARA: It's two in the morning, Ed!

ED: So where is everybody? Are these the proofs? *(He takes the proofs from Clara and starts to page through them.)*

CLARA: Oh, my god. Maybe if I drove a stake through his heart...

ED: I love this girl.

CLARA: I'll go make coffee...

BELINDA: Ed—we didn't know you were still here.

ED: I've been over in editing. So, what, are you quitting? Deadbeats. Nobody's got any stamina anymore. My first season in television, I worked with three guys who never went home. I mean, literally. We'd work until four every night, then they'd go back and sleep in their offices. I didn't have an office, so I had to drive to Santa Monica, and back three hours later. My marriage was the only one that survived the season... *(Reading.)* Whoa, you lost the arm and a leg joke?

BELINDA: Oh—

REN: I just thought, you know, he's facing his mortality, we don't need to hear one-liners. And it gives the scene a little more room so that there's an emotional context. For the characters.

ED: An emotional context? He's sounding like a real writer, isn't he? It's a great script, Ren... *(He chuckles, looking at the pages before him.)* So, you guys didn't do anything to the A scene?

BELINDA: Oh—

ED: The lawn mower run doesn't work, does it? I mean, it's a good area, it's just not real enough...

REN: Yeah. I had some ideas but...

ED: Well, you want to do this now? I mean, we're still working, right?

REN: *(Enthusiastic.)* Yeah! Great...

BELINDA: Great!

ED: Great.

(Lights change.)

SCENE XII

CLARA AND BELINDA: Clara and Belinda Get Drunk
Clara and Belinda are in a bar.

CLARA: ...So I go over to Bill's house, right, he's the fucking director what am I supposed to say? Besides, why the hell not, he makes the whole thing sound like an afternoon around the pool with his wife and kids, fun, I could stand to go swimming, this city is so hot and disgusting. So I get there and it turns out that Marguerite and the kids have gone to Jackson Hole for the week. Okay. I'm cool, I'm acting like no big deal, it's still a swimming pool, I'll stay for an hour or something and at least get wet. So he's sitting here and I'm swimming, and I get out of the pool and he's acting like my dad or something, smiling like—it's just creepy, he keeps talking about what a great group we have on the show, it's such a family, do I want something to drink? Do I want to try out the Jacuzzi? And I'm like, no, Bill, I just want to get some sun. And he gets kind of jolly and paternal, and he says, come over here. Let me give you a hug. I'm like, excuse me? I'm in my bathing suit, I'm all wet, he's in his bathing suit, and he wants to give me a *hug*. And he's just sitting there smiling and holding his arms out like Buddha or something—

BELINDA: Oh, gross—

CLARA: And he just keeps sitting there, you know? He doesn't move. So to give him a hug, you have to sit on his lap.

BELINDA: No. Come on.

CLARA: It was completely creepy.

BELINDA: So, did you do it? Did you sit on his lap?

(Clara looks at her, then away.)

BELINDA: Oh, fuck. This town is amazing. It's like they've institutionalized sexual harassment.

CLARA: Welcome to Hollywood.

BELINDA: They're so blunt about it out here. I mean, at least in academia the harassment was—*subtle.*

CLARA: And it doesn't get you anywhere, either. I mean, the whole point of putting up with harassment is that you get something out of it, right? Explain that to Bill. He had my spec for three weeks. That's why I went over there. Guess what? He still hasn't read it. Next time he asks me to sit on his lap, I'm going to tell him to fuck off and die.

BELINDA: You should've told him the first time.

CLARA: Look, don't give me that shit, I'm just doing the best I—

BELINDA: No, I'm sorry, I didn't—fuck, I know, it's—

CLARA: I shouldn't care, you know? I shouldn't even be out here. This town is bad. The first week I'm here, I'm walking around these gorgeous neighborhoods, Santa Monica, Beverly Hills, thinking, where the fuck are the black people? I drove through Compton just for the fuck of it, and that scared me so bad I went back to Beverly Hills. I called my dad in Dallas, he pulled some strings and got me a job on the lot, so then I'm walking around this major fucking studio, thinking, oh man, I work in the big house now. Fucking Bill says sit on my lap, I almost said, Yassir, Massa. You walk around the lot, maybe catch a glimpse of Whoopi or Denzel off in the distance, they're like fucking gods, you know, we aren't even on the same planet. And everybody keeps telling me how lucky I am. All my friends? I get paid three hundred bucks a week to run errands for white people, and I'm a lucky girl because I got a *job* on the fucking *lot*. I saw an angel on a street corner, and I didn't even think twice. Wings and shit. The whole nine yards. I didn't even blink. She said, get out now, girl, the day of judgment is at hand, get the fuck out of LA, and I said, what, are you kidding? I got a job on the lot!

(Pause.)

BELINDA: You saw an angel?

CLARA: Oh fuck, they're everywhere now, you see them all over, what's the big deal? They're in catalogues, for God's sake. Notecards and shit. There was some Broadway play about angels, they're making a miniseries of it over on the other side of the lot. The place is crawling with angels. Six hundred extras with wings; the whole soundstage looks like this huge, stressed out birdbath. I don't know. The whole thing, it'll kill you if you think about it too hard. Oh, who cares, right? Some of them are real. They have to be. Don't they?

BELINDA: I guess. Yeah, sure.

(Clara drinks, depressed. Belinda looks at her.)

BELINDA: You wrote a spec?

CLARA: Every PA on the lot has written a spec.

BELINDA: Well, I'll read it for you.

CLARA: Oh, that'll do me a lot of good. No offense.

BELINDA: No, come on, I know a lot about writing. I used to teach writing. And contrary to what those guys may think, writing is not a competitive sport. You should let me look at it.

CLARA: Okay. Thanks. *(Pause.)* You're not going to last out here, you know.

BELINDA: What?

CLARA: I mean, what the fuck are you doing, having drinks with one of the PA's? What is the matter with you? Don't you have a brain in your head?

BELINDA: What?

CLARA: You're not going to last.

(They stare at each other. Lights change.)

SCENE XIII

STEVE: What Is Comedy?

The writers' room. Everyone is screaming at each other. Once again, Ed is not there.

BELINDA: The scene dies; the whole thing just grinds to a halt—

STEVE: It's just the joke, if we come up with a better—

BELINDA: It's not the joke, it's the scene. We've been waiting for fifteen minutes to find out if she got the job, oh, suspense is building, did she get it, did she—

REN: Maybe there's something in the perfume area, there's got to be a joke in—

BILL: Perfume, that's funny.

SALLY: Perfume that smells like cheese, maybe?

REN: That's funny.

SALLY: 'Cause it's the cheese state, right—

BELINDA: Wisconsin is the cheese state.

STEVE: They're right next to each other. We can fudge it.

REN: Perfume that smells like fudge.

SALLY: For chocolate lovers.

(They laugh.)

SALLY: Oh, this is a terrific area, Ren. You are so funny.

BELINDA: Look, all I'm saying is, we're waiting for this information, so if it comes out at the beginning of the scene, there's nothing driving the rest of it.

STEVE: Wait, wait wait. Everyone who smells the stuff hates it, right? Perfume that smells like chocolate. Who would buy this shit? Then a huge fat man comes up to the counter—

REN: Oh, that's perfect—

(Everyone except Belinda is laughing.)

STEVE: He's like, in a trance—

BILL: And Sissy's put the perfume on, right? She's been trying it on, while she talks about dating again—

STEVE: And the fat guy waddles over—

BELINDA: Oh, come on, you guys, not fat jokes; aren't we above anything?

STEVE: Not if it's funny.

BELINDA: Yeah, but come on, this isn't that funny, and besides, Ed keeps talking about the show being real, and there's nothing real about a fat man and chocolate perfume. Come on, you guys. We could make this really good. I mean, they're going to put it on television, television is where people now, in our culture, go to hear stories about our lives, and stories are what keep us human. There are so many stories to tell, some days I feel like I'm just *choking* on stories, and if we're not...I don't know—*diligent*—if it's just *shit,* then, what— *(She notices that they are all staring at her.*) I'm sorry. I just think that, you know, twenty-five million people are going to watch this, and it really does bother me that we're always turning Sissy into such a moron. We don't have to. The problem here is just a little more structural, and if we figured out a way to—

STEVE: Oh yeah, structure always makes me laugh. Those hilarious structures they teach you in graduate school always lay me flat.

(They all laugh.)

BELINDA: That was mean.

STEVE: What?

BELINDA: That was a mean thing to say. The joke is mean, and you are being mean. Now. Here. You're being mean to me.

SALLY: Oh, dear. Did you get up on the wrong side of the bed, Belinda?

BELINDA: No. I did not get up on the wrong side of the bed. I can't remember what side of the bed I got up on; it was so long ago. Look, I'm sorry, I just—this isn't funny. It's just mean.

BILL: Oh, brother.

STEVE: Well, comedy is mean. If you can't take it, then—

BELINDA: No, I can take it. I guess I just never understood it. Comedy is mean. Wow. See, I always thought comedy was wit, and surprise, and insight. But I guess if you can't come up with that stuff, mean will do just as well. Oh. Was that a mean thing to say? Gosh, you should write it down; maybe we could use it in the scene.

(Ren snickers. Sally looks at him; he lets the smile drop and doodles. Sally picks up the pencil.)

SALLY: All right, where were we? Perfume counter…

BELINDA: Fine. Go ahead and write that damn joke. It will never make it in. Ed is going to hate it.

STEVE: Look—

BILL: No, she's right. Ed is going to hate it.

SALLY: I think it's funny.

BELINDA: Well, let's just ask him. Let's call over to editing and ask him. That way we don't waste any more time; it's after midnight already—

SALLY: I think it's funny.

REN: Yeah, me too.

BILL: Oh, yeah, it's hilarious. But I think she's right. It's really not Ed's kind of joke.

(Pause. There is a moment of tense silence.)

REN: So, what else can we use there, there's got to be something else we can put in there.

(Pause. They think.)

ED: *(Enters.)* Hey, how's it going, you hacks? Anybody crack this thing yet?

REN: Ed!

SALLY: Ed, hi—

BILL: You finish the cut?

ED: *(Shaking his head.)* It's not coming together. Jim's a fucking mess. Maybe if you took a look at it. *(Off script.)* Whoa You're still in the D scene?

SALLY: Well. We've been kicking around a few—We were talking about maybe finding a joke in the perfume area.

ED: Perfume jokes? Yikes.

SALLY: No. We had some really funny ideas.

BELINDA: I just think the problem is—

ED: I don't want to know what the problem is, I want to know what the solution is! Jesus, fucking perfume jokes. Do I have to do everything myself? *(He exits. All are left in a tense silence. Lights change.)*

.

SCENE XIV

CLARA: Is There Coffee?

Morning. The writers' room. Clara is cleaning up. Belinda enters, frazzled. She carries a rough draft manuscript.

CLARA: Hey. How's it going?

BELINDA: I don't know. Ed called me on Friday and said he needed my episode first thing Monday, so I spent the whole weekend writing. How was the weather?

CLARA: Gorgeous.

BELINDA: What a surprise. Can you type this?

CLARA: Sure. I can't wait to meet Benny.

BELINDA: *(Not quite hearing her.)* What?

CLARA: Benny. Sissy's ex-husband.

BELINDA: What about him?

CLARA: Your episode's about Benny, isn't it?

(Belinda stares at her.)

CLARA: Ed had a meeting with the network last week. They were about to cancel us, so he told them about all the great scripts coming up, and he said you were writing this hilarious episode about Benny. He's been telling everybody.

BELINDA: What?

CLARA: That's why he needed the script this morning. They're casting Bennys this afternoon.

(Bill enters.)

BILL: Hey, how's it going? How's our little machine? I can't wait to meet Benny. Clara, is there coffee?

CLARA: Do you have eyes? Look at the coffee pot. Look at it.

BILL: I love this girl.

BELINDA: Bill, I didn't know anything about Benny.

BILL: Benny, Sissy's ex-husband. It's such a hilarious idea, bringing him on. I can't wait to see what you did with him.

BELINDA: I didn't do anything with him.

BILL: Ed said he called you on Friday—

BELINDA: He did call me on Friday, but he didn't tell me anything about Benny! I thought Benny was an off-stage character, we've been talking for months about how we were never going to see Benny—

BILL: The network wanted Benny. We're casting Benny this afternoon.

BELINDA: There's no Benny.

BILL: You didn't write anything for Benny? Oh, Jesus. What the fuck are we supposed to use for sides?

STEVE: *(Enters.)* Hey, how's it going? So, today's the big day we meet Benny. Clara, is there coffee?

CLARA: Why are people always asking me that?

BILL: *(To Steve.)* She forgot Benny.

STEVE: She what?

BELINDA: *(Overlap.)* I didn't forget Benny, no one told me!

STEVE: Aren't we casting Benny this afternoon?

BILL: Except we have no sides.

CLARA: You want me to type this, the way it is?

BILL: No.

BELINDA: It's all I've got—

STEVE: You forgot *Benny?* Whoa.

BELINDA: I didn't forget him.

BILL: Ed's gonna have a fit.

ED: *(Enters.)* Hey, how's it going? Can't wait to meet Benny. Clara, is there coffee?

CLARA: I can't believe how difficult this coffee thing is for everybody. No one can tell if it's here. No one can pour their own cup…

ED: I love this girl.

BELINDA: Ed, you didn't tell me about Benny.

(Ed turns and looks at her. She forges ahead.)

BELINDA: I just spent the whole weekend working on my script, because you said you needed it today, but you didn't say anything about Benny. And I can do it, if you want me to invent this guy Benny, that's fine, I can do that, I can write a whole episode about Benny, I can do anything with Benny that you want, but you have to tell me. You told everybody else. Why didn't you tell me?

ED: *(Stares at her.)* Look, you've got an hour. It's no big deal. Just introduce Benny. Write a little scene for him. Maybe something on a stoop in the rain on a college campus. It can be a flashback, we'll give everybody funny hair. I wrote a scene like that for my movie and it never got in. It was hilarious.

STEVE: I remember that scene. It was.

ED: So, you guys up for some hoops this afternoon?

BILL: Isn't it supposed to get pretty hot today?

STEVE: I heard it was gonna be in the nineties.

ED: Wimps.

(They go. Clara watches Belinda, who sits at the table.)

CLARA: You still want me to type that?

BELINDA: This episode's not about Benny. Benny belongs in it about as much as the fucking tooth fairy. I'm going to have to rewrite it from scratch, I just spent the weekend working on an episode that's completely USE-LESS, I was up till four last night, I haven't had a day off in MONTHS and he's acting like I'm the one who's nuts. WHAT THE FUCK IS THE MATTER WITH THESE PEOPLE?

CLARA: Belinda…Don't let them get in.

BELINDA: What?

CLARA: You want some coffee? Let me get you some coffee. Here. Have some coffee. *(She pours Belinda coffee.)*

(Lights change.)

SCENE XV

BELINDA: After Two

Belinda sits in the writers' room. She smokes. After a moment, Ren enters.

REN: Belinda?

BELINDA: Oh, Jesus. You scared me.

REN: What are you doing here? Everything's done, isn't it?

BELINDA: Yeah, I was just having a cigarette. I probably shouldn't be smoking in here. You know Sally's just going to throw a fit. Don't tell her I said that.

REN: Are you okay?

BELINDA: Yeah, sure.

(She smokes. He watches her.)

REN: You going over to the garage?

BELINDA: No, you go ahead. I'll be out of here in a minute.

REN: I don't mind waiting.

BELINDA: Look, I'm fine, all right?

REN: It's after two.

BELINDA: Yeah, so maybe we'll get lucky; maybe some nice little psychopath will find me alone and come after me with a hatchet. It'd be a real break for you, Ren; once I'm out of here they're going to make you a producer like that.

(She snaps her fingers. He looks at her.)

BELINDA: Sorry.

(Clearly, she's not. After a moment, Ren crosses, takes a cigarette and lights it. He sits. She watches him.)

REN: So, what's up with you?

BELINDA: Nothing's up. I'm just a little depressed.

REN: How come?

BELINDA: Gee, I don't know. I just moved three thousand miles to the ugliest city in America, I work eighty hours a week, I don't get any sleep, my writing is for shit and everybody hates me. I don't know why I'm depressed. If you can't be happy here, you can't be happy anywhere. Right?

REN: What are you talking about? Nobody hates you. They all love you here.

BELINDA: Secretly, they hate me. Maybe I'm not depressed. Maybe I'm paranoid.

REN: Maybe you are.

BELINDA: *(Snapping.)* Yeah, what would you know about it, Golden Boy?

REN: Belinda—

BELINDA: I'm sorry. I'm a little tense. I started therapy this week; I think it's making me—

REN: Really? You're in therapy?

BELINDA: Yeah, so what, you've never been in therapy? *Everyone* does therapy—

REN: Feeling a little defensive about it?

BELINDA: *(Beat.)* Maybe. Defensive, depressed and paranoid. Good thing I'm in therapy.

(Pause.)

REN: What made you go?

BELINDA: *(Matter of fact, almost good humored.)* I couldn't get off the floor. Saturday morning. I got up and took a shower, and then I went back to my bedroom, and I was looking for this shirt, in a pile of clothes on the floor, and I just...put my head down and started crying, and I couldn't get up. I couldn't get off the floor, for like...three hours. *(Pause.)* Pretty weird, huh?

REN: Jesus, Belinda. Why didn't you call me?

BELINDA: What?

REN: You should've called me. I could've come over and made you lunch or something. We could've gone to a movie. Something.

BELINDA: It's okay. I improvised and went into therapy instead.

REN: What is it, are you lonely?

BELINDA: *(Pause.)* Look, I'm fine—

REN: Do you want to go have a drink?

BELINDA: Oh, no, come on—

REN: What, you're just sitting here anyway—

BELINDA: I don't need you feeling sorry for me.

REN: Yes, you do. You need someone to feel sorry for you and then be really, really nice to you for a whole hour or something. Come on, we'll go to an all-night supermarket, buy a bottle of champagne and drink it in the parking lot.

(He takes her by the hand and pulls her up. She leans her head against his shoulder for a second)

REN: Come on, you're okay.

BELINDA: I know! It's just—nothing. Thanks.

(They look at each other. After a moment, he leans in slowly and kisses her. After a moment of uncertainty, she kisses him back. She pushes him away. They look at each other. After a moment, they kiss again. The kiss quickly becomes passionate and they wind up on the table. Blackout.)

END OF ACT I

ACT II
SCENE I

CLARA: The Angel In Los Angeles
Clara wears wings and sunglasses and speaks to the audience.

CLARA: This is the way the universe works: Everything moves from imagination to reality. Such is the force of creation. As soon as anyone imagines anything, it is only instants away from becoming real. Magic is the power that makes this happen. Science also has power, but in a smaller way. You think of objects—a telephone, a refrigerator, an airplane, and then, they exist. From the imagination, to the real.

    In America, somehow this process has been reversed. Americans look at something that is only imaginary, and then transform the real into that imagined thing. Little girls look at billboards of impossible women and say, that is what I want to be. People watch moving images of beings who could never exist, and say, that is what we are. The real yearns to be imaginary. And so, America is evaporating. This problem is particularly acute in Los Angeles, a city which is, frankly, about to lift off. Maybe that is why they call it the City of the Angels. Although that too is something of a misnomer. Really, we don't like it here.
(Lights change.)

SCENE II

REN: The Rookie Phenom
Ren and Belinda are in bed in his apartment. He is reading a script. She is going through catalogues.

BELINDA: You hear the one about the megalomaniac baseball team?
REN: No.
BELINDA: Norman Lear has first base, Jim Brooks has second, Cosby third, and Ed has the whole outfield.
(Ren smiles, scribbling.)
REN: Come on, he's not that bad.
BELINDA: You know what he told me about that stupid movie he made, I saw that thing, it's the worst movie ever, right? Am I right?

REN: It's not *Citizen Kane*. Okay. It's the worst movie ever.

BELINDA: Exactly. He told me, it was his autobiography. The thing is an adaptation of somebody else's *book,* this other guy wrote the book, and Ed is running around telling everybody it's his autobiography.

REN: He was being metaphoric.

BELINDA: Ed is incapable of being metaphoric. I mean, with all due respect, the guy's a fruitcake, and you're just defending him because he's decided you're his "son." The fact that you grew up in somebody else's house notwithstanding.

REN: Hey. If Ed's decided I'm his son, who am I to say I'm not?

BELINDA: Oh, it's all bullshit anyway. And if I hear one more word about how decent it all is, I may truly puke.

REN: What is the matter with you all of a sudden? What happened to television being like a campfire and you're the great storyteller?

BELINDA: Oh, come on—

REN: No, you come on. You watch a rerun of *The Odd Couple* some night. That show was a thing of beauty. Tony Randall's commitment and, and timing and *pathos*—

BELINDA: Pathos?

REN: Yeah, pathos, you don't see that—I mean, I've read Moliere—

BELINDA: Moliere? How did Moliere—

REN: Yeah, big surprise, the dumb jock reads Moliere.

BELINDA: I didn't say—

REN: And frankly, I don't see the difference.

BELINDA: The difference? Between Tony Randall and Moliere?

REN: Yeah, that's right. What's so fucking different, Miss Ph.D. in English? You tell me what's so different.

BELINDA: *(Overlap.)* Could we not bring my Ph.D. into this, I'm not—

REN: Just answer the question.

BELINDA: You want me to tell you the difference between Tony Randall and Moliere.

REN: That's right. Why is fucking Moliere so much better than Tony Randall?

BELINDA: I don't know, he just is.

REN: He just is, that's a real compelling argument—

BELINDA: All right. The sophistication of his language, his profound understanding and compassion for human nature even while he's satirizing social—

REN: He's telling the same stories we are. Who gets the girl. Fathers and sons competing with each other—

BELINDA: Oh, come on, Ren, theatre and television are completely different experiences. The theatre is much more—vivid, it's more *humane*—

REN: Yeah, I have seen some class A shit in the theatre.

BELINDA: Of course, but—

REN: In fact, most of what passes for theatre is class A shit. The only people who write for the theatre these days are people who can't get work in television.

BELINDA: Oh, is that so?

REN: And I've read your fucking *New Yorker,* too. Boy, that's good writing.

BELINDA: Ren!

REN: What?

BELINDA: What's the matter?

REN: Nothing. *(Pause.)* I just, I think there's been some great television, and I'd like to write some. Someday. I mean, we're telling stories, right? You're the one who made me feel like this. When you talk about it, sometimes, you make it sound like something holy.

BELINDA: Well, I'm full of shit.

REN: No, you're not.

BELINDA: Yes, I am! Christ, we spend all this time, as a group, going over and over these damn scripts—who *ever* decided that writing was a group activity, that's what I want to know. And you know what else I want to know? Why, if we're going to do ten drafts of a script, it doesn't get better! Why not just shoot the first bad draft? Why shoot the *tenth?* Why do Steve and Sally get to fuck up my work? Why does Ed? I mean, all of this—it isn't about storytelling. It's not even about product. It's just about power.

REN: Then why are you doing it?

BELINDA: *(Pause.)* For the money. *(Pause.)* I mean, I've never had money. I know, you think it's chicken feed, but this is more money than I've ever *dreamed* of, this is—That's the thing about selling your soul. No one tells you how much they'll actually pay you for it.

REN: You're not selling your soul. I can't believe you. I'd kill to be able to write like you, and all you do is run it down. Never mind.

(He goes back to the script. She watches him, uncertain, a little embarrassed.)

BELINDA: I'm sorry.

REN: You don't have to be sorry. I'm sorry. I'm sorry you don't enjoy this more.

BELINDA: *(Making up.)* I'm starting to enjoy it. I'm starting to enjoy it a lot.

REN: Well, you should. Ed is crazy about you. And you love him. Whether you want to admit it or not.

BELINDA: I never said I didn't like Ed. I think he's a nut, and I'm also desperate for his approval. It's an ongoing topic of discussion between me and my therapist.

REN: Well, stop worrying about it. You know, he's bumping up your next episode. He called me yesterday, raving about it.

BELINDA: *(Pause. Positively glowing.)* He did? He liked my script?

REN: He loved it. He loves you. He loves the way you fight—

BELINDA: Forget Ed. What do you like?

REN: I don't like anything at all.

(They kiss.)

REN: Okay. That's all you get.

BELINDA: Come on…

REN: I'm working!

(Giggling, she falls back, watches him for a moment, then looks through her catalogues.)

BELINDA: *(Musing.)* Hey, Ren? What did you do when you first started making money? I mean, was there a moment when all of a sudden, you had money? You didn't have any, and then you just, had a lot?

REN: Yeah, sure.

BELINDA: What did you do?

REN: I don't know, I…I bought, uh, a box of chocolates. You know, like, a five pound box of See's chocolates, and I…Fed-Exed it to my grandmother.

BELINDA: You sent your grandma chocolates? That is so—

REN: Yeah, okay—

BELINDA: It's adorable!

REN: So what did you do?

BELINDA: I bought sheets. I realized I've been sleeping on the same sheets since college; they're always so expensive, I could never justify buying new ones. So I bought these pretty sheets, with colors, and…I'm sorry, I'm embarrassed now. After that spectacular grandma story, I sound so—

REN: No, you don't.

BELINDA: It's just so weird, actually having it. I don't quite know how to spend it.

REN: Tell you what. This weekend, we'll go to San Francisco, rent a suite at the Ritz, and never leave. Order up room service for two days.

BELINDA: Oh, yeah? What will we be doing for two days?

REN: We will be watching basketball on TV.

BELINDA: *(She laughs.)* You are so mean.

REN: Basketball is a beautiful thing.

BELINDA: So how come you quit? I mean, you were a big college star, right? Why didn't you keep going?

REN: Because I was awful. I was the worst basketball player, ever.

BELINDA: But you were in all those big games, weren't you?

REN: Yeah, "big games." That's the NC double A to you, babe. I didn't really play in those games. The coach basically kept me on the team because he liked me.

BELINDA: I don't believe you. Ed says you're great.

REN: Compared to Ed, I am. He is old and weak, and I am young and hard.

BELINDA: *(Laughing.)* Ed's no good?

REN: Terrible.

BELINDA: How's Bill?

REN: Sucks.

BELINDA: Wait a minute. If you guys all stink, maybe I could play with you.

REN: No.

BELINDA: *(Baiting him.)* Why not?

REN: *(Beat.)* You're not tall enough.

(He kisses her as she laughs. Blackout.)

SCENE III

BELINDA: The Family of Mann III
The Mann family kitchen. Dave and Willy are arguing.

UNCLE WILLY: The situation is not grim, Dave. Not grim at all.

DAVE: The car is a lemon. I took you into my home, put a roof over your head, and you sold my daughter a lemon. Your own niece!

UNCLE WILLY: Now, Dave, you're not looking at this right.

DAVE: I'm looking at a lemon!

UNCLE WILLY: You know, cars are like people, Dave. Each one has a different personality and no one is perfect.

DAVE: Don't start this, Willy. I don't want to have to hurt you.

UNCLE WILLY: But we all try to make ourselves better. Don't we? I know I do. I know I'm always searching for my best self. Well, cars search too.

DAVE: Willy, she's had this car for less than twenty four hours and the fuel line is leaking, smoke is coming from somewhere…everywhere…

UNCLE WILLY: Is there ever a good time for trouble, Dave? For some of us, it comes early, and for some it comes late. But trouble is an important part of life's journey! You would never call a person a lemon, Dave.

DAVE: Oh, I might.

UNCLE WILLY: No, not you. Not my big brother Dave. I loathe you, you big lug.
(Sissy enters, followed by Buddy, who has soot on his face.)

UNCLE WILLY: Sissy! Aren't you looking like a fresh spring morning.

SISSY: Thank you, Uncle Willy. Uncle Willy, is there something wrong with my new car? It's spouting dust everywhere. Buddy was trying to help—

BUDDY: Anything for you, Sis—

SISSY: But it just keeps blowing up!

UNCLE WILLY: Oh, no, that's perfectly natural for—

DAVE: Sweetheart?

SISSY: Yes, Daddy.

DAVE: You know I love you.

SISSY: Oh, thank you, Daddy.

DAVE: Could you go back outside for a minute? I'm going to have to hurt Uncle Willy, and I don't want you to have to see it.

SISSY: Oh.

UNCLE WILLY: Sissy—you know, Sissy, what would go beautifully with your hair today? A 1982 Volvo with new whitewalls and a moonroof.

SISSY: *(Sweet.)* Oh, Uncle Willy. You always say the sweetest things. *(Abrupt.)* I'm sorry, do I have—do I have to say this? This is so stupid.

UNCLE WILLY: I don't even have that. What is that?

SISSY: I can't make this work. It's not even funny.
(Willy looks at her script. Bill enters, flustered.)

BILL: What's the problem? Jesus. What's the problem now? Monica, you're supposed to cross—

BUDDY: What? They cut my—I had a whole speech there.

SISSY: It's bullshit, Bill. Come on, you know it is.

DAVE: *(Overlap.)* I don't have these pages, either. What color is that, salmon? I don't have salmon pages.

BUDDY: Salmon? I didn't get salmon pages.

UNCLE WILLY: I haven't seen any salmon pages.

BILL: Oh, Jesus. Could someone call up to the writers and— *(Yelling out.)* Who the fuck fucked up this time?

SISSY: I mean, *I* can write better than this. Bill!

BILL: Look, Monica, this is not a fight you want to pick. Ed's under a lot of pressure right now, and besides, the writing on this show is excellent; you should see the shit they make you say on other shows. *(Yelling out.)* Could someone take care of this, please? Are we getting new pages?

SISSY: "You always say the sweetest things" is excellent? What am I, a complete moron?

DAVE: Sweetheart, you want Shakespeare, go to New York. You can do it in Central Park; they'll pay you three hundred bucks a week. Here, you make ten thousand a week doing shit. So shut up.

BILL: People. People!

DAVE: And could you get him to say the line right? It's I *love* you, not I *loathe* you. He's doing it on purpose.

BILL: It sounded fine to me, Jim.

UNCLE WILLY: I say the line that's written.

DAVE: He said I *loathe* you!

BUDDY: So where are these salmon pages? I don't have 'em.

CLARA: *(Enters, frantic.)* Here they are! I'm sorry. *(She starts to pass out pages.)*

BILL: So what the fuck is going on, Clara? This is, we can't have this. We lost, like, fifteen minutes here trying to figure out if everybody's even in the same scene.

CLARA: I don't know what happened, Bill. I wasn't here this morning when the pages were distributed.

BILL: So who's in charge of this, can you tell me that?

CLARA: I don't know, Bill; I'll find out as soon as I get this—

BILL: *(Snapping.)* Don't you fucking raise your voice to me!
(There is silence on the set.)

BILL: I don't need some little shit PA talking back to me. You fucked up. You cost this operation thousands of dollars because you were fucking careless. And now you're going to stand there and tell me this isn't your fault?

CLARA: I think I have a right to defend myself.

BILL: You have no fucking rights, you little shit! What makes you think your job affords you any dignity at all? You're a PA! You're nothing! And you fucked up. Do you understand? Do you understand anything at all? You're shit. You are nothing but shit here. No one wants to hear what you did wrong. Get out of here. *(Pause.)* Get out!
(She goes. He turns back to the actors.)

BILL: Okay, the show's over. Could we do some work here? *(He sits.)*
(Lights change.)

SCENE IV

BUDDY: We Could Help
Steve is sitting in the writers' room. Belinda enters.

BELINDA: Oh, hi. Where is everybody?

STEVE: I don't know. I thought we were meeting.

BELINDA: Well, yeah, I thought so, too. Clara?
(Clara enters.)

BELINDA: Do you know where everybody is?

CLARA: Bill's on the set, Ren and Ed are editing, and Sally's at wardrobe.

BELINDA: I thought we were meeting.

CLARA: Ed postponed till after lunch.

BELINDA: Oh, okay. Great.
(Clara exits. Belinda starts to go.)

STEVE: As long as we've got time, we could go over your script.

BELINDA: Oh. By ourselves?

STEVE: Well, I took a pass at it last night. I mean, it's good. I just had some ideas about the second act. To pop the comedy a little.

BELINDA: Oh. Well, shouldn't we wait until the whole group is together so that we don't…repeat?

STEVE: Are you doing something else right now? I just want to help. This is your first show, and I've done this a lot, and I consider it my responsibility to—help. Is that a problem?

BELINDA: No! No, of course not, I—

BILL: *(Enters.)* Is Ed in here? Where is everybody?

BELINDA: Ed's in editing with Ren, Sally's in wardrobe.

BILL: Great. Jim just had a major meltdown.

STEVE: What happened?

BILL: Apparently, Monica was on the *Today* show this morning, so he's livid. Some asshole reporter said, on the air, that she's the real star of the show. So now nothing's right. Jim's costume's fucked, the scene's fucked, I'm fucked—

STEVE: Oh, Jesus.

BELINDA: You want me to go get Ed?

BILL: Please. He's not going down to the set for this kind of shit. What are we doing for lunch?

BELINDA: I don't know. I was gonna grab Ren. I'll tell Ed you're looking for him.

BILL: Oh, you're going over there?

BELINDA: Yeah, Ren and I are supposed to have lunch.

REN: *(Enters.)* Hey, you ready?

BELINDA: Oh, you're here.

REN: Ed had to go do an interview.

BILL: Where are you going? Commissary?

BELINDA: Actually, I think we were going to go off the lot for a change. You
   want to come?

BILL: No. You go ahead.

   (They go. Bill shakes his head.)

BILL: Can you fucking believe it?

STEVE: What?

BILL: Ren and Belinda. They're sleeping together. Man, it didn't take them
   long.

STEVE: You're kidding.

BILL: You couldn't tell? Shit. I just hope Ed doesn't find out. He hates that
   shit. And Sally's going to have heart failure.

STEVE: Sally? Why should she care?

BILL: Jesus, Steve. Where are you?

SALLY: *(Enters.)* I'm sorry I'm late. Oh, aren't we meeting?

STEVE: Ed postponed till after lunch.

SALLY: Oh, God. I hate it when he does this. We're falling behind already and
   it's much too early in the season. We don't even have our pickup yet, and
   he's already—

BILL: We're fine. Belinda's new script just came in; it's terrific. Did you read it?

SALLY: Of course I read it. I think it needs work.

BILL: What, are you kidding? It's great. It reads like a fucking *Cheers* episode.
   If we've got an Emmy script, that's the one. Well, I'll go see if Jim's
   calmed down. He's going to be hell until we get the pickup.

   (He goes. Sally and Steve sit in silence for a moment.)

SALLY: What is he talking about? That script needs a lot of help.

STEVE: I agree.

SALLY: I can't believe this. I mean, where is she? We could be working on it,
   even if Ed's not here. We could take an initial pass.

STEVE: She's having lunch with Ren.

SALLY: You're kidding. It's eleven thirty in the morning. What are they going
   to lunch now for?

STEVE: Apparently, they're sleeping together.

   (They look at each other. Lights change.)

SCENE V

SALLY: She's Great

Ed is in his office. Sally enters.

ED: Hey, what's up?

SALLY: Nothing major. I just have some Polaroids for you to look at. Jim keeps changing his mind about what he's wearing this week. He wants you to look at it. *(She hands him the Polaroids.)*

ED: Oh, Jesus. Like I got nothing better to do.

SALLY: I told him, but he's gone completely insane. Ever since Monica did the *Today* show, he's been impossible.

ED: He's just uptight about the numbers. Everybody's got a lot riding on this. Here, this one.

SALLY: Great, that's the one everybody likes. So, are we going to take a pass at Belinda's script before it goes to table?

ED: Well, there's not a lot to do on it. I thought she and Ren and I would just take a look at it tonight, see if we can punch anything up.

SALLY: Oh. Sure. You don't want Steve and I to stick around, then?

ED: Yeah, you know, you guys, we should get you going on another couple of scripts, so if you could put some things together, ideas, that's probably the best use of your time.

SALLY: Sure. That sounds great. *(Pause.)* Belinda's script really is terrific. Everyone's saying it could be our Emmy.

ED: Really?

SALLY: That's what Bill was saying. The crew is wild for it.

ED: Well, Jesus. I don't know about any Emmys. She's a kid. It's her third script.

SALLY: Oh, I know. That's just what people are saying. I mean, she and Ren are just great. You know, Ren's good, and she's really good.

ED: They're both good.

SALLY: But she's special, she really is. Everyone's noticed it.

ED: Yeah. I was the first to notice it, remember? I hired her.

SALLY: Oh, I know. She's really a find. Oh, one other thing. I was talking to some reporter this morning, from *Redbook* or something, who went off on this kick about not knowing how Dave fit into the show. Now—I tried to get her off this, because that idiot on the *Today* show said exactly the same thing to Monica.

ED: Oh, Jesus. Jim's going to throw a fit.

SALLY: That's what I thought. Anyway, I'm just not sure I convinced her, and the next thing you know, we're going to be in one of those situations where everyone's saying the star isn't the star—

ED: Yeah, yeah, yeah—

SALLY: Do you want to give her a call?

ED: Yeah, sure.

SALLY: I'll have Clara send the number over.

BELINDA: *(Enters.)* Hey, what's going on?

SALLY: What do you mean?

BELINDA: *(Pause.)* Well—Ren and I are over in the writers' building. Where is everybody? Aren't we starting the rewrite soon?

SALLY: Steve and I are taking the night off.

BELINDA: You are?

ED: Yeah, I thought the three of us could handle it. There's not a lot. Mostly we just need to take a pass and see if we can't make Dave more central to the episode.

BELINDA: *(Slight pause.)* What?

ED: Yeah, I just think, you know, we gotta keep our focus on our guy. Keep him central. He's the person everyone's coming to see. I just don't think this script really answers the question Why is this important to Dave? just yet.

BELINDA: Well—

ED: *(A little dangerous.)* You have a problem?

BELINDA: No! I just, you know, it's—this episode's not really *about* Dave. Off the top of my head, I just don't see how we're going to graft him in.
(Ed stares at her. There is an uncomfortable pause.)

SALLY: Have a fun rewrite! *(She goes.)*
(Lights change.)

SCENE VI

The Family of Mann IV
The lights come up low on Ed, in his office.

ED: *(Quiet.)* I don't feel good. I don't *feel* good. You think I don't know what's going on? You think I'm stupid? I know what they want. Fighting amongst themselves. Trying to destroy each other. When I'm the one they're really after. You think I don't know that? You think I can't see it in their eyes? They're cannibals! They'd eat me alive if they could. That's what happened to the gods, you know. Their children ate them. For their strength. Why should I be any different? Well, fuck them. Fuck them all. Not one of them could handle this. Not ONE. The networks. The fucking numbers. Reporters. The assholes who advertise on this fucking show. FUCKING ACTORS. Every fucking day I deal with shit, with FUCKING SHIT, I keep everyone from destroying those fuckers, I spend my life providing for all of them, and they TURN on me. You think I don't KNOW?

GINNY: Dave? Are you all right, sweetheart? Why are you sitting in the dark?

DAVE: What, darling?

GINNY: Oh, you poor darling. You're upset about something!

DAVE: Oh, no.

GINNY: But you are, sweetheart. Your little forehead is getting all bunched up. Oh. Let me take care of you. Let me make you a cup of tea. Buddy! Sissy! Come down here and take care of your father! He's upset.

DAVE: That's okay, Ginny. Let the kids sleep.

GINNY: No, I want them down here, Dave, so you can see what a fortunate man you are. Your whole family is with you. Your kids, your brother. A lot of people might think, what a lot of good-for-nothing freeloaders. But you're glad they're here!

DAVE: I guess I am.

GINNY: I must admit, I sometimes worry. Maybe it would be better for Willy and the kids if they went out and lived their own lives. But it wouldn't be better for *you.*

DAVE: You think so, honey?

GINNY: I know it. You like it like this. Everyone here, under your control.

DAVE: Under my power.

GINNY: It makes you feel great.

DAVE: That's true.

GINNY: And that's why we stay. To make you happy. That's the only reason. Kids! Where are you? Your father needs you!

DAVE: Is that true, Ginny? You're all here, for me?

GINNY: Of course it is, sweetheart!

(*Buddy and Sissy enter.*)

BUDDY: Hey! What's everyone doing up?

GINNY: We were just talking about how glad we are to have you kids back home with us. You see, most people don't understand how perfect our world is.

DAVE: What could be better? I'm the king, and everyone else serves my needs. In return, I protect you and give you things. Money. Presents.

BUDDY: We earn some of that stuff, Dad. Yesterday, I did mow the lawn.

DAVE: Yes, you did, son. Not as well as I would have. But what the hey.

SISSY: Oh, Daddy. I love you so much. Would you like some more tea?

DAVE: That would be great, honey.

GINNY: I'm just going to go stand off in the corner here, Dave. I know how much you prefer the company of these young, healthy kids. If you need anything, just give a holler.

DAVE: Thanks, Ginny. You're so understanding.

UNCLE WILLY: Hey! What about me?

BUDDY AND SISSY: Uncle Willy!

DAVE: Come on over here, Willy, you old coot, and let me shove my fist up your ass!

(Dave and Willy laugh heartily.)

REN: Hey, are you two having good manly fun over over there? I want to get in on this! How about I shove my fist up your ass!

(They laugh.)

UNCLE WILLY: And then I'll shove my fist up your ass!

REN: And then I'll shove my fist up your ass!

(They laugh.)

DAVE: And then we can all play basketball! And you girls can cheer us on!

SISSY: *(Dry.)* Yeah, that sounds like fun.

(The men all stop laughing. They stare at her.)

SISSY: *(With forced enthusiasm.)* I mean, that sounds like *fun!* That sounds like fun!

(They continue to stare at her.)

BELINDA: I'm trying, all right? And how much longer am I going to have to hold this fucking teapot?

GINNY: Sissy!

BELINDA: Oh, come on, he's not actually buying this shit, is he? I mean, do you really need me here? Can't I just go read a book?

DAVE: Sissy, are you feeling left out?

BELINDA: Left out? No. Pissed off is closer to what I'm running into here. I mean, this is so boring. Do any of you know people who are like this? And would you want to? Why are we doing this?

DAVE: *(Beat.)* You're not Sissy. You're not my daughter at all. Where's Sissy?

BELINDA: I ate her. *(She laughs maniacally.)*
DAVE: Sissy? Sissy! SISSSSYYYY!
   (As Dave howls and Belinda laughs, the others turn and scatter. Blackout.)

SCENE VII

CLARA: Ed Wants To See You
   Belinda stands at the door of Ed's office.

BELINDA: You wanted to see me?
ED: Yeah, come on in. Have a seat.
   (She does. Ed looks up and speaks easily but abruptly.)
ED: I've been thinking about this, and I don't think you'll ever be happy here, and I think you should leave the show. It's up to you, but that's what I think.
   (Pause.)
BELINDA: *(In shock.)* Okay.
   (Ed looks at her, stunned and outraged.)
ED: All right. Fine. *(Pause.)* That's all.
   (He gestures to the door. She stands and looks at him, confused.)
BELINDA: Wait a minute. Is this really what you want? You want me to leave the show. That's what you want?
ED: I think…you are never going to be happy here, and…it's up to you, but I think you should leave.
BELINDA: Yesterday you told me I was talented, and valuable and—now you want me to leave? I don't understand.
ED: It's your decision.
BELINDA: For heaven's sake, Ed, you're the executive producer. If you want me to leave, it's not my decision!
ED: It's interesting to hear you say that. You didn't seem to feel that way yesterday.
BELINDA: Yesterday, what? You mean last night? What did I say? I said, I thought that grafting Dave into the episode might not—
ED: I don't graft. I DON'T GRAFT. And if you're not willing to rewrite, then—
BELINDA: You wanted to rewrite an episode that worked!
ED: I decide what works!

BELINDA: Two days ago, you loved that episode. Everyone loves that episode—

ED: *(Overlap.)* And if one day I say it works and the next day I say it's shit, then that's the way it is. You clearly don't understand the process. When I was working on my movie, I would go home every night and rewrite scenes for the next day!

BELINDA: But I was willing to stay! I didn't think it was necessary, but I would have done it—

ED: You didn't think it was necessary? You're making these decisions now?

BELINDA: You were the one who called off the rewrite. You said we'd do it today! Ed, listen. I am not trying to contradict you. I have nothing but admiration for your movie…and your…brilliance. But yesterday, I listened to you with that reporter on the phone, and I thought, you seemed to be panicking. I just thought it was my job to reassure you that the episode was good, and you didn't have to panic.

ED: I don't need some little girl telling me what's good and what's not.

BELINDA: *(Flaring again.)* Look, if you're going to stick fruit loops in one of my episodes because someone crossed their eyes at you over lunch, I think I have a right to at least—

ED: Your episode? Your episode? Let me tell you something. There isn't any episode that's *yours*. There is only *my* show. *I* write this show. Don't you ever talk about your episodes again.

BELINDA: Oh, Jesus, everybody talks about their episodes, we always—Ren practically blew a gasket last week because you bumped his episode in the release order and you didn't ask him to leave!

ED: That was a different situation. I was in a different mood then.

BELINDA: So I'm being fired because you're having a bad day?

ED: It's up to you.

(Pause.)

BELINDA: I'll have my agent give you a call.

(She goes. Ed's head twitches for a moment, then he sits. Clara enters, carrying a script.)

CLARA: Hey, Ed, you wanted to look at proofs for next week? *(Pause.)* Ed?

ED: Belinda's out of here. She's out.

(Clara stares at him, stunned. Lights change.)

SCENE VIII

REN: Belinda Blows A Gasket

Ren's office. Belinda paces, furious and frantic. Ren sits, confused.

BELINDA: Then, THEN he gives me the line about that fucking movie, when he was working on his MOVIE, he went home every night and rewrote scenes for the next day. I'm thinking, oh, and what a blinding achievement that piece of shit was, Ed.

REN: Belinda, you have to keep it down; the secretaries—

BELINDA: I don't give a *shit* who hears. That fucking piece of shit fired me over nothing; he's screaming at me that no little girl is going to tell him anything; can you FUCKING believe that prick called me a little GIRL—

REN: BELINDA. You have to be quiet now. You just, you have to be quiet.

BELINDA: I'm sorry. I'm sorry.

(She starts to cry. He crosses and holds her.)

BELINDA: I just don't—what happened? I mean, you hear about this shit going on, but who the fuck knew it actually did?

BILL: *(Enters.)* What's going on? We can hear you guys yelling in here all over the building, what's—

BELINDA: Ed asked me to leave the show.

BILL: What? Oh, fuck. Oh, Jesus.

BELINDA: That fucking *prick*—

REN: Belinda.

BILL: He didn't mean it.

BELINDA: He was very specific, Bill—

BILL: What did he say?

BELINDA: He said he thought I should leave the show! But it's up to me. Is that the most passive aggressive bullshit you've ever—

REN: *Belinda.*

BILL: No, he means it. I mean, he means you don't have to go. You have to go back in there and apologize.

BELINDA: What? What am I apologizing for?

BILL: Look, you're upset, you're crying, just go back and tell him you're sorry, it's all he wanted. He doesn't want you to leave.

BELINDA: I'm not going to cry for him.

REN: You're crying now.

(She stares at him.)

REN: What? If you can cry for us, you can cry for him, what's the difference?

BILL: Look. Ed is under a lot of pressure, his wife is bugging him to get out of television, the show isn't getting the numbers he wanted, he wants to get rid of Steve and Sally, but he can't—

BELINDA: So he got rid of me instead?

BILL: No, he doesn't want to get rid of you. That's not what he wanted. He just wants your loyalty. He needs you to say, I'm here for you, Ed.

BELINDA: While he's telling me to leave?

BILL: He didn't say that. He said it was up to you. You cannot leave him.

BELINDA: He told me to leave!

BILL: That's not what he told you.

REN: Look, what did he say? What did you do to piss him off?

BELINDA: I didn't—I don't know, it was—

BILL: Look, you can't fall apart on us, Belinda. The show needs you. There can be no ego involved here!

BELINDA: What do you mean, no ego, I don't even know what that—

BILL: You do not exist. Do you understand me? The only person who exists here is Ed. He is the executive producer. It is his show, his vision, and you do whatever he wants.

BELINDA: He wants me to leave the show!

REN: He said it was up to you.

BELINDA: Oh, man. Don't you both fucking gang up on me—

BILL: You cannot leave him. No writer has ever left Ed and gone on to work on anything of significance. Anywhere.

BELINDA: What?

BILL: All I'm saying is no writer has ever left Ed and gone on to work on anything of any significance.

BELINDA: What are you saying, I only exist in relation to Ed? If I leave, I cease to exist, I'm no longer a writer, is that what you're fucking telling me?

BILL: This is not about ego, Belinda!

BELINDA: I mean, I love this! He fires me on a whim, and now you're telling me that if I don't get down on my knees and beg for my job back, I'm being egotistical!

REN: Okay, okay, I'm taking you home—

BELINDA: Don't you touch me!

REN: Belinda, Jesus, would you stop, would you just—

BILL: She cannot leave the lot. I'm telling you, I've seen this happen before; she has to go back now, before he gets used to the idea and can't even—

REN: I'm just saying if we send her in there now, while she's still acting like a raving lunatic, it's not going to—

BELINDA: Well, thank you very much and could you all not
    if I'm not even in the room? Jesus, you guys are starting
    Ed.
BILL: Belinda, Ed is a genius.
BELINDA: He's not a genius, he's a TV producer! *(Pause.)* And, a m   .a-
    niac. And a madman. And what's more, everybody knows it. *(She goes.)*
REN: Oh, Christ.
BILL: That's it. It's over.
REN: Come on, let's go talk to him. She's, they're both so emotional.
BILL: You don't understand. It was a test, and she failed it. *(Pause.)* It's over.
    (He shrugs. Ren stares at him, confused. Lights change.)

SCENE IX

BILL: A Whole Different World
    Ren and Ed are in Ed's office.

ED: Hey! How's it going?
REN: Great. It's really—
ED: I'm glad you're here; I was gonna call you. You want to go do some editing?
REN: Yeah, sure.
ED: Also, we're going to have to stay late and take a look at next week's script.
    It's not quite working and Belinda's gonna leave the show, so I thought
    you and I could take a pass at it.
REN: Yeah, I just saw her. She's real upset.
ED: She's a talented girl; she'll be fine. Sometimes these things just don't work
    out.
REN: She really doesn't want to leave, Ed.
ED: I gave her a choice.
REN: Yeah, but, I, I think she didn't understand—see, I just think she's kind
    of insecure. This is all really new to her, I mean, we've all done it before,
    one way or another, and she's from a whole different world. That's all I
    think it is. And Sally really is—I know you guys have been through a lot
    together, but she's not been great to Belinda. You know how competitive
    women can be. She's—it's mostly when you're not around, but she gives
    her a hard time, and you know, it's clear to everyone else that it's because
    she's threatened, but how's Belinda supposed to know that? And she's

good, everyone knows that, but she's just, she's figuring out how it all works, so she's a little...I don't know. She makes some mistakes. But she loves the show, I know she loves being here, that's mostly what it is, I think.

(Pause.)

ED: So, what are you saying? Are you two sleeping together? Is that what you're telling me?

(Pause.)

REN: Would that be a problem?

ED: No! Jesus, no, I told you, I think she's great. I'm just—I mean, personally, I wouldn't be able to sleep with someone who's a better writer than I am. But hey, I think it's great. She'll land on her feet.

(They look at each other. Lights change.)

SCENE X

BELINDA: Producer

Belinda lies on Ren's bed. She holds a bottle of scotch, out of which she drinks. Beside the bed, there is a beautiful ten-speed bicycle, wrapped in red ribbon. Ren enters. Pause.

REN: How are you?

BELINDA: Fine. How are you?

REN: Okay. Not so great. You know.

(She doesn't answer. He sees the bicycle.)

REN: What's that?

BELINDA: It's a bicycle. Someone delivered it about fifteen minutes ago.

REN: For me? I mean, it's...for me?

BELINDA: Well, it's not for me.

(Curious, Ren crosses to look at it. He finds a card and starts to open it.)

BELINDA: It's from Ed. He's making you a producer.

(Pause.)

REN: Yes. I know.

BELINDA: Oh. You saw Ed.

REN: Of course I saw him, Christ, what do you think, I went over after you left and—

BELINDA: You went to see him? Oh. Did you talk about me?

REN: Yes, as a matter of fact, we did. I told him this was all a huge mistake.

BELINDA: You told Ed—*the* Ed—that he was making a huge mistake?

(Pause. Ren does not answer.)

BELINDA: No, that's not what you told him. You told him *I* was making a huge mistake. By not begging for his love while he tromped all over me, I made a huge mistake. Thank you for your support. It means so much to me that you went in and explained that to your good friend Ed!

REN: Belinda—

BELINDA: Yeah, too bad it didn't work. I mean, you went in to beg for my job, and came out a producer. Poor Ren. You can't do anything right.

(Pause.)

REN: All you had to do was cry.

BELINDA: Fuck you. You think it's so fucking easy to cry for that creep, then you do it, you fucking woman.

(Pause.)

REN: I'm not going to talk to you right now. You're drunk.

BELINDA: Oh, that's rich. You can talk to a man who is completely insane well enough to get yourself that precious fucking producer button, but one drunken female has you tongue-tied.

REN: Jesus, you are—you know, you are just as bad as he is.

BELINDA: Not possible. No one's as bad as Ed. No one's as good as Ed. Only Ed exists, remember? You better remember, or he'll get you, too.

(She drinks from the bottle. He reaches for it. She pulls away.)

REN: Give me the bottle.

BELINDA: You know what I think is interesting? You told me to fight. You said, he loves you. He wants you to fight for what you believe in. He wants you to fight for your script.

REN: Belinda—

BELINDA: You sent me in there, to fight, and I got fired, and now you're a producer. I find that very interesting.

REN: That's not what happened.

BELINDA: Isn't it? Then you tell me what happened. You—you tell me—

REN: Give me that. Would you give me that?

(She shoves him away.)

BELINDA: No. NO. Get your hands off me. Stay—just don't—

(Pause. Ren sits on the bed.)

BELINDA: Why don't you tell me to go? Just tell me to go.

REN: I'm not going to do that. I don't understand any of this. I think I'm falling in love with you, and—it's not right what he did. I don't know what I'm going to do.

(He rubs his eyes. She watches him. Lights change.)

SCENE XI

BILL: Loyalty
Steve, Sally and Bill are in the writers' room.

SALLY: Well, I think it's definitely what needed to happen. She just wasn't fitting in. Already, you can feel how relieved everyone is.

BILL: I just don't know what we're gonna do for scripts now. I mean, she was a machine.

STEVE: I've got a lot of ideas. We can pick up the slack.

BILL: No, I know, I just—

SALLY: I think Ed always overrated her, frankly. I mean, she wrote fast, but we had to do a lot of work on her material.

STEVE: She wasn't funny. I didn't think. She just wasn't funny.

BILL: Well, she certainly wasn't loyal.

STEVE: And she just made everyone tense. I don't know *what* Ren sees in her.

SALLY: Oh, please. That's not going to last.

(Ren enters, frazzled. Sally is immediately sympathetic.)

SALLY: Ren! How are you?

REN: Oh, I'm fine. I'm sorry I'm late, I just, you know. Is Ed around?

BILL: He's at the network.

REN: Something going on?

BILL: You know. The usual shit. They're talking about the pickup.

REN: Oh, Jesus.

SALLY: *(Sympathetic.)* How's Belinda?

REN: She's fine. A little rattled.

SALLY: She'll be fine.

REN: Oh, yeah. She's already got, like, six job offers.

SALLY: *(Too polite.)* Really?

REN: Yeah, it's amazing how fast people hear somebody's available. You know, there's always work for someone who can write. She doesn't know what she's gonna do. You know, I don't think she's ready to just, dive into another show.

BILL: Fuck her.

SALLY: Bill.

BILL: No, I mean it. We give her her break, Ed hires her when she's nobody and now everybody wants her. Ed created her, and now she's off fielding offers from every shithead in town.

SALLY: Look. We're all upset by what happened—

BILL: No, look, I'm sorry, Ren, I know there's something going on between you two, but I'm not going to lie about how I feel.

REN: No, I know. I understand that.

BILL: I think a person should show a little loyalty. That's just how I feel.

REN: I agree, Bill.

BILL: I mean, Ed doesn't—Ed is not in this because he needs the power, or the money or anything. This is all a huge headache for him, and he has so much money, he doesn't have to do it anymore. He doesn't have to do anything unless he thinks it's going to benefit mankind.

REN: I know that.

BILL: So when she goes in there and tries to take over the show, how is he supposed to take that?

REN: I don't think that's what—

BILL: That's how it looked, all right? I mean, how else is he supposed to take it? And the next thing you know, she's calling her agents in. I don't think it's right. I think Ed deserves a little better than that.

REN: I understand what you're saying.

BILL: Do you?

(Beat. Ed enters.)

ED: Hey, you hacks, how's it going?

BILL: Great!

ED: (Sober.) You guys got a minute?

(Pause.)

BILL: Sure. Sure! What's up?

ED: Well, you know, I know things have been a little tense around here lately, the numbers haven't been what we hoped and I know everyone's been pretty worried and wondering about what kind of life *The Family of Mann* has to look forward to. So I wanted everyone to know as soon as it happened. I just got back from the network and...we've got our pickup.

(He laughs. Everyone cheers.)

ED: I think this is a real vote of confidence for us from the network. They're under a lot of pressure to come up with shows that they really think are

going to fly, and they're backing us a hundred percent. So I'd like everyone to just take a minute to feel good about all your hard work, and I
think that we can now look forward to a lot of years together.

(Everyone cheers again.)

ED: And don't worry about the numbers; everybody at the network assures
me that it's not going to matter. They're going to stand behind us no
matter what, and we all know that there is someone out there who's
eventually going to find us and say, thank god. Something real, and
decent for a change.

(They all hug and applaud.)

SALLY: Oh, isn't it wonderful?

BILL: Fantastic.

REN: That's great news, Ed.

ED: Yeah, it looks like we got a show for our new producer to produce! Now,
get back to work. Hacks... *(He goes, laughing.)*

BILL: Well, how about that?

SALLY: What a relief!

STEVE: I wasn't worried.

(They all laugh.)

SALLY: Ren, we never congratulated you on your promotion. I think it's terrific.

REN: Thanks.

SALLY: Well, I guess if we're going for a whole season—

BILL: Hey, we're going longer than that. Seven years—

SALLY: Then we better get back to work!

BILL: All right! So what's Jim doing in this scene? Besides standing around
with his fist up his ass.

STEVE: *(Snickers.)* You think that's physically possible?

BILL: It's the only way Jim's gonna get it.

STEVE: "Hey hey, Ralph! What are you doing?"

BILL: "I'm fucking myself, Norton! It's the wave of the future! You wanta
watch?"

REN: "Hey hey hey hey!"

BILL: "Norton—you're the greatest!"

*(Bill and Steve laugh. Ren tries to smile. Clara enters. She wears her wings
and passes out yellow sheets, menus and scripts.)*

CLARA: Here are the lunch menus. Polaroids from wardrobe. Casting sheets.
New second acts. Anything else?

BILL: Yeah, how would you like to give me a blow job?

(Clara looks at him. The others laugh. The laughter dies out.)

CLARA: Actually, Bill, you know what I'd really like, is to cut it off and shove it down your throat.

(Steve goes, "whoaaaa...." Bill stares at her, cold. She stares back. Lights change.)

SCENE XII

CLARA: Out In The Cold

Belinda sits on a bench, smoking a cigarette. A bedraggled Clara, still wearing her wings, approaches.

BELINDA: Hey. How's it going?

CLARA: Fine. Shitty, fine. *(She picks up the cigarettes from the bench and takes one.)* This city is, you know, man. This city is smoking. They're finally rioting over on Rodeo Drive.

BELINDA: They are?

CLARA: They should be. I mean, if I was gonna riot, that's what I'd do. I'd fucking burn Beverly Hills to the ground, that's what I'd do.

BELINDA: Bad day, huh?

CLARA: Please. Would you look at this place? Earthquakes. Fires. Riots! Floods! It's downright apocalyptic around here. The city of angels, my ass. This is Sodom and Gomorrah, and all this bad behavior is having an impact on the weather. The day of righteousness is at hand. Armageddon is starting at the corner of Wilshire and Fairfax, right down there in front of the May Company. I think it's already started.

(She smokes. Belinda watches her.)

BELINDA: Clara?

CLARA: Yeah?

BELINDA: You've grown wings. You know that, don't you?

CLARA: You can see them?

(Belinda nods.)

CLARA: Oh, thank god. Oh, Jesus. I thought I was losing my fucking mind, I got these major wings growing out of my back and nobody's even mentioned it! I mean, I go in that fucking room, and fucking Bill—I got fucking wings growing out of my back and he's asking me for a blow job!

BELINDA: He what?

CLARA: He asked me for a blow job. In front of everybody! Can you believe it?

BELINDA: What did you say?

CLARA: I told him I'd rather cut it off and shove it down his throat. Some angel I'm gonna make.

(They laugh.)

CLARA: You can see them? You actually see these things?

BELINDA: Yeah, they're pretty.

CLARA: You like them?

BELINDA: I think they're beautiful. Are they real?

CLARA: I guess! I mean, they kind of itch, you know? And they don't come off, which makes it real hard to get any sleep. And sometimes, at night, they just move. On their own. They beat. They're anxious about something.

BELINDA: Me too.

CLARA: Yeah, me too.

BELINDA: Where'd they come from?

CLARA: I don't know. I was just sitting at my desk, right, everyone's screaming at me, and I start thinking about flying off, imagining what that would be like, to just float away. Fly off, into the sunset. The next thing I know, fucking wings. Growing out of my back.

(Beat.)

BELINDA: You imagined them. *(Pause.)* I can't, I can't imagine anything except buying a gun and shooting Ed, in an alley. *(Beat. Trying to collect herself.)* Clearly, wings are a much better way to go.

CLARA: Yeah. I think so. And I'm going to use them. I'm getting out of this town. I don't know why I stuck around this long. Unfinished business, I guess. You want to touch them? Go ahead. You can touch them.

BELINDA: No, I—no.

CLARA: It's okay.

(Clara reaches over and takes Belinda's hand. She places it on one of her wings. Belinda starts to cry. Clara takes her in her arms and rocks her. Lights change.)

SCENE XIII

REN: A Great Opportunity
The writers' room. Ren is looking at scripts. Belinda pokes her head in.

BELINDA: Hi.

REN: Belinda! What are—what are you doing here?

BELINDA: I just cleaned out my office. And, I was looking for you, actually. Everyone's gone, aren't they? I looked around, and—

REN: Yeah. Ed's over in his office. But everybody else left an hour ago. You're safe.
(Awkward pause. She looks around.)

REN: So. What'd you do today?

BELINDA: I went to the tar pits.

REN: Again?

BELINDA: Yeah, you know, there's something about it I really find comforting. I think it's that dramatic recreation of the mastodon getting sucked into the tar. You know, the one you can see from the street. Her husband, and her little baby bellowing woefully at her from the bank. I find it kind of touching in a way that's unusual for Los Angeles.

REN: So how many times is that?

BELINDA: I don't know. Five or six.

REN: Just this week.

BELINDA: I've only been out of work this week. Give me a little more time, I may set a record. *(Pause.)* I bumped into Clara.

REN: You did?

BELINDA: Yeah.

REN: She had a kind of a run in with Bill. Did she tell you?

BELINDA: Actually, what she said was he asked her for a blow job. In front of a whole roomful of writers.

REN: Well, she gave as good as she got.

BELINDA: You notice anything different about her? About the way she looks or anything? Like, wings or anything?

REN: Wings?

BELINDA: Yeah, you know. Wings. *(Pause.)* Never mind. She says she's not coming back.

REN: Yeah. She made that pretty clear.

BELINDA: This city is smoking, you know? Clara told me that, at the tar pits, and I thought she meant that they were rioting again, but that's not it. I figured it out. She's talking about television.

REN: Really?

BELINDA: I think so. It's us that's burning. You know, we're, like, putting our lives into this cauldron, and turning up the heat so high—with the pressure, and the money, and the power, it's making us all white hot until our essence just burns away. You know, the best of us, the stuff that makes us human, it evaporates. And we're left with sitcoms. Maybe that's what all the smog is. It's not car exhaust. It's us, burning ourselves up.

REN: Belinda—

BELINDA: And then hanging there, in the air, like a disease. Like television. What is it? What are we becoming?

(Pause. The door bursts open. Ed enters.)

ED: Hey, how's my new producer? *(Beat. He takes her in.)*

BELINDA: Ed.

REN: I was on my way over, Ed, she just stopped by for—

BELINDA: It's okay. *(Beat.)* I was picking up my stuff, Ed.

(Beat. They wait for Ed to respond.)

ED: *(To Ren.)* I'll be in my office, okay? Whenever you're ready. *(He turns to go.)*

BELINDA: God, aren't you even going to let me say good-bye?

(He stops and waits for her to continue. She crosses and holds out her hand. He turns to Ren.)

ED: Whenever you're ready. No rush.

(He goes. Beat. Belinda looks at her hand.)

BELINDA: Whoa. I've been dissed. *(She laughs.)*

REN: Oh, shit. I have to go.

BELINDA: Oh, come on, Ren, relax. What's he gonna do if you don't hop, fire you? Pretty soon, he's not going to have any staff at all! *(She laughs.)*

REN: I don't have time for this! This is bad, don't you get it? It's bad that he saw me with you! *(Beat.)* I'm sorry.

BELINDA: *(Beat.)* Oh, no.

(She looks at him. He looks away.)

REN: Look. I'm as sorry as anyone about what happened to you, but you have to understand, this is a great opportunity for me, and I need to protect myself here.

BELINDA: Don't do this.

REN: Don't—oh, that's great. Now *I'm* the villain.

BELINDA: No, you're not the villain, that's not— *(Regrouping.)* Look. I'm sorry I haven't been paying attention to what's going on with you, the position that you're in now, I—I've been so upset, it's like this whole place has poisoned me, and I'm trying to get myself back—

REN: This place is fine.

BELINDA: No, it's not, Ren, it's destroying people! And I think the longer you stay here, the more it infects you, and pretty soon you can't imagine anything else—

REN: What did you think you were going to find here? I mean, why is this all such a big surprise to you? I'm just a dumb jock from Illinois, and I knew it was going to be like this. Why didn't you just go back and tell Ed you were sorry?

BELINDA: Because he would do it again.

REN: Of course he would! He's the boss! That's what bosses do! I don't get why—how can you stand there and act like what's happened to you is so terrible? You had a good job, with people who admired you, and you gave it all up for pride—

BELINDA: Yes, I have pride—

REN: So the boss blows off steam in your direction, so what? He's under a lot of pressure. He's entitled. What's your problem?

BELINDA: Apparently my problem is I really do want people to be decent!

REN: It's a sitcom, Belinda! It's a fucking sitcom!

BELINDA: Well, this sitcom is a lie, and you're selling your soul to write it!

REN: Oh, no. That was never me. That's you, remember? I happen to like this show. I think it's funny, and smart, and *decent*. I'm proud to write for it, and I'm proud to work with Ed. I think I can learn a lot from him. I intend to try.

BELINDA: *(Pause.)* Ren. What are you—are we on feed? Is this being piped into Ed's office? *(She looks for the hidden mic.)* Ed-d-d...

REN: I have to go. *(He goes for his knapsack.)*

BELINDA: No. Please, listen to me. If you just go along with it all, you'll lose yourself.

REN: Look, I can't do this. Really, I can't fight with you anymore. I just can't. I have to go. *(He heads for the door.)*

BELINDA: Hey. What are you and Ed doing? Are you rewriting my script?

REN: *(Beat.)* Yes, We are.

BELINDA: Well. Have a good time.

REN: Look. We all do what we have to do.

BELINDA: I know that! I know.

REN: I'll call you, okay?

BELINDA: Sure.

> *(He goes. She sits, for a moment, looking at the room. From the darkness around him, the Mann family begins to take shape. They move in, whispering their lines. She turns.)*

BELINDA: What? What do you want out of me? WHAT?

> *(They fall silent. She turns and looks at them as they surround her. She turns, finally, and looks at the script before her.)*

BELINDA: Scene One: The Mann Family Kitchen.

> *(She looks at them, throws the script on the table, picks up her box and goes. The Family of Mann leans in to read the script. Blackout.)*

END OF PLAY

VIEW OF THE DOME

ORIGINAL PRODUCTION

View of the Dome was originally produced in New York by The New York Theatre Workshop on September 13, 1996. It was directed by Michael Mayer. The cast was as follows:

SENATOR GEOFFREY MADDOX/RICHARD . . . . Jim Abele

TOMMY/LANCE/REPORTER/SENATOR B . . . . Patrick Breen

ANNABETH GILKEY/MARJORIE/JUNETTE/
    REPORTER/BELLA . . . . Candy Buckley

E.T. BLACK/GOVERNOR/REPORTER/AUGUST/
    RUSH/SENATOR C . . . . Tom Riis Farrell

EMMA. . . . . Julia Gibson

DAVID/ANCHORMAN/SHEILA. . . . . Dion Graham

ARTHUR WOOLF/LEONARD/SENATOR A . . . . Richard Poe

Scenic Design. . . . . Neil Patel

Costume Design. . . . . Michael Krass

Lighting Design . . . . Frances Aronson

Sound Design . . . . Darron L. West

Production Stage Manager . . . . Lisa Iacucci

Assistant Stage Manager. . . . . Charles Means

Character doubling enables the play to be performed with seven or eight actors.

SET

A fancy restaurant. One table with four chairs, and another table with one chair off to the side. All of the action takes place in the restaurant, even the action that doesn't.

A restaurant. Two tables. One seats four people in a lively debate. At the second a single woman sits alone.

ANNABETH: I was mentioning to the senator what an extraordinary coincidence—is this vinaigrette? I don't think this is the vinaigrette.

TOMMY: No, that's it—

ANNABETH: Are you sure?

ARTHUR: Yes, I've got the same thing. It's a raspberry—

ANNABETH: But this looks like it has cream in it.

TOMMY: No, I don't think so—

ANNABETH: In any event, I was telling the senator how extraordinary I thought it was, when I heard Arthur speaking about the call to public service, how close your two positions actually are, and how rare it is to hear politicians, even aspiring politicians, actually speak of civic duty—

SENATOR: Yes. I think the last time someone even said the words up on the hill they were quietly taken aside and stoned.

(They all laugh.)

ANNABETH: Exactly. So I said to Arthur, you have to meet the Senator and tell him your ideas. But when you get to the part about "civic duty"—keep your voice down.

(They all laugh again. The laughter stops suddenly as Emma raises her eyes and speaks to the audience.)

EMMA: Do any of you find this interesting? Some of you must. Every night of the week, all across America, near strangers who want something from each other gather and enact a social ritual involving food which nobody has to pay for because it's being expensed. And then everyone talks about nothing for a couple of hours, somehow sliding into the cracks the mysterious subject of What They Want, and then everybody goes away, pondering the even more mysterious subject of What They Got. It's called a political dinner.

SENATOR: So, Arthur, you're thinking of taking a run at Congress?

ARTHUR: Well, I'm afraid it's gone a little farther than that. I declared my candidacy last week.

SENATOR: *(Mock dismay.)* Oh, dear. Then I've come too late.

(They all laugh again.)

EMMA: I happen to think political dinners are a huge crashing bore. Nevertheless, I would give anything to be sitting at that table.

ANNABETH: Oh, the escargot are excellent. Geoffrey—Senator—I think they're even better than the ones we had in Nice.

SENATOR: The ones *you* had. I'm afraid I'm too much of an American to actually consume a garden slug.
(*They laugh.*)
EMMA: I walked in with those people.
SENATOR: Are you a snail man, Arthur?
EMMA: In fact, I drove them here.
ARTHUR: Well, I'm afraid—
SENATOR: Careful.
ARTHUR: Absolutely not.
ANNABETH: Oh. stop. (*She feeds him a snail.*)
EMMA: You have no idea where this sort of thing can lead. This is what happened. (*She stands and crosses to the table indicating Arthur.*) Two weeks ago, I received a phone call from this man's wife. Her name is Natalie, she and Arthur and I are old friends, and she wants to know if I will have dinner with them tonight.
ARTHUR: The challenge of any society is balancing the rights of the individual against the rights of the community. America, built on the dream of rugged individualism, is directly challenged by communism, which annihilates the individual and promotes only the dream of the community. But just as communism finally destroyed itself, crumbling under the weight of its singular dream, so shall we fall unless we find a way to support a dynamic interchange between self and society.
EMMA: Now, the fact is, I am a sucker for this kind of shit.
ARTHUR: This is the job of a leader. To protect the individual, and the community, at the same time.
EMMA: Arthur was one of my professors in law school. While everyone else was busy grinding my imagination to smithereens, Arthur spoke of—
ANNABETH: Dreams! Another word you don't hear on the hill...
SENATOR: They stone you for that too, Arthur.
ARTHUR: Mea culpa, mea culpa!
(*They all laugh.*)
EMMA: So me, Arthur, and Natalie are going to dinner, when Tommy calls to tell us Annabeth Gilkey has arranged for us to meet Senator Geoffrey Maddox in her office. We planned to hook up with Natalie after, but she gets a head cold and bags the trip.
ANNABETH: He's so delightfully idealistic, isn't he, Geoffrey?
ARTHUR: Oh. I don't—
ANNABETH: No, no, it's charming! Mr. Smith Goes To Washington. It reminds me of you, Geoffrey.

SENATOR: Well, I don't—

ANNABETH: Oh, to a tee! And the time is right for this. Public mood.

SENATOR: You might be—

ANNABETH: Who gives a shit about the presidency, we've gotta take the House back. I mean those fascists on the right are just driving me nuts. Gingrich, and Robertson, those idiot freshmen oh, my God, Rush Limbaugh, when is he gonna go away.

SENATOR: The situation is difficult right now.

ANNABETH: I know, it's late, the primary is only a couple months away, but let's face it, we've got *no one* who stands a chance and Geoffrey, I'm telling you, I can *do* something with this. And you know I wouldn't say it if it weren't true. *(She smiles at him.)*

EMMA: Annabeth Gilkey is living proof that it is in fact possible to sleep your way to the top, in any field. She is the kind of person who, if she owned a fur coat, it would be made of puppies.

(The scene changes to Annabeth's office. The Senator leaves.)

EMMA: We arrive at Annabeth's office fifteen minutes early.

ANNABETH: Emma! How lovely to see you again! I didn't know you were coming.

EMMA: Why wouldn't I be coming?

ARTHUR: Is my tie all right?

EMMA: *(Checking it.)* It's fine

ARTHUR: I'm so nervous

EMMA: He's gonna love you—

ARTHUR: I just hope I get a chance to explain my ideas to him.

TOMMY: You were great with the governor.

ANNABETH: The governor? Arthur, you *are* moving up quickly.

EMMA: He's a friend of my dad's.

ANNABETH: How darling.

EMMA: Arthur knocked him dead. We're on our way!

ANNABETH: You already have a whole organization, Arthur. What's your title, Emma?

EMMA: *(Fixing tie.)* We haven't gotten to that yet.

ARTHUR: Chief of staff.

(They laugh.)

ANNABETH: How darling.

EMMA: Okay, see you guys at the restaurant. Give my best to the senator.

ANNABETH: Actually, the senator's had to postpone.

(There is an awkward disappointed pause.)

TOMMY: Oh?

ARTHUR: Oh.

ANNABETH: Oh, stop! Such long faces. He's just running late. He's going to join us. Where were you going?

EMMA: Chardonnay.

ANNABETH: Fabulous. *(She picks up the phone and punches a button.)* Jennie? It's Annabeth. The Senator asked me to call and let him know where we'd be having dinner. We're heading over to Chardonnay, can you let him know? Thanks, you're a doll. *(She hangs up, bright.)* Shall we? *(The scene changes back to the restaurant.)*

EMMA: *(To audience.)* So all of us get into my car and we drive across town, to a very nice, very discreet French restaurant.

ANNABETH: I *love* this place.

EMMA: Where I have made a reservation.

ANNABETH: And I hardly ever get over here.

EMMA: To have dinner with my friends and colleagues.

ANNABETH: Now, how do you want to do the seating, Arthur? Four and one? *(Emma looks over as Arthur considers this.)*

ARTHUR: *(Quickly.)* Oh, yes. That's exactly right. Four and one.

ANNABETH: David—We'll need a table for four, and a table for one.

DAVID: Right this way.

EMMA: *(To audience.)* I wish I could say that it took me a minute to get this, but unfortunately I understood immediately what was going on.

TOMMY: Wait a minute. There are going to be five of us, aren't there? When the senator gets here—

EMMA: *(To Tommy.)* Apparently, Annabeth and Arthur would prefer that I ate at a separate table.

ANNABETH: We'll set you up at the best single they have. David, can we get her the view of the capitol dome?

DAVID: Anything for you, Annabeth.

ARTHUR: Emma, you understand. This is strictly business.

EMMA: Of course!

ARTHUR: The senator—

EMMA: I know.

DAVID: It's a little close to the kitchen and there is a draft, but I think you'll be very pleased with the view.

ARTHUR: *(To Annabeth.)* I can't tell you how much I appreciate your help arranging this, Annabeth—

ANNABETH: I didn't do it for you, Arthur. I did it for all of us. Now, you and

Tommy need to fill me in on your campaign strategy before the senator gets here.

ARTHUR: Of course! Tommy—

(They all sit at their respective tables.)

EMMA: *(To audience.)* So they get to work. I order a drink.

(She does. The waiter delivers it.)

EMMA: The senator arrives.

(He does. The waiter knocks the drink on Emma in his rush to serve the senator. More and more rattled.)

EMMA: And while they chat, I eat alone. I don't have a book with me because I didn't realize that I would be eating alone. I don't have a newspaper because, same thing. I don't have anyone to talk to because, well, that's obvious. Plus, the service is terrible because everyone in the restaurant is obsessed with "Geoffrey," the senator, once he gets here. So, I sit alone for two hours, wondering why the hell I went along with this, why Arthur went along with it, why Tommy went along with it, and why the fuck the vinaigrette has cream in it!

(Everyone bursts into laughter at the next table. Emma stabs her salad, eating angrily.)

SENATOR: Oh, look at the time! I'm going to miss that fundraiser altogether.

ANNABETH: Well, maybe you should—

SENATOR: I wish. But I've *got* to put in an appearance. You'll join me, of course.

ARTHUR: That would be delightful—

SENATOR: That's the last time you'll say that, Arthur. If all goes well for you, and I'm sure it will, you will get very tired of fundraisers.

ARTHUR: That's very kind of you.

SENATOR: We'll have to call a cab, I'm afraid. I sent the car ahead with my wife—

ARTHUR: No no, that's not a problem. We have a car.

SENATOR: Wonderful!

ARTHUR: Yes, we drove down from Baltimore with my dear friend Emma. Emma— *(He brings the Senator over to Emma's table.)*

EMMA: Hello! Yes—

ARTHUR: The senator is heading over to that DNC fundraiser. He'd like us to come along.

SENATOR: You came down together? Why didn't you have dinner with us?

EMMA: *(Smiling.)* Apparently, I'm not important enough to sit at your table.

(She laughs. They laugh. Arthur gives her a hug.)

SENATOR: Certainly not.

ARTHUR: Oh, no, it wasn't that—

ANNABETH: Aren't we heading over? We'd better go soon, or Geoffrey may just turn into a pumpkin. Think of how that would look in the morning papers.

(They all laugh again. The scene changes.)

EMMA: What a surprise. The fundraiser is a huge crashing bore. It's just like a political dinner, except the drinks are watered, everyone stands up and for some reason there's a military band…At times like this, one cannot help but wonder about the rituals of white people.

(The Senator exits. Music plays. As before Emma stands off to one side.)

ANNABETH: *(Waving, working the room.)* Frank, how are you? I *loved* what you said on Nightline the other night. I thought Cokie Roberts was going to *hit* you. Paul, meet Arthur Woolf. Maryland's next congressman from District 2.

TOMMY: Al Gore's here.

SENATOR: Emma! Here you are off in a corner again. I've been looking for you.

EMMA: You have?

SENATOR: Would you like to dance?

EMMA: Here? Now?

SENATOR: With me?

EMMA: Maybe the evening won't be a complete disaster after all. I'd love to.

(The music changes into a tango. Emma and the Senator dance.)

SENATOR: So what do you do, Emma?

EMMA: I'm a lawyer.

SENATOR: Really? My wife is a lawyer.

EMMA: Yes, we've met. I was opposing council on that Bennington suit.

SENATOR: That was you? You really made her work.

EMMA: Not hard enough. She whipped the pants off me.

(The Senator dips her.)

SENATOR: Sounds fascinating.

(Annabeth snaps into action.)

ANNABETH: Arthur, let's dance.

ARTHUR: Shouldn't I be mingling?

ANNABETH: That depends on what kind of a dancer you are. If you're any good at all, this is a much better way to get people talking about you.

(She whips him around and dips him. Very quickly there are dueling tangos.)

SENATOR: So how do you know Arthur, Emma?

EMMA: He was one of my professors, my first year of law school.

SENATOR: And now you work for him?

EMMA: Unofficially.

SENATOR: Sounds romantic.

EMMA: Arthur? No.

SENATOR: Excellent. *(He dips her again.)*

ARTHUR: Don't you think I should put together a policy statement?

ANNABETH: That's a wonderful point, Arthur. The problem is, no one reads policy statements.

ARTHUR: But everyone says they're sick of the status quo. We have to provide people with options.

ANNABETH: Americans are afraid of ideas.

ARTHUR: Then we have to teach them that there's nothing to be afraid of.

ANNABETH: Oh, Arthur. You are just perfect. I can work with this, I really can. *(Suddenly flashbulbs go off. Arthur looks up, startled. Annabeth smiles for the camera.)*

ANNABETH: Perfect.

SENATOR: Now, just a minute there. This is perfectly innocent. *(He goes off after the photographers.)*

ANNABETH: I'm telling you, Arthur, my way is easier. We're going to be all over the newspapers by Tuesday. *(She follows the Senator off. Arthur and Tommy look at each other. Arthur heads after Annabeth. Tommy helps Emma up.)*

TOMMY: I'm sorry, Em. Arthur gets nervous at these things. He just started; he doesn't know what he's doing yet. I mean, that thing in the restaurant...

EMMA: *(Dusting herself off.)* It wasn't his fault. Annabeth set me up.

TOMMY: Still. He shouldn't have let it happen.

EMMA: Look, it's okay.

TOMMY: You sure?

EMMA: Yes!

TOMMY: You are such a sport. I'll talk to him about it, okay? *(The scene changes. The phone rings. The waiter comes in and sets the phone before her. It stops ringing and Arthur steps into the light.)*

ARTHUR: Emma, could you call me? I need to talk to you about something.

EMMA: So, not only am I to be humiliated, now I have to listen to people apologize about it. Might as well get it over with.

ARTHUR: Hello?

EMMA: Arthur. Hi. I'm returning your call.

ARTHUR: Listen, Emma. I wanted to talk to you about that evening in the restaurant.

EMMA: You know, Arthur, let's just forget about it, okay? It was just an awkward situation.

ARTHUR: Yes, it was, and I really feel that I need to say something about it. I mean, I appreciate everything you've done to help this campaign get off the ground, the money you've given, the introduction to the governor, bringing Tommy on board, the fundraisers you've organized, that's been great, but I have to say, I was really upset with you for the way you behaved the other night.

EMMA: What?

ARTHUR: When you said that you weren't important enough to sit at our table, I felt that you were trying to punish me. And I don't appreciate it. I was going to Washington for an extremely important meeting, something you seem to have completely forgotten—

EMMA: I didn't forget—

ARTHUR: It was not appropriate for you to be there!

EMMA: Whoa! Wait a minute—

ARTHUR: Well, now you're upset. I can't talk to you.

EMMA: Yes, I'm upset. You're yelling at me.

ARTHUR: I'm not yelling, I'm making a point!! If you didn't like the seating arrangements, you should have left the restaurant.

EMMA: I was trying not to create a scene—

ARTHUR: Well, you didn't exactly succeed, now did you? You were an embarrassment and I won't have it. Do you understand me? I won't have it.
(Arthur hangs up the phone. Tommy enters.)

TOMMY: You okay?

EMMA: Arthur seems angry.

TOMMY: I'm really sorry, Em. Arthur's just, he's a little crazy right now, and somehow, it all got kind of unloaded on you.

EMMA: Why? I didn't do anything!

TOMMY: Well, you did say that thing to the senator about not being important enough to sit at his table.

EMMA: That was true! I was invited to dinner, I *drove* everybody there, and then you guys made me sit at another table! I can't believe I drove. I don't know, that just makes it worse somehow. I *drove*.

TOMMY: I know, it's crazy.

EMMA: And I was willing to let it go! I mean, when it was over, I was like,

okay, that was awful, but now it's over, time to move on, and
called *me*—

TOMMY: I know. When he told me he was going to do that, I thought, 1
wouldn't, it's just putting salt in the wound, but...

EMMA: He told you? I mean, he told you that he was going to call me and
scream at me?

TOMMY: Yeah. And I thought, what a bad idea.
(Beat.)

EMMA: But you didn't say that. I mean, you didn't tell him not to. Call me.
(Beat.)

TOMMY: Look, let's not blow this out of proportion. These things happen
early in a campaign. People are nervous. Things just need to settle out.
Let me talk to him.
*(Annabeth and Arthur enter. The scene changes. Emma steps to one side and
watches.)*

ANNABETH: I really don't understand why she's making such a big deal about
this. I mean, really. She is not the one running for office here.

TOMMY: I just think her feelings were hurt.

ANNABETH: Her *feelings?* What do her feelings have to do with anything?

TOMMY: She's done a lot for us. And she is a friend.

ANNABETH: If she were truly a friend, she would understand what our prior-
ities are here. I mean, Arthur has better things to do than running
around apologizing for some girl's hurt feelings.

ARTHUR: Apologize? Now she expects me to apologize?

TOMMY: No, that's not—

ARTHUR: Is she insane?

TOMMY: Arthur, she's given us money, she introduced you to the governor—
she introduced you to me, for crying out loud—she took a leave of
absence from her job to help us out—

ARTHUR: That doesn't give her the right to try and take over the entire campaign.

TOMMY: Arthur—

ARTHUR: No, you listen to me. I know you're friends with Emma, and that
has put you in an awkward position here. I respect that. But I also ask
that you respect me. I cannot let her wounded ego interfere with what
I'm trying to do. What's happening here is bigger than that. The country is at sake. If she can't learn to make a few compromises, then she
doesn't belong. And if you don't understand that, then you don't belong,
either.

understand.

I think this all just blew out of proportion.

That's all I'm really trying to say.

ANNABETH: Of course you are. And Emma has been a big help to you, Arthur, she has! She told me as much.

ARTHUR: Well, yes, but—

ANNABETH: I think we should conserve our resources, The senator seemed quite taken with her. That could be useful in the long run; he can get skittish during a tough campaign. Besides, if she apologizes, there's no reason why she can't come back.

ARTHUR: No. I suppose not. If she apologizes.

ANNABETH: You'll tell her, won't you, Tommy? Come on, Arthur. We don't want to be late for that lunch with 20/20.

(They go. The scene changes.)

EMMA: They want me to what?

TOMMY: Since the senator liked you so much, they think you could be useful. But you have to apologize.

EMMA: And what exactly am I apologizing for?

TOMMY: Well, it's a difficult situation for everyone. You do share responsibility for this, Em. And he's in no position to apologize to you. I want you around. I think you should do it. *(He goes.)*

EMMA: I decide to talk to other people. Be an adult. Get a broader perspective. I call my friends.

(Another woman Marjorie sits across from her. They are having lunch. Emma launches in.)

EMMA: It's like, Keats, okay? That negative capability thing? Believing in two completely contradictory ideas at the same time, I always thought that was something deeply profound, like the Heisenberg Uncertainty Principle, if you know where that electron is, you cannot know how fast it's going, or, or Kierkegaard, knowing the universe is going to annihilate you and yet embracing the belief in a just God, all of these things, the resonating of opposites, it always seemed so huge to me, and then it turns out it's not that at all. It turns out, it's just a moment in your life, or a person who you thought was one thing who is in fact also its opposite, or not people, maybe, but the things that we yearn for, small tiny things that then make everything else you thought you knew disappear. And I don't know if I can do it. I mean, maybe I did idealize Arthur, but that still doesn't alter the fact that he fell into that whole nasty in-crowd logic so quickly, and I know he wants this badly, but can a dream destroy your ideals? Are integrity and kindness truly the hope of fools? I don't know what to think anymore.

(Marjorie stares at her, takes a piece of bread. Pause.)

MARJORIE: You remember last year when we were playing Pictionary, and you accused me of cheating?

EMMA: What?

MARJORIE: You did, you accused me of cheating. *(Pause. Insistent.)* On New Year's Eve, we were playing Pictionary, and you said, "come on, come on!"

EMMA: Yes?

MARJORIE: I'm just saying, you know, you're not perfect, either. All this talk about integrity? And *you* accused *me*. Of cheating.

EMMA: Marjorie!

MARJORIE: Look, I have a lot of anger in me, okay? And maybe I should have told you at the time, but this is just not easy for me, and my friends just have to learn to accept my anger because, you know, I have a right to express it. My group feels very strongly about this.

(Pause.)

EMMA: I decide that maybe friends are not who I should turn to at this time. Maybe a total stranger, a chance encounter, a foreign perspective will help me understand the mysterious workings of the human heart. Like Diogenes, I go in search of an honest man.

(She turns to sit at a bar. There is a drunken man there.)

E.T. BLACK: Okay, here's the thing: I'm, like, do you know who I am? I'm E.T. Black. That doesn't mean anything to you, does it? E.T. Black. You've never heard of me. Nobody in this whole place knows who I am. But I'm like, the biggest screenwriter in Hollywood. One of the biggest. Any one of my scripts, I could write anything here, right now, on a napkin, and it would get made. I've got an academy award. You think I'm making this up. But it's because you don't know who I am.

EMMA: Well, I don't go to a lot of movies.

E.T. BLACK: What are you talking about? Everybody goes to movies. What, do you just sit at home and let the television like suck your brains out, is that what you do?

EMMA: No, I'm busy, I'm a busy person.

E.T. BLACK: Oh, little Miss Important, is that who you are? Huh? Too important to go to the movies, is that what you're saying?

EMMA: *(Rising to go.)* You know, maybe I...

E.T. BLACK: No, you talk to me! You said you have a question! Well, I have questions, too! Do you know who I am? I'm E.T. Black! I'm the biggest screenwriter in Hollywood! My movies get made! Nobody reads books anymore! They go to see my movies! If this were the nineteenth century or something I'd be Charles Dickens! *City Slickers?* I wrote that. That thing about starting a stampede with a coffee grinder? That was my idea. *Total Nonsense. Harriet the Spy.* I did the final rewrite on that, most of that is mine. I mean, I'm filthy rich, I'm fuckin'...filthy rich, and nobody asks me what I think about anything. If this were the nineteenth century, I'd be hanging out with Ruskin. Fucking Ruskin would be having lunch with me. Disraeli. Winston Churchill.

EMMA: Winston Churchill was World War II.

E.T. BLACK: What?

EMMA: Well, you said, if this was the nineteenth century, and Winston Churchill didn't live in the nineteenth century, he—

E.T. BLACK: Fuck you! Do you know who I am? You have no idea who I am!

EMMA: Do you think people are good?

E.T. BLACK: Have you been to Hollywood? No. The answer to that is no.

EMMA: Do you think a dream can destroy ideals?

E.T. BLACK: Ideals? What the fuck is an ideal? Who are you, anyway? Ideals are like, nothing. Fucking Plato forgot to tell you that part. I mean, I thought we were talking about reality. Jesus. You are really sad, lady.

EMMA: We're not talking about me.

E.T. BLACK: No? No? I mean, you wanted the truth, you just, now you don't like it, is that it? I mean, I didn't make this shit up. Do you know who I am? I'm a fuckin' world-famous screenwriter, and I'm telling you the way things are. There are things I *know.* Power and money are *it.* Because people aren't just afraid of death, they're *mad* about it, death is what drives us insane, and we think if we collect enough...you know... *(He starts to drift off.)* Maybe...if we have enough...if we're whores...you know, fucking... if we live without meaning...we can beat God at his own fucking game...

(His head is on the table. Emma watches him for a moment.)

EMMA: I don't know why it took Diogenes so long to find an honest man. I got one my first time out. I gotta get away from all this. Far away. Alaska. I'll take a cruise. Those things are great. Everyone takes care of you. All you really have to do is look at the world through binoculars and think. Or not think. Rest. Figure things out. *(She looks at the world through binoculars for a moment.)* Alaska really is spectacular. Oh, look, a whale! *(She continues to look. After a moment.)* Yeah, going to Alaska was a great idea. There's just one thing I forgot. Dinner.

(Leonard and Junette enter, dressed for dinner.)

LEONARD: Leonard Larson, from Minnesota. And this is my wife, Junette. It looks like we're at the same table!

JUNETTE: We'll be eating together all week!

EMMA: It turns out that Leonard's wife has an identical twin sister named June. June was born first, which is why Junette is named Junette.

JUNETTE: *(Bright.)* It's true!

EMMA: You can't make this stuff up.

JUNETTE: So did you see that glacier today? My goodness.

LEONARD: Just great.

JUNETTE: And tomorrow, I guess we're gonna stop in Valdez.

LEONARD: See the pipeline. I been looking forward to that, let me tell you.

JUNETTE: Oh, I don't know...

LEONARD: What?

JUNETTE: That pipeline tour. I just don't know.

LEONARD: *(Disappointed.)* Well, we don't have to. I just thought...

JUNETTE: I don't know.

LEONARD: I was kinda looking forward to it.

JUNETTE: Well.

LEONARD: We don't have to.

EMMA: Instead of seeing the pipeline, Leonard and Junette take a bus tour of the Worthington Glacier Mountain Pass, which carries you through Keystone Canyon, past Bridalveil Falls, three thousand feet up the side of a mountain. There, Leonard, who has a heart condition, goes into arrest.

JUNETTE: It was pretty scary, let me tell you!

LEONARD: It's nothing!

EMMA: He doesn't survive the night.

LEONARD: *(Bright.)* I guess we should've gone to see the pipeline! *(Less bright.)* I woulda liked to see that.

EMMA: Junette, I'm sorry.

JUNETTE: *(A little confused.)* Oh, well, those things happen. Nice meeting you, Cathy.

(She and Leonard go.)

EMMA: All told, I learn nothing on my cruise, except that Alaska is very far away, and the human race is at best a touching disappointment.

(The scene changes. Tommy enters. He and Emma meet in a restaurant.)

TOMMY: Hey, how's it going?

EMMA: Fine Just got back from Alaska.

TOMMY: Yeah, I heard. Must've been fantastic.

EMMA: It was very beautiful.

TOMMY: I bet. How was the cruise?

EMMA: Lotta food. Gained a few pounds.

TOMMY: I've heard that about those things.

EMMA: The Love Boat, with lots of old white people. Dutch crew, Nigerian porters. It was an exercise in imperialism with bad night club shows and bingo. They actually had sit-down aerobics.

TOMMY: *(Laughing.)* Oh, no.

(Long pause.)

EMMA & TOMMY: So— *(They laugh.)*

EMMA: Go ahead.

TOMMY: No, you.

EMMA: I was just going to say…that, I did a lot of thinking while I was up there at the ends of the earth, and I got kind of lonely, frankly, and I don't want to lose you. *(Beat.)* There was this old couple on the boat— ship, I mean, the ship—and at first I found them truly annoying, they were from "Minnesota," but they were also so *together* you know, and then they lost each other, over a mistake, a foolish mistake, and I don't want that to happen to us. I mean, I don't really know what that whole thing in the restaurant was, but it was just a moment, a foolish mistake, and it doesn't matter as long as you and I are okay, because you are so dear to me, Tommy—

TOMMY: Emma. *(Beat.)* Um.

EMMA: What?

TOMMY: This is awkward. *(Beat.)* You should have let me go first.

EMMA: *(Beat.)* Why?

TOMMY: Arthur feels that you have been a destructive influence. He, things aren't going as well on the fundraising, as he had hoped, the primary is right around the corner and he's very frustrated. He needs an outlet to express that frustration, and you seem to be providing that outlet.

EMMA: I wasn't talking about Arthur.

TOMMY: Yes you were.

EMMA: No. I wasn't. *(Beat.)* Why are you?

TOMMY: Well. I am his campaign manager.

EMMA: And what am I?

TOMMY: You? You're nobody. *(Beat.)* You should have apologized, Em.

EMMA: I didn't do anything. I didn't have anything to apologize for.

TOMMY: Yeah, well, I'm the guy's campaign manager. You can't expect me to side against him.

EMMA: *(Getting mad.)* Side against Arthur, what does that mean?

TOMMY: Emma, come on. You're putting me in an awkward position. You have to at least acknowledge that.

EMMA: No, actually, I don't think I do.

TOMMY: Emma.

EMMA: What? I mean, what are you telling me, that you're cutting me off because Arthur's gone paranoid, that it wasn't enough for him to insult me in a restaurant, now he's got to take away my friends, too?

TOMMY: Look—

EMMA: No, you look! This is ridiculous! Tommy, are you really willing to throw me away over nothing? Can you really just throw people away like that?

TOMMY: I'm sorry. I said what I have to say. I have to go. *(He starts to go.)*

EMMA: Don't you dare walk away from me. I got you this job! No one would hire you! You were a huge drunk, and no one would even talk to you! I practically saved your life!

(He gives her a look.)

EMMA: Well, it's true.

TOMMY: I had some problems. I've worked them out. I hope I haven't disappointed you or Arthur.

EMMA: *(Apologizing.)* No, of course not. You've...you seem to be doing a great job. How would I know? I don't know. Because no one will talk to me, because now I'm nobody. *(Beat.)* I just want this all to go away. I want it to have never happened. I don't understand it.

TOMMY: Why don't you just let go of this?

EMMA: I've been trying to.

TOMMY: No. You haven't.

EMMA: There's something I have to talk to you about, Tommy—

TOMMY: I am not talking to you anymore! *(Beat.)* Look. I'm not trying to be mean, but you know—there's no big mystery here. You act like what's happened to you was crazy; well it wasn't. People just love to create a pecking order. It's everybody's favorite pastime, deciding who is more important than whom. This is why communism never worked. Oh, we're all equal. Yeah, right. It doesn't even work that way biologically. It doesn't work for monkeys, why should it work for us? You just ended up on the bad end of it for once. To Arthur, you were the least dangerous. The most expendable. It made him feel better to insult you so he did it.

EMMA: *(Cold.)* What happened to Mr. Smith Goes to Washington? Democracy? A Man of the People?

TOMMY: He's still that. On a profound level, he has not compromised his ideals. I mean, this is just politics. And I have to go. *(He stands.)*

EMMA: Fuck you.

TOMMY: Fine. I did my best.

EMMA: Your best isn't very good. You're weak.

(He looks at her doesn't answer and goes. Emma sits alone.)

EMMA: I mean, you think you have something to say, and then you find out that you don't because no one's listening. Is that possible? Like a tree falling in the forest, thoughts and feelings directed at no one don't exist? This is starting to BOTHER ME. ARTHUR!

(She turns mid-roar to find Arthur and Annabeth in a big indiscreet clinch. For a moment she doesn't put it together.)

EMMA: Oh, I'm sorry, I was looking for—

(Annabeth and Arthur shriek and pull apart guiltily shoving their clothes together.)

ARTHUR: This isn't what it looks like. We are both consenting adults, my marriage has been in trouble for many years—

ANNABETH: Arthur. Arthur! It's Emma, Arthur.

EMMA: Hi.

ARTHUR: Oh, my god.

EMMA: What are you doing, Arthur?

ARTHUR: How did you get in here?

EMMA: The kid at the desk said you were free. He said go on in—

ARTHUR: *(To Annabeth.)* He's fired.

ANNABETH: I'm on it.

EMMA: Oh, Arthur. Annabeth? Oh, ick. Oh.

ARTHUR: And get her out of here.

ANNABETH: Gladly.

EMMA: I'm not going anywhere!

ARTHUR: I'm calling security.

EMMA: Fine, call security. I'd love a scene. So would the press, I'm sure! *(Pause.)*

ANNABETH: Just hold off for a second, Arthur. I'm sure that won't be necessary. What do you want, Emma?

EMMA: *(Beat.)* I want my money back.

ARTHUR: What?

EMMA: I gave you five thousand dollars for your campaign because I thought you were something that it turns out you're really not. I want my money back.

ARTHUR: *(To Annabeth.)* She's insane.

ANNABETH: Arthur, could you go into the next room please? I'll handle this. Just wash your face, we have to be at the Rotary Club in fifteen minutes. *(Firm.)* Arthur. I'm handling this.
(Arthur goes. Annabeth considers Emma.)

EMMA: Wow. He walks, he talks, and you can't see the wires.

ANNABETH: Emma, you're sounding like a bad soap opera. What you're doing here, I don't know, but I find it tacky.

EMMA: *I'm* tacky?

ANNABETH: You're embarrassing yourself. Your obsession with Arthur is abnormal. He told me you were in love with him. I didn't believe him. But this? Clearly, he was not imagining things. I'd think about that before I started babbling nasty little rumors to the press. Your motives aren't exactly pristine.

EMMA: My motives are fine. I'm not in love with Arthur. I'm mad at him because he squashed my ideals.

ANNABETH: *(Laughing a little.)* What?

EMMA: Oh, never mind. *(Mouths: Why do I even bother?)*

ANNABETH: You know, just for the record, I wanted you back. Geof Maddox was really taken with you and that sort of thing works with him. If you actually cared about Arthur, that might have occurred to you.

EMMA: What are you saying?

ANNABETH: I'm saying if you wanted to help, you had your chance. All this talk about broken ideals. This is nobody's fault but your own.

EMMA: I can't follow this. Just give me my money, and I'll go.

ANNABETH: That is not going to happen.

ARTHUR: Give her the money. *(Arthur stands in the doorway.)*

ANNABETH: I don't think that's wise, Arthur.

ARTHUR: If it will get her out of here, give her the money.
(Annabeth shrugs reaches into her jacket and pulls out a checkbook. She writes a check and hands it to Emma.)

ANNABETH: Don't come back, Emma. It's embarrassing.
(She goes. Emma looks at the check, at the audience as Arthur brings the podium downstage. Emma listens.)

ARTHUR: Without question, America has fallen into a crisis of imagination.

This great, troubled country, still the strongest force for freedom on this earth, seems to be slipping from our grasp. The two-party system has collapsed upon itself, imploding every issue into a middling sameness. Our leaders have shrunk into mere politicians, squabbling endlessly over nothing. And the most powerful voice now heard in our land is the shrill shriek of the hate-monger, claiming our airwaves, our heartland, claiming the highest legislative body of our nation. But we can tolerate this crippling cynicism no longer. We must build a bridge from our past to our future, and embrace the spirit of those democratic ideals, our own, which for the past two hundred years have provided a beacon for our suffering planet. "We hold these truths to be self-evident: that all men are created equal, that they are endowed by their Creator with certain inalienable rights, that among these are Life, Liberty and the Pursuit of Happiness." There is no quibbling here. There is only vision. Hope. The conviction that the human spirit can and will transcend its own pettiness. Only that conviction will save us now.

EMMA: I keep going back over that night. What I could have done to stop it. *(The restaurant comes together around her again. The others take their places as she speaks.)*

ANNABETH: Now, how do you want to do the seating, Arthur? Four and one? *(Emma looks over as Arthur considers this.)*

ARTHUR: *(Quickly.)* Oh, yes. That's exactly right. Four and one.

ANNABETH: David— *(She waves the waiter on.)*

EMMA: And it always seems inexorable, in an odd way.

ANNABETH: We'll need a table for four, and a table for one.

DAVID: Right this way.

EMMA: The whole thing was so smooth. Like they'd practiced it.

TOMMY: Wait a minute. There are going to be five of us, aren't there? When the senator gets here—

EMMA: *(To Tommy.)* Apparently Annabeth and Arthur would prefer that I ate at a separate table.

ANNABETH: We'll set you up at the best single they have. David, can we get her the view of the capital dome?

DAVID: Anything for you, Annabeth.

EMMA: Like a secret handshake.

ARTHUR: Emma, you understand. This is strictly business.

DAVID: It's a little close to the kitchen and there is a draft...

EMMA: And the only reason it was even this gracious was because graciousness is our excuse.

ANNABETH: Now, you and Tommy need to fill me in on your campaign strategy before the senator gets here.

EMMA: I'm just lucky we don't live in Rwanda.

ANNABETH: Arthur, this is awkward. Should I shoot her?

ARTHUR: Oh, yes. That's exactly right. Go ahead and shoot her.

(Annabeth draws a gun and shoots Emma, who goes down. Annabeth then turns and pockets it.)

TOMMY & ARTHUR: Good shot! Good shot, Gilkey!

EMMA: I'm lucky this isn't the Vatican.

TOMMY: Arturo, why are these women talking?

ARTHUR: Good point. Guards! ANNO. DOMINI PATRI CHRISTO. NINA, PINTA, SANTA MARIA. AMEN.

(The waiter grabs Emma; Tommy grabs Annabeth; they force them down as Arthur dismisses them with a cross.) .

EMMA: I'm lucky this is America. Where democracy is a goal to which we, and our leaders, aspire.

ANNABETH: Now, how do you want to do the seating, Arthur? Four and one?

(Emma looks over as Arthur considers this.)

ARTHUR: (Quickly.) Oh, yes. That's exactly right. Four and one.

ANNABETH: David— (She waves the waiter on.) We'll need a table for four, and a table for one.

DAVID: Right this way.

(The waiter starts to move a place setting to the separate table.)

EMMA: So why should I go along with this nonsense?

TOMMY: There are going to be five of us, aren't there?

EMMA: I mean, if they want to play this game, I can play too, right?

ARTHUR: Emma, you understand.

EMMA: No, I don't, actually. I'm sitting here.

(She sits at the table. They all stare at her.)

ANNABETH: (Horrified.) What is she doing?

EMMA: You invited me to dinner.

TOMMY: What are you *doing?*

ARTHUR: WHAT ARE YOU DOING?

EMMA: I want to meet the senator.

(They all scream. Arthur has a heart attack. Emma leaps up from the table. Annabeth goes to Arthur's dead body. She glares at Emma.)

ANNABETH: He's dead. You killed him.

DAVID & TOMMY: MURDERER!

SENATOR: ASSASSIN!

EMMA: I'm sorry.

ARTHUR: You are an embarrassment.

EMMA: I'm sorry.

TOMMY: You're nobody.

EMMA: But, I drove.

ANNABETH: David, can we get her the view of the capital dome?

DAVID: Anything for you, Annabeth.

EMMA: Because finally there was nothing to be done.

DAVID: Anything for you, Annabeth.

EMMA: Somehow, it was a moment that would not be denied.

DAVID: Anything for you, Annabeth.

ARTHUR: *(Again speaking.)* We must reclaim that idealistic heritage which was, at one time, our birthright. With the courage of our forebears we will reshape ourselves as a country and people of discipline, wisdom and compassion.

(Loud cheers and applause, as if at a convention. Arthur acknowledges.)

EMMA: I know it's vague, I know it's just rhetoric. But this is my problem. When people say things like that, I believe them. Or, I used to.

(The Governor enters. The others exit as they take a seat in a restaurant.)

GOVERNOR: Emma!

EMMA: Hello Governor!

GOVERNOR: Emma, I warned you.

EMMA: Oh, come on.

GOVERNOR: I mean it!

EMMA: I am not calling you "Uncle Jack." Everyone will think you're my sugar daddy.

GOVERNOR: If that's the way you feel about it… *(He turns to go.)*

EMMA: *(Protesting.)* Uncle Jack…

GOVERNOR: *(Sitting.)* Much better. How's your dad?

EMMA: Oh, you know. The same. Lots of gardening, golfing, fighting with mom.

GOVERNOR: Your mother is a saint.

EMMA: She knows.

GOVERNOR: And your friend Arthur won the primary. This must be a very exciting time for you.

EMMA: Actually, I'm not involved in his campaign anymore.

GOVERNOR: No? You were so high on him.

EMMA: I found some things out. It's complicated.

(The waiter brings tea. She sips it.)

GOVERNOR: *(Worried.)* Oh?

EMMA: I just had to put some distance there. It's nothing.

GOVERNOR: If it's nothing, then why don't you tell me?

EMMA: Because you're the governor.

GOVERNOR: It's sounding more and more like something you should tell the governor.

EMMA: I don't want to get anybody in trouble.

GOVERNOR: Emma, you introduced me to this man. I endorsed him. If there's something there that could come back and bite me, I need to know about it.

EMMA: No. There's nothing. Really.

(The Governor thinks about this, seems satisfied, and goes for his tea.)

EMMA: Just a little bit of erratic behavior. I'm sure it's nothing that you need to worry about.

GOVERNOR: What kind of erratic behavior?

EMMA: I don't want to damage Arthur! But the stress of the campaign seems to be making him increasingly unstable. He kind of lashed out at me at dinner, recently. It was very humiliating. And then when I tried to patch things up, he just became enraged. It got worse and worse until finally I just had to disengage myself from the whole thing.

GOVERNOR: Well, what set him off?

EMMA: Honestly, Uncle Jack, I don't know. Nothing, as far as I can tell. It was actually kind of psychotic. I mean, not psychotic. Psychotic is too strong. I'm sure it's just stress! But maybe you should keep an eye out. Just in case it happens again with, you know. Someone important, God forbid.

GOVERNOR: You're important, Emma.

EMMA: Thanks, Uncle Jack. Do we have to talk about this? I hardly ever get to see you. Let's talk about something else.

GOVERNOR: *(Paternal.)* Of course. Let me just make a phone call.

(He goes. Emma watches then sips her tea. Beat.)

EMMA: *(Musing.)* Wow. That was easy. I didn't even have to lie.

SENATOR: Emma? *(The Senator approaches delighted.)* Well, this is a pleasure. I haven't seen you since…

EMMA: That fundraiser.

SENATOR: With your friend, Arthur. I see he's doing well in the polls.

EMMA: Actually, I think he's slipping.

SENATOR: Surely not. Annabeth tells me he's a huge hit.

EMMA: You don't think his rhetoric is sounding a little empty these days?

SENATOR: Well, whose isn't?

(He laughs. She laughs with him.)

EMMA: So true. They're throwing that big lunch for him today. You're probably on your way in, huh.

SENATOR: As a matter of fact, I am. Are you at my table?

EMMA: That would be novel, wouldn't it? Actually, I was going to skip it.

SENATOR: (Disappointed.) Oh.

EMMA: Well, you don't have to go, do you? As I recall, you hate these things.

SENATOR: Annabeth has me down for the keynote address.

EMMA: Cause I was hoping we could sneak off. Go get some seafood or something.

SENATOR: (Suggestive.) Lobster bisque?

EMMA: Lobster bisque.

SENATOR: Tuna tartare?

EMMA: Tuna tartare.

SENATOR: Creme brulee?

EMMA: Senator!

SENATOR: You're right, it's too risky. Well. (He starts to go.)

EMMA: Then again, I've always liked creme brulee.

SENATOR: Emma. You're not talking about lunch.

EMMA: I'm not?

SENATOR: You're talking about politics.

EMMA: I'm very interested in politics. (Listening intently she steers him to the other side of the stage.)

SENATOR: It is a fascinating subject. You want to know what my life is like?

EMMA: Yes, I do.

SENATOR: I'm a prominent man. People are out to get me.

EMMA: It's so unfair, the system these days.

SENATOR: My home life is a mess. I never see my family.

EMMA: That's awful.

SENATOR: I don't make a lot of money. I go to battle every day up there on the hill, my work is murderously dull and the electorate I serve hates me. Why would anyone live this life?

(He casually drapes his arm around her. She sees where this is going but doesn't want to stop it.)

EMMA: Service?

SENATOR: Power! When I walk into a room, people applaud. My picture is in the newspapers, which quote the things I say. I eat delicious food. And women want me. Why should I give that up? It's the only reward I get.

(He is undressing her.) Without the danger, I'm a petty bureaucrat. With it, I'm a senator!

(They fall into bed. Across the stage, Annabeth, Tommy and Arthur look about. Tommy, Annabeth and Arthur enter. Tommy is on cellphone.)

TOMMY: We can't find the senator.

ARTHUR: *(Panicking.)* What do you mean, you can't find him? He's giving the keynote speech!

ANNABETH: *(Overlap.)* Goddammit!

TOMMY: *(Reporting from phone.)* He's not backstage. He's not on the floor.

ARTHUR: Annabeth, you take care of this.

TOMMY: He's not picking up his cellphone.

ANNABETH: I hate it when he does this!

ARTHUR: You said put yourself in my hands! You said I'll take care of everything!

TOMMY: *(Reporting.)* There's a chance he's still in subcommittee—

ANNABETH: Get real. He's off screwing some campaign worker. The man is positively led around by his dick. Arthur, get Leon Panetta. He's always available. Tommy, call Jimmy Carville, he owes me bigtime. Somebody dig me up a Kennedy!

(They go.)

EMMA: Make no mistake, the senator and I had a wonderful time. I needed it. It made me feel better. And there was an element of poetic justice that frankly added a certain zing to it all. Hey!

(The half-naked Senator takes her picture with a Polaroid camera. They playfully fight over it and take pictures of each other. They romp.)

SENATOR: I want to be able to see you whenever I want.

EMMA: In subcommittee hearings? I always wanted to be in politics. *(She snaps a picture of him.)*

SENATOR: Just be careful who you show that to. Emma…

(She keeps snapping pictures as he stands.)

EMMA: You look delicious…

(He checks his watch.)

SENATOR: Oh my God. Look at the time. I gotta get to that dinner.

(The mood changes immediately. Emma watches him dress.)

EMMA: What dinner? The one for Arthur?

SENATOR: *(Beat.)* Yeah.

EMMA: I thought you weren't going to that.

SENATOR: Annabeth gave me such a hard time. I've missed the last three because of you, young lady. I can't skip another one.

EMMA: Did you tell her about us?

SENATOR: No. She may have guessed, though. Did you two have a fight or something?

EMMA: What makes you say that?

SENATOR: Just a vibe I get.

EMMA: Don't go. Come on, don't go. Please?

SENATOR: Emma. I have to.

EMMA: Because Annabeth says so.

SENATOR: Emma. Don't be a child.

EMMA: Don't treat me like one.

SENATOR: Oh, brother.

EMMA: What does she have on you?

SENATOR: Nothing.

EMMA: If she told you to dump me, would you?

SENATOR: You and I are having a wonderful time, Emma. Don't get like this.

EMMA: What would you do if she told you to dump me?

SENATOR: You're being ridiculous.

EMMA: Answer the question.

SENATOR: *(Point blank.)* I'd want to know her reasons. And if they were good, I'd follow her advice. But it's not going to come to that, okay?

EMMA: No, not okay. For almost six weeks now, you and I—

SENATOR: Wait a minute. There's no "you and I here." What is—I knew this was going to happen. You girls, you always think you have rights. Well, you don't, okay? I'm a public figure, for god's sake. You know what you're doing? You're trying to control policy. You think you have the right to do that just because you're a good lay?

EMMA: I'm a what?

SENATOR: Look. You started this.

EMMA: That's not precisely how it happened.

SENATOR: Well, Annabeth never did this. She understands, this is business.

EMMA: And what business is that?

SENATOR: *(Beat.)* You shouldn't have pushed.

(He grabs the photos and splits. She takes this in for a moment.)

EMMA: I do think there are moments in life when you realize that everything you thought about yourself and the world were just never true. And that knowledge brings with it, frankly, great temptation.

(She reaches into a pocket and pulls out one last Polaroid. An anchorman appears in a spotlight.)

ANCHORMAN: And the hotly-contested race for Maryland's second district just got hotter. In an already scandal-ridden electoral season, a new star has appeared on the horizon as a young campaign worker has stepped forward to accuse congressional candidate Arthur Woolf and his sponsor, Senator Geoffrey Maddox of some rather exceptional forms of sexual misconduct. On the basis of rumor and innuendo alone, the polls are already fluctuating wildly. And while few facts are as yet available, pundits are leaping to comparisons with Donna Rice, Paula Jones, Jennifer Flowers, Fannie Fox, Kristine Keeler, Camila Parker Bowles, Lucy Mercer, Jessica Hahn, Rita Jenrette, every woman who's ever *met* Bob Packwood, Judith Exner, Kim Novak, Sherry Rowlands, and Marilyn Monroe. We take you live to Baltimore, Maryland.

(Emma turns and speaks. Flashbulbs pop.)

EMMA: Three months ago, I accompanied the candidate and his campaign manager to a dinner and a fundraiser. At the time, I was not an important part of the campaign—they even sat me at a different table in the restaurant—but as soon as the senator showed interest in me, things changed. Arthur made it clear that I should be…"nice" to the senator. He really needed his endorsement, so I was basically told to do whatever had to be done. If I cooperated, he said, I would be rewarded.

ANCHORMAN: And you took that to mean sexual favors?

EMMA: That is what it meant, yes.

ANCHORMAN: And were you compensated for these favors?

EMMA: Only recently. The senator and I met for the last time a week ago, and I told him I was pregnant. At that time, he decided he wanted nothing more to do with me. When I told Arthur, he gave me a check for $5000 and told me to get an abortion. I realized then that I could no longer participate in their sick, twisted morality.

ANCHORMAN: You realize that both the candidate and the senator have denied your allegations.

EMMA: Well, that doesn't surprise me. They're both pretty heavily into denial. Anyway, I have the check, and some pictures of myself with the senator. *(She shows these things to the Anchorman.)* Oh. And here's my doctor's report. I'm just starting my second trimester. *(She shows it to the Anchorman.)*

ANCHORMAN: *(Clears his throat, to audience.)* As I said, the offices of both the candidate and the senator have issued denials at this time. However, several supporters of opposing candidate Oliver Riley have hailed this young woman as a heroine and a prophet for the new morality. They are calling for a senate investigation into this matter.

(He nods and exits. Emma looks at the audience.)

EMMA: This town is about spin. They spun the story one way, I spun it another. Oh. Did I tell you I was pregnant?

(Flashbulbs pop. A crowd of reporters descend.)

REPORTER #1: Emma—

REPORTER #2: Over here, Emma—

REPORTER #3: Emma, could we have a statement?

EMMA: I made a mistake. I didn't stand up for myself. I'm doing that now.

REPORTER #1: Is there anything you want to say to Senator Maddox?

EMMA: I'm sorry he's going to be hurt by this, but frankly he should've kept it in his pants.

(They laugh.)

REPORTER #2: And, why have you decided to come forward with this story now? By your own admission, you were quite happy with this arrangement for months. What made you change your mind?

EMMA: I just realized that men who could behave like this had no business serving in the highest legislative body of our land. I mean, I talk to people, and there's this sense that we can do better, we can be a better people, but we need leaders who will understand our hunger of spirit. Our yearning. Our hope that humanity is not merely degraded.

REPORTER #3: We're living in the gutter but looking at the stars, huh?

REPORTER #1, 2 & 3: Yeah, yeah, yeah, yeah. *(They go.)*

EMMA: I can't believe it took me so long to figure this out. When you're good, everybody stomps on you. When you're bad, you end up in the newspaper. I'm going to be in the newspaper!

RICHARD: Can I speak with you?

(Emma looks over. Richard a carefully dressed party organizer smiles at her politely.)

EMMA: Actually, I'm kind of tired. The press conference went longer than I thought.

RICHARD: Yes, I saw. I'm Richard Riley. People in my organization were impressed with what you did. You're a brave woman.

EMMA: Thank you.

RICHARD: Well, I'm afraid what you're doing is going to lead you into a lot of very difficult, very frightening situations. You are aware of that, aren't you?

EMMA: Actually, I hadn't really thought about what happens next—

RICHARD: Of course not. You were just trying to do what was right. Let the world know who these men are.

EMMA: Yes.

RICHARD: Unfortunately, Washington is not a town that respects someone with a really pure motive. People here don't seem to understand that once in a while, maybe someone just wants to do what's right.

EMMA: No. They don't.

RICHARD: Why don't you let us help you?

EMMA: Well—who are you?

RICHARD: We are the Keepers of the American Promise.

(Bella and August enter, bustling about Emma, making her comfortable.)

BELLA: She's pregnant, Richard! Would you offer her a seat?

(August gives her a chair.)

AUGUST: Congratulations. I know that might be hard for you to hear, under these circumstances—

EMMA: Well—

BELLA: But babies are great. You're going to have a great time.

EMMA: I hope so. I'm a little—

AUGUST: We think you're very brave.

BELLA: Very.

AUGUST: Aren't politicians awful?

BELLA: Just terrible. What they did to you.

EMMA: It was pretty—

AUGUST: It's certainly time for a change. Washington just doesn't understand what people want any more.

BELLA: What *good* people want.

EMMA: Who are you again?

BELLA: Emma. Some of the fine points of our philosophies are not going to match up. But we want you to know that you are not alone. The system doesn't work anymore. A lot of people realize that. And we're trying to organize, on a grassroots level, to rebuild the country from the bottom up. Our schools. Our cities. Our communities. These are the things we're concerned about. I think that's what you're concerned about, too.

RICHARD: Besides, they fucked you over. Forgive me, for such language, but they did.

AUGUST: Richard, I really think—

RICHARD: Look. Unless we spell things out, they're going to crucify her. Emma. This is the hill. No one gives a shit about women here. And no one cares about the truth. Remember Tailhook? Remember Anita Hill? That's what's going to happen to you. You are about to become the biggest lesbian fantasizing lovesick crazy bitch the world has ever seen. Unless you let us help you.

EMMA: Help me how?

(Lance, a flaming costume designer approaches carrying sweaters and skirts.)

LANCE: God, no. Absolutely not. Everything has to go. SHEILA! I'm going to need the rack of Laura Ashley. *(Fingering Emma's jacket.)* Oh, this is *fabulous*. Rayon and wool, right? These new blends are unbe*liev*able. What size are you? Six? And you can eat anything, right? I hate you, I really do. *(He holds up a hideous pink sweater.)*

EMMA: I'm not wearing this.

LANCE: Sweetheart, you can't go out there as a fallen woman, it's completely unsympathetic. Even Ingrid Bergman couldn't pull it off. *Notorious?*

EMMA: That's my favorite movie!

LANCE: *(Impersonating Ingrid Bergman.)* Why won't you believe me, Dev? Just a little bit.

LANCE & EMMA: Oh, Dev! Dev! Dev!

LANCE: She's fabulous, of course, but people just didn't want to see it. And with all due respect, dear, your story is wretched enough. You don't want to look the part. We have to go much more Midwest…

EMMA: Nobody wears this stuff. Even in the Midwest.

LANCE: I wouldn't lie about clothes this ugly. Isn't this hideous? I love it! SHEILA!

(Sheila enters, pushing a rack of Laura Ashley dresses as Lance continues to dress a resisting Emma.)

SHEILA: *(Frazzled.)* I don't know, Lance. This is all I could find and I was sure we had just a mess of them from that Junior League tag sale…

LANCE: Those whores. They promised me a lot of at least twenty. Oh, this is just pathetic…

EMMA: I'm not wearing this!

SHEILA: That's not my battle, honey. You and I are gonna accessorize. Some pretty earrings. A little something at the neck. I love your hair. Is that your real color? Wait a minute, what happened to that little gold rosary?

EMMA: I don't know…

SHEILA: I'm telling you, this stuff will make all the difference. Cause when you look good, you feel good. And when you feel good, you do good. That's what I say. It's not strictly true, but what the hell.

(She drapes it on her arm as Richard enters, businesslike, and oversees the final touches.)

RICHARD: Here's the new statement. The rosary's too much.

SHEILA: I like it…

RICHARD: It's too Catholic. We need a broader appeal.

(Sheila goes after her with a hairbrush. Richard hands Emma some pages.)

EMMA: I can't say this. These people used to be friends of mine.

RICHARD: Wait until you hear what they say about you.

(Annabeth, Arthur and Tommy enter as the others leave.)

ANNABETH: That fucking *cunt*.

TOMMY: Has anyone tried to talk to her? I mean, maybe if we just tried to have one conversation. She can't be completely crazy—

ANNABETH: Have you read the newspapers?

TOMMY: I'm just saying—

ANNABETH: Fuck her, I'm not talking to that bitch. I'm taking out a fucking contract on her life. I told you, Arthur, I told you not to give her the money—

ARTHUR: If you didn't want to give it to her, you shouldn't have given it to her! You were the one who made out the check!

ANNABETH: Only because you told me to!

ARTHUR: I said, call security! I said, she's insane!

ANNABETH: That's my point! How the hell did you ever let her into this fucking campaign?

TOMMY: Things were fine when she was involved. The whole mistake was kicking her out in the first place—

ANNABETH: I'm sunk. I'm fucking dead meat in this town. Geoffrey Maddox won't return my fucking phone calls, did you know that? Has anyone thought about that? You introduced her to a major fucking senator and she fucked us both, Arthur, that's not the sort of thing people forget around here—

ARTHUR: You take care of this, Annabeth. You said, put yourself in my hands, I'll take care of everything—

ANNABETH: I swear, if it was legal I'd take out a fucking contract on her life. I'd rip that baby out of her womb with my bare hands if the press wouldn't be so shitty about it.

TOMMY: You think she's really pregnant, then?

ANNABETH: Of course she's fucking pregnant! It was the first thing I checked!

TOMMY: So, who's the father? I mean, we don't really think it's Senator Maddox, do we?

(Silence. Arthur and Annabeth look at him, exhausted.)

ANNABETH: We don't know, Tommy. He won't return my phone calls. He has distanced himself from our campaign. *(Beat.)* I'm fucking sunk in this town.

TOMMY: So what do we do?

ANNABETH: I'll spread some money around her firm, see who I can get to smear her.

TOMMY: You're not going to come up with anything.

ANNABETH: Don't be smug. There's always somebody who got passed over for a promotion, or got turned down for a date. Arthur, what about law school?

ARTHUR: What about it?

ANNABETH: She fuck any of her professors? Cheat on a test? Plagiarize anything?

ARTHUR: I'll come up with something.

ANNABETH: Tommy, you'll make the statement.

ARTHUR: *I'll* make the statement.

ANNABETH: Arthur, you have to stay above this.

ARTHUR: They're not above it.

ANNABETH: Of course they're not, they're *republicans.*
(Richard stands at a podium and reads a statement.)

RICHARD: We insist that this matter be given the fullest scrutiny.
(Tommy approaches the other podium.)

TOMMY: This woman was only peripherally involved in Mr. Woolf's campaign, for a very short period of time.

RICHARD: This man was running a prostitution ring out of his campaign headquarters!

TOMMY: The candidate was aware that she had a history of mental illness dating back to when she was once a student in law school, but it was our understanding that those problems had been resolved.

RICHARD: If, as Mr. Woolf claims, this young woman is emotionally disturbed, that makes their behavior even more reprehensible!

TOMMY: We have documentation from several psychiatrists and ex-boyfriends. She is a nymphomaniac and a pathological liar.

RICHARD: We have also uncovered evidence that the campaign funds used to pay this woman off may have come from an illegal foreign bank account connected to several failed Savings and Loans. I wouldn't be surprised if this conspiracy reached all the way to the presidency.

TOMMY: Oh, for heaven's sake!
(The two men's arguments start to overlap.)

RICHARD: You are not going to sweep this under the rug. Your candidate and

Senator Maddox were incapable of controlling their penises, well, you can just reap the rewards of that, because you're in the big leagues now, buster, and the rules of the game have been made pretty damn clear these past few years, so—

TOMMY: *(Overlap.)* I'm sick to death of you and your little troop of fanatics, ranting on and on about what's right and true and godly when none of you give a shit about the truth, or god for that matter, all you care about is winning and you'll stoop to absolutely any kind of lie you Bible thumping CONTROL FREAK!

(Richard and Tommy square off. Emma enters, watching. Emma carries a bowl of popcorn. She has been transformed into a modern-day virgin type.)

RICHARD: FORNICATOR!

TOMMY: HYPOCRITE!

RICHARD: HOMOSEXUAL!

TOMMY: NEO-NAZI!

RICHARD: LIBERAL!

TOMMY: Oh, fuck you, you fascist scum.

RICHARD: Yeah, fuck you, too.

(They reach across the divide and shake hands, congratulating each other as after a debate. Rush Limbaugh comes on the television.)

RUSH: I'm sure I should be surprised, but I'm not. The new way to get elected, according to the democrats, is to pimp your campaign workers for political favors. Have you heard about this one? A candidate for congress told one of his campaign workers to sleep with a well-known senator in order to get an endorsement. And you thought you had seen it all. Not yet! Now, this woman is apparently some sort of ex-feminazi, and it's hard to have sympathy for her because out of party loyalty, I guess, she actually went along with this sick arrangement for at least three months. Yeah, she's a real prize. Scratch a feminist, find a prostitute. And it turns out she's pregnant! And I for one am not sanguine about her shall we say "maternal instincts," are you? The chances of this little tyke running afoul of the law are just a little too rich for my blood. More police, more court costs, more prisons—more of your tax dollars being spent to address the misdeeds of the liberal elite! Not to mention the cost to the victims of this whore's demon seed! It's a good thing we have the death penalty, that's all I have to say! I mean, if it were up to me, I'd say we should just drown the kid at birth!

EMMA: Oh, my God!

RUSH: Oh, what did you expect, a baby shower? *(He goes.)*

LANCE: Doll, you do know how to stir things up.

EMMA: I just don't know about this. Why do I have to look like the Virgin Mary? Everybody knows I'm *not* the Virgin Mary.

LANCE: Hey, you're getting a little bit of a pooch here.

EMMA: I am not.

LANCE: Oh my god. Isn't that the most beautiful thing you've even seen? *(Calling off.)* Sheila get the baby clothes!

EMMA: *Baby* clothes. I'm only twenty weeks!

LANCE: Oh come on, aren't you getting excited? Little shoes and socks and those tiny baby overalls, hats, little tiny baseball caps—

EMMA: It is kind of great. I felt the baby move the other day.

LANCE: Ohmygod. Can I? *(He holds his hand over her stomach.)*

EMMA: Well, sure, but you probably won't feel anything. It doesn't happen all that…

(He starts, holds up his hand. She falls silent as he feels the baby move.)

LANCE: Is that it?

EMMA: That's it.

LANCE: Just that little flutter?

EMMA: Wait a minute.

(They pause.)

LANCE: *(Laughing.)* Isn't that something?

(They smile at each other.)

LANCE: You're so lucky. I can't wait to have children.

EMMA: You want children?

LANCE: I love children. You should have seen me in my heyday. I was the baby-sitting queen of America.

EMMA: Really?

LANCE: Oh honey, I'm telling you, they were lining up around the block. My dance card was *full.* Some nights I had four or five of 'em in my mother's living room crawling all over me, crawling all over each other, diapers everywhere—I was in pig heaven.

EMMA: It sounds awful.

LANCE: I'll tell you this much, there's nothing better than putting a baby to sleep. Children are life's holy blessing.

EMMA: Yeah, it's what they grow into that worries me.

LANCE: I think I could be satisfied with maybe seven or eight. Course, I have to find the right woman first.

(He goes back to work. Emma looks at him.)

EMMA: It must be hard.

LANCE: What's that?

EMMA: Well, you know. Being a gay man who wants kids.

LANCE: *(Beat.)* What makes you say that?

EMMA: Well—I don't know. It's hard for gay men to have kids, isn't it? It just seems to me there'd be a lot to work out. Logistically.

LANCE: And what makes you think I'm a homosexual?

EMMA: *(Beat.)* Well, gee, Lance, I mean—Oh. You're kidding, right?

LANCE: You think this is funny?

EMMA: Well—No. I'm sorry. Let's forget I said it.

LANCE: I don't want to forget it. What you've accused me of is very serious. I don't see how you can ask me to forget this!

EMMA: I'm not accusing you of anything! I just thought—I mean, come on, you're so—flaming. Lance—

LANCE: Homosexuality is a sin. It is a perversion of nature. The Bible is very clear about this.

EMMA: The Bible?

LANCE: You don't believe in the Bible?

EMMA: Well, I don't know. I mean, some of it seems okay, but—

LANCE: You can't pick and choose among the word of God, Emma. Do you know what you're saying?

EMMA: I didn't, I just—look. I don't think there's anything wrong with, you know. Being gay. So, I'm sorry. I misunderstood.

LANCE: Yes. You did.

EMMA: So I'm sorry.

(Beat.)

LANCE: It's all right. But you should read your Bible. It—what you're talking about—is disgusting to God.

EMMA: I'm sorry to hear that.

LANCE: It's just that I've been accused of this before. This is why—for years people trusted me with their children, and I loved every one of them. You would've had to strike me dead before I let anyone hurt those children.

EMMA: I know that.

LANCE: Then someone decided it was unnatural. I was unnatural. I never had a girlfriend, it just didn't happen, all of a sudden, people started thinking—well, I don't have to tell you, you thought the same thing. And they decided their children were not safe. I just, I can't take this lightly, Emma.

EMMA: I'm sorry.

(Lance exits.)

SHEILA: Emma! You're on in five minutes.

(Emma turns, confused. The lights come on her.)

EMMA: Oh, I'm sorry—I'm just so confused about all this—

SHEILA: Honey, no. Confusion's bad. They'll just eat you up.

EMMA: Oh! I don't know.

SHEILA: Now, you can do this! I know you can! The world wants to hear from you. All those normal people out there, they're sick of these politicians. They want to hear some real talk about the way things are. They want to hear the truth. Come on now. Tell us who you are.

EMMA: I'm a concerned citizen.

SHEILA: That's right.

EMMA: I am not insane.

SHEILA: We know you're not. Emma, just tell the truth.

(The Senators arrive.)

SENATOR A: You are not on trial here. This is a simple investigatory hearing which should allow us to gather the facts.

SENATOR B: The senate is grateful to you for bringing these matters to our attention. And may I just take a minute to assure the public, I knew *nothing* about this prostitution ring. I was in no way involved.

(He laughs, uneasy. The other Senators look at him as they set up before her.)

SENATOR C: I'd like to begin by asking the witness to provide us with a short synopsis of events beginning I think with the evening you first met Senator Maddox. According to your statement here, the meeting took place in a restaurant here in Washington.

EMMA: Yes.

SENATOR C: *(Reading off his copy of her statement.)* You came with the candidate and his party with the intention of meeting the Senator, but you ended up sitting at another table. Is that correct?

EMMA: Yes.

SENATOR C: Why was that?

EMMA: I never was entirely clear about that.

SENATOR A: You came together?

EMMA: Yes. I drove.

SENATOR A: You drove! And then the candidate, who I believe is a friend of yours—

EMMA: Was a friend of mine, yes.

SENATOR A: He asked you to sit at another table?

EMMA: Yes.

SENATOR B: Not very good manners.

> (*The Senators concur.*)

SENATOR A: Not good manners? It was downright rude! Didn't that hurt your feelings?

EMMA: Yes, actually it did—

SENATOR A: I should think so! Did he ever apologize?

EMMA: No, in fact, he became angry with me.

SENATOR B: He became angry with you? Why?

EMMA: You know, I never could really figure that out, either.

SENATOR C: Now, wait a minute. I just want to make sure I've got this straight. He completely humiliates you by asking you to sit at another table, and then *he* gets mad at you.

SENATOR A: That takes some nerve! I mean, she *drove*.

SENATOR C: So what did you do?

EMMA: Well, then I tried to suggest we just put it behind us, but he was more and more angry—

SENATOR A: Unbelievable!

EMMA: It just seemed to keep going, no matter what I did—

SENATOR C: It became a point of pride? He decided he was too important to deal with it, and you got left in the dust?

EMMA: I guess.

SENATOR A: I hate it when men do that. You give them a little bit of power, and their manners go right out the window.

SENATOR B: But he wasn't even elected yet!

SENATOR A: Well, it's a good thing. Can you imagine how insufferable he'd be if he actually got in congress?

SENATOR B: Oh, my god.

SENATOR A: We've all missed a speeding bullet if you ask me.

EMMA: He's really not that bad.

SENATOR A: Oh, no. Don't defend him. There's no excuse for this kind of nonsense.

EMMA: But the guy he's running against is no saint, either.

SENATOR C: Why? What did he do?

SENATOR A: Did he do this?

> (*He bonks Senator B on the head with a gavel. Senator C stands up and pulls his nose. For a brief, hysterical moment, they whack each other crazily and then sit down.*)

SENATOR A: Is that what he did? Because we won't stand for that!

SENATOR B: The idea!

SENATOR C: This is the senate! We insist that people BEHAVE!

(Senator A bonks him on the head. Senator C glares at him.)

SENATOR C: Why, I oughta…

(And they all go at each other again, in a fast, furious slapstick fight.)

EMMA: Hey! HEY!

(They all stop and stare at her.)

EMMA: What are you doing?

SENATOR A: We were just making a point. If your friend wants to be in congress, that means you have to behave better, not worse, than everyone else.

SENATOR C: Well put.

SENATOR B: I couldn't agree more.

SENATOR C: I have everything I need.

SENATOR A: Same here.

SENATOR B: *(To Emma.)* Thank you for your time. The country needs people as civic minded as you are.

(They start to exit.)

EMMA: Wait a minute! I mean—don't you want to talk about this prostitution ring?

SENATOR C: What about it?

SENATOR B: I knew *nothing* about it. I just want to make sure everyone knows that.

EMMA: Well, of course you didn't, you moron, it didn't exist! I made it up!

(She stops herself. Pause.)

SENATOR C: What are you trying to tell us, Emma?

EMMA: All right, look. The men I was working for disappointed me greatly. I did feel the need to let people know, and this was a way I thought I could do it. I mean, if I just told my story, no one would care, petty acts of meanness and cruelty don't seem to make an impression on people anymore. To get anybody's attention, you need a big, vulgar scandal, even though, if you asked me, what actually happened was worse than this stupid story I made up. But no one would understand that, and I was angry, so…I'm sorry. I never meant—

SENATOR C: No need to apologize.

SENATOR B: I couldn't agree more.

SENATOR C: I have everything I need.

SENATOR A: Same here.

SENATOR B: *(To Emma.)* Thank you for your time. The country needs people as civic minded as you are.

(They exit. Sheila enters.)

SHEILA: Emma! You're on in five minutes.

(Emma turns, confused.)

EMMA: Oh, I'm sorry—I'm just so confused about all of this—

SHEILA: Now, what I'd tell you about confusion!

EMMA: Oh—I don't know…

SHEILA: The world wants to hear from you! All those people out there! Someone real's gotta tell the truth! Normal people are sick of this shit! The truth will set you free! Hallelujah! Praise Jesus! *(She starts to sing in tongues.)*

EMMA: Sheila?

SHEILA: *(Fast to switch back to reality.)* Emma. Just tell the truth.

(She goes. Emma looks at the audience.)

SENATOR C: *(Voice over.)* WHY DON'T YOU TELL US WHAT HAPPENED THAT NIGHT?

EMMA: I was introduced to Senator Maddox. He seemed interested in me. It was suggested that I should be nice to him because it might help Arthur's campaign. *(Beat.)* That is what I did.

(The lights change. The Senators leave. Emma sits alone on stage. Lance enters.)

LANCE: Hey. How you doing?

EMMA: Oh. Lance. Hi.

LANCE: I thought it went good. The hearing.

EMMA: Yeah, it went fine.

LANCE: I mean, you seemed a little nervous at first.

EMMA: Did I?

LANCE: But you looked fabulous.

EMMA: Thanks.

LANCE: Richard really thought it went well. And I thought—to tell you the truth, I think you're the bravest person I've ever met.

EMMA: Oh. No.

LANCE: To stand there and admit to the whole country what you've done wrong—

EMMA: Yeah, well—

LANCE: And then to do whatever you have to, to set it right, no matter what the cost—

EMMA: It's really not what you think, Lance.

LANCE: It's meant a lot to me. I've learned a lot from you.

(Pause. Emma sighs.)

LANCE: *(Continuing.)* I'm sorry I took your head off the other day.

EMMA: It's okay. I shouldn't have said anything.

LANCE: No. You were right. *(Pause.)* When you said, that you thought I was—that way. You were right.

EMMA: *(Beat.)* I was?

LANCE: I've tried to fight it. I've prayed a lot. I see a counselor. But I just don't seem to be able to overcome it.

EMMA: Well, Lance, maybe that's because there's really nothing wrong with it. Have you thought about that?

LANCE: That's what the devil would like me to believe.

EMMA: Oh. The devil.

LANCE: Anyway. You don't need to hear about my problems. I just wanted you to know. You were so brave about admitting your sins. I thought I should do the same.

EMMA: Lance, you're fine—

(Richard enters.)

RICHARD: You were wonderful, Emma! Your testimony means a great deal, not just to us, but to the entire country.

LANCE: I was just telling her.

RICHARD: Lance, do you think that tomorrow we could go for a slightly more sophisticated look? I think we've erred too much on the side of caution. She looked like a perverse school girl out there.

LANCE: Maybe a blazer—

RICHARD: And lose the headband. Emma, we've made some revisions in your testimony. We came up with some evidence that implicates the first lady, and it would be good if you could lay some groundwork for that. *(He hands her pages.)*

EMMA: No, no, no. I'm not doing this anymore. This is bullshit. I'm not going back there. I'm not testifying any more.

RICHARD: I think you are. Lance, I'd like to speak with Emma alone, please.

LANCE: I'll be praying for you, Emma. *(Lance exits.)*

EMMA: You know, this whole thing is a lie. You know I made it up. Don't you?

RICHARD: Of course.

EMMA: And that doesn't matter to you.

RICHARD: Not one bit. Sit down, Emma.

EMMA: I'm not doing what you tell me anymore, Richard. You're a bunch of fucking hypocrites, couching all this bile and hate in terms of righteousness—

RICHARD: Now, I'm not going to have a conversation with you about hypocrisy, Emma. With all due respect, you could teach a class. I said, sit down.

(She does.)

RICHARD: I mean, what do you think this is? What do you think is going on here? Do you honestly think you can just do whatever you want and there will be no consequences? For god's sake, we could take your child from you. We could send you to jail. And if you cross me, we'll do it. Do you understand that?

EMMA: *(Beat.)* You can't take my baby.

RICHARD: Well, it's wonderful to hear that that concerns you. I wasn't sure. So, you want this baby. You care about this baby.

EMMA: Yes.

RICHARD: Then you listen to me. You've perpetrated a fraud on the entire nation! You've tried to interfere with the workings of the senate! You're clearly mentally unstable. So if we want that kid, we're not going to have any trouble getting it. And then we're going to give it to some nice, Christian family to raise. Am I getting through to you? *(Pause.)* Look. There's no need to throw threats at each other. You came here because you belonged here. You didn't like the way people were behaving, so you decided to punish them. No one held a gun to your head. You did it because it made sense to you. You're just like us. You understand righteousness, and anger, and retribution. You understand the human condition. So stop whining, and play by the rules. Don't ever talk back to me again. *(He goes. Beat.)*

EMMA: *(To audience.)* All right. I admit it. I've made some mistakes. But, you know, I didn't start this. You saw what happened. You were with me every step of the way. And it all made sense to you, I mean, I didn't hear anyone trying to stop me, now did I? YOU'RE IN THIS EVERY BIT AS DEEP AS I AM. I'm sorry. Once again, it seems that I am in need of a little perspective.

(Marjorie enters as the stage changes into a bar. A drunk sits at another table.)

EMMA: *(To Marjorie.)* It was, somebody said this, I remember, but I can't remember who, said this thing about culture and objectivity, that when a culture values objectivity and, you know, *reason,* then that's good, because that means we're all in this together, we're trying to find this collective objective *thing,* right? But that doesn't always happen, sometimes whole cultures, whole, like, America, slide toward subjectivity, everything is me me me, and then, all hell breaks loose, no one is talking to each other anymore, it's like we've all got these reflector sunglasses on and the reflector part is on the inside, so we just keep looking at ourselves until we're completely blind and then there's nothing holding us together anymore, and I didn't mean to do it, but I got angry, and I thought anger was a good thing, because it helps you fight for change, but it's also dangerous because it's so sub*jec*tive, you think you're helping the world, and you're the problem! That's just it, isn't it, the lesson is, there's nothing you can do. I'm sorry. I've just, I've done terrible things and I don't know how to set it right.

(She drinks. Marjorie smiles at her, happy.)

MARJORIE: Hey, I saw you on TV today.

EMMA: What?

MARJORIE: I thought you looked great. That dress you had on was adorable. That's a good look for you. Kind of young.

EMMA: Marjorie—

MARJORIE: Oh, come on, cheer up! I mean, this is very exciting. They were talking about you on the news, too. And I was like, wow. I know her.

EMMA: What were they saying?

MARJORIE: Oh, you know. I don't know. But you should be having a great time. Everyone is paying all this attention to you. You get to meet all these famous people.

EMMA: I'm in the middle of a terrible scandal.

MARJORIE: Yeah, but you're on TV! I mean, this stuff doesn't happen everyday. I think you should enjoy it, is all I'm saying.

EMMA: Well, you're in a good mood.

MARJORIE: Oh, yeah. I feel great. I'm on prozac, did I tell you?

EMMA: No, actually, you didn't.

MARJORIE: Oh, yeah. I love it. You should try it. I mean, with all due respect, Emma, you're getting a little negative these days.

EMMA: I realize that. I was counting on you to be negative too. That's sort of why I called you.

MARJORIE: Well, yeah, but I'm on drugs now.

EMMA: So you said.

MARJORIE: OK. I love you.

EMMA: *(Sour.)* I love you, too.

(Marjorie goes. The drunk at the next table calls at her as she leaves.)

E.T. BLACK: Hey! Do you know who I am?

MARJORIE: Oh, of course! Hi! How's it going?

E.T. BLACK: You know me?

MARJORIE: Oh! No. I thought you were someone else. I'm sorry. *(She smiles and goes.)*

E.T. BLACK: *(To his drink.)* Well, fuck you, I don't know who you are, either. *(He drinks. After a pause, Emma calls from her table.)*

EMMA: Hey, E.T.

E.T. BLACK: What?

EMMA: I know who you are.

E.T. BLACK: You do?

EMMA: You're E.T. Black. You're a famous screenwriter.

E.T. BLACK: You know who I am? Wait a minute. You know who I am? *(The drunk stares at her, stands and slowly staggers over to her table.)*

EMMA: Yeah, you're E.T. Black. I met you here a couple months ago.

E.T. BLACK: Fuck. Did I sleep with you?

EMMA: No.

E.T. BLACK: I can't remember anything anymore…Wait a minute. I know who you are.

EMMA: Yeah, we met a couple months ago.

E.T. BLACK: You're the girl from the senate hearings. Not Anita Hill, the other one. With the weird story. I know all about you.

EMMA: *(Cold.)* Good.

E.T. BLACK: Yeah, Hollywood is all over you. You got everything—sex, money, politics, a good part for a woman. They want me to write a movie about you.

EMMA: They do?

E.T. BLACK: Nobody's called you yet? Well, isn't that a fucking kick. They're pitching your story to me, and they don't even own the rights. Assholes. Listen, when they come after you, first thing they're gonna do is try and rob you blind. Don't be stupid. Hire a lawyer and hold out for seven figures.

EMMA: Thanks for the tip.

E.T. BLACK: Yeah, like you need to be warned about how the world works.

EMMA: And you'll write the screenplay?

E.T. BLACK: Oh, fuck, no. I passed. I'm not getting involved with this. I mean, with all due respect, sweetheart, that story you told is a complete whopper.

EMMA: *(Beat.)* Is that so?

E.T. BLACK: Oh, come on. I may be a drunk, but I'm still a writer. I can tell when something's made up.

EMMA: I don't know what you're talking about.

E.T. BLACK: Yeah, of course you have to take that position. And most of them will fall for it. I said to these guys, these producers, she's *lying*, and they all stared at me like I was insane, of course, they all tell so many lies per second they can't tell the difference anymore, but what am I supposed to do? You can't fictionalize a piece of fiction, where would that fucking put you? You keep building on something fake and the next thing you know, you got just some psychic no man's land, the American government, or Hollywood, some weird fucking place where nothing has to make sense anymore, it just has to move or make money. Everyone keeps acting like two lies make a fucking truth, when that isn't exactly how it works, hasn't that *occurred* to anybody? How long do they expect me to go along with this? That's all I'm saying! I'm E.T. Black, I'm a *writer*, for God's sake, if this were the nineteenth century I'd be having lunch with *Disraeli* and these guys just keep paying me to lie, but there are limits, all right? There are fucking limits!

EMMA: You won't write my story.

E.T. BLACK: No I will not.

EMMA: Because you have too much integrity. Is that what you're saying?

E.T. BLACK: Sweetie, it shows up at the oddest times. *(He stands to go.)*

EMMA: I just put a spin on things. Everybody does it.

E.T. BLACK: Yeah. That's the first one you tell yourself. You know—you're gonna have a kid. You should be thinking about these things.

EMMA: Oh, I am.

E.T. BLACK: And you shouldn't be drinking. It's not good for the baby.

DAVID: It's apple juice.

E.T. BLACK: Well, that's good. Don't start drinking, okay? It doesn't help. You think it does, but it doesn't.

EMMA: Thanks for the tip.

(He goes.)

EMMA: *(To audience.)* So, it turns out I have less integrity than a Hollywood screenwriter.

DAVID: Hey, are you E.T. Black?

E.T. BLACK: You know I am. I drink in here all the time.

DAVID: I love your work, man.

E.T. BLACK: You're just saying that.

DAVID: No, I'm not. You're the best writer in America.

E.T. BLACK: Really?

DAVID: Ever since you started drinking in here, I went out and rented all your movies. You're a fucking genius man.

E.T. BLACK: You watched my movies?

DAVID: Yeah. Look, I got this killer idea for a screenplay. Takes place in

Washington. All these white people are just like they're fucking nuts, okay, and there's this brother who sees everything, he's around all the time but nobody figures out that he's watching, and going, man, the country is fucked up, people suffering and dying on the streets, children with guns, it's like a war out there, and none of these fuckers see any of it, they're totally lost in this non-reality and it's like Anacosta or South East, different country man, they could give a shit, and every night this guy he's out there serving escargot, Puilly Fusses and Coque whatever to these people who are talking about taking food out of the mouths of children—like it's good *policy*, it's good *politics*. And he's gotta be polite to these idiots. What do you think that does to somebody's *heart*? What do you *think*? (*Beat*.) Anyway, this brother, the one watching them, he finally says fuck you, fuck you all, do your own fucking dishes, and then he blows up the White House.

E.T. BLACK: It's been done. (*Beat.*) If you blew up the dome, that would work.

BARTENDER: Yeah, it could be the dome.

E.T. BLACK: Let's talk about this.

(*He staggers off with the Bartender. Emma calls after them.*)

EMMA: But that's not how we started! It's not!

(*Arthur enters, hopeful and excited.*)

ARTHUR: I don't know. It's such a huge undertaking—

EMMA: Arthur, don't do this to me! It's taken me months to talk you into this, you can't back out now!

ARTHUR: I just think we should be realistic! I don't have a chance of winning—

EMMA: Come on, this is America. All sorts of idiots get elected to congress. If they can do it, you can too. Arthur! You've been talking about running as long as I've known you, and you're never going to get a better opportunity. I talked to my friend Tommy about you, he's been managing campaigns for a long time, not this high profile, but he knows the ropes. He says you have a shot. At least talk to him. Tommy!

ARTHUR: Tommy? Is this your young man?

EMMA: Sort of.

ARTHUR: "Sort of?"

EMMA: It's still early. But it's going well.

(*Tommy enters.*)

TOMMY: So, is he going to do it?

EMMA: He's going to do it.

TOMMY: Excellent.

(Emma and Tommy kiss.)

ARTHUR: I didn't say that!

TOMMY: The party's in complete disarray, sir. The old standbys are terrified and well they should be. Everybody's looking for a dark horse. If you want to run, there's never going to be a better time.

ARTHUR: *(Considering.)* And you can help me?

TOMMY: Yes. I can.

EMMA: Come on, Arthur. Wouldn't it be worse not to try? What's the worst that can happen?

(Beat.)

ARTHUR: I'll do it.

EMMA: Yes!

(She and Tommy kiss again. There is a brief celebratory moment as they all hug and congratulate each other.)

ARTHUR: *(To Tommy, joking.)* Now I have to call Natalie and tell her the bad news.

(He heads off. Tommy calls after him.)

TOMMY: Get her down here! We can use all the help we can get!

(He goes. The mood changes. Emma watches him as a Bartender crosses, pours him a drink and hands him the bottle.)

TOMMY: *(Cool, drinking.)* Hello, Emma.

EMMA: Tommy.

TOMMY: I thought that was you.

EMMA: Hi.

TOMMY: Hi. *(Beat.)* You're looking good.

EMMA: Thanks.

TOMMY: I mean, you look good. You just had a baby, right? I heard you had your baby.

EMMA: Six weeks ago.

TOMMY: Well, you look great.

EMMA: Thank you.

TOMMY: So, what'd you have?

(He pours himself a drink. She watches.)

EMMA: A boy.

TOMMY: Wow. That's great.

EMMA: Yes. It is.

TOMMY: So. Is it mine?

(Beat.)

EMMA: No, actually. "It" is mine.

TOMMY: Yeah, that virgin birth stuff may have worked with your friends over in Christian la la land, but I happen to know better. *(He pours himself another drink.)*

EMMA: You're drinking again.

TOMMY: How very observant of you. Yes. I have, for the moment, fallen off the wagon. It's temporary.

EMMA: It won't solve anything.

TOMMY: What would you know about it?

EMMA: Nothing. It's just, someone told me that.

TOMMY: Drinking doesn't solve anything. There's a news flash. I don't expect it to solve anything. I'm more interested in the way it blots things out.

EMMA: How's Arthur?

TOMMY: A little depressed. Losing kind of does that to you.

EMMA: He'll be fine.

TOMMY: Oh yeah. He was a newcomer, no one expected him to win. In fact, to tell you the truth, most people thought it was pretty impressive that he got as far as he did. A major scandal his first time out. The party boys took note. They want him to try again.

EMMA: Is that right?

TOMMY: *(Nodding.)* Hoping for a liberal backlash. If the religious right hates him so much, he can't be all that bad, something like that. Annabeth thinks he's got a shot. Politicians, every last one of them, they're like this special breed of human beings made out of cork and Teflon...
(He reaches for the bottle. Emma tries to stop him.)

EMMA: Come on, Tommy
(He moves it away from her.)

TOMMY: You could have returned my phone calls.

EMMA: I didn't see the point.

TOMMY: The baby is the point, Emma. The baby is the point.

EMMA: I just told you. It's not your kid.

TOMMY: Yeah, and I'm telling you. You're a big liar. I never thought you were. But then you got up, in front of the whole country and told the most spectacular set of fibs I ever heard. So I wouldn't stand there and act like just because words come out of your mouth we all have to believe them. I want to see the baby.

EMMA: That is not going to happen.

TOMMY: *(Furious.)* I have a right. That is *my* son.

EMMA: *(Warning.)* Tommy.

TOMMY: HE'S MY SON.

EMMA: Listen to me. He is not your son.

TOMMY: You just can't keep lying about this, Emma. Not about this.

EMMA: Like you're so honest. If you were so sure about this, why didn't you say something during the hearings? You had plenty of opportunities. You could have just slid it in between all those stories about how deranged I am.

TOMMY: I wasn't sure then. I'm sure now.

EMMA: That's convenient.

TOMMY: I didn't want to be involved!

EMMA: So, you got your wish.

TOMMY: You can't stop me. I'll demand a court order. I'll get paternity tests.

EMMA: *(Impatient.)* No one is going to grant you parental rights. You come forward now, and everyone's going to think you collaborated in this fraud waged on the U.S. Senate. Plus you're a big old alcoholic. I'm not afraid of you.

TOMMY: *(Beat.)* You're a cold bitch.

EMMA: Fine.

(She stands to go. Tommy grabs her arm to stop her. There is a very brief struggle. Embarrassed, he lets her go.)

TOMMY: I'm sorry.

(He sits. She watches him.)

TOMMY: I guess none of us are who we thought we were, huh?

EMMA: I guess not.

TOMMY: Emma, please. What happened that one stupid night, it was so small, why can't you just let it go?

EMMA: Look, you're the one who dumped me. Over nothing, over Arthur being a prick about seating arrangements. And now my child has no father. So don't tell me how small that evening was. That evening was not small.

TOMMY: You should have told me about the baby—

EMMA: I tried! But you could barely speak to me, remember? Arthur said to get rid of me, so you did. You didn't think twice. You didn't flinch.

TOMMY: That's not how it was.

EMMA: You couldn't throw me away fast enough.

TOMMY: We all made mistakes.

EMMA: Forget it. I got one good thing out of this whole mess, and I'm not going to screw it up. None of you people are coming near that kid. He is not your kid.

TOMMY: You can't keep away the whole human race.

EMMA: There are good people somewhere. I'll find them.

TOMMY: You thought Arthur was good. You thought you were good. *(Beat.)* Please. Let me see the baby.

EMMA: No.

TOMMY: You can't protect him.

EMMA: I have to go. *(She goes.)*

TOMMY: YOU CAN'T PROTECT HIM!

(He slumps in his chair. Emma looks at the audience.)

EMMA: You should see my boy. He's quite beautiful; he is, in fact, the most beautiful thing I've ever seen. My doctor tells me that the reason babies are so adorable is that if they weren't, we'd leave them by the side of the road. Which, I think, says more about us than it does about them. So how do you raise a child in a world that has people in it? How can I teach him to be good when I know that goodness will not protect him? I don't actually want to raise a little idealist; they turn into the most god-awful cynics. And I don't particularly want to watch his heart break when he learns what people are really like. But I look at him, and he is so clearly good, I don't know if I can bear to teach him anything else.

ANNABETH: Now, how do you want to do the seating, Arthur? Four and one?

(Arthur, Annabeth, and Tommy enter, taking their seats. Emma looks over as Arthur considers this.)

ARTHUR: *(Quickly.)* Oh, yes. That's exactly right. Four and one.

EMMA: And yet I fear the anger of the righteous.

ANNABETH: David— *(She waves the waiter on.)* We'll need a table for four, and a table for one.

DAVID: Right this way.

(David, the waiter starts to move a place setting.)

TOMMY: Wait a minute. There are going to be five of us, aren't there? When the senator gets here—

EMMA: What's that quote about those small unremembered act of meanness that make up a man's life?

DAVID: Kindness. Small, unremembered acts of kindness.

EMMA: Are you sure?

ANNABETH: We'll set you up at the best single they have.

EMMA: I suppose the best I can do is to teach him to watch carefully. To struggle for objectivity. To believe always that the human spirit can and will transcend its own pettiness.

ANNABETH: David, can we get her the view of the capital dome?

DAVID: Anything for you, Annabeth.

EMMA: And when someone asks him to sit at another table…

ARTHUR: Emma, you understand.

EMMA: He can go peacefully. Whole unto himself, without surrender.

ARTHUR: This is strictly business.

EMMA: *(To Arthur.)* It's all right, Arthur. I prefer it over here.

    (David hands her a paperback.)

EMMA: Thanks.

END OF PLAY

THE ONE-ACT PLAYS

When I was asked to provide cast information for the first productions of all the following plays, I went into a small panic because the truth is, I don't actually remember who did what when, and there are no records. They were all done in tiny theatres, mostly in New York, everyone worked for no money, and all the shows had very limited runs of no more than ten or twelve performances each. Some shows we did only once or twice. There were no sets, no critics, no stars and no movie deals. We performed for ourselves and each other, for our friends, and for anyone else who loves the theatre. We did it for the sheer fun of it, and to keep our craft honed. We had the time of our lives.

The casts of these various productions included some of the most gifted actors it has been my pleasure to work with. An incomplete, unalphabetized list includes: Kristen Flanders, Richard Poe, Julie White, Rebecca O'Brien, Tim Ransom, Dee Freeman, Stephan Umsted, Willie Garson, Merrill Holtzman, Lisa Beth Miller, Billy Strong, Fisher Stevens, Gina Gershon, Connie Shulman, Linda Larson, Kristine Nielsen, Gayle Keller, Reed Birney, Cathy Curtain, Marcelline Hugot, Mary Joy, Patty Cornell, Miriam Healy, Eric Lutz, Chris Romeo, Paula Plum, Colleen Quinn, Chris Baskus, Janine Robbins and Adina Porter. This list is extremely incomplete because, as I've said, I can't remember who did what when. (There was a really great actor named Danny something who did *Does This Woman Have A Name?*, and I just can't remember his last name.)

The directors who shaped these performances include Mary Pat Green, Pamela Grace, Michael Stuno, Geoffrey Nauffts, Arnold Mungioli, Beth Schachter, Tracey Brigden, Jace Alexander and Suzanne Brinkley. All of them have my special thanks for their uncompromising support and guidance, and their endless hours of work.

Most especially, I would like to thank the theatres which supported me and my collaborators in this endeavor. They include: Naked Angels, Alice's Fourth Floor, Manhattan Class Company, West Bank Cafe, Manhattan Punchline, the Miranda Theatre, and New Georges, and, in Los Angeles, Theatre Neo, and Naked Angels West Coast.

The one-act is the theatrical equivalent of the short story. The arc is brief, the focus intent; much is made of little. I find it a thrilling form to work in, and I am proud of these pieces. I hope that actors and theatres continue to give them a life.

DOES THIS WOMAN
HAVE A NAME?

CHARACTERS

SARAH: An actress in her late twenties; pretty in a hometown-girl way, smart, both sarcastic and direct at the same time

MEL: A writer in her late twenties, complicated, introspective

JON: Mel's lover, a lawyer; he wears suits; nice guy

SET

A very bare room, representing Mel's apartment. There are three pieces of furniture: a cot, a table with a computer and printer on it, and a chair. A long sheet of computer paper covered with type spills out of the printer and onto the floor. A telephone with a long cord sits on the bed.

SCENE I

Lights up on Mel's apartment. Mel sits at the computer, staring at the screen but listening to Sarah, who sits on the bed, talking on the telephone. She holds a pad of paper on a clipboard and writes as she listens.

SARAH: Hi, can I help you? *(Pause.)* That's right, it is. Has Micki explained to you our procedure? Fine. Now why don't you tell me who you'd like to talk to, and what you'd like to talk about? *(Long pause. She scribbles as she listens.)* Uh huh. *(Pause.)* Uh huh. *(Pause.)* Uh huh. *(Long pause.)* Does this woman have a name? *(Pause.)* Uh huh. *(Pause.)* Yes, of course, I'll explain that to her. Absolutely. And can you give me a number where you can be reached in about fifteen or twenty minutes? *(Pause. She writes.)* And who should I tell Inga to ask for? *(Pause.)* All right, Marco. I'll give Inga your message. *(She hangs up.)* This isn't going to work.

MEL: Just let me look at it, okay?

(She holds out her hand. Sarah hands her the pad.)

SARAH: He wants to talk to *Inga*. Inga. I'm sorry, but really, Swedish accents are just not sexy. "Yah, Marco, yah, yah—"

MEL: You have to shut up while I think about this.

(She starts to type rapidly while looking at the notepad. She types.)

SARAH: This isn't going to work.

MEL: What is this, I can't read your handwriting—is this something about a blow job?

SARAH: Yeah, he wants a twenty-four hour blow job.

MEL: You have got to be kidding.

SARAH: That's what he said. I mean, what am I supposed to do with that? Blow jobs over the phone. Get real. I can't believe guys actually have fantasies about this stuff. I mean, if someone gave me a twenty-four hour blow job, I'd probably die.

MEL: *(Deadpan.)* But what a way to go.

SARAH: No, I don't think so. Oh, my God, are you kidding? That sounds horrible. Death by a blow job? Oh. Ugh.

MEL: Yeah, but I bet Marco likes it.

SARAH: No. Come on. Are you putting that—Mel, come on. You can't write that. I can't say that; I'll start laughing or something—

MEL: *(Grinning, typing.)* Marco is going to love it. *(She types.)*
(Blackout.)

SCENE II

Lights up on the apartment, the next night. Mel sits at the computer; Jon stands. He wears a trench coat. He sets down his briefcase.

JON: *(Bewildered.)* You're doing *what?*

MEL: It's just for a little while.

JON: Mel—

MEL: I know.

JON: Oh, man. Is it the money?

MEL: Of course it's the money. I just—I can't do office work anymore; it makes me really stupid, and I get home too tired to write; it's pointless—

JON: *(Overlap.)* God, Mel, if you need money, I can give you money—

MEL: I can't take your money—

JON: I make a fortune—

MEL: I can't take any more of your money, Jon! *(Pause.)* And I can't take any more from my parents, either. I mean, at some point, you go, it's time to be a grownup—

JON: You are a grownup! You just sold two stories; it's happening for you—

MEL: *(Overlap.)* I can't live on two stories a year—

JON: You could move in with me.
    (Pause. She looks at him.)

JON: Okay. Sorry. Forget I mentioned it. You're right. Doing phone sex makes much more sense than moving in with the man you love. I don't know what I was thinking.

MEL: Come on. I just don't think that would solve anything. I can't stop trying to take care of myself.

JON: I'm not asking you to. I'm just saying. You could stay home and write. You're doing so well, I just think if you—

MEL: I am not doing well! I'm completely broke!

JON: You're an artist! You're supposed to be broke!

MEL: Nobody in America is supposed to be broke.

JON: Artists are.

MEL: No, even artists—

JON: Yes, you are. It's romantic.

MEL: Trust me. Being broke is not romantic.

JON: It's very romantic.

MEL: It's a pain in the ass.

JON: It's good for you. You're supposed to live with the poor and record their struggles.

MEL: Yeah, well, the poor don't have parents and boyfriends bailing them out all the time.

JON: But if they did, you can bet they wouldn't argue about it. They'd just say, you want to give me money? Free money? Why, thank you—

MEL: Jon—

JON: I'm telling you, you'll never be an important artist until you learn to say yes to free money.

MEL: *(Pause.)* Jon. I'm not going to take your money.

JON: Mel—

MEL: It won't be for long. I promise. In two or three weeks I can make enough to live for maybe four months. And anyway, it's really not as bad as it sounds. I just write the stuff. Sarah does the actual call.

JON: Sarah? I should have known.

MEL: Don't start—

JON: Was this her idea?

MEL: It doesn't matter who's idea it was—

JON: Mel—

MEL: Could we not fight about this, please?

JON: *(Pause.)* Fine.

(Tense pause. Mel crosses and takes him by the lapels.)

MEL: Come on. Lighten up. There are some benefits to this.

JON: I'll bet.

MEL: Really. Last week I did some job-related research, and I learned some very interesting things.

JON: I'm sure you did.

MEL: I did.

(She pulls his face down and whispers something in his ear. He pulls away, trying not to smile.)

JON: Mel—Mel—

(She pulls him back and whispers again. He starts to laugh, puts his arm around her. She wraps her legs around him. Sarah enters, carrying a shoulder bag and a six-pack of beer.)

SARAH: Ooops. Don't mind me.

(Jon pulls away from Mel.)

JON: Hello, Sarah. How nice to see you.

SARAH: Hey, Jon. So, Mel, doing some warm ups for our shift, huh?

MEL: Something like that. *(She goes to the computer.)*

JON: So, I hear you two are working together. Congratulations. This whole set-up is very enterprising.

SARAH: I know, you think it's sick—

JON: No, hey—

SARAH: It's survival work, okay? I mean, you try being an actress in this city.

JON: I wouldn't want to.

SARAH: I just don't want any shit about it, okay?

JON: I understand.

SARAH: Good. You know, I have to say, you're being pretty open-minded about this. Most guys, I bet they'd freak out if their girlfriend was doing phone sex.

JON: You think so?

SARAH: Oh, yeah.

(The phone rings. They all stare at it for a moment. Pause. It rings again. Sarah picks it up.)

SARAH: Hello?

(Blackout.)

SCENE III

Lights up on Mel and Sarah, Mel on the bed, Sarah sprawled all over the floor, somewhat entangled in the phone, surrounded by streams of computer paper. Sarah holds a strip of paper and reads from the end of it. She speaks rapidly, stream of consciousness style.

SARAH: Yes yes oh yes oh yes oh oh my arms my eyes my breasts oh your tongue oh the soil of the garden slides between my teeth, my saliva moistens it yes I feed you with my tongue in your mouth yes I am transformed into mud my legs my thighs my sex between your legs yes yes OOOOOh. Ohh. Yes. Yes. *(She holds the phone away from her ear for a moment.)* Hello? You okay? You okay there? *(Pause.)* Yeah—yeah, that one got away from both of us. Listen, Sir Michael, we're going to have to wrap up now. Yeah, I'm afraid so. No, it has; it's been twenty minutes—yes, I'm sure. Yes. Yes. Okay. Yes. Bye now—Goodbye. *(She hangs up decisively and looks at Mel for a moment, then reads off the paper, expressionless.)* "I am transformed into mud my legs my thighs my sex between your legs yes yes oh oh yes yes." Where do you get this shit?

MEL: James Joyce, Monique Wittig—and some I made up.

SARAH: I don't know, Mel. I think this stuff is a little too creative.

MEL: All you gave me was garden fantasy. That's all I had to go with.

SARAH: I know, but—

MEL: Did he ask for his money back?

SARAH: No.

MEL: All right then.

SARAH: *(Going back over the script.)* Oh yeah, this was my favorite part: "Yes you plant me oh oh your mouth consumes the ripe fruit of my breasts you plow me under you make me earth your tree shoots in my body oh oh oh."

(Mel laughs. Jon enters, carrying a bag with Chinese food cartons and a six-pack of beer.)

JON: It's so nice to see people enjoying their work.

MEL: Hi, hi, hi.

(She crosses and kisses him several times. While they kiss, Sarah starts to open the food.)

SARAH: Plow me. Shoot your tree in me. Yes yes yes. Oh.

(Jon looks at her. Mel pulls away and helps Sarah with the food.)

JON: What is that?

MEL: "That" is Molly Bloom.

JON: That is not Molly Bloom.

SARAH: It's a gardener fantasy.

(She eats. Mel pops a beer.)

MEL: We had a bunch of weirdoes tonight, didn't we? The shoe shine guy? And then that guy who wanted to have sex with Joan of Arc?

SARAH: I don't know. I can see that.

MEL: You know, I hate to admit it, but this is kind of fun, in its own weird way. Don't you think it's kind of fun? I mean, I can't believe how easy this is. It's like having the reverse of writer's block. I feel very fertile.

JON: Fertile?

MEL: Fecund. Blossoming. And just for the record, I'm getting a great deal of sick satisfaction out of the fact that none of these guys would take a second look at me on the street because I'm not some sort of live version of a Barbie doll, but I'm the one they come to for their orgasms. I mean it. Phone sex may just be my calling. I feel very fulfilled. I'm writing up a storm, and for once, I'm making a living at it.

JON: So—what are you saying? You're giving up writing?

MEL: No, of course not.

JON: Have you written anything since you started this?

MEL: Jon, could we not—

JON: Have you?

MEL: I was in the middle of a dry spell anyway—

JON: Great. That's—

MEL: Oh, come on, I'm just—never mind.

JON: Mel—

MEL: *What?*

JON: Nothing. Forget it. Sorry. Forget it. *(Pause.)* So, do you ever get any time off from this fulfilling job?

MEL: What?

JON: Don't you get a couple days off once in a while? You guys have been working straight since this started.

MEL: Well—

SARAH: We just did that cause we needed the money. But Micki's flexible, we can take a couple days whenever we want.

JON: Good. Then maybe you should do that.

MEL: Jon—

JON: Because one of the partners down at the firm has a house on the cape which he isn't using this weekend.

SARAH: Why, Jon. What a wonderful idea. I'd love to.
(Jon looks at her.)

SARAH: Oh, chill out. I'm kidding.

JON: What do you say? *(He crosses to Mel, puts his arm around her.)*

MEL: I don't know.

JON: What don't you know?

MEL: I just—I don't know, okay?

JON: *(Coaxing.)* Mel—

MEL: *(Quiet.)* I just don't know.

JON: Come on— *(He kisses her.)*

SARAH: Oh, man—You guys—I'm sorry, but could we not have a public sex scene here? I mean, I'm from the midwest, okay?

JON: Sarah—do you think we could maybe have a little privacy here?

SARAH: I'm hungry!

JON: Sarah—

SARAH: All right. I'm sorry. I'm going.

MEL: It's all right, Sarah. *(She pulls away from Jon, crosses to the table to look at the food.)*

JON: It's not all right, Sarah.

SARAH: I don't know. Doesn't look to me like you're getting anywhere, Jon.

JON: Sarah, please. I'm a desperate man.

MEL: You are not desperate.

JON: I am too.

MEL: You are not.

JON: I am. Can you get the weekend off?

MEL: I said, I don't know.

JON: Great.

(*Pause. He sits. Mel stares at the food. Sarah watches them.*)

SARAH: So you two are having trouble in bed, eh?

JON: As a matter of fact, we are.

MEL: Could we not discuss very private matters in front of Sarah please?

SARAH: For God's sake, Mel, we have been talking about nothing but the most intimate sexual acts all day. You can't get coy now. So what's the problem?

MEL: There is no problem! I just—when you think about sex all day it's hard to get excited about it.

JON: I have never found that to be true. Back in high school, when I thought about nothing else, I still wanted it. I swear.

MEL: I'm just having trouble relaxing lately, okay?

SARAH: I'm relaxed. I'm horny as hell. I agree with Jon, talking about it just makes me want it. It's like being in a play, you know; this always happens whenever I do a really sexy part. I mean, the guy I'm working with can be a total loser but the stuff I have to say finally gets to me; it's like the script makes me want to have sex. I have had more stupid affairs with crazy actors because of this kind of thing.

JON: Well, maybe you need to set up something with one of your customers.

SARAH: Oh, gross. Jon. That is really disgusting.

JON: You just said—

SARAH: I said, you know, the script makes me want to have sex. These guys on the phone make me want to throw up.

JON: Mel thinks it's noble that you two are reaching out to their humanity. You're touching their souls—

SARAH: Yeah, well, Mel doesn't have to talk to them.

MEL: I didn't say it was noble. I just said it was—I don't know, *real.*

JON: That's not what you said; you said it was your life's calling.

MEL: All I meant was—

JON: What you said was—

MEL: (*Snapping.*) Jon, I know what I said! (*Pause.*) I was just—I was kind of kidding, okay? It just—it's been a while since I had anything published and you get tired of writing for nobody. It feels—different—writing for somebody.

JON: Even if they're sleezeballs.

MEL: Even if they're sleezeballs.

(Pause. She sits and looks at the pages of text, distracted. Sarah eats. Jon watches Mel.)

MEL: I should clean this place up. It's getting—I should just clean it up.

JON: Don't you want some food? You must be hungry—

MEL: No, thanks, I'm not. I'm really not.

JON: I brought all this food—

MEL: I know. I'm sorry. It's great, it's really—I'm just not real hungry. *(She picks up one of the cartons and looks at it. She sets it down. Blackout.)*

SCENE IV

Mel sits at the desk, counting money, which she then puts into a bank deposit envelope. She fills out deposit slip. She is singing lightly, under her breath. Jon lies on the bed, watching her.

JON: They pay you in cash?

MEL: What? No. Sarah gets a check, and she—pays me.

JON: Ah. How much is that?

MEL: Four thousand, six hundred and twenty-three dollars.

JON: Four thousand, six hundred and twenty-three dollars.

MEL: Yeah.

JON: How long did it take you to make that? Three weeks?

MEL: Something like that.

JON: And you're going to quit now? *(Pause.)* You said you were going to quit after three weeks.

MEL: Yeah, well—I don't know. Sarah and I thought if we worked another week or so, we'd both have a kind of buffer—

JON: A buffer.

MEL: Yeah. Look, I gotta go to the bank and deposit this. It makes me really nervous to have it here.

JON: I still make more than you.

MEL: What?

JON: I make more than you. I pull in about two thousand five a week. I told you; I make a fortune. Lawyers make a fortune in this city.

MEL: I know, I just—I didn't know it was that much.

JON: I know. You never asked. I always thought that was weird. We've been going out for almost a year, and you've never asked me how much I made.

MEL: I don't care how much you make.

JON: Sure you do.

MEL: No, I don't.

JON: And you can live on that for how long? Four months?

MEL: Yeah. Yeah, about that.

JON: You're the only person I know who can make five thousand dollars last that long.

MEL: I know lots of people who live on less.

JON: If I gave you five thousand dollars, I wouldn't even feel it. I wouldn't even know it was gone.

(Pause. She does not answer.)

JON: If I gave you five thousand dollars, you'd have ten thousand. You could live on that for six months and still have enough left over to go out to dinner once in a while. Buy yourself some new clothes. Stay at home and finish your novel. Spend some time with your boyfriend. It would be sort of like having a grant, you know, the Jon Diehl Grant for Continuing Achievement in the Arts.

MEL: I'm not going to take your money, Jon.

JON: How come you can take money from these perverts but you can't take it from me?

MEL: I *earn* money from these perverts, okay?

JON: Earn. Right. That is—you are so fucking middle class—

MEL: Could we not—

JON: No, look, I haven't said anything; I've been very good, but this has gone on long enough. When you started this, you said—

MEL: Look, it's my life—

JON: *Take my money. Please. Would you please take my money?*

MEL: NO. *(Pause.)* Look. It just—you have to believe me; it would be bad for us, it would be really bad—

JON: Worse than this?

MEL: YES. I need to take care of myself; that's important to me—

JON: You're not taking care of yourself!

MEL: Look, I'm not going to be your little pet girlfriend—

JON: Don't get feminist on me; you're a fucking whore!

MEL: Get out.

(He looks at her, tries to speak, gives up, and exits. Blackout.)

SCENE V

Lights up on Sarah, on the phone. Mel is on the bed. Sarah reads.

SARAH: *(Oriental accent.)* Yes, under the rising moon I feel you as a gift of the Buddha. You have a beautiful body, Victor-san, which I wash with the tears of all my sisters— *(Pause.)* Excuse please?

(Pause. She stops reading. Mel looks at her.)

SARAH: Yes, Victor-san, I am—uh, moment please— *(She covers the phone. To Mel.)* He's getting all pissed off— *(Into phone.)* Yes, Victor-san, I want to put you in my mouth—

MEL: No, what are you doing?

SARAH: He's all pissed off because it's not sexy enough. *(To phone.)* Yes, Victor-san, oh, oh, you are large and lovely—

MEL: Sarah, stick to the script.

SARAH: *(To phone.)* Yes, Victor-san, I am true geisha—I was raised by Buddhist monks in Beijing—

MEL: No, Sarah, what are you doing? *(She tries to grab the script.)*

SARAH: *(Dropping accent.)* Look, I'm doing the best I can, all right? What do you want here? *(Pause.)* Well, I was getting to that. Yeah, I was, if you would just let me— *(To Mel.)* Write me something, would you? He's losing it.

(Mel hunts for a pencil.)

SARAH: *(To phone.)* Look, would you just calm down for a second—

MEL: Just go back to the script—

SARAH: I can't go back to the script; he knows it's an act. Write me something!

MEL: I can't find a pencil!

SARAH: *(To phone.)* Yeah, yeah, I'm here. Look, Victor, I'm just sitting here thinking how great it would be to—what? *(Pause.)* Look, you don't have to—look— *(Pause.)* What? *(Pause.)* That's really—no, look, you're getting all—LOOK—

MEL: Hang up on him.

SARAH: *(To phone.)* Stop it. *(Pause.)* Stop it.

MEL: SARAH, HANG UP ON HIM.

SARAH: STOP IT.

(Mel hits the phone, hanging up, then grabs the receiver from Sarah. The two women stare at each other.)

SARAH: Fuck you.

MEL: Sarah—

SARAH: No, fuck you. What the fuck is this shit? You give them all this fancy shit, and I end up—fuck you. You're just supposed to give them what they want. What is the matter with you?

MEL: Why didn't you just hang up on him?

SARAH: You're not supposed to hang up! You're supposed to tell them that they're great and they can do whatever they want to you! Christ, what do you think is going on here? What is this crap, geisha girls—

MEL: He wanted a geisha girl!

SARAH: He wanted to come! *(Pause. She kicks the papers viciously.)* Fuck. I can't believe—I can't believe you're getting a fifty percent cut for just sitting over there and playing games with your little computer while I take this shit.

MEL: Sarah—

SARAH: WHAT? You think it's great; you're having the time of your life dreaming up your little stories; well, it's not so funny when you have to listen to these guys whacking off, okay?

MEL: I'm hardly having the time of my life!

SARAH: Yeah, well you could have fooled me. You don't even need this, with your rich boyfriend—

MEL: That has nothing to do with—

SARAH: He WANTS to support you! Why the fuck are you doing this shit? If I didn't have to, do you think I'd be doing this?

MEL: I don't have a rich boyfriend, all right?

SARAH: Oh, right—

MEL: I don't have a rich boyfriend anymore!

SARAH: Oh, that's just—you are so fucking stupid—

MEL: Oh, shut up—

SARAH: You are so stupid!

MEL: I KNOW!

(They both sit. Pause.)

MEL: Are you all right?

SARAH: I'm sorry. It's just, some of these guys are really creeps.

MEL: What did he say?

SARAH: Mel, just don't ask, okay?

MEL: I'm sorry.

SARAH: No, I'm sorry. You broke up with Jon?

MEL: I guess.

SARAH: Fuck.

MEL: Yeah.

SARAH: What happened?

MEL: I don't want to talk about it. I'm sorry about this. You're right; the scripts are getting too weird. I'll tone it down.

SARAH: It's not the weirdness. It's just—you gotta keep things sexy, you know?

MEL: I thought that was sexy.

SARAH: Okay, then don't keep them sexy. Just keep them gross.

MEL: *(Pause.)* I thought that was gross.

SARAH: Okay, then just keep them—disgusting.

MEL: It was about to get disgusting. He freaked out just when it was about to get really, really disgusting.

SARAH: Okay, then. Just make sure they stay really, really—

MEL: Repulsive.

SARAH: Appalling.

MEL: Revolting.

SARAH: Filthy.

MEL: Feculent.

SARAH: What? No, now, see—

MEL: I'm kidding. I'll just keep it—nasty.

SARAH: Nasty. That's good.

MEL: Gross.

SARAH: Gross.

MEL: Sick.

SARAH: Sick.

MEL: Disgusting.

SARAH: Disgusting.

> *(They look at each other. Blackout.)*

SCENE VI

Lights up on Mel and Sarah, Mel at the computer, Sarah on the bed, on the phone. The Chinese food cartons, beer cans, and computer paper from previous scenes litter the stage. A half bottle of scotch stands on the desk; Mel takes a hit from it as she watches Sarah.

SARAH: *(On phone.)* ...And who would you like to talk to and what would you like to talk about? *(Pause. She writes.)* Uh huh. Uh huh. Uh huh. *(Pause.)* And does this woman have a name? *(Pause.)* Yes, I understand that, but which of these girls would you like to speak to? *(Pause.)* Yes, but if you had a preference— *(Pause.)* I see. I'm sorry, sir, but I assume Micki told you—I mean—well, usually our girls work alone—well, of course, I understand that, but—well, yes sir, we do offer that service, but this just may take a little longer, I have to talk to Micki about this—yes, sir. Well, yes, of course that is a factor. Could you give us your number? We'll call you back in fifteen to twenty minutes. *(Pause.)* And who should we ask for? *(Pause.)* Okay, Jean-Paul, we'll call you right back. *(She hangs up and looks up at Mel.)* We got a problem. This guy has a lesbian twin fantasy and he wants to talk to both of us.

MEL: What?

SARAH: He wants two girls. I'm calling Micki; we're not doing anymore weir-does.

MEL: Wait a minute; what did he say?

SARAH: I don't know; he's got some lesbian thing which is totally out of con-trol—I thought the whole point of those lesbian fantasies was that you watched them. Could you tell me why anybody would want to have a lesbian fantasy over the phone? I mean, anybody other than a lesbian. *(Mel takes the pad. Sarah reaches for the phone.)*

MEL: Just hold it for a second, okay? He's willing to pay what? What is this—

SARAH: Triple.

MEL: Triple?

SARAH: Yeah, can you believe that? Four hundred and fifty bucks for phone sex. The things people spend their money on make me sick, they really do.

MEL: God, he must be loaded.

SARAH: I don't care. He could give the money to charity or something. Support the arts. But what is he doing? He's sitting in a hotel room somewhere, thinking about lesbians, and jacking off. The world is in bad shape, I'm telling you. I'm just going to tell Micki I can't do this one.

MEL: You could do two voices. You could do this.

SARAH: Oh, no—

MEL: Yes, you could do that low cigarette voice and then the Betty Boop thing; he'll never know—

SARAH: I cannot—Mel—I can't pull this off. I'm just not good enough, and it's too weird. We agreed, after that geisha thing, no more weirdness. *(Mel takes the pad, sits at the computer and begins to type.)*

MEL: I'll keep it sexy; I promise. Look at it this way: if we get repeat business from this guy, we'll be millionaires in a month. Maybe he'll tell his friends about us.

SARAH: Mel, if I fuck it up, we're screwed; I'm not allowed to hang up again! That other guy made Micki give him the money back—

MEL: Lesbian twins—this is easy; we can do this good twin-evil twin Madonna-whore thing—

SARAH: I can't do it.

MEL: Sarah—

SARAH: *(Real rage.)* WHAT?
(They stare at each other. Pause.)

MEL: *(Quiet.)* Don't you get it? Don't you fucking get it, yet? We can win this. We can beat them at their own fucking game.

SARAH: Man, I don't know what you're talking about, Mel—

MEL: Yeah, you do. We can win this.
(Blackout.)

SCENE VII

Lights up on Mel on the phone, reading from a script. Sarah sits across from her, leaning against the bed; she also has a script in her hands.

MEL: *(Speaking gently.)* I guess I would have to say Sandra's feet are the most beautiful part of her body. She has the feet of a Madonna, and when she slides them over my—oh, ohhhh… *(She groans into the phone and hands it to Sarah.)*

SARAH: Yeah, you like that, don't you? Jennifer likes it when I—well, I don't know how to put it. Oh, what the hell. When I step on her. And I don't mind. It feels all right to have her body under my feet. Particularly when I'm wearing my spikes…

MEL: *(Writing while she speaks.)* Step on me, Sandra—Ooohhhhh—

SARAH: Just like I'm doing now— *(She hands the phone to Mel.)*

MEL: Oh, don't stop, Sandra—your feet, your beautiful feet—put your feet in me— *(She hands the phone to Sarah.)*

SARAH: Jennifer, yes, yes—let me caress your body with my heels, let me—
 Oooohhhh. Oh, I'm sorry, Jean-Paul, this is just getting—it's getting—
MEL: OOHHHH.
SARAH: Yes, yes, I…oh…I know, but—it's hard to describe what we're doing,
 it's like—it's like—
 (Mel hands her a sheet. She reads.)
SARAH: The taste of cold steel.
MEL: Ohhh.
SARAH: *(Pause.)* Blood between your teeth.
MEL: Oooohhh…ohhhh…
SARAH: One hand, reaching into your chest, under your ribs, holding your
 heart until it stops.
MEL: Ohhhh…
SARAH: The face of God.
MEL: *(Screaming.)* OOOHHHHH.
 (Sarah covers the phone and looks at her. Mel laughs silently.)
SARAH: I'm sorry, Jean-Paul, we got a little carried away with ourselves here.
 What? Yes, well—uh huh. Uh huh. *(Pause.)* Uh huh. Yeah, well, I—just
 a minute— *(She hands the phone to Mel.)* He wants more.
MEL: What?
SARAH: He wants more, and I'm not dealing with this. You take care of it. He's
 got another five minutes or something.
MEL: I can't—
SARAH: Either hang up or deal with it. I warned you about this.
 *(She lights a cigarette shakily and turns away. Mel looks at her, looks at the
 phone, puts it to her ear.)*
MEL: Jean-Paul? This is Jennifer. Uh huh. Yes, I'm having a great time, I—oh,
 yes, I do like that.
 *(Jon enters behind them and watches. They do not see him. As she continues,
 the words become more and more difficult.)*
MEL: Yeah, why don't you—oh I wish you would—step on me. Are you wear-
 ing spike heels? Oh, yeah, that feels so— *(Pause.)* You want— Okay.
 Okay. Stick it in me. Hurt me. Yeah, I want you to. Put your hand into
 my—ribs, I want you to— *(Pause.)* Yeah. Yeah, cut me open. *(Pause.)*
 What? *(Pause.)* Yeah. Um, rip my arm off. Oh, yeah. Make me bleed.
 Yes. Stick it in me and tear me open, that's what I want. I want you to—
 butcher me. Open. Oh. YES. Hurt me. YES. I want it. YES. I— *(She holds
 the phone away from her ear, looks down. Pause. She picks up the phone and
 speaks quickly for a moment.)* Sorry, Jean-Paul, your time is up. Bye.

(She hangs up the phone. Silence. Sarah looks at her.)

SARAH: You are something else.

JON: Yeah, she's a remarkable girl all right.

(Both Mel and Sarah jump, then turn to see Jon. He moves into the room.)

SARAH: Jon, for God's sake, you scared me to death. When did you get here?

JON: A while ago. You girls put on quite a show.

SARAH: Oh, that was—

JON: Please. You don't have to explain it to me. It was self-apparent what that was.

MEL: How did you get in?

JON: I have a key, remember? Long ago you gave me this key as a sign of your undying love etc. etc.; we had a little ritual. *(He throws the key on the desk.)*

MEL: I remember.

JON: I thought you might have forgot. I mean, we haven't talked in so long. I wanted to tell you: Your phone must be broken. I mean, I really, I just cannot get through—

MEL: Jon—we're in the middle of our shift, you know—

JON: I know. I wasn't doing anything tonight and I hadn't seen you for a while so I thought I'd come over and watch. You don't mind, do you?

MEL: Well, yeah, I kind of do—

(He picks up the scotch bottle, looks at it, takes a hit.)

JON: So, Mel, you're taking up acting! You're really very good. That was quite convincing.

MEL: Thanks.

JON: Sounded like Jean-Paul enjoyed it a lot.

MEL: He seemed to.

JON: You too. You seemed to be having a lot of fun. It must be fun to actually perform your own work. Makes it a little more real, I guess.

MEL: Well, actually—

SARAH: It was just the one guy. He wanted this lesbian twin thing, and he was offering a lot of money, so—

MEL: Look, I don't have to defend myself—

SARAH: I'm just trying to explain to him—

MEL: I don't have to explain anything, either!

SARAH: You're not explaining it; I am! *(Pause. To Jon.)* It was just the one guy. He said he'd pay triple. It was an offer we couldn't refuse.

JON: I should say not. This is American capitalism at its finest. If you have enough money, you have the right to buy anything. Such as dismemberment fantasies.

MEL: Don't get moralistic on me. You're a fucking lawyer.

SARAH: You guys—

JON: That's right. I'm a fucking lawyer. And as one prostitute to another, I'd like to welcome you to the glorious world of exploitation.

SARAH: You guys—

MEL: There is nothing wrong with what I'm doing! I mean, I didn't invent this game. This is not something my gender needs, you know?

JON: Gender wars! Of course! That's what this is!

MEL: CHRIST, that's what the whole fucking world is!

JON: I'm sorry, I thought we were just talking about phone sex!

SARAH: WOULD YOU BOTH SHUT UP? *(Pause.)* Man.

MEL: I just don't appreciate this, you know? If you have a problem with this, you shouldn't come over here. I'm not going to quit because you're getting territorial about your woman.

JON: Oh, PLEASE. THAT IS NOT WHAT THIS IS ABOUT.

MEL: *(Pause.)* Jon—

JON: I'm sorry. *(Pause.)* I just—it's been so long since we even tried to talk to each other, Mel. Please. Could we just—

MEL: *(Overlap.)* I didn't think we had anything more to say to each other—

JON: Oh, that was it, huh? One fight and that's it—

MEL: It was hardly one fight—

SARAH: You guys, come on, I really don't want to hear this!

(The phone rings. They all stare at it.)

SARAH: Christ. *(She answers it.)* Yeah. *(Pause.)* Oh. Micki, hi—*(Pause.)* Yeah, yeah, that's right, I was about to call you about that; that last guy gets an extra charge— *(Pause.)* He did? Why? *(Pause.)* Now? Christ. *(She covers the phone and talks to Mel.)* Jean-Paul wants a second go around.

MEL: Oh, God.

(Jon starts to laugh.)

SARAH: *(Back into phone.)* He was a real creep, Micki, I'm not doing him again.

MEL: Yes, we'll do it; it's fine. If he wants to fork over another four hundred fifty, that's fine— *(She types.)*

SARAH: *(To Mel.)* What? *(Pause.)* He did? Yeah, well, that's what he wanted; I just gave him what he—No, no, it was just me; I did two voices and—

JON: *(Yelling.)* Don't believe it, Micki! They're pulling a fast one on you!

SARAH: JON— *(Into phone.)* well, yeah, a friend stopped by a few seconds ago, but he's leaving— *(To room, phone uncovered.)* You're going to have to take off, Jon—

JON: *(Yelling.)* I'm not going anywhere!

SARAH: CHRIST. Mel, would you please take care of this?

MEL: Jon, this isn't funny.

SARAH: *(Into phone, overlap.)* I know, Micki, but I'm not gonna do it.

JON: *(Overlap.)* I want one too, Mel.

MEL: Oh, please—

SARAH: *(Into phone, overlap.)* I know. He's leaving—

JON: *(Yelling to Sarah.)* I'M NOT GOING ANYWHERE. *(He pulls out his wallet.)* Come on, Mel, write one for me.

SARAH: You guys, I'm not kidding, could you work this out later?

MEL: *(To Jon.)* For God's sake, could you please not try to teach me a lesson? I don't need this, okay?

JON: I'm not trying to teach you anything; I'm trying to buy myself an orgasm since that seems to be the only way I'm going to get one. Now, can I buy one or not?

MEL: Oh, for God's sake—

SARAH: *(Yelling into phone.)* Yes, I told you, everything is fine here; this is just going to take a little while, all right?

JON: Tell him to call back! They're busy now! *(To Mel.)* So what's the going rate now? Four-fifty?

MEL: Forget it.

SARAH: Just give him to someone else. I need to take care of this.

JON: Here, this is a hundred and something; can I give you a check for the rest? *(He drops a handful of dollars on the desk.)*

SARAH: *(To phone.)* I know that, but—

MEL: YOU'RE NOT SCORING ANY POINTS HERE, JON.

JON: I'M NOT TRYING TO SCORE POINTS, MEL. I'M TRYING TO BUY SOME PHONE SEX.

SARAH: *(Yelling into the phone.)* I REALIZE THAT, MICKI, BUT I DON'T GIVE A SHIT. *(She slams down the phone.)* Now could you tell me what exactly the problem is here?

JON: Are you two running a business or not? My money is as good as Jean-Paul's, and I was here first.

SARAH: *(To Mel.)* Is he kidding?

MEL: Apparently not.

SARAH: Look. I'm just going to leave now. I'm going to leave for an hour and you two can fight or make out or do whatever it is you have to to get this out of your systems.

JON: Are you turning me down?

SARAH: Yes, Jon, I am; I am not going to give you phone sex. I won't do it. *(She heads for the door.)*

JON: You realize of course that it's illegal to refuse legal tender offered in exchange for services which are offered to the general public in the capacity of—

SARAH: *(Overlap.)* Jon, I don't give a fuck!

JON: I'll just go to Micki. This is a business deal; if I can't arrange it through you, I'll go to Micki. Is this her number?
(He picks up the clipboard, crosses to the phone and picks it up. Sarah pulls it away from him.)

SARAH: Oh, man. *(Pause.)* This is cute, Jon, really, but wouldn't you rather work this out some other way? Preferably, some way that does not have me right in the fucking middle of it?

JON: *(Pause.)* This is a business deal. That's all it is.
(Pause.)

MEL: Fine. *(She picks up the clipboard.)*

SARAH: Come on, Mel, please. Don't do this. It's too much. Don't do it.

MEL: And who would you like to talk to?

JON: Joan of Arc. *(Pause.)* Molly Bloom. Scarlett O'Hara. The Virgin Mary. *(Pause.)* You.

MEL: And what would you like to talk about?
(Blackout.)

SCENE VIII

Jon lies on the bed. Sarah sits on the floor, speaking into the phone, reading from a manuscript. Mel sits at the desk, watching.

SARAH: *(Reading.)* Hey baby, how you doing?

JON: Fine.

SARAH: You been waiting for me?

JON: Yes.

SARAH: You been waiting long, baby?

JON: I thought you forgot. I thought you weren't coming.

SARAH: I'm here. I've always been here. I'm just invisible. Didn't you know that?

JON: No.

SARAH: I'm right here, lying right alongside you, my body is pressed right up against yours. Don't you feel me? Don't you feel my hand running down your chest? Don't you feel my breath on your neck? Don't you feel my heat?

JON: No.

SARAH: Yes you do, baby. I'm right here. It's just there's too much heat; we're burning up together and you don't know what's me and what's you anymore. That's all it is. But I'm here all right. My hands are dipping into you; I'm running through your veins. I'm the invisible woman. I made myself invisible for you, so I could be with you all the time.

JON: No. You're never here.

MEL: Just listen.

SARAH: *(Looks at her, continues.)* I think of you all the time. You're all I think of. Ever. The taste of your skin. The feel of your bones. It's all I want. I want you in my mouth. I want you inside me. I want you to make me invisible. Whatever you want, that's what I want. Isn't that what you want?

JON: I want—

SARAH: I know what you want. I know. I'll give you whatever you want. That's what I'm here for. My hands are here. My mouth is here. Underneath you. Down the length of you. My legs winding round you like vines, like roots, like water. I cling to you like water. My hands pass down you like rain. Like blood. Listen, the world does not exist. Only my hands. On you. We grow together. We evaporate. I evaporate. As you emerge.

(Pause.)

JON: That's not what I want. *(Pause.)* You got it wrong. That's never what I wanted. I just wanted you.

MEL: *(Pause.)* You don't know what you want.

JON: I just want you, Mel. I just want you. Mel. Mel.

(Pause. Mel looks at him from a great distance. Sarah looks away. Blackout.)

END OF PLAY

THE BAR PLAYS

SPEAKEASY

CHARACTERS

KAY: Mid-twenties
SUZ: Mid-twenties
BILL: Twenty, handsome in an unimaginative way
MARGY: Eighteen, Bill's cousin
TED: Twenty-two, Bill's friend
LOUIS: Thirty
MEG: Thirty, Louis's wife
BARTENDER

SET

The interior of a quiet, slightly seedy bar decorated in period as a speakeasy. There is a bar and three simple tables with chairs. Low blues play throughout. It should be unapparent where the music is coming from.

Lights up. The bartender lounges behind the bar, clearly not having much to do. Louis and Meg sit at the table far right, not speaking. They both have a beer. Kay and Suz stand at the bar, also with beers.

KAY: I don't know. The only thing that makes me feel better about this century is thinking about all the other ones. I mean, I get all worked up about how horrible things are—people are so petty and mean and *stupid* it just makes me want to throw up, but then I start thinking about, I don't know, the fourteenth century or something, the middle ages, when they were all whacking each other to bits and dying of bubonic plague and priests were rapists, whatever, and I realize we're just the same, the human race hasn't changed a bit, there's no justice or logic and there never *has* been. And that makes me feel better in a weird way. Because it's not that we're getting worse, it's just that we've always been this bad.

SUZ: Well, you are just going to be a lot of fun tonight. I can tell.

(Bill, Ted and Margy enter and cross to the center table. Bill grabs an extra chair from the empty table left and they sit.)

MARGY: There's no one here.

BILL: It's still early.

MARGY: There's no one here. How did you find this place?

BILL: I don't know. I been coming here a while. I like it. It's sorta moody, you know, like one of those places in the past. Gangsters. You know?

TED: Speakeasy.

BILL: Yeah.

MARGY: I don't know.

BILL: What's not to know?

MARGY: It's dark and there's no one here, okay?

(Bill looks at her, doesn't comment, and goes to the bar. Suz and Kay watch him.)

SUZ: Ouch.

KAY: You like him?

SUZ: Like him? No, no. I just find him appealing in a trivial, cheap, wouldn't it be fun to use each other sort of way.

KAY: Oh.

SUZ: Hi.

(She leans in front of Bill to get a pack of matches from the bar. She smiles at him, pulls back, and lights a cigarette. Bill watches her, smiles, gets his drinks and goes back to his table. The whole move takes very little time. Kay watches.)

KAY: I had a one-night stand once.

SUZ: Only once? Kay—

KAY: I thought it was stupid.

SUZ: Well, that's not generally my response, but I suppose—

KAY: Hey, I enjoyed it. You know? Of *course* I enjoyed it. While we were, you know, I don't know, doing it, I enjoyed it a lot. But afterwards—I left my earrings there, you know, so I called him later that week, and he was like, oh yes, right, they're here. Come on by and pick them up. So I went by that afternoon and you know, he left them in an envelope by the *mail* boxes, for Christsake. A little envelope with my name misspelled on it. I mean, what am I supposed to—what do you do with something like that? Do I need to put myself through that, like, several times or something? I don't think so.

SUZ: I'm sorry, but I don't know what you're talking about.

KAY: I don't know.

(She looks off, distracted. Suz shakes her head.)

LOUIS: It's not you.

MEG: Great. Well, I'm glad to know that. That makes me feel much better. Thank you.

LOUIS: What do you want me to say?

MEG: I don't know. But "it's not you" is not what I want you to say. I know it's not me. That much, I know.

LOUIS: I just meant—

MEG: It's just like, I don't know, you think "it's not you" is going to make me feel better. It doesn't make me feel better, all right?

LOUIS: Fine.

(He picks up his beer and drinks. Meg looks at him, frustrated, then crosses to the bar angrily. Bill watches her. Margy watches him.)

MARGY: She's too old for you.

BILL: You think so?

MARGY: Please.

BILL: I don't know.

TED: You'd have better luck with the one at the bar.

BILL: You think so?

TED: Please.

(They both laugh knowingly.)

MARGY: Could you two maybe not be too totally gross about, you know, I mean, really.

BILL: You know I mean really?

MARGY: You know what I mean.

BILL: *(Leaning in, flirtatious.)* No, I don't. What do you mean? Why don't you tell me what you mean?

MARGY: Forget it.

BILL: You're so cute.

(He crosses to the bar and leans up against it next to Meg. She ignores him while she waits for her drink. Margy watches him angrily.)

TED: He's too old for you.

MARGY: What?

TED: You're not his type.

MARGY: I don't think—

TED: Why don't you get over it? It's not going to happen. He doesn't even know you're alive.

MARGY: I don't know what you're talking about.

TED: I'm just saying.

MARGY: What are you saying?

TED: What is the matter with you? Do you think this tough little bitch act is attractive or something?

MARGY: It seems to work for you.

TED: What? *(Pause.)* I don't know what you're talking about.

MARGY: Yeah, right.

(She turns to watch the bar. Meg has her drink and is about to go back to her table. Bill leans in slightly. She looks at him full in the face for a long moment, then silently goes to her table. Bill watches her, smiling. Suz watches him.)

SUZ: Oh, shit.

MARGY: Shit.

(Bill crosses back to his table.)

KAY: What?

SUZ: Nothing.

KAY: What, you think—

SUZ: I don't think anything, okay? It's not that big a deal. It's not like I was in love with the guy. I just think he's cute. Christ.

KAY: What are you getting so pissed off about?

SUZ: I'm not pissed off, I'm just, you know—you're being kind of a pain. I just thought we were going to have a drink. I don't get what's going on with you tonight.

KAY: Nothing, I just—

SUZ: I mean, everything is so troubled and, and, and—*morose* with you lately. The universe. The human race. Nothing is easy. Nothing just is what it is. Just have a drink, would you? Pick somebody up. Would you like, just live your life?

KAY: I'm sorry.

(Suz shrugs coolly and drinks. Kay looks away. Bill continues to watch Meg, who leans in to talk to Louis.)

MEG: You have to say something to me. You can't just do this and then sit there like—it doesn't make any sense, Louis. I have to have a reason if— it's my life, okay?

LOUIS: Meg—

MEG: It's my life.

LOUIS: I don't know what you want me to say. I don't know.

MEG: Anything. Say anything.

LOUIS: I said, it's not you—

MEG: *Say something else.* Please.

LOUIS: There's nothing else to say. It's just, nothing makes any sense to me anymore. I don't feel anything, I don't think anything, I just don't— that's all. I know this isn't fair to you. I'm not saying it is. Our marriage is fine. I just don't want it anymore. I don't want anything. I know this is a terrible thing to do to you. I know. I just don't know what else to do.

MEG: Can we wait?

LOUIS: For what? I mean, I get up every morning, I put on my clothes, I live on the planet, I breathe the air, I see the sky. I look at the moon. And that is what is happening to me. There's no room for another person there. We could wait, but it would only make you unhappy. It wouldn't change anything. Nothing will change. I honestly don't know how I ever convinced myself that I could love you in the first place. I just don't know.

MEG: *(Pause.)* You are such a *shit.*

LOUIS: I know.

(She suddenly throws a drink in his face. Everyone in the bar looks at her. She looks at them for a moment, picks up her purse and crosses the room silently. As she passes Bill, she stops for a brief moment and looks at him, then continues out. Bill grins at Margy and Ted.)

BILL: See you guys later.

(He follows her out. All except Louis watch him go.)

KAY: Did you see that? I'm sorry, but it just can't—it can't be that easy. I mean, what about diseases? What about—

SUZ: Kay, *please.*

KAY: What?

MARGY: *(To Ted.)* What?

TED: Nothing.

KAY: *(Looking at Louis.)* He's cute. Don't you think he's kind of cute?

SUZ: I don't think anything.

KAY: I wonder why she left.

SUZ: Why don't you go ask him?

KAY: Maybe I will.

SUZ: Good.

KAY: Fine.

    (She stands and crosses tentatively. Louis looks up and sees her.)

KAY: Hi.

MARGY: *(To herself.)* I hate this place. It's dark. There's no one here.

KAY: Can I join you?

    (Blackout.)

END OF PLAY

BIG MISTAKE

CHARACTERS

BRIAN: Early thirties, something of a bully
PAUL: Early thirties, confused but friendly
LORNA: Early thirties, stubborn, controlled, intelligent
ANNIE: Early thirties, friendly, talkative

SET

A bar

NOTE

Because there is so much hostility between the men and women for most of the piece, it is important that the actors play against that hostility with a veneer of politeness and social agility. This veneer is, of course, worn through rather quickly.

A small, tasteful bar. A female bartender smokes a cigarette at the bar. A couple of well-dressed young men, Brian and Paul, sit at a table right, sipping beers. An empty table is near the door.

PAUL: I don't know. She's big enough to fucking kill me.

BRIAN: She's not that big.

PAUL: She's pretty big.

BRIAN: She's little. She's, like, five-something, five three or something—

PAUL: She's bigger than that.

BRIAN: She's little.

PAUL: She works out like a fucking maniac. I mean, she's got all those muscles. She's big. Have you ever seen her in that blue sleeveless thing? She could probably break my arm.

BRIAN: I think she looks good.

PAUL: She looks great. I'm just saying.

BRIAN: So don't ask her out. No one's begging you.

PAUL: It's just—it's kind of weird, that's all I'm saying.

BRIAN: I think she looks good.

PAUL: Okay, I know, I'm a jerk, I'm a nerd, I can't take the competition, so sue me—

BRIAN: I didn't say that—

PAUL: I just found life a little more comfortable before women spent so much time in gyms. I mean, you had a little more freedom to be an asshole, you know what I mean?

(They laugh. Lorna and Annie enter. Annie is talking a mile a minute.)

ANNIE: So this guy is like pouring me champagne, right, and the fire is going, and he's got like—his place is un-fucking-believable; oriental rugs, antique armchairs, he's even got a fucking Picasso on the wall, I'm not kidding—I mean, I don't consider myself a materialistic person but at a certain point you can't help being *affected,* you know what I mean?—and we're sitting on this overstuffed ottoman-loveseat-fur-futon thing, and his foot is sort of sliding up underneath my butt and moving down my leg, and I'm going my GOD—I mean, I am—my brain cells are about to blow out my ears, you know, my arms have already gone limp, and from this great distance I hear somebody say, "Oh, wow. This is a great movie." And I'm—I go, excuse me? My electrodes are turning to butter, and he's got the TV on. I didn't even notice, right, and they're showing Nightmare On Elmstreet Two and this guy is suddenly *transfixed.* Catatonic. I mean, I'm going, "Hello. Helllooooo—"

(During this monologue, Lorna takes off her coat and turns to wave to the bartender. She and Brian lock eyes for a moment. She sits down quickly.)

LORNA: Oh, shit.

ANNIE: Exactly.

LORNA: No, I mean, oh shit we better get out of here.

ANNIE: Why?

BRIAN: Oh, shit.

LORNA: Look, could we just go?

PAUL: What?

ANNIE: Why?

LORNA: Don't look, don't—

(Annie looks over at the men. All are suddenly looking at each other. Brian waves. Lorna raises her hand and waves back stiffly.)

ANNIE: You know them?

PAUL: You know them?

LORNA: Yeah. *(She slips her coat off and sits at the table by the door.)*

ANNIE: Look, if you want to go—

LORNA: Forget it. It's too late.

(Brian stands.)

ANNIE: What do you mean, too late, you just stand up and walk out—

LORNA: *Forget it.*

ANNIE: Oh, no. I don't have a good feeling about this.

BRIAN: Hey. Lorna. How's it going?

LORNA: Fine. Hi. Good to see you.

(She holds out her hand to shake. He leans in and kisses her on the cheek. She stiffens.)

BRIAN: Yeah, it's great to see you, too. It's been a while.

LORNA: Yes, it has. You're looking well.

BRIAN: You too. You look good.

LORNA: Thanks. Thank you.

BRIAN: Can I buy you ladies a drink?

LORNA: No. Thanks. We aren't going to stay long.

BRIAN: What can I get you?

LORNA: Really, we're fine. Thank you.

BRIAN: You're not going to let me buy you just one drink?

LORNA: It's not necessary. Really.

BRIAN: I know it's not necessary. That's not why I offered.

LORNA: I'm fine, all right?

BRIAN: I can see that. I just want to buy you a drink.

(Pause.)

LORNA: Thanks. That would be lovely.

BRIAN: White wine, right?

LORNA: Actually, I'm drinking vodka gimlets these days.

BRIAN: Great. Great! I never trust women who only drink wine. *(To Annie.)* And what can I get you?

ANNIE: I think I'd better have a martini.

BRIAN: Great. I'll be right back.

(He goes to the bar. Annie looks at Lorna. During their dialogue, Brian crosses to Paul, and speaks with him for a moment. Paul nods and crosses to Annie and Lorna's table.)

ANNIE: I have a really bad feeling about this.

LORNA: It'll be fine.

ANNIE: We should just go. Now. We should just go now.

LORNA: That would not be wise.

ANNIE: What do you mean, that would not be wise? What is that supposed to mean?

LORNA: I just mean I would prefer not to do anything that might provoke him, okay?

ANNIE: Provoke him to what?

LORNA: Let's just have a drink with him, okay?

ANNIE: Oh, God. So, what, did you sleep with this guy?

LORNA: I would prefer not to talk about it.

ANNIE: I have a really bad feeling about this.

LORNA: We'll just let him buy us the drink, stay for a few minutes, and go. Okay? It'll be fine.

ANNIE: You slept with him? How many times?

LORNA: I don't want to talk about it.

ANNIE: More than once?

LORNA: Yes. More than once.

ANNIE: Oh, god.

(Paul crosses.)

PAUL: Hi.

LORNA: *(Smiling but chilly.)* Hi.

PAUL: I'm a friend of— *(He indicates Brian at bar.)* Paul Bishop.

(They shake.)

LORNA: Hi. I'm Lorna. This is my friend Annie.

PAUL: Oh, *you're* Lorna. Nice to meet you! Brian's told me a lot about you.

ANNIE: *(To Lorna, accusing.)* Brian? That guy's Brian?

BRIAN: Here you go.

ANNIE: Lorna!

(Brian arrives with the drinks as Paul sits.)

LORNA: Thank you. Brian. This is really lovely of you.

BRIAN: Not at all. I'm just glad to see you.

LORNA: Me too. You look good.

BRIAN: So, you all have made friends already, huh?

ANNIE: Apparently.

PAUL: Have we met? You look real familiar.

ANNIE: I don't think so.

PAUL: No, I'm not kidding. You look like somebody I knew in a previous life, or something.

ANNIE: I don't think I have any previous lives. I mean, I think this is probably my first time around. Or something.

PAUL: Oh. Yeah.

ANNIE: Yeah.

(Pause.)

BRIAN: So, what have you been doing with yourself?

LORNA: Not much. You?

BRIAN: Got a new job.

LORNA: Good.

BRIAN: Yeah, I finally just got sick of it at DeCourcey's. I mean, you can only put up with so much shit, you know? You know. I mean, you heard it all. So I finally just told him to fuck off. I'm on my own now.

LORNA: Really?

BRIAN: Well, you know, for the most part. I'm managing a smaller place. In the village. Nobody gives me any shit.

LORNA: Good.

BRIAN: Yeah, it's great. You still with—

LORNA: Yeah.

BRIAN: You are?

LORNA: Sure.

BRIAN: I thought you were pretty sick of it there.

LORNA: It's gotten a lot better.

BRIAN: Sure, but—

LORNA: We had a bunch of meetings about it. It's a lot better.

BRIAN: Yeah, but—I'm sorry. I just thought you were pretty set on getting out of there.

LORNA: I was. But it's gotten a lot better.

BRIAN: Well, good.

LORNA: Yeah.

    (Pause.)

PAUL: *(To Annie.)* Are you a lawyer?

ANNIE: Uh, no.

PAUL: Oh. You look like a lawyer. I thought maybe—

ANNIE: No, I'm in retail.

PAUL: Yeah? Where?

ANNIE: Macy's.

PAUL: Maybe that's where I know you from.

ANNIE: You work with Macy's?

PAUL: Well, I shop there.

ANNIE: What do you mean?

PAUL: I mean, I've bought a couple of things there.

ANNIE: So? I mean, what do you think, I'm a sales girl or something? I say I'm in retail, so you think I'm a clerk, or something?

PAUL: No, I just—never mind.

ANNIE: I'm a buyer. I'm not like, a shopgirl on the floor, okay?

PAUL: I didn't mean anything. I mean, I thought you were a fucking lawyer, okay? I didn't think you were a shopgirl. I thought you were a lawyer. I was just trying to figure out why you looked so familiar, okay?

ANNIE: I'm sorry.

PAUL: I'm just, you know—Christ.

LORNA: You guys—

ANNIE: I'm sorry. I just—I am, I'm a little defensive. Look, I don't know you, and I just, I didn't have a great day, so—I'm sorry, okay?

PAUL: *(Chilly.)* Fine.

ANNIE: *(Pause.)* Fine.

PAUL: Christ.

ANNIE: Look, I'm sorry, okay?

PAUL: Sure.

BRIAN: *(To Lorna.)* So, you seeing anybody?

LORNA: Excuse me?

BRIAN: I asked if you were seeing anybody. What, is that too personal or something? I'm just making conversation. I'm just trying to be friendly. You don't have to answer—

LORNA: No, it's fine—

BRIAN: I don't care—

LORNA: Yes, I am seeing someone. Well, a couple people. Nothing too serious.

BRIAN: Oh. *(Pause.)* Do I know them?

LORNA: I don't think so.

BRIAN: What, somebody from work or something?

LORNA: No, you don't know them.

BRIAN: Well, try me.

LORNA: You don't know them.

> *(Pause.)*

BRIAN: Okay. Sure. Fine. I was just asking. You know. Making conversation. *(Pause.)* I'm seeing somebody.

LORNA: Well, good.

BRIAN: Yeah, she's great. An actress.

LORNA: Yeah, actresses. They're great. They're always so stable.

BRIAN: *(Pause.)* What is that supposed to mean?

LORNA: It doesn't mean anything.

BRIAN: *(Starting to snap.)* No. I mean it.

ANNIE: Look at the time. God, I'm sorry, Lorna, I completely lost track of things here—

> *(The following two conversations begin to overlap as tempers rise, but should remain distinct until the very end.)*

PAUL: Oh, please.

ANNIE: Excuse me?

BRIAN: I mean it, what is that supposed to mean? Actresses are so stable. What is that?

PAUL: If you want to leave, just leave. Don't make up some cute little song and dance about it. No one's going to beg you to stay.

LORNA: It's just an observation.

ANNIE: Well, thank you. It's been lovely meeting you.

BRIAN: It wasn't an observation. It was a dig.

PAUL: I wish I could say the same.

LORNA: Brian, I don't care who you go out with. I hardly know you anymore. Why would I care?

ANNIE: Listen, asshole, no one begged you to come over and have a drink with us.

PAUL: So excuse me for being friendly.

BRIAN: Oh, you care.

ANNIE: What I can't excuse is your rudeness.

LORNA: Excuse me, but I am not the one prying into my ex-lover's affairs; I don't *care!*

PAUL: *My* rudeness? I ask you about your job and you practically take my head off—

BRIAN: That's right, you don't care, but you just got to make sure that I *know* you don't care; you have to sit there acting cool and superior and hostile—

ANNIE: Look, I just came in here to have a drink! I was in no mood for some stupid male pick up crap—

PAUL: Pick up? Excuse me, honey—

LORNA: *I'm* the one who's hostile? You come over and practically shove these fucking drinks down our throats and I'm hostile. Oh, that's perfect—

ANNIE: Oh, you weren't trying to pick me up? That stupid line about past lives was not a pick up?

BRIAN: If you didn't want the damn drink, then why the fuck are you sitting here? If you weren't even going to be friendly—

PAUL: I thought I knew you from somewhere!

LORNA: Oh, is that the trade off? You buy me a drink so I have to be nice to you?

ANNIE: WELL, YOU DON'T!

BRIAN: YES. THAT'S THE TRADE OFF.

PAUL: THANK GOD.

LORNA: Fuck you.

(Pause. They all glare at each other. Brian and Paul begin to speak almost simultaneously. Their speeches should overlap completely until their finish; likewise, Annie and Lorna's responses should overlap until the bartender cuts them off.)

BRIAN: You women. You don't know what you want anymore, do you? On the one hand you got us treating you like queens, buying you drinks, bringing you flowers, it's all so nice and friendly as long as you're on the receiving end. But as soon as we ask for *anything*—a little conversation, a smile, a little *affection,* god forbid, you got more walls than a fucking prison; you got nothing but attitude and excuses. You keep saying you want a relationship, but as soon as you got one, all you can do is turn us down in bed! You got us jumping through so many hoops we don't know if we're coming or going, and then when we say time out, could someone tell me what's in this for me, you'd think we were threatening rape! Well, it's not going to last, sweetheart. The day is coming when you're all—all of you—you're gonna get yours.

PAUL: *(Overlap with Brian.)* You women. Could someone please tell me what you want from us? I can't talk to any of you anymore; it's like a battle zone around here! I was just trying to have a drink and unwind! I didn't

ink a reference to past lives was going to start world war three! It was
a joke, all right? I was kidding! I was nervous! I don't believe in reincar-
nation; I barely believe in God. I was trying to start a conversation about
something stupid because I happen to know that our mutual friends
here would kill each other if we gave them half the chance. I was trying
to help. And just for the record, I don't care if you're a sales clerk or a
garbage collector or the president of the United States! You looked familiar! I think you're pretty! So sue me!

ANNIE: Listen, asshole, I admit I snapped at you, but you know, I also apologized! You're the one who couldn't get over the fact that I had a bad day.
I had a bad day, all right? I had a bad day! And frankly, you caught me
at a bad moment. My so-called best friend here had just agreed to have
drinks with the most legendary psycho of her sexual past, so at the very
instant you started talking about past lives, I was a little tense. I'm still a
little tense. You're not helping my tension, all right? I mean, could we
just let this go, please? I have a splitting headache and while I might have
found you cute at first, you're really starting to get on my nerves. It's
time to GET OVER IT.

LORNA: *(Overlap with Annie.)* You can stop crying about what "we" want,
Brian; you're not interested in what we want. The only thing you've ever
been interested in is what you can get. It's always the same thing with
you; we say no, and you say yes, I'm buying you this drink whether you
like it or not, and now I own you. The world is so simple, isn't it? You
get your way, and when you don't, it's only because we haven't behaved,
we're breaking the rules somehow. If you can't control us, it's because
we're fucking up, and that gives you the right to do whatever you want.
We say no, you say yes; that's rape from start to finish, and we're not the
ones who invented it.

BARTENDER: Excuse me. Hey. HEY. *(Pause.)* Look, I know what you're up
against, but could you, like, keep things down? Some of us like to pretend we're civilized.
(He exits. Pause.)

PAUL: You thought I was cute?

ANNIE: What?

PAUL: You just said, you thought I was cute. At first. You thought I was cute
at first.

ANNIE: At first, yeah.

PAUL: Oh, shit. I know what it is. You remind me of my sister's best friend.
Molly. You remind me of Molly. I had a crush on her for eight years or

something. Grade school. High school. Christ. That's what it is. I'm sorry. That's all it was.

ANNIE: Molly?

PAUL: Yeah. You look just like her. Or you don't, actually, you don't look like her at all, but you remind me of her. She always looked like she was either going to laugh or punch you. She was great. I mean, I was two years younger than her; she didn't even know I was alive, but…she was really great.

(Pause.)

ANNIE: That is so corny.

PAUL: Sorry.

ANNIE: No. No. *(Pause.)* Do you want to have dinner with me?

PAUL: *(Pause.)* Yes.

ANNIE: Lorna?

PAUL: Brian—

(They turn to look at Lorna and Brian, who seem to not even know they are still in the room. Pause.)

ANNIE: Right. *(To Paul.)* We're out of here.

(They exit. For a moment, Brian and Lorna do not move. They both turn and look at each other, steely.)

LORNA: Well. It looks like we have some unfinished business.

BRIAN: Looks like.

LORNA: Do you want to start?

BRIAN: Oh, no. Ladies first.

LORNA: I need another drink.

(She holds her empty glass out to him. It is a dare. He takes it. They stare at each other. Black out.)

END OF PLAY

DRINKING PROBLEM

CHARACTERS

RENNY: Attractive but somewhat haggard woman in her late thirties, talkative

THE BARTENDER

SET

A bar

Renny sits at the bar, alone. An empty lowball glass with melting ice sits before her. She finishes a second drink and aligns the second glass carefully alongside the first, then waves the bartender over.

RENNY: I would like another, please. Could I have another? The same.
(The bartender nods and reaches for the glasses. She stops him.)
RENNY: Oh no, could you—could I keep the glasses? I find it helpful to have something to look at. They're a visual aid. I mean, you look at a bunch of glasses kind of lined up, like a little row of soldiers or something, a firing squad, and that has impact. You know?
(The bartender shrugs, pulls an identical glass from behind the bar and pours her a huge scotch on the rocks, hands it to her, makes a note of it on her bill.)
RENNY: Thank you. I appreciate it. You're very kind. *(She looks at the drink.)* You know, these are really the biggest drinks I have ever seen in my entire life. These drinks are huge. How can you afford this? How much do they cost, ten dollars or something?
(He pushes her tab toward her. She looks at it. He cleans as she speaks.)
RENNY: Ah. Yes, I see. That's very reasonable. Yes. Thank you. *(Pause.)* You don't talk, huh? You just—everything is sort of responded to non-verbally, huh? Hey, I respect it. It's a choice. I'm just observing. You know. It's very effective; I can already feel this sort of transference thing going on. I mean, most of therapy—psychology, psychiatry, whatever, the human brain, I think it's a crock, but that transference shit just cuts a little too close to the bone, if you know what I mean. I mean, I'm already—I've been talking to you here for what, two minutes or something, and I'm already projecting all sorts of nasty little thoughts and emotions onto you. Hey, I can't help it, all right, it's just transference, you know, it's a force of nature, it just happens. Like rain or something. Except I don't know, I think that's a crock too, frankly. First of all, "transference" is like the *worst* name for anything; it sounds like "cash register" or something; I just don't know what it means. And second of all—I mean, the main point is—you're completely— you're like a wall, there's nothing there, why shouldn't I think you're thinking all sorts of horrible thoughts about me? Either you're nice or you're not nice. Either you're generous or you're not generous. If you're generous, you smile, or you let your little face crinkle up with sympathy, or you nod or shake your head or something, and if you're not generous, you just sit there with no expression. Because you want the other person to feel like shit, but you

don't want to take responsibility for doing that. I'm not saying that's what you're doing. I'm just saying, those fucking therapists don't tell you about that part. *(Pause. She drinks.)* I've never been in therapy. I just think about it a lot. Because I think it sounds like such a great idea: you go and talk to someone about your problems and then your, like, your life is solved. The whole idea just charms me to death. But I can't help it, I just—it seems to me that if it really worked that way, the world would not be quite such a huge mess. So I figure there's a little bit of a scam going on here. That's why I never went into therapy. But I respect people who do. I do. I think that shows a lot of—I don't know, I think it's a very hopeful thing to do. It's like, believing in God. Falling in love. Going into therapy. It's the same sort of thing, you know? Could I have another?

(The bartender pauses for a moment, unsure.)

RENNY: No, I'm not finished. There's still a considerable amount here. Do I have to finish this one before you'll give me another one? Is that like, bartender rules or something?

(He goes and makes her another drink.)

RENNY: I didn't think so. I mean, you see this on television all the time, some guy lining up drinks and then knocking them back one after another... not that I'm going to do that. I just want to see what it looks like. I bet it looks kind of nice. We'll have one that the ice is all melted in, one with ice, one half full of scotch, and one completely full of scotch. It will be a variation on my visual aids theme.

(He hands her the drink. She sets it next to the others.)

RENNY: Oh, yes. That's nice. That's very nice. They look like children or something. *(She picks up the half full glass and downs it, then sets it back down.)* And now they're soldiers. *(She picks up the fourth glass and looks at it.)* I don't think this is a good question to ask you at this point in time, but I'm going to ask it anyway. Do you think I have a drinking problem? Don't answer that. *(Pause. She smiles at him.)* You were about to really let loose, weren't you? You were just going to let me have it. But you know, you don't have all the facts. It's very important, when someone asks you a delicate question like that, to be sure of your facts. That's the problem with the world today. Everybody's got an opinion, you know, but they don't have the facts! They just *think* they do. Okay. Here's a fact: I hardly ever do this. I mean, I'm sitting here getting wasted for no good reason, and that's not great, but I *never* do this. Hardly ever. But—BUT I do drink every day. Not every day. Almost every day, though. Not a whole lot. A glass of wine before I go to bed, or, you know, a gin and tonic before dinner. And then once in a while at a party, I'll get trashed and then I wake up at five in the morning and feel horrible and hate myself. And that's like, okay, not great, but I don't think that's a drinking problem. I don't. I saw this thing on television about Richard Burton, and *that* man had a problem; he drank like three bottles of vodka a day. Can you imagine? You'd have to get out of bed in the morning and start drinking in the shower or something. I mean, I don't do that. But I do like the way it makes me feel. And that kind of bothers me because you know, there's some part of me that says that life should be enough. You should be able to just be a happy person without this...But I have to be frank. Life just isn't enough, all right? And I am very tense. *(She knocks half the fourth scotch back, shudders.)* Oh, God. I'm going to wake up at five in the morning and feel really, really awful. Oh, well. I feel pretty good now. I hate that. I mean, it's like you have to pay for every fucking second of peace you scrounge for yourself, you know? Who made up that rule? One piece of chocolate cake costs like, I don't know, a week of calisthenics or something. And it's not like this for everyone; you see guys shoving down chocolate cake like their lives fucking depended on it and then when I put on a couple of pounds, they look at me like I've killed a puppy or something; whenever a woman gains a couple pounds it's like a moral offense against the universe. You get tired of it, all right? You get tired. It's just, there's so much shit that gets thrown at you. And then when you fight back, when you say, hey, I'm just going to have a piece of chocolate cake, all right, I'm going to have four scotches, it makes me feel better, all right, so fuck you—all fucking hell breaks loose. You wake up at five in the morning, wishing you were dead. And it's not your fault. It's not my fault! It's like that Chinese water torture, you know, one fucking drop isn't going to drive you out of your mind, but you know, number 8,712 is not so funny! That's all I'm saying, all right? That's all I'm saying!

(Pause. They look at each other. The bartender is clearly listening to her, and has been for a while.)

RENNY: You see? Now you're listening. Now I can see you're a real person. You don't have to say anything. That's not what I wanted. This is what I wanted. This is all I ever wanted.

(They stare at each other for a long moment. The lights fade.)

END OF PLAY

SEX WITH THE CENSOR

CHARACTERS

WOMAN: A prostitute

MAN: The censor

SET

A bare room. A small cot covered with a bedspread has been set to one side. There is also a chair.

(Lights up. A provocatively dressed woman sits on the bed. A man stands across the room, by the chair. He wears a suit.)

WOMAN: So, how do you like it? Sitting, standing, or are you a traditional kind of guy?

MAN: What?

WOMAN: Tell you what; we'll improvise. *(She stands and crosses to him.)* Just see what happens, huh?

(She reaches for his jacket, as if to take it off him. He backs away from her.)

MAN: Don't do that.

WOMAN: Oh. Sorry. Some guys...

MAN: I don't want you to do that.

WOMAN: Whatever. *(She turns and takes off her skirt. Underneath she wears black stockings and panties.)* No shit, most guys like, you know, to be undressed. I think it reminds them of their mother, although I don't know why you'd want to be thinking about your mother at a time like this. I mean, I know about the whole psychology thing, Oedipus, whatever—we do, we talk about that stuff—but I have to say I never believed most of it. That guys want to fuck their mothers. That just, frankly, that makes no sense to me. I mean, if it's true, you guys are even crazier than I thought, you know what I mean? I mean, no offense or anything.

MAN: Stop talking.

WOMAN: *(Unbuttoning her blouse.)* Oh, sorry. I know, I kind of run on. Especially late in the day; I get tired and anything that comes into my head comes right out of my mouth. I don't know. A lot of guys like it, which is lucky for me because I just, I don't even really know when it's happening—

MAN: Don't do that.

WOMAN: Excuse me?

MAN: Don't take your shirt off.

WOMAN: Oh. Okay. *(She starts to button up again.)*

MAN: No. Leave it like that. I want to see that I can't see.

WOMAN: What?

MAN: If you button it, I can't see. I want to see that I can't see.

WOMAN: Oh. Sure.

(She stands for a moment, in the unbuttoned shirt and stockings. He stares at her. He is fully dressed.)

WOMAN: So...are we ready to get going here? I mean, I don't mean to rush things, but it's been my experience that it kind of helps to hit the ground running, you know, just let her rip, and since you're not particularly interested in small talk, we probably should just get to it, huh? *(Pause.)* So are we, what? You need a hand with this clothes thing here?

MAN: No.

WOMAN: No.

(Pause. They stare at each other.)

WOMAN: Okay, sure, you're shy. I'm sensitive to that. We'll just take this real slow. *(She reaches for his jacket carefully.)*

MAN: Don't touch me.

WOMAN: Honey, that's not going to be entirely possible under the circumstances here—

(She tries to take the jacket off him. He shoves her, hard.)

WOMAN: Hey, don't get rough with me, asshole. That's not the deal, all right?

MAN: I told you. I don't want you to touch me. We don't do that.

WOMAN: Well, what do we do?

(He looks at her. He pulls the chair over, back to the audience. He sits in it.)

MAN: Stand here.

(He points in front of him. She crosses warily and faces him. His back is to the audience.)

WOMAN: *(Irritated.)* So, what, you just want to look, is that it? Fine. Whatever. But it's the same price, okay? We're not sailing into discount land because you're in some sort of fucking mood here, okay?

MAN: Don't say that.

WOMAN: I'm just telling you the rules.

MAN: No, I tell you the rules.

WOMAN: Listen—

MAN: I don't want you to use that word. You've used it twice. I don't want to hear that word.

WOMAN: What word?

MAN: You know the word.

WOMAN: What word? You mean fuck?

MAN: I don't want to hear it.

WOMAN: Sorry. I mean, I just, I thought that's what we were here for.

MAN: I DON'T WANT TO HEAR IT.

WOMAN: Okay, fine, I won't say anything. I'll just stand here. You can pay me to stand here; that's fine by me. Fucking weirdo. Sorry.

(He sits, staring. Pause.)

MAN: Tell me what you want.

WOMAN: Tell you what I—you want me to tell you what I want?

MAN: Yes.

WOMAN: Okay. I want to wrap this up and go home and see my kid. It's been a long day—

MAN: No.

WOMAN: No.

MAN: No.

WOMAN: That's not what I want.

MAN: No.

WOMAN: Okay, then you tell me what I do want because I mean, I am in the dark here, all right? Usually, I have to say, usually there is not a lot of confusion about how to proceed, but—

MAN: Stop talking.

WOMAN: Stop talking. Right. I forgot.

MAN: Tell me what you want.

(Pause. She looks at him.)

WOMAN: *(Matter of fact.)* Okay. Let's try this. I want you.

MAN: Yes.

WOMAN: Yes. That's a yes. Here we go. I want you…inside of me.

MAN: Yes.

WOMAN: Two yesses. This is a trend. I want to suck your cock.

MAN: No.

WOMAN: No. That's not what I want. Okay, fine, I—fuck, I don't know what the fuck—

MAN: NO.

WOMAN: No, sorry, I didn't mean to use that word, I meant, I mean, I meant DARN. Darn.

MAN: Yes.

WOMAN: Yes. Darn. Sorry. I'm a little slow, darn it. *(Pause.)* I want you…in my mouth?

(He does not respond.)

WOMAN: I want…to touch you.

MAN: *(Quiet.)* No.

WOMAN: But I can't.

MAN: Yes.

WOMAN: I want you to look at me…and not see me.

MAN: Yes.

WOMAN: Yes. I want to stand in front of you naked, with clothes on.

MAN: Yes.

WOMAN: I get this. You want to have sex without sex.

MAN: *(Aroused.)* Yes. Tell me what you want.

(Pause. The Woman stares at him for a long moment, then turns and picks up her shoes.)

WOMAN: No. I won't do it. This is sick, this is really—

MAN: Do you want the money or not?

(Pause.)

WOMAN: Yeah. I want the money.

MAN: Then tell me what you want.

(Pause. The woman sets her shoes down, turns and looks at him.)

WOMAN: I want…I want you in me outside of me.

MAN: Yes.

WOMAN: I want you to touch me…without feeling me. I want words with no voice. Sex with no heart. Love without bones.

MAN: *(Overlap.)* Yes. Yes.

WOMAN: *(Overlap.)* Skin without skin. I want blind eyes.

MAN: Yes.

WOMAN: I want you to stare me dead. I want you to lick me dry. I want you to take my words. Wipe me clean. Make me nothing. Let me be nothing for you. Let me be nothing. Let me be nothing.

MAN: *(Overlap.)* Yes. Yes. Yes!

(He comes without touching himself. She watches him, dispassionate. There is a long pause. They stare at each other.)

MAN: You disgust me.

WOMAN: Yeah. I know. That'll be $200. Sir.

(Blackout.)

END OF PLAY

WHAT WE'RE UP AGAINST

CHARACTERS
STU: White, thirty
BEN: White, thirty

SET
An office

Stu and Ben sit at a drafting table. Stu reaches into the bottom drawer of a file cabinet, finds a bottle of scotch, and pours drinks.

STU: All I'm saying is there's—

BEN: Rules. That's what I'm trying to—

STU: A *sys*tem.

BEN: Yes, Jesus, I—

STU: Things don't just happen, history, events—

BEN: I know, this is not—

STU: We *create.*

BEN: Exactly. A company. I tried to—

STU: You look at anything, the boyscouts, some fucking *convent,* and maybe it doesn't seem like—

BEN: You just can't—

STU: It's part of something much more *com*plicated. You can't just act like that's not true.

BEN: That's my point. She's a fucking bitch. That's all I'm saying.

STU: I'm not *saying* that. That is not what—

BEN: Okay, okay, fine, but—

STU: You cannot give them that.

BEN: I'm not giving them anything. I'm just saying, she doesn't belong. I don't know why they hired another fucking woman, it's not like—

STU: Look, they want to work, women want to work, they should have the opportunity. I'm not saying—fuck, that's just—you know that's what they think, they all have their little meetings and tell each other that we don't *want* them, we're *threat*ened, when that's not the issue. You can't give them that. Because that's not the problem.

BEN: Stu, you just said she—

STU: She *tricked* me. The bitch tricked me, that is my point. She is a lying, deceitful, dishonest little manipulator. I don't mind working with her. But, she is a cunt. That, I mind.

BEN: That's what I'm—

STU: No, that is not what you're saying, Ben. These are two very different things. I welcomed her. I was happy when they hired her, I said, I want to work with this woman.

BEN: Oh, come on—

STU: Excuse me?

BEN: What? I'm just saying—

STU: What are you saying, Ben?

BEN: I'm *saying*, shit, I'm saying you didn't want her any more than the rest of us. What do we need another woman for? Janice is, we have one of them, I don't know what—

STU: This isn't an issue of sex. That's what I'm telling you. Are you fucking listening to me?

BEN: Yes, I'm listening, you're not—

STU: It's the system I'm talking about. It's not whether or not she's a *woman*. It's the fact that she has no re*spect,* this is my point. She comes into my office and says, we need to talk, Stu, and I'm, okay, I'm fine, I can talk, I don't have a problem with this. She has questions. I'm fine with this. She wants to know why I won't let her work. Now, that is not what is happening, I explain that to her. She is a new employee, how long has she been here, five months, six months, this is not—the experience isn't there. That is my point. When the experience is there, she'll be put on projects. She wants to know how she can get the experience if we won't let her work. This is a good question. And so I tell her: Initiative. Initiative, that is how the system works, that is how America works, this is what they don't under*stand.* No one *hands* you things. You *work* for them. You *earn* them. You prove yourself *worthy.* So she says to me, what about Webber? And I say, what about him? And she says, you let him work. He's been here four months, and you put him on projects.

BEN: Oh, that fucking—

STU: Exactly. She's jealous. The bitch is jealous. She doesn't care about the work, she just cares, she's competitive, Webber got ahead of her and she doesn't like it. She's after his balls. So I say to her, that's got nothing to do with you. Nothing. This isn't about competition. This is about business. We use the best person for the job. If you prove yourself, through initiative, to be the best person, to be *worthy,* we will use you.

BEN: So what'd she say to—

STU: I'll tell you what she said. This fucking bitch, she stopped by Webber's office and picked up a copy of that mall extension you guys are working on, the Roxbury project—

BEN: What? What'd she do that for?

STU: So she's got your design, right—

BEN: That thing's not finished, Stu. Did she show you that? She had no business doing that. We are not finished with that.

STU: So she says to me—

BEN: I cannot believe that bitch, trying to make us look bad! We haven't solved the duct thing yet, okay, we're still working on it! I can't be*lieve*—

STU: Would you shut up, Ben? I'm trying to ex*plain* something to you. She's not after your balls, she's after Webber—

BEN: I'm just saying, we're still working on that. We've got *ideas.*

STU: I'm not talking about your *ideas,* Ben, I'm trying to tell you something! She brings me your design, she tells me she got it from Webber, and then she says, I can see putting Ben on this, he's got se*nior*ity. But why does Webber get to work, and not me? What is so good about what he does? Tell me why Webber got this project and not me. She's pissing me off now, because I explained this to her, it's not about competition, I *said* that, but if she wants to play this game, fine, *fuck* her, I'll *show* her why Webber got the project. So I go through it. Every detail. I show her how every fucking detail indicates that Webber has experience. I prove it to her. And you know what she says to me? "I designed that."

BEN: What?

STU: The bitch put Webber's name on one of her designs. She came up with her own fucking design for that fucking mall, and then she pretended it was Webber's. She tricked me.

BEN: You're shitting me.

STU: This fucking *woman* stands there—she stands there, and says to me, "This is my point, *Stu.* It's not about the work, it's about point of view. When a woman designs it, it's shit, and when a man designs it, it's great." So I say to her, no this isn't about point of view, this is about power, you fucking bitch. You're trying to cut off my balls here. She says, look at the design, Stu, you know it's good, and I say, I don't give a shit if it's good. You want to play by these rules, I can play by these rules. It's shit. Get out of my face.

BEN: You said that?

STU: She says, I want to work. Why won't you let me work? And I say fuck you. What you want is power. You fucking cunt, don't lie to me. You come in here and try and cut off my balls, I welcomed you, and this is what you do.

BEN: Fucking bitch.

STU: This is what we're up against.

BEN: Fuck.

(Pause. They think about this.)

BEN: But it was good?

STU: What?

BEN: The design. You said—

STU: Fuck you, are you fucking listening to a word I'm saying?

BEN: Yes, I'm listening, I just—I was wondering what she did with the air ducts.

STU: What? What are you saying?

BEN: I'm saying, you know, Webber and I—those fucking ducts are all over the entryway there, and we can't—

STU: Fuck you, Ben, you are not listening to a word out of my mouth.

BEN: Yeah, I know, she's a cunt, I'm just saying, you said the design was good, so I was just wondering—

STU: The design is shit.

BEN: Yeah, but if she's got an idea—

STU: She's got nothing, Ben. *Nothing.* You give her nothing.

BEN: Why not?

STU: Excuse me? What? Excuse me?

BEN: If she's got one fucking idea—

STU: She *tricked* me.

BEN: Yeah, but you don't let her work, Stu. She's right about that. You let Janice do more, and her work is for shit.

STU: What are you—what is your fucking point, Ben?

BEN: I don't have a point! I just want to see that fucking design. Webber and I have been going over that fucking duct thing for weeks and we can't crack it. So, if she's got a solution, I want to see it. Did she have a solution or not?

STU: Yeah. She did.

BEN: Well, I want to see it.

STU: No.

BEN: She's here now, fuck, they hired her and we had nothing to say about it, she's being paid, why shouldn't we use her?

STU: I'll tell you why. Because then, she's won. She didn't wait. She didn't play by the rules. It's context. If she had waited, it would've been different. If she had respect for the system. But she has no respect. This is what we're up against.

BEN: That's a load of shit, Stu.

STU: I'm what? Excuse me, did you, what did you—

BEN: Look, Stu—

STU: If she were here, listening to us, you know what she'd do?

BEN: Hopefully, she'd tell me what she did with those fucking ducts—

STU: No. That is not what she'd do. I'll tell you what she'd do. Two men, having a simple conversation, we're having drinks. Right? Is there anything wrong with this? But she sits here and she listens to us, and then she goes and tells her little friends. She goes back to her little group, and she says,

"They said this, and they said that, they called me a bitch, they called me a cunt" and she and her friends, they all act like this is some big fucking *point*. But there is no *point*, Ben. This is what they don't understand. There is a system. Things fit together. It's not about point of view. It's just about the way things are. They want things to be the way they're not. They don't get it, and they're trying to make us pay for that. But they are not going to win. It's the system. That's all it is. The system. *(They stare at each other. Blackout.)*

END OF PLAY

THE CONTRACT

CHARACTERS
PHIL: An agent
TOM: An actor

SET
An agent's office

Two men sit in an office. Phil sits at a desk, reading Tom's resume.

PHIL: Yeah, this is—

TOM: I also dance. Plus, I condensed. That's not everything.

PHIL: Oh—

TOM: I mean, it's representative. There's a ton more stuff, I just thought—

PHIL: No question. The thing is, your type—

TOM: I don't really see myself as a type. There's much more range, you know different—

PHIL: Character—

TOM: Yeah, character-type work, and, um, improvisation—

PHIL: This is what I'm saying. A character actor, what are you, mid-thirties—

TOM: Early. Early thirties, although I often read, last year, I played a twenty-three year old junkie, in an independent, and it was—

PHIL: *(Slightly impressed.)* A junkie? Cause there's maybe, they're hot this year—

TOM: You want tape on that? Cause I could get you that tape. The junkie tape—

PHIL: Yeah, I—

TOM: I mean, it was excellent, I didn't have a lot to do, but there's a great cameo of me nodding off, it's killer stuff—

PHIL: No, you know what you should do? All this, you do a lot of theatre, right? This is mostly like stage stuff?

TOM: Yeah, a lot, my training is—

PHIL: Fantastic. I love the theatre. Why don't you give us a call, next time you're in something, we'll stop by and take a look, okay?
(He pushes the resume toward Tom. Tom does not take it.)

TOM: Well but isn't that why you called me in? Cause you saw the showcase and—

PHIL: It would just be great to see you in something bigger. Get more of a sense of what you can do.

TOM: Yeah but you called and asked me to come in and now—

PHIL: Hey can I be candid? *(Looks at resume.)* Tom? I mean, this is a tough business, it's best to be candid, right?

TOM: Oh absolutely, that's—

PHIL: Cause I'm sort of not really getting your tone here. I mean I called you in cause I think you have talent, I might want to, you know, *represent* you someday and now I'm getting like a ton of attitude here.

TOM: No, you're not getting attitude. I just—

PHIL: I'm just saying. Don't talk to me like a jerk.

TOM: I'm not talking to you like a jerk. You're talking to me like—You call me in, I take time out of my schedule—

PHIL: Your very busy schedule— *(He waves the resume, unimpressed.)*

TOM: I told you, that's not—besides, who cares what's on my—Harrison Ford was a *carpenter* for god's sake—

PHIL: If you were Harrison Ford, believe me, this conversation would be very different.

TOM: You called me. *You* called *me*—

PHIL: Yes, I called you and you jumped. You jumped at this. I mean, you want representation or not? You want it or not?

TOM: Of course I want it, I—

PHIL: All right. I am the representation. I am what you want. I am the object of desire in this town. Got that? It's not some fucking starlet tits out to here. It isn't a gold BMW. It's me. You want to work, you want to see your face on the big screen, the fucking tube, whatever—

TOM: Look, I—

PHIL: *(Very reasonable.)* I am what gets you that. I am what makes this town run. So when I say jump, you don't say why. I mean, what, you have a problem with authority? You didn't like your dad or something? Tell it to your shrink. Keep it out of my damn office and just do what I say.

TOM: Why are you yelling at me?

PHIL: Oh, now I'm—

TOM: Yes, you're not even representing me and you're, you're—

PHIL: I said I *might.*

TOM: Oh well that's—

PHIL: Look. I didn't invent the world. I didn't make up the rules. I'm giving you advice here. This is free! Do you know what you are? You're an actor! No one gives a shit about you! You're a total nobody! The fact that I'm even speaking to you is going to be the most significant thing that happens to you all year. You should be fucking genuflecting, and I mean literally hitting your knees when I say boo, and what do I get instead? What do I *get?* "You called me up and now you aren't being nice to me." This is show business, you moron! Nobody's nice to anybody! Especially actors. You guys are the lowest form of life. Oh yeah, I know everybody says that about agents, but they're wrong. I mean, we're slime, okay, I don't argue that, but we're slime that *you* need, and *you* want, so you are lower even than me, and that means I don't *have* to be nice to you. *You* have to be nice to me!

TOM: I just—I don't—that's nuts. You're nuts.

PHIL: I'm *what?*

TOM: I mean, I'm an actor. How can you—I'm an *artist.* Laurence Olivier, for god's sake—this is an art form and you're—yeah, okay, I understand that it's not show friends, it's show business, but—we're talking about telling *stories,* reaching in and communicating our hu*man*ity, and if you can't even—if decency means *nothing* anymore, then why—I just don't accept that. I'm sorry, but I don't. I've given up everything to do this work, my family thinks I'm completely—I've maxed out all—I mean, I am fucking broke every second of my life, and I know that I'm just another actor but that's not—this is a *noble thing.* Do you understand that? We are as puppets dancing for the gods. We spin meaning out of nothing, out of oblivion we make *art,* and you—well. You're not—I can't—you don't—No.

PHIL: Did you finish a sentence in there? I mean, did you actually say something?

TOM: I don't want you to represent me.

PHIL: You *what?*

TOM: You're a bad person. *(Tom takes his resume and puts it in his knapsack.)*

PHIL: Oh. Well. You cut me to the quick, Tom. I, I just don't know what to say.

(Tom is heading for the door.)

PHIL: Hey! What are you doing?

TOM: I'm leaving.

PHIL: Did I say you could go? Cause I don't remember saying that.

TOM: I, I didn't ask.

PHIL: Tom. This is really—sit down. Would you sit down? Come on. I mean, I like you Tom, would I be even talking to you if I didn't—sit down. Come on.

(Tom does.)

TOM: I'm really confused.

PHIL: I don't see why.

TOM: I'm getting very mixed signals from you.

PHIL: How so, Tom? Cause I'm being as candid as I possibly know how to be. I mean, most people in this town—some of that stuff you said, you could've really pissed some people off with that. And you know, someone like me, if I were vindictive, I could call every casting agent I know and tell them, you know, you're a difficult guy, and that would be it. Your career would be over.

TOM: Is that a threat?

PHIL: It's just a fact. Nobody wants to deal with anybody who's difficult. Life's too short, babe. You want to have a conversation about, what do you call it—

TOM: The work?

PHIL: "The work", people aren't gonna put up with that. Humanity, noble, decency, art—Tom. People are not gonna put up with it.

TOM: Why are you saying these things? I was going to leave. I am leaving— (He stands.)

PHIL: You leave when I tell you to leave!

(Tom looks at him, confused.)

PHIL: I mean, there's something you're not getting here, Tom. I am your friend. I see an actor with talent, I ask him to come in, he's clearly confused about how the world works but I like him so I decide to teach him a few useful lessons. I am your friend. And if you ever want to work as an actor, get paid, actually have a real acting job instead of some stupid *theatre* thing, then you will LEAVE when I SAY LEAVE.

(They stare at each other.)

TOM: You know, Nietzsche was not right.

PHIL: Oh, Jesus—

TOM: Yes, Nietzsche, the philosopher said—

PHIL: I'm trying to tell you something, Tom—

TOM: And I'm trying to tell you, the guy was like obsessed—

PHIL: Yeah, that's fascinating, I'm so—

TOM: So we did this acting exercise in grad school, which was based on a Nietzschean model of humanity and basically the exercise was all about who's going to win the scene, because Nietzsche has this theory about the will to power but—

PHIL: DON'T YOU FUCKING TALK TO ME ABOUT NIETZSCHE!

TOM: (Cowed but continuing.) It's just that it's a very limited model of humanity. As an actor you have to draw on many aspects of…you know what? I can see that this is really important to you, so you know what I'm going to do? I'm going to let you win the scene. (He sits back down.)

PHIL: You're what?

TOM: Whatever you want, Phil. I'll do whatever you want. You want me to stay, leave, whatever. That's what I'll do.

PHIL: I want you to listen.

TOM: I'm listening.

PHIL: I want you to get with the picture.

TOM: That's what I'm doing.

PHIL: I mean, which one of us knows this town, you or me?

TOM: You.

PHIL: That's right.

TOM: That's right. And I really appreciate everything you've said to me. You really put me on the right path and I appreciate it.

PHIL: You should.

TOM: I do.

(Tom looks at him. Phil studies him, uncomfortable.)

PHIL: What are you doing?

TOM: I'm letting you win the scene.

PHIL: You're *letting* me? What do you mean, you're—

TOM: I don't mean anything.

PHIL: You said "let."

TOM: That's not what I meant at all. What I meant was it just took me a while to understand what you were trying to tell me, and I'm just, I'm saying you're right. You are right. You're amazing. It's a thrill meeting you and thank you for your time.

PHIL: *(Suspicious.)* You're acting, aren't you?

TOM: Do you want me to be acting?

PHIL: Yeah, that's funny. I mean, you're a real comedian.

TOM: If that's what you want me to be.

(He strikes a little shticky pose for him. Phil laughs a little. Tom joins him. They have a good chuckle together. Phil looks at him, liking him again.)

PHIL: So…was this whole thing an act? One big mind-fuck? Nietzsche and art and humanity—you been putting the whole thing on, right? You're fucking with my head so I'll sign you. Am I right? I mean, 'cause that's kind of brilliant.

TOM: Well…

PHIL: I mean, I could work with that. 'Cause then we understand each other. You know, then we're on a wavelength.

TOM: *(Some growing concern.)* Oh…oh. Oh, oh, oh.

PHIL: *(Snapping again.)* Oh what? Are we understanding each other or not? I mean, am I winning this scene or not?

TOM: Yeah. Yeah, of course.

(Phil studies Tom, then points his finger at him and starts laughing. Tom laughs too, a bit uncomfortably.)

PHIL: I like you. I like you. *(He thinks for a minute, then suddenly yells.)* Hey SUZIE! Get me a set of standard contracts, will you?

(Tom looks around, concerned.)

TOM: Oh. You want to—

PHIL: I'm gonna sign you, Tom! Welcome to Hollywood.

(He shakes his hand, laughing. Tom laughs too. The laughter goes on for quite a while. Tom ends up looking a little sick.)

(Blackout.)

END OF PLAY

KATIE AND FRANK

CHARACTERS

KATIE: Early thirties, scattered, angry, but not crazy
FRANK: Early thirties, on his own track

SET

A room with a bed or a couch or a chair, a door and a phone. The door leads to the bathroom.

Katie lies on the bed. Frank is in and out of the bathroom.

KATIE: I talked to your mother the other day.

FRANK: *(Off.)* What?

KATIE: Your mother called yesterday.

FRANK: Oh yeah? *(He crosses through, wearing an open shirt and nice trousers. He is absurdly handsome.)*

KATIE: I told you. Last night.

FRANK: No you didn't.

KATIE: Yes, I did, remember, after you got home from work, I said—

FRANK: I don't remember.

KATIE: It was just yesterday.

FRANK: I don't remember.

KATIE: It was—

FRANK: Katie. I don't remember.

(Having found his socks he returns to the bathroom. She lies on the bed, thinking.)

KATIE: It was after therapy. I remember telling you because I was so upset, I mean, I came from therapy, I was feeling *good,* you know, I was just feeling, sitting here feeling good for a change and then your fucking mother called.

FRANK: *(Off.)* That's nice. That's very nice

KATIE: Well, I told you to call her and you didn't. The last time? Whenever that was, last week, and I told you to call her but you didn't so then she called me yesterday to scream at me. *(Suddenly loud.)* AND I TOLD YOU THIS LAST NIGHT AND NOW YOU'RE SAYING YOU DON'T REMEMBER.

(Frank appears in the doorway, annoyed.)

FRANK: Katie. Do you mind? I'm about to walk out the door here and I don't have time for one of your whatever these things are.

KATIE: Where are you going?

FRANK: *(Off.)* Work.

KATIE: It's Saturday.

FRANK: *(Off.)* I work on Saturdays.

KATIE: Yeah, so you say.

FRANK: Katie, please!

KATIE: *(To herself.)* Yeah, fuck you, Frank. Why don't you call your fucking mother for once?

(Frank appears.)

FRANK: I mean, I thought you were feeling better. I mean, you said, a minute ago, that after therapy yesterday, you felt better. Did you not say that?

KATIE: Yes I did. I did feel better. But—

FRANK: So why don't you hang onto that? Huh? I just don't—your life is not some huge fucking torture here. I don't know why it always has to be like this.

KATIE: Well, I'll tell you why it has to be like this. It has to be like this because you won't call your mother.

FRANK: I can't talk to you when you're like this.

KATIE: This is my point! This is my whole point! Why don't you call your mother? You know when you don't call her she blames it all on me, and then I end up taking endless hours of shit from her on the phone. Is he there? Well why didn't he call me? Did you tell him? I just don't understand why if you told him he doesn't call. Like it's my fault, you know, God forbid it should ever be *your* fault. It's just, why don't you tell her? Why don't you ever call her and say I'm sorry I forgot to call. Katie told me you called but I *forgot*. That's all I'm *saying.*

FRANK: You're going to drive me nuts.

(He crosses through, truly annoyed, finds his tie and exits again. Katie watches him.)

KATIE: *(Sad, to herself.)* I just don't understand why it's all my fault. *(Beat. Quiet.)* My therapist says you don't listen to me.

FRANK: *(Out of the bathroom like a shot.)* Oh, no. No no no. That's the one thing I said to you, when you went into therapy, I will pay for this, but I will not be *blamed.* You are not dumping all your problems on me. That is not an option here.

KATIE: I didn't—

FRANK: It's not an option, Katie! *(He goes back into the bathroom.)*

(Beat.)

KATIE: I bought a gun.

(Frank sticks his head out, looks at her.)

KATIE: *(Innocent.)* What?

FRANK: *(Disgusted.)* Nothing. Nothing. *(He goes back in the bathroom.)*

KATIE: I did. This morning. I went out and bought a gun. It's absurdly easy, you know, you walk into a store and just, like, buy it. Actually, you go in on Monday and pay for it but they don't give it to you until today because of this *waiting* period, they make you wait before they give you the gun just in case you want to change your *mind,* like they think if some woman comes in here going you know, I hate my husband, I think

I'll just put a bullet between his eyes, that they need to give her a few days to consider that. Which doesn't seem like great logic to me, frankly. If you're thinking about shooting your husband it seems to me an extra week is just going to make you more determined to do it. Unless that's what they're hoping for.

FRANK: *(Entering.)* Where's the toothpaste?

KATIE: We're out.

FRANK: We're out.

KATIE: No, wait, there's some in that little, one of those travel things I put together. The blue thing in the back of the towels.

(He glares at her pointedly for a moment, and goes.)

KATIE: So anyway, this gun —

FRANK: *(Off.)* I can't find it!

KATIE: It's in the blue thing!

FRANK: I TOLD YOU, I CAN'T— *(Silence.)* Never mind.

(Silence. She continues.)

KATIE: I could have gotten more than one, you know. They make you wait, but you can buy as many as you want. I asked the guy about it. I said, if I wanted to buy like, eleven guns or something wouldn't you worry about that? Wouldn't that seem kind of hostile to you? And he said it was my right. To buy that many guns. Like that made it okay.

(She is vaguely bemused by this. Frank appears in the doorway.)

FRANK: This is ridiculous you know. This toothpaste situation? I mean, I'm just squeezing here, for this *squidge,* it's not even, when was the last time you went to the store? I understand that you're *troubled* but I don't think it's asking too much that you occasionally get it together to go to the store and buy a fucking tube of toothpaste. All right? I do not raise my voice to you, but I feel a little strongly about this.

(He exits again. She reaches under the bed and gets her purse. She pulls out a gun.)

KATIE: So anyway I have this gun because it's my *right.* Which means, I think, that's it's probably my right to shoot you. Because okay this is why: It's my right to buy a gun, I buy a gun because I hate my husband, it's my right to hate my husband because well we don't need to go into that but let's just say the reasons are VERY CLEAR therefore, it's my right to shoot my husband. What's that called? A logical syllogism. I think therefore I am. I hate you and therefore we are. Therefore you're dead you lying fucking bastard, you lying fuckface, you liar liar liar—

FRANK: This isn't funny, Katie. *(He appears in the door, tying his tie. He sees the gun and stops.)* What's that?

KATIE: I told you. I bought a gun.

FRANK: That's not a gun.

KATIE: I told you, Frank. They'll sell a gun to any idiot who asks for one. Did I not just tell you this? Do you listen to a word out of my mouth? This is what my therapist says—

FRANK: Hey—

KATIE: No, this is just what she's talking about, and then you *complain,* you say I'm *blaming* you when it's the truth. YOU DON'T LISTEN.

FRANK: Katie, put the gun down.

KATIE: I'm not going to put it down. I just got it. It's brand new. I'm getting used to it. I like the way it makes me feel. It's my right to feel this way.

FRANK: I'm calling your useless therapist—

(He starts to move for the phone. She points it at him.)

KATIE: Oh now you're calling her. I asked you, I *asked* you to go with me and you couldn't be bothered because she's a fucking idiot, but now you want to talk to her because I have a gun is that it?

FRANK: Katie, you're clearly losing it.

KATIE: Gee Frank I wonder why that is. *(Beat.)* Anyway, it doesn't matter. I can be completely fucking out of my fucking mind and it's still my right to own a gun, and it's my right to point it at you and it's my right to feel what I feel. Some country, America. *(She has the gun right up against his head.)*

FRANK: *(Really scared now.)* Katie. Katie.

KATIE: What Frank?

FRANK: Come on, honey. Put the gun down.

KATIE: Frank. This is the first time you've listened to me in years. Why would I put the gun down?

FRANK: Honey—

KATIE: Honey. That's a good one.

FRANK: What do you want, Katie? What do you want?

KATIE: *(Beat.)* I want you to call your mother, Frank. And I want you to say, Mom, how are you? Katie told me you called, and I forgot to call you back.

FRANK: *(Resisting.)* Katie—

KATIE: Pick up the phone. *(The gun goes to his head again.)* Pick up the phone, Frank.

(He does. Blackout.)

END OF PLAY

GREAT TO SEE YOU

CHARACTERS
JILL
LIZA
RUDY

PLACE
A restaurant table

.

A woman, Liza, sits alone. A man and a woman, Rudy and Jill, stand before her.

JILL: *(Excited.)* Hi—

LIZA: Oh—

JILL: It's so great to see you! You look exactly the same!

LIZA: So do you.

JILL: Oh, no—

RUDY: Hi.

    (They sit.)

LIZA: Wow, it's great to see you.

RUDY: Yes.

LIZA: I wasn't sure, Rudy said you'd probably have to work—

JILL: When I heard you were in town, I got someone to take my shift! I mean it's been, god—

LIZA: A while.

JILL: Years, right?

LIZA: Something.

JILL: And what are you here for?

LIZA: Well, my parents live here.

JILL: Oh that's right. So vacation!

LIZA: A visit.

JILL: Well, it's just great that you could make time for us. I mean, I know you have to rush in and out of town.

LIZA: Of course I wanted to see you. It's been so long. *(There is an awkward pause.)* So how are your kids?

JILL: Just great. Benny's in preschool now, he's just a holy terror. And Doug's in second grade.

LIZA: Really? I mean, I can't—that's so big.

JILL: They love it here. Really love it. I'm so glad we moved back.

LIZA: It's a great town.

JILL: Heartland. If you're gonna raise kids, what else can you do?

LIZA: Well.

RUDY: How's your little girl?

LIZA: Great. She's great. Little. I mean, littler than—anyway. She's with her dad in England right now.

JILL: Oh that's right, your husband's British!

LIZA: Well, we're not—we never actually got—anyway.

JILL: Oh. You didn't—

LIZA: We're together. I mean, we're fine, everything's, we just never actually—
    I have a thing about the church, as you'll recall.
RUDY: *(A slight smile.)* Yes.
JILL: You didn't want to even—
LIZA: Actually, I have a thing about the government, too. Institutions in general.
JILL: Aren't you worried, about how it might…well, legally it does limit your
    rights. And internationally I mean, if you got married you'd be able to
    work in England, wouldn't you?
LIZA: I can pretty much do that. I mean—you know, my work takes me there,
    a lot, and anyway, that wouldn't be why we did it. So I could work.
    (Beat.) It's hard to explain.
JILL: No! We completely understand.
    (Pause.)
RUDY: So how is your work?
LIZA: Good. You know, very, it's a trip.
RUDY: You still with Sotheby's?
LIZA: Yeah. I worked the Jackie Kennedy auction, that was, good lord.
JILL: Oh, it must've been thrilling.
LIZA: Oh yeah. You know, touching history, that whole thing. And the people.
JILL: It must've been, just—great.
LIZA: It was kind of surreal actually. Of course the whole New York glitterati
    thing was going, like every celebrity in the city was there, even the ones
    who are above that sort of thing, and then they're all rubbing elbows
    with every rich conspiracy freak in the nation, I mean literally every
    nutjob with cash pulled favors and got themselves in there, so it was a
    scene.
JILL: Well. Your life is a lot more exciting than ours.
LIZA: Oh, no, that's—no.
RUDY: Are you still painting?
LIZA: *(Beat.)* No.
JILL: Well, Rudy's going back to writing, did he tell you?
LIZA: *(Interested in this.)* No, that's great. I mean, I know you've—
RUDY: No——
JILL: Yes, he took the tests and everything! I tell all my friends my husband
    the doctor wants to quit his practice and become a novelist. They think
    it's a scream, but I think he should do it, don't you? I mean, it worked
    for Michael Crighton, didn't it? *(Checking her watch, reaching for her*

purse.) Oh shoot, I have to call the sitter. The boys are at her house this week, because she has some sort of car thing, and I'm just not—here it is. *(She finds a piece of paper in her purse, and goes. There is an awkward pause.)*

LIZA: I'm glad she came. I wasn't sure she could.

RUDY: No, she took off.

LIZA: That was nice of her.

RUDY: You look great. You look exactly the same.

(Liza nods, looks away, sad.)

LIZA: It's weird being back. I mean, good weird, sort of.

RUDY: I'd love to meet your little girl someday.

LIZA: Oh yeah. Next time. Usually, I bring her.

RUDY: You come often?

LIZA: No, not often. *(Beat, goodnatured.)* So, you took some test to be a writer?

RUDY: *(Embarrassed.)* Oh—

LIZA: I didn't know there was a test. What is it, like, "draw this dog?"

RUDY: It wasn't anything. G.R.E.

LIZA: Oh, for graduate school?

RUDY: *(Embarrassed.)* It's not gonna happen. She loves it here, the boys love it here. It was a stupid idea.

LIZA: Can't you just write in your free time? *(Beat.)* What sort of thing do you want to write?

(Rudy shakes his head.)

LIZA: Are you all right?

RUDY: *(Too quick.)* Yes. I'm fine.

LIZA: You just seem—

RUDY: No. I'm fine. I don't seem anything.

LIZA: I'm sorry.

RUDY: Why? I mean, why are you sorry?

LIZA: Well, you seem—never mind. Oh, man. Maybe this wasn't such a good idea.

RUDY: No. Maybe it wasn't. I mean—Why are you here, anyway?

LIZA: *(Now irritated.)* Why am I here? I'm here because you—oh, man.

RUDY: What? I what?

LIZA: You didn't—that letter wasn't—

RUDY: It was just a card.

LIZA: It wasn't just a card, Rudy, it was very—between the lines, you were so—

RUDY: I wasn't anything between the lines. You don't know me anymore. I'm sorry, but you don't. You show up here, acting like—we haven't spoken in years, for god's sake. Years. You don't have the right to act like you know me.

LIZA: Yeah, well, you don't have the right to send me cards that say "I think of you every day."

(Jill returns.)

JILL: The machine was on. Can you believe that?

RUDY: Was it?

JILL: I mean, I like this baby-sitter, don't get me wrong, but it is unusual, bringing the boys to her house, and then for her to have the machine on. I suppose they could have gone to the library, but her car is not working, as we know, so that is just not very likely.

RUDY: Do you want to go over there?

JILL: No no. I'm just a little concerned is all.

LIZA: I understand, if you need to go.

JILL: No no no. I'm fine! And I never get to see you!

LIZA: I meant both of you could go. All of us. Maybe this just isn't a good time.

(Jill is surprised at this, and considering it.)

JILL: Oh. Well. Maybe we should, honey.

RUDY: *(Beat.)* If something were wrong, she'd call us. She has the number here, and the cellphone, and the beeper.

JILL: Absolutely.

RUDY: Yes.

(There is another unfortunate pause.)

LIZA: *(Trying.)* So, you guys bought a house?

JILL: It's great. So beautiful, you wouldn't even believe it. One of those Victorian painted ladies, well it's not painted, but it's in that school.

LIZA: And you probably paid like three cents for it, right? Everything's so affordable here, I can hardly stand it. Our place in Manhattan, it's like two floors of a brownstone, a million five. Ridiculous.

JILL: A million?

LIZA: *(Now embarrassed.)* A million five.

JILL: Well. You must be doing very well. Of course, Sotheby's.

LIZA: Well, Michael does—he's in international real estate, and that's pretty much taken off. People buying things in other countries, it really rocks and rolls, over there in that market.

JILL: *(A little joke.)* And you haven't married this man?

LIZA: *(Beat.)* No. We're not married. *(Beat.)* We do have a kid, though, which always seems, to me, like the bigger commitment, actually.

JILL: Oh absolutely. Absolutely. Rudy and I just had our tenth anniversary.

LIZA: Ten? Really?

RUDY: Yes.

LIZA: Congratulations. I, you know, I didn't know it had been that long.

JILL: Oh yes. It was so romantic. I stole him away, he was completely surprised, but I arranged for us to spend the weekend in this lovely little B and B across the river.

LIZA: Sounds great.

RUDY: It was.

JILL: He didn't even know where we were going. I picked him up at the clinic and just said, we're not going home—his sister was staying with the boys—and I had everything we needed in the car. I had this beautiful basket of fruit and wine and cheese, and then I had bought this, you know, a peignoir, completely see through, it was gorgeous, all black lace, I had to work out for weeks just to feel good about wearing it. So we get to this place, this B and B, and I didn't know it when I booked the room, but it's run by these Baptists, I kid you not, and there's a sign right at the front, where you sign in, no alcohol. Can you imagine? No alcohol. So I think well, it's our anniversary, they can't keep us from just having a glass of wine, besides, there was something just kind of decadent about sneaking a bottle into our room so that's what we did. So then we get to our room, which is just so beautiful and quaint and private, and I made Rudy go into the bathroom so I can set everything up, and I open the wine, and lay out the fruit and I put on the peignoir, and I get on the bed, and I say you can come out now! And I start jumping on the bed. I don't know why I did it, but I just felt like it. *(She is laughing now.)* So there I am, jumping on the bed, completely naked under this beautiful peignoir, and he comes out and I jumped right on him and knocked him over, and he got this terrible gash in his head, from the table by the side of the bed, and he's bleeding all over and I've twisted my ankle, and then all those Baptists are knocking on the door, saying is everything all right in there? And there's that bottle of wine, and I'm stark naked on the floor, and Rudy's bleeding—it was a riot, just a riot.

(She smiles at Liza, who seems more or less stunned by this story.)

LIZA: Wow.

JILL: Oh, it was great. We laughed all night. After things calmed down.

LIZA: Yeah, had I known what fun marriage could be, maybe I would have tried it by now.

JILL: You should. You really should. We're so happy.

RUDY: Shouldn't we have seen a waiter by now?

JILL: You know you're right. *(Waving.)* Excuse me?

RUDY: Honey. Why don't you go ask? You need to check on the boys anyway.

JILL: I won't be a minute.

(She heads off. Liza looks down, then.)

LIZA: I have to go.

RUDY: Don't be ridiculous.

LIZA: God, could you not—

RUDY: If you left now, she'd know something was wrong.

LIZA: Rudy, she won't know anything. She lives completely on her own planet, as far as—

RUDY: Don't—

LIZA: No, don't you—you did what you had to do. I don't know why. You never bothered to tell me.

RUDY: That woman is my wife.

LIZA: Okay, she's your wife, and you sit there like a demented brooding lump of clay whenever she's around, and send sad evasive touching cards to your ex-girlfriend behind her back! Yeah, you guys make marriage look great.

RUDY: That is not what is happening here.

LIZA: Yeah, okay Rudy.

(She stands and starts to go. He reaches over and grabs her arm to stop her. She stops. He continues to hold her arm.)

LIZA: Rudy. Let go of my arm.

RUDY: You are not leaving.

LIZA: Rudy, let go. You're right, we don't know each other anymore. This is stupid. I have a lot to do this afternoon, I'm only in town for the day anyway. Christ, it was ten years ago, who cares, now, who cares? *(Beat.)* Although why you had to go and get married to—

RUDY: You left.

LIZA: We were breaking up every other day, back then, it was ridiculous, we were making each other miserable. We're making each other miserable now! I have a kid. And you still probably go to church. Don't you. Don't you?

RUDY: Yes.

LIZA: Well.

(He kisses her hand.)

LIZA: Rudy, stop it, we're in public and your wife is around the corner and I refuse to be part of some tawdry scene.

(Jill reappears just as Liza breaks away and sits back down.)

JILL: Caught you!

(Oblivious, she laughs. Liza is distracted, Rudy sullen.)

JILL: Well, I was a complete failure. Couldn't find a waiter and left the phone number for the sitter in my purse. So I'm wandering out there like a fool and missing our whole visit! I'm sure someone will help us any minute.

LIZA: I don't know about that. Something's clearly gone wrong. Hasn't it? I mean, clearly, they've forgotten we're back here.

RUDY: I think they're a little shorthanded today.

LIZA: This never happens in New York, or London. I mean, those places are constantly packed but you get service right away.

JILL: *(A little testy.)* They're probably more used to it. Lots of people coming and going. It's just a little slower paced here, that's what we love about living here.

LIZA: Absolutely. *(Looking about.)* Who recommended this? Jill, you were the one who likes this place?

RUDY: *(Edgy.)* I do.

LIZA: Oh. 'Cause when I spoke with Jill, she said she picked the restaurant.

RUDY: She picked this one because I like it.

LIZA: I'm sure the food is great.

JILL: Well the atmosphere is really—

LIZA: Absolutely. Such a lovely corner. Lovely private corner. The atmosphere's fantastic, that's why they can't find us. We're not here to eat anyway; we're here to *visit. (She slaps the table for emphasis.)* You guys look great. Time is serving us all so well.

JILL: Did Rudy tell you, we're thinking of having another baby?

LIZA: *(A beat.)* No. He didn't mention it.

JILL: Well, by adoption. That's what we're thinking. I just desperately want a girl, and the only way to guarantee that is to get one already cooked, so to speak! I know it takes forever, even for people like us, a stable family et cetera et cetera so we are looking into foreign adoption, which makes me a little nervous, because of all the reports about how disturbed and sick those children are, but I think if we keep our focus on maybe South America. Some cute little Guatemalan baby, something like that. Of course for some reason most of them are boys so maybe it really is my fate to just be surrounded by boys!

LIZA: *(At her wit's end.)* If you want a girl, why don't you go to China?

JILL: We thought of that. I just think that culturally it's too far.

LIZA: Further than Guatemala?

JILL: Oh yes.

LIZA: Wow. Okay. I uh, actually, never thought of it that way.

RUDY: We're very excited.

JILL: Oh, just thrilled.

LIZA: *(Distracted and mean.)* You don't know your sitter's phone number by heart?

JILL: Excuse me?

LIZA: Before, when you tried to call, you left the number here.

JILL: Oh. You know, you're right, but she's got one of those numbers it's just impossible to remember! There's not like two fours or three ones, nothing, every number is different and none of them are sequential—you know, six seven eight or two three four. That's why. And I have the number right on my refrigerator door, so if she doesn't show up, I know right where to go.

LIZA: What if you're at work, what about that?

JILL: If I'm at work, she's at my house. Besides, I carry it with me, that's what I do. I carry it with me. Here it is.

LIZA: Oh you're right. There it is. So you could call.

JILL: I think they're fine.

LIZA: Well, if you're comfortable, sure. I just thought, since before you didn't get through.

RUDY: They're fine.

LIZA: It's me. I just wouldn't be comfortable.

JILL: *(Conceding.)* You're right.

RUDY: No, they're fine.

JILL: It'll just make me feel a little better. I'll be right back.

(She goes. Liza calls after her.)

LIZA: And check on the waiter while you're at it!

RUDY: *(As soon as Jill's gone.)* Are you proud of yourself?

LIZA: *(Angry.)* I don't know. Are you?

RUDY: I have nothing to be ashamed of.

LIZA: That is what you married. That.

RUDY: How dare you.

LIZA: How dare *you?* Is that how you two talk to each other? Is that it? And you're gonna adopt a kid. Oh that's a good idea. You guys have the most dysfunctional relationship this side of my parents and—

RUDY: There is nothing—

LIZA: You're a genius and she's a dingdong!

RUDY: I am hardly a genius.

LIZA: Yeah you're right. I gotta qualify what I used to think about you, having met your—

RUDY: Do not—

LIZA: I'd like to kill you. *(There is a tense pause.)* You slept with her, didn't you? Before you got married. She was the one. You didn't get her pregnant, you just slept with her because all that Catholic shit inside you was finally making you a little too nuts, so one night you lost it and you slept with whoever was around, and it was her, and then you had to marry her. That's what happened. You couldn't sleep with me, even though you loved me, you had to sleep with whoever, and then—

RUDY: I love her.

LIZA: You loved *me.* And with all due respect, I don't believe that one person could love both of us, Rudy.

RUDY: Shut up.

LIZA: You stop sending me letters!

(She stands to go. He stands to stop her. She leans over and kisses him. In no time flat they are making out passionately. It goes on for quite a long time, and goes really too far. Occasionally one of them looks up and around, vaguely worried that someone—say, Jill—is going to see them, but their concern is generally much too fleeting. The table settings go flying. Finally, they stop, breathless, and silently part. Liza goes back to her side of the table. They both sit, silent, not looking at each other for a long moment. Liza makes a halfhearted attempt to straighten out the tablecloth. Jill returns and sits.)

JILL: *(Oblivious.)* Well, I spoke to the maitre'd. Apparently one of his waiters didn't show up today but he said he would get right on it. Has anyone been over here? What happened to the table? Well, now this is really ridiculous. *(Waving off.)* But I did get hold of the baby-sitter. They were out back on her swingset. I just don't understand why she couldn't take a phone with her, that's all. Really, this is—well, the table is a mess! *(She briefly looks back and forth between them, not comprehending what's going on.)* Well, I hope you two got through all your reminiscing while I was gone because I am not leaving this table again.

LIZA: Yes. We got through it.

JILL: Good! It's so good to see old friends. Really, you look great. *(Taking Rudy's hand.)* Doesn't she look great? *(Looking off.)* And here comes the waiter! Now everything's in place, and we can just have a lovely meal. *(Happy, she waves to the approaching waiter. Blackout.)*

END OF PLAY